THE DARK SIDE
OF VALUATION

FINANCIAL TIMES

Prentice Hall

In an increasingly competitive world, it is quality of thinking that gives an edge. An idea that opens new doors, a technique that solves a problem, or an insight that simply helps make sense of it all.

We must work with leading authors in the fields of management and finance to bring cutting-edge thinking and best learning practice to a global market.

Under a range of leading imprints, including *Financial Times Prentice Hall*, we create world-class print publications and electronic products giving readers knowledge and understanding which can then be applied, whether studying or at work.

To find out more about our business and professional products, you can visit us at www.phptr.com

Pearson Education

THE DARK SIDE
OF VALUATION

Valuing Old Tech, New Tech, and New Economy Companies

ASWATH DAMODARAN

FINANCIAL TIMES
Prentice Hall

An Imprint of PEARSON EDUCATION
London • New York • San Francisco • Toronto • Sydney
Tokyo • Singapore • Hong Kong • Cape Town • Madrid
Paris • Milan • Munich • Amsterdam

Library of Congress Catalog-in-Publication Data

Damodaran, Aswath.
    The dark side of valuation : valuing old tech, new tech, and new
economy companies / Aswath Damodaran.
        p. cm.
    Includes bibliographical references and index.
    ISBN 0-13-040652-X
    1. Valuation. I. Title.

HG4028.V3 D352 2001
658.15'5--dc21

00-051649

Editorial/Production Supervision: *Jan H. Schwartz*
Acquisitions Editor: *Tim Moore*
Marketing Manager: *Tc Leszczynski*
Buyer: *Maura Zaldivar*
Editorial Assistant: *Allyson Kloss*
Cover Design Director: *Jerry Votta*
Cover Design: *Anthony Gemmellaro*
Art Director: *Gail Cocker-Bogusz*
Series Interior Designer: *Meg VanArsdale*
Interior Compositor: *Vanessa Moore*

FINANCIAL TIMES
Prentice Hall

© 2001 Prentice Hall PTR
Prentice-Hall, Inc.
Upper Saddle River, NJ 07458

Prentice Hall books are widely used by corporations and government agencies for training, marketing, and resale.

The publisher offers discounts on this book when ordered in bulk quantities. For more information, contact: Corporate Sales Department, Phone: 800-382-3419; Fax: 201-236-7141; E-mail: corpsales@prenhall.com; or write: Prentice Hall PTR, Corp. Sales Dept., One Lake Street, Upper Saddle River, NJ 07458.

Printed in the United States of America

10 9 8 7 6 5 4 3 2 1

ISBN 0-13-040652-X

Prentice-Hall International (UK) Limited, *London*
Prentice-Hall of Australia Pty. Limited, *Sydney*
Prentice-Hall Canada Inc., *Toronto*
Prentice-Hall Hispanoamericana, S.A., *Mexico*
Prentice-Hall of India Private Limited, *New Delhi*
Prentice-Hall of Japan, Inc., *Tokyo*
Pearson Education Asia Pte., Ltd.
Editora Prentice-Hall do Brasil, Ltda., *Rio de Janeiro*

*To my wife, Michele, who is the voice of reason
and sanity in our household, and to my children,
Ryan, Brendan, Kendra, and Kiran,
for helping me keep things in perspective.*

CONTENTS

CHAPTER 3   THE PRICE OF RISK: ESTIMATING DISCOUNT RATES   53

CHAPTER 11 REAL OPTIONS IN VALUATION 353

CHAPTER 12 VALUE ENHANCEMENT 403

PREFACE

Do the old rules still apply? Do we need new valuation metrics, or are the old metrics flexible enough to deal with the companies that constitute the new economy? Can you value a company that has no earnings, no history, and no comparable firms? These are the questions that I have heard repeatedly over the last few years. I have always believed the fundamentals that determine value are the same, no matter what company you value and what market it is in. Increasingly, though, I have faced skeptical audiences who are unwilling to take this belief at face value and have demanded proof that America Online, Amazon.com, or Priceline.com can be valued with traditional models.

The genesis for this book was a paper I did on valuing Amazon.com in March 2000, where a discounted cash flow model yielded a value of $34 per share. Since the stock was trading at $80 at that time, there were many who viewed the valuation as either excessively pessimistic or as missing something. The interest in the paper led me to think about writing a book, but I expanded it to cover both new technology and old technology firms. While there are differences in estimation that arise across these firms, I believe that they have far more in common. Why technology firms? I believe that traditional valuation books and models (and I count my book on investment valuation among the culprits) have tended to concentrate on valuing manufacturing or traditional service firms. Technology firms are different. They expand by investing in research and through acquisitions and not by building plant and equipment.

Many of them have astronomical growth rates in revenues and often, very little in current earnings. Their assets are often patents, technology, and skilled employees. I look at how the notions of capital expenditures, operating income, and working capital have to be redefined for these firms.

I begin this book by laying out the facts on the growth of technology and, in particular, new technology stocks in the equity market and argue that although the principles of valuation might not shift, the focus can change as firms move through their life cycles. This discussion is followed by an extended section (Chapters 2–7) on applying traditional discounted cash flow models to value technology stocks, with an emphasis on the estimation of cash flows, growth, and discount rates for these firms. In the next three chapters, I look at the use of relative valuation to value technology companies, both in terms of adapting existing multiples (such as price-earnings and price-to-sales ratios) and developing new ones (value per Web site visitor, for instance). In Chapter 11, "Real Options in Valuation," I consider an argument made by many for the large premiums paid on technology stocks (i.e., they represent real options to expand into a potentially huge e-commerce market), and consider some questions that a skeptic should ask before accepting this argument. In Chapter 12, "Value Enhancement," I consider how managers of technology firms can enhance the value of their firms through better investment and financing decisions.

The book is structured around the valuations of five technology firms—Motorola, Cisco, Amazon.com, Ariba, and Rediff.com. The first three are household names but represent three different points in the technology spectrum. Motorola is an old technology firm with substantial investments in existing assets. It is also a firm that has fallen on hard times in the last few years, largely as a consequence of poor investments and strategic choices. Cisco is one of the great success stories of the 1990s, but a great deal of the market value of the firm reflects expectations about the future. It is also a firm that has chosen to grow through acquisitions and has done it very well. Amazon.com is the poster child (for better or worse) for the new economy stocks that have entered the market in recent years, and the popular press has documented its ups and downs in extensive detail. Ariba and Rediff.com are more recent entrants into the new economy, with Ariba representing the promise (and peril) of the Business-to-Business (B2B) Internet model, and Rediff the potential of an Internet portal serving a market (India) that could be a huge market in the future.

One of the limitations of valuing real companies is that your mistakes are there on the printed page for all to see over time, but that prospect does not bother me. At the risk of giving away the punch line, I do find discounted cash flow values for all five companies: Motorola ($32.39), Cisco ($44.92), Amazon.com ($34.37), Ariba ($72.13), and Rediff.com ($19.05). For what it is worth, at the time that I did the valuations in June 2000, I found Amazon to be overvalued at $48 per share and Cisco to be overvalued at $64.88. Motorola at $34.25 per share and Ariba at $75 per share were fairly valued, and Rediff.com was significantly undervalued at $10 per share. By the time I finished the book, Amazon had dropped in value to $30 per share, and Cisco was trading at $51. Motorola had gone from being fairly valued to undervalued, Ariba saw its stock price double, and Rediff remained undervalued. I have no doubt that you will disagree with me on some of the inputs I have used, and the values that you assign these firms will be different from mine. What I would emphasize, therefore, is not the values that I arrive at for these firms, but the process by which I got there.

Finally, I want this book to be useful to a wide audience: individual investors who hold technology stocks in their portfolios, equity research analysts, venture capitalists, and managers at technology firms. There are portions of the book that I must confess are not easy reading, but I have tried as much as I can to provide an intuitive rationale for everything that I do. Technology firms, notwithstanding the back and forth of markets, are here to stay, and valuing them is something we all need to grapple with. I hope you find this book useful in that endeavor.

Acknowledgments

I would like to thank Russ Hall, who read through the manuscript and helped make it clearer, and Louis Columbus, who made several useful suggestions that I incorporated into the book. I would also like to acknowledge Tim Moore, who has sped this book through the publication process.

THE DARK SIDE
OF VALUATION

In 1990, the 10 largest firms, in terms of market capitalization, in the world were industrial and natural resource giants that had been in existence for much of the century. By January 2000, the two firms at the top of the list were Cisco and Microsoft, two technology firms that had barely registered a blip on the scale 10 years prior. In fact, six of the 10 largest firms,[1] in terms of market capitalization, at the beginning of 2000 were technology firms, and amazingly, four of the six had been in existence for 25 years or less.

In an illustration of the speeding up of the life cycle, Microsoft, in existence only since 1977, was considered an old technology firm in 2000. The new technology firms dominating financial markets were the companies that used the Internet to deliver products and services. The fact that these firms had little in revenues and large operating losses had not

1

deterred investors from bidding up their stock prices and making them worth billions of dollars.

In the eyes of some, the high market valuations commanded by technology stocks, relative to other stocks, were the result of collective irrationality on the part of these investors and were not indicative of the underlying value of these firms. In the eyes of others, these valuations were reasonable indicators that the future belongs to these Internet interlopers. In either case, traditional valuation models seemed ill suited for the firms that best represented the new economy.

DEFINITION OF A TECHNOLOGY FIRM

What is a technology firm? The line is increasingly blurred as more and more firms use technology to deliver their products and services. Thus, Wal-Mart has an online presence and General Motors is exploring creating a web site where customers can order cars, but Wal-Mart is considered a retail firm and General Motors an automobile manufacturing firm. Why, then, are Cisco and Oracle considered technology firms? There are two groups of firms that are designated, at least in popular terminology, as technology firms. The first group includes firms like Cisco and Oracle that deliver technology-based or technology-oriented products—hardware (computers, networking equipment) and software. You could also include high-growth telecommunications firms such as Qualcomm in this group. The second group includes firms that use technology to deliver products or services that were delivered by more conventional means until a few years ago. Amazon.com is a retail firm that sells only online, leading to its categorization as a technology firm, whereas Barnes and Noble is considered a conventional retailer. This group is further broken up into firms that service the ultimate customers (like Amazon) and firms that service other businesses, often called Business to Business (B2B) firms. As the number of technology firms continues to expand at an exponential rate, you will undoubtedly see further subcategorization of these firms.

There are more conventional measures of categorizing technology firms. Services such as Morningstar and Value Line categorize firms into various industries, though the categorization can vary across services. Morningstar has a technology category that includes firms such as Cisco and Oracle but does not include Internet firms like Amazon. Value Line has separate categories for computer hardware, software, semiconductors, Internet firms, and telecommunication firms.

THE SHIFT TO TECHNOLOGY

The shift in emphasis toward technology in financial markets can be illustrated in many ways. Look at three indicators. In Figure 1–1, note the number of firms that were categorized as technology firms each year from 1993 to 1999.[2]

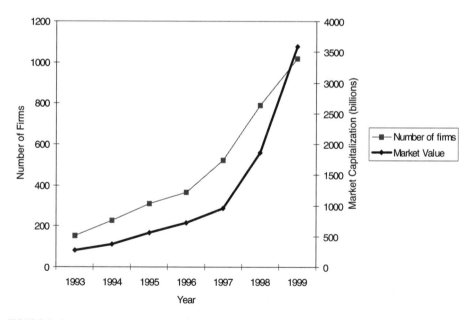

FIGURE 1–1
The Growth of Technology (*Source:* Standard and Poor's, *www.standardandpoors.com,* June 15, 2000, McGraw Hill)

The number of firms increases almost tenfold from 1993 to 1999. The growth in the number of firms is matched by the increase in market capitalization of these firms, also shown in Figure 1–1.

While the overall market has also gone up during the period, technology stocks represent a larger percentage of the market today than they did five years ago. Figure 1–2 shows the percent of the S&P 500 represented by technology stocks.

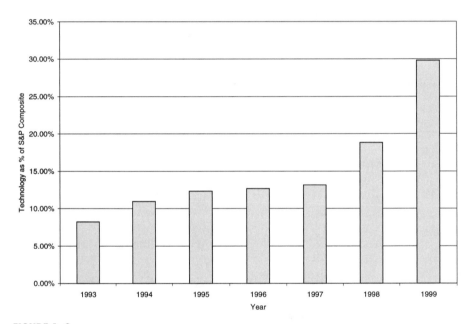

FIGURE 1–2
Technology as a Percent of the S&P 500 (*Source:* Standard and Poor's, *www.standardandpoors.com,* June 15, 2000, McGraw Hill)

In 1999, technology stocks accounted for almost 30% of the S&P 500, a more than threefold increase over the proportion six years earlier.

The growth of technology firms can also be seen in the explosive growth of the market capitalization of the NASDAQ, an index dominated by technology stocks. Figure 1–3 graphs the NASDAQ from 1990 to 2000 and contrasts it with the S&P 500.

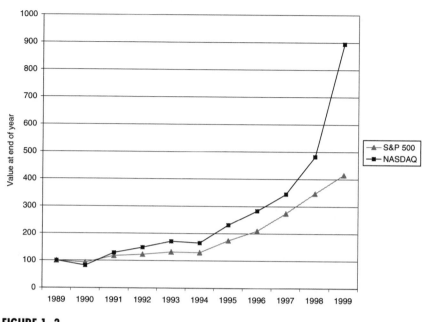

FIGURE 1–3
NASDAQ vs S&P 500 Growth of $100 Invested in 1989

While both indices registered strong increases during the 1990s, the NASDAQ increased at almost twice the rate of the S&P 500. In fact, the effect of technology is probably understated in this graph because of the rise of technology in the S&P 500 itself.[3]

Finally, the growth of technology is not restricted to the United States. Exchanges such as the JASDAQ (for Japan), KASDAQ (for Korea), and EASDAQ (for Europe) mirror the growth of the NASDAQ. In an even more significant development, the conglomerates and manufacturing firms that had conventionally dominated Asian and Latin American markets were displaced by upstarts, powered with technology. In India, for instance, InfoSys, a software firm with less than two decades of history, became the largest market capitalization stock in 1999.

OLD TECH TO NEW TECH

While there has been a significant shift to technology in the overall market, there has been an even more dramatic shift in the last few years toward what are called new technology firms. Again, while there is no consensus on what goes into this categorization, new technology firms shared some common features. They were younger, tended to have little revenue when they first came to the market, and often reported substantial losses. To compensate, they offered the prospect of explosive growth in the future. The surge in public offerings in these firms coincided with the growth of Internet use in homes and businesses, leading many to identify new technology firms with the Internet.

The growth of new technology firms can be seen in a number of different measures. No firms were categorized as Internet companies by Value Line in 1996, whereas there were 304 in that category by 2000. Second, the increase in market value has been even more dramatic. Figure 1–4 graphs the

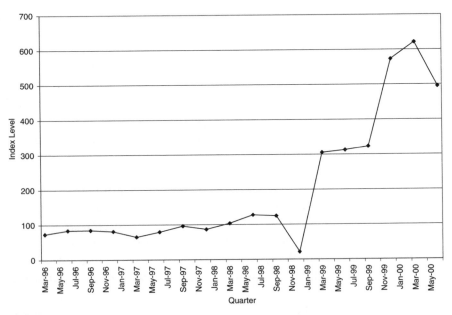

FIGURE 1–4

Inter@ctive Week Internet Index (*Source: www.zdnet.com/intweek,* June 2000, Ziff Davis)

Inter@ctive Week Internet Index, an index of 50 companies classified as deriving their business from the Internet from its initiation in 1996 to June 2000.

This index, notwithstanding its tenfold jump over the four-year period, actually understates the increase in market value of Internet companies because it does not capture the increase in the number of new Internet companies going into the market in each of the quarters. At their peak, these Internet companies had a value of $1.4 trillion in early 2000. Even allowing for the decline in market value that occurred in 2000, the combined market value of Internet companies in June 2000 was $682.3 billion.[4]

What did these firms have to offer that could have accounted for this extraordinary increase in value? By conventional measures, not much. The combined revenue of Internet firms in 1999 was $18.46 billion, about one-third of the revenues in 1999 of one old economy firm, General Electric.[5] The combined operating loss for Internet firms was $6.7 billion in 1999, and only 23 of the 304 firms had positive operating income. In contrast, GE alone had operating income of about $10.9 billion in 1999. In summary, then, these were firms with very limited histories, little revenue, and large operating losses.

EXTENSION OF THE VALUATION METRICS

Dozens of valuation metrics exist; two of them have been widely used over time to measure the value of an investment. One is the *price-earnings ratio*, the ratio of the market price of a security to its expected earnings, and another is the *price-to-sales* ratio, the ratio of the market value of equity in a business to the revenues generated by that business. On both measures, technology firms, and especially new technology firms, stand out relative to the rest of the market.

Consider, first, the price-earnings ratio. The price-earnings ratio for the S&P 500 stood at 33.21 in June 2000, while Cisco traded at 120 times earnings at the same point in time. Figure 1–5 compares the price-earnings ratios for three technology sectors (computers, semiconductors, and computer software)

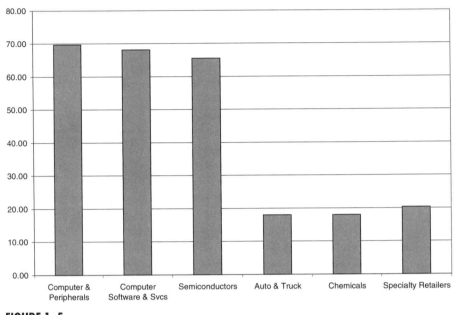

FIGURE 1-5
PE Ratio Comparison across Sectors

with the price-earnings ratios for three nontechnology sectors (automobiles, chemicals, and specialty retailers).

The average PE ratios for the technology sectors are much higher than the ratios for nontechnology sectors. In fact, the price-earnings ratio for the entire S&P 500, an index that, as noted in Figure 1–2, has an increasingly large component of technology stocks, has increased over the last decade from 19.11 in 1990 to 33.21 today. Some, or a large portion, of that increase can be attributed to the technology component.

The new technology stocks cannot, for the most part, even be measured on the price-earnings ratio metric, since most report negative earnings. To evaluate their values, look at the price-to-sales ratio. Figure 1–6 summarizes the price-to-sales ratio for the six sectors listed above, as well as for Internet firms.

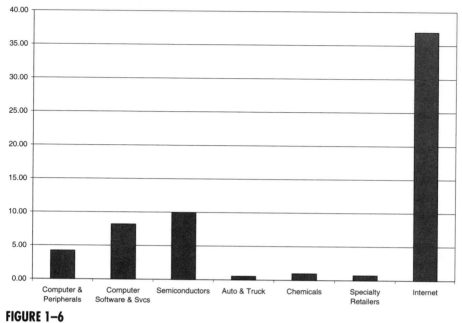

FIGURE 1-6
Price-to-Sales Ratios by Sector

Technology firms, and especially new technology firms, therefore command much higher multiples of earnings and revenues than other firms. Can the difference be attributed to the much higher growth potential for technology? If so, how high would the growth need to be in these firms to justify these large price premiums? Is an appropriate assessment being made for the risk associated with this growth? These are the questions that have bedeviled investors and equity research analysts in the last few years.

THE IMPLICATIONS FOR VALUATION

When valuing a firm, you draw on information from three sources. The first is the *current financial statements for the firm*. You use these statements to determine how profitable a firm's investments are or have been, how much it reinvests to generate future growth, and for all of the inputs that are required in any valuation. The second is the *past history of the firm*, both in terms of earnings and market prices. A firm's earnings and revenue history over time let you make judgments on how cyclical a firm's business has been and how much growth it has shown, and the firm's price history can help you measure its risk. Finally, you can look at the *firm's competitors or peer group* to gauge how much better or worse a firm is than its competition and also to estimate key inputs on risk, growth, and cash flows.

While you would optimally like to have substantial information from all three sources, you may often have to substitute more of one type of information for less of the other if you have no choice. For example, the 75 years or more of history on each of the large automakers in the United States compensate for the fact that there are only three of these automakers.[6] In contrast, there may be only 5 years of information on Abercombie and Fitch, but the firm is in a sector (specialty retailing) where there are more than 200 comparable firms. The ease with which you can obtain industry averages and the precision of these averages compensate for the lack of history at the firm.

What makes technology firms, and especially new technology firms, different? First, they usually have not been in existence for more than a year or two, leading to a very limited history. Second, their current financial statements reveal very little about the component of their assets—expected growth—that contributes the most to their value. Third, these firms often represent the first of their kind of business. In many cases, there are no competitors or a peer group against which they can be measured. When valuing these firms, therefore, you may find yourself constrained on all three counts when it comes to information.

How have investors responded to this absence of information? Some have decided that these stocks cannot be valued and should not therefore be held in a portfolio. Their conservatism has cost them dearly as technology stocks have powered the overall markets to increasing highs. Other analysts have argued that while these stocks cannot be valued with traditional models, the fault lies in the models. The latter have come up with new and inventive ways, based upon the limited information available, of justifying the prices paid for technology stocks.

NEW PARADIGMS OR OLD PRINCIPLES: A LIFE CYCLE PERSPECTIVE

The value of a firm is based on its capacity to generate cash flows and the uncertainty associated with these cash flows. Generally, more profitable firms have been valued more highly than less profitable ones. In the case of new technology firms, though, this proposition seems to be turned on its head. At least on the surface, firms that lose money seem to be valued more than firms that make money.

There seems to be, as viewed from the outside, one more key difference between technology firms and other firms in the market. Technology firms do not make significant investments in land, buildings, or other fixed assets and seem to derive the bulk of their value from intangible assets. The simplest way to illustrate this divide is by looking at the ratio of market value to book value at both technology and nontechnology firms. Like the price-earnings and the price-to-sales ratios, the price-to-book-value ratio at technology firms is much higher than it is for other firms. Figure 1–7 compares the price-to-book-value ratio for technology sectors to that of nontechnology sectors.

The negative earnings and the presence of intangible assets is used by analysts as a rationale for abandoning traditional valuation models and developing new ways that can be used to justify investing in technology firms. For instance, comparison of Internet companies in their infancy was based on their value per site visitor, computed by dividing the market value of a firm by the number of viewers to their web site. Implicit in these comparisons is the assumption that more visitors to a site translates into higher revenues, which, in turn, are assumed will lead to greater profits in the future. All too often, though, these assumptions are neither made explicit nor tested, leading to unrealistic valuations.

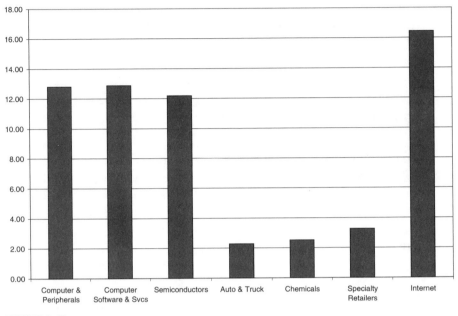

FIGURE 1–7
Price-to-Book-Value Ratios by Sector

This search for new paradigms is misguided. The problem with technology firms, in general, and new technology firms, in particular, is not that they lose money, have no history, or have substantial intangible assets. It is that they make their initial public offerings far earlier in their life cycles than firms have in the past and often have to be valued before they have an established market for their product. In fact, in some cases, the firms being valued have an interesting idea that could be a commercial success but has not yet been tested. The problem, however, is not a conceptual problem but an estimation problem. The value of a firm is still the present value of the expected cash flows from its assets, but those cash flows are likely to be much more difficult to estimate.

Figure 1–8 offers a view of the life cycle of the firm and how the availability of information and the source of value change over that life cycle.

	Startup or Idea Companies	Rapid Expansion	High Growth	Mature Growth	Decline
Revenues/ Current operations	Nonexistent or low revenues/ Negative operating income	Revenues increasing/ Income still low or negative	Revenue in high growth/Operating income also growing	Revenue growth slows/ Operating income still growing	Revenues and operating income growth drops off/ may decline
Operating history	None	Very limited	Some operating history	Operating history can be used in valuation	Substantial operating history
Comparable firms	None	Some, but in same stage of growth	More comparable firms at different stages of life cycle	Large number of comparables, at different stages	Declining number of comparables, mostly mature
Source of value	Entirely future growth	Mostly future growth	Portion from existing assets/Growth still dominates	More from existing assets than growth	Entirely from existing assets

FIGURE 1–8
Valuation Issues across the Life Cycle

13

■ *Startup*: This phase represents the initial stage after a business has been formed. The product is generally still untested and does not have an established market. The firm has little in terms of current operations, no operating history, and no comparable companies. The value of this firm rests entirely on its future growth potential. Valuation poses the biggest challenge at this firm since there is little useful information to go on. The inputs have to be estimated and are likely to have considerable error associated with them. The estimates of future growth are often based on assessments of the competence of existing managers and their capacity to convert a promising idea into commercial success. This is often the reason why firms in this phase try to hire managers with a successful track record in converting ideas into dollars: it gives them credibility in the eyes of financial backers.

■ *Expansion*: Once a firm succeeds in attracting customers and establishing a presence in the market, its revenues increase rapidly, though it still might be reporting losses. The current operations of the firm provide useful clues on pricing, margins, and expected growth, but current margins cannot be projected into the future. The operating history of the firm is still limited and shows large changes from period to period. Other firms are generally in operation, but usually are at the same stage of growth as the firm being valued. Most of the value for this firm also comes from its expected growth. Valuation becomes a little simpler at this stage, but the information is still limited and unreliable and the inputs to the valuation model are likely to be shifting substantially over time.

■ *High Growth*: The firm's revenues are growing rapidly at this stage, but earnings are likely to lag behind revenues. At this stage, both the current operations and operation history of the firm contain information that can be used in valuing the firm. The number of comparable firms is generally highest at this stage, and these firms are more diverse in where they are in the life cycle, ranging from small, high-growth competitors to larger, lower-growth competitors. The existing assets of this firm have significant value, but the larger proportion of value still comes from future growth. More information is available at this stage, and the estimation of inputs becomes more straightforward.

- *Mature Growth*: As growth starts leveling off, firms generally find two phenomena occurring. The earnings and cash flows continue to increase rapidly, reflecting past investments, and the need to invest in new projects declines. At this stage in the process, the firm has current operations that are reflective of the future, an operating history that provides substantial information about the firm's markets, and a large number of comparable firms at the same stage in the life cycle. Existing assets contribute as much or more to the firm's value than does expected growth, and the inputs to the valuation are likely to be stable.

- *Decline*: The last stage in this life cycle is decline. Firms in this stage find both revenues and earnings starting to decline as their businesses mature and new competitors overtake them. Existing investments are likely to continue to produce cash flows, albeit at a declining pace, and the firm has little need for new investments. Thus, the value of the firm depends entirely on existing assets. The number of comparable firms tends to become smaller at this stage and they are all likely to be either in mature growth or decline as well.

Is valuation easier in the last stage than in the first? Generally, yes. Are the principles that drive valuation different at each stage? Probably not. In fact, valuation is clearly more of a challenge in the earlier stages in a life cycle, and estimates of value are much more likely to contain errors for startup or high-growth firms. The payoff to valuation is also likely to be highest with these firms for two reasons. The first is that the absence of information scares many analysts away, and analysts who persist and end up with a valuation, no matter how imprecise, are likely to be rewarded. The second is that these firms are most likely to be coming to the market in the form of initial public offerings and new issues, and therefore need estimates of value.

ILLUSTRATIVE EXAMPLES

The estimation issues and valuation challenges are different for firms at different stages in the life cycle. Consider five technology firms that span the life cycle, from idea or startup to mature growth.

- *Motorola*, a company that started off manufacturing televisions and then found success making semiconductors is one example. In recent years, Motorola has found success in telecommunications with its cellular phone venture, though it has had its share of disappointing investments (such as the Iridium venture). As technology firms go, Motorola is an old firm that is still viewed as having some growth potential.

- In early 2000, *Cisco*, for a brief period, became the largest market capitalization firm in the world, an astonishing feat given its short history. In many ways, Cisco is the growth firm that young startups would like to emulate and, as such, is an example of a high-growth firm. It is also a company that has had unique success in building itself up through acquisitions of smaller firms with promising technology and converting that technology into commercial success.

- *Amazon.com* became a symbol for the new technology firms, both because of its visibility and because it operates a business that is easy to understand—it is a retailer. Are the drivers of value different for a dot.com than they are for a brick and mortar firm? Valuing Amazon might provide an answer to this question.

- *Ariba* is also a new-technology/Internet firm that offers business solutions to other businesses. There is more of a technology component to Ariba than there is to Amazon, and valuing it allows you to examine whether firms that sell to other businesses (B2B) are different, from a valuation perspective, from firms that sell to the final consumer. It is also a younger firm than Amazon and has barely made the transition form the idea stage to producing revenues.

- As a final example, you will look at *Rediff.com*, an initial public offering at the time this book was written. Rediff.com is a portal serving the Indian market and chose to go public on the NASDAQ. The valuation of a firm very early in its life cycle, the effects of country risk on value, and the consequences of having limited historical information are all examined in the valuation of Rediff.com. In addition, there is the very real possibility that Rediff could make the shift into other businesses, such as online retailing, in the near future, especially if it succeeds in its initial push to raise capital and expand its presence in the market.

SUMMARY

Technology stocks account for a larger percent of the market capitalization of stocks than ever, mirroring the increasing importance of technology to the economy. As more and more technology firms are listed on financial markets, often at very early stages in their life cycles, traditional valuation methods and metrics often seem ill suited to them. Although the estimation challenges are different for these firms, you will discover through this book that the fundamentals of valuation do not and should not change when you value technology firms.

ENDNOTES

1. The six firms were Cisco, Microsoft, Oracle, Intel, IBM, and Lucent. Of these, only IBM and Intel were publicly traded firms in 1975. Microsoft went public in 1986, Oracle in 1987, and Cisco in 1990. Lucent was spun off by AT&T in 1996.

2. The Bloomberg categorization of technology firms is used to arrive at these numbers.

3. In other words, a large portion of the increase in the S&P 500 can be attributed to the growth in market value of technology stocks like Microsoft and Cisco.

4. The Value Line categorization of Internet firms is used to arrive at this value.

5. General Electric reported revenues of $51.5 billion in 1999.

6. The big three auto makers are GM, Chrysler, and Ford. In fact, with the acquisition of Chrysler, only two are left.

2

Show Me the Money: The Fundamentals of Discounted Cash Flow Valuation

In the last chapter, you were introduced to the notion that the value of an asset is determined by its expected cash flows in the future. In this chapter, we begin making this link between value and expected cash flows much more explicit by looking at how to value an asset. You will see that the value of any asset is the present value of the expected cash flow from that asset. This proposition lies at the core of the discounted cash flow approach to valuation. In this chapter, we explore the fundamentals of this approach, starting with an asset with guaranteed cash flows and then moving on to look at assets where there is uncertainty about the future. In the process, we cover the groundwork for how to value a firm and estimate the inputs that go into the valuation.

DISCOUNTED CASH FLOW VALUE

Intuitively, the value of any asset should be a function of three variables: how much the asset generates in cash flows, when these cash flows are expected to occur, and what uncertainty is associated with these cash flows. Discounted cash flow valuation brings all three of these variables together by computing the value of any asset to be the present value of its expected future cash flows:

$$\text{Value} = \sum_{t=1}^{t=n} \frac{CF_t}{(1+r)^t}$$

where

n = Life of the asset

CF_t = Cash flow in period t

r = Discount rate reflecting the riskiness of the estimated cash flows

The cash flows vary from asset to asset—dividends for stocks, coupons (interest) and face value for bonds, and after-tax cash flows for real projects. The discount rate is a function of the riskiness of the estimated cash flows; riskier assets carry higher rates, safer projects carry lower rates.

We begin this section by looking at valuing assets that have finite lives (at the end of which they cease to generate cash flows) and conclude by looking at the more difficult case of assets with infinite lives. We look at firms whose cash flows are known with certainty and conclude by considering uncertainty in valuation.

VALUING AN ASSET WITH GUARANTEED CASH FLOWS

The simplest assets to value have cash flows that are guaranteed, that is, assets whose promised cash flows are always delivered. Such assets are riskless, and the interest rate earned on them is called a *riskless rate*. The value of such an asset is the present value of the cash flows, discounted back at the riskless rate. Generally, riskless investments are issued by governments that have the power to print money to meet any obligations they otherwise cannot cover. Not all government obligations are riskless, though: some governments have defaulted on promised obligations.

The simplest asset to value is a bond that pays no coupon but has a face value that is guaranteed at maturity; this bond is a *default-free zero coupon bond*. Using a time line, you can show the cash flow on this bond, as in Figure 2–1.

FIGURE 2–1
Cash Flows on N-year Zero Coupon Bond

The value of this bond can be written as the present value of a single cash flow discounted at the riskless rate.

$$\text{Value of Zero Coupon Bond} = \frac{\text{Face Value of Bond}}{(1 + r)^N}$$

where r is the riskless rate on the zero-coupon and N is the maturity of the zero-coupon bond. Since the cash flow on this bond is fixed, the value of the bond varies inversely with the riskless rate. As the riskless rate increases, the value of the bond will decrease.

Consider, now, a default-free coupon bond that has fixed cash flows (coupons) occurring at regular intervals (usually semiannually) and a final cash flow (face value) at maturity. The time line for this bond is shown in Figure 2–2 (with C representing the coupon each period and N being the maturity of the bond).

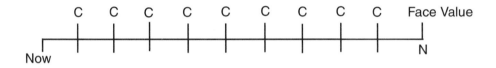

FIGURE 2–2
Cash Flows on N-year Coupon Bond

This bond can actually be viewed as a series of zero-coupon bonds, and each can be valued with the riskless rate that corresponds to the time when the cash flow comes due:

$$\text{Value of Coupon Bond} = \sum_{t=1}^{t=N} \frac{\text{Coupon}}{(1+r_t)^t} + \frac{\text{Face Value of Bond}}{(1+r_N)^N}$$

where r_t is the interest rate that corresponds to a t-period zero coupon bond and the bond has a life of N periods.

INTRODUCING UNCERTAINTY INTO VALUATION

In valuation, you have to grapple with two different types of uncertainty. The first arises in the context of securities like bonds, where there is a promised cash flow to the holder of the bonds in future periods. The risk that these cash flows will not be delivered is called *default risk*; the greater the default risk in a bond, given its cash flows, the less valuable the bond becomes.

The second type of risk is more complicated. When you make equity investments in assets, you are generally not promised a fixed cash flow but are entitled instead to whatever cash flows are left over after other claimants (like creditors) are paid; these cash flows are called *residual cash flows*. Here, the uncertainty revolves around what these residual cash flows will be, relative to expectations. In contrast to default risk, where the risk can only result in negative consequences (the cash flows delivered will be less than promised), uncertainty in the context of equity investments can cut both ways. The actual cash flows can be much lower than expected, but they can also be much higher. For the moment, we can label this risk *equity risk* and consider, at least in general terms, how best to deal with it in the context of valuing an equity investment.

VALUING AN ASSET WITH DEFAULT RISK

We begin this section by discussing how to assess default risk and adjust interest rates for it, and then consider how best to value assets with default risk.

Measuring Default Risk and Estimating Default-Risk Adjusted Rates. When valuing investments where the cash flows are promised but where there is a risk that they might not be delivered, it is no longer appropriate to use the riskless rate as the discount rate. The appropriate discount rate here includes the riskless rate and an appropriate premium, called a *default spread*, for the default risk. There are two parts to estimating this spread.

The first part is assessing the default risk of an entity. Banks do this routinely when making loans to individuals and businesses; investors buying bonds in firms get some help, at least in the United States, from independent ratings agencies like Standard and Poor's and Moody's. These agencies measure the default risk and give the bonds a rating that measures the default risk. Table 2.1 summarizes the ratings used by Standard and Poor's and Moody's to rate U.S. companies.

TABLE 2.1 Ratings Description

STANDARD AND POOR'S		MOODY'S	
AAA	The highest debt rating assigned. The borrower's capacity to repay debt is extremely strong.	Aaa	Judged to be of the best quality with a small degree of risk.
AA	Capacity to repay is strong and differs from the highest quality only by a small amount.	Aa	High quality but rated lower than Aaa because margin of protection may not be as large or because there may be other elements of long-term risk.
A	Has strong capacity to repay. Borrower is susceptible to adverse effects of changes in circumstances and economic conditions.	A	Bonds possess favorable investment attributes but may be susceptible to risk in the future.
BBB	Has adequate capacity to repay, but adverse economic conditions or circumstances are more likely to lead to risk.	Baa	Neither highly protected nor poorly secured; adequate payment capacity.
BB,B, CCC, CC	Regarded as predominantly speculative, BB being the least speculative and CC the most.	Ba	Judged to have some speculative risk.
		B	Generally lacking characteristics of a desirable investment; probability of payment small.
D	In default or with payments in arrears.	Caa	Poor standing and perhaps in default.
		Ca	Very speculative; often in default.
		C	Highly speculative; in default.

(*Source:* Standard and Poor's, *www.standardandpoors.com*, June 15, 2000, McGraw Hill; Moody's, *www.moodys.com*, June 1, 2000, Moody's Investor Services)

While ratings agencies do make mistakes, the rating system saves investors a significant amount of the cost that would otherwise be expended doing research on the default risk of issuing firms.

The second part of the risk-adjusted discount rate assessment is coming up with the default spread. The demand and supply for bonds within each ratings class determines the appropriate interest rate for that rating. Low-rated firms have more default risk and generally have to pay much higher interest rates on their bonds than do highly rated firms. The spread itself changes over time, tending to increase for all ratings classes in economic recessions and to narrow for all ratings classes in economic recoveries. Figure 2–3 summarizes default spreads for bonds in S&P's different rating classes as of December 31, 1999.

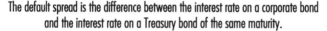

The default spread is the difference between the interest rate on a corporate bond and the interest rate on a Treasury bond of the same maturity.

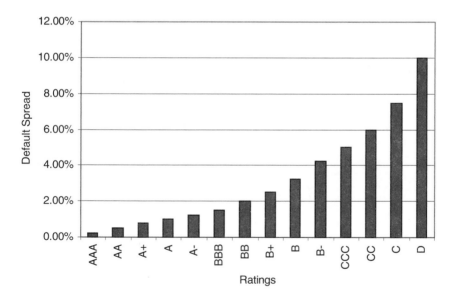

FIGURE 2–3
Default Spreads and Ratings (*Source: www.bondsonline.com*, July 7, 2000, Bonds Online Group, Inc.)

These default spreads, when added to the riskless rate, yield the interest rates for bonds with the specified ratings. For instance, a D-rated bond has an interest rate about 10% higher than the riskless rate.

Valuing Corporate Bonds. The most common example of an asset with just default risk is a corporate bond, since even the largest, safest companies still have some risk of default. When valuing a corporate bond, you generally make two modifications to the bond valuation approach you developed earlier for a default-free bond. First, you discount the coupons on the corporate bond, even though these no longer represent expected cash flows but are instead promised cash flows.[1] Second, the discount rate used for a bond with default risk will be higher than that used for a default-free bond. Furthermore, as the default risk increases, so will the discount rate used:

$$\text{Value of Corporate Coupon Bond} = \sum_{t=1}^{t=N} \frac{\text{Coupon}}{(1 + k_d)^t} + \frac{\text{Face Value of Bond}}{(1 + k_d)^N}$$

where k_d is the market interest rate given the default risk.

VALUING AN ASSET WITH EQUITY RISK

Having valued assets with guaranteed cash flows and those with only default risk, let us now consider the valuation of assets with equity risk. We'll begin with an introduction to estimating cash flows and to considering risk in investments with equity risk, and then we'll look at how best to value these assets.

Measuring Cash Flows for an Asset with Equity Risk. Unlike the bonds valued so far in this chapter, the cash flows on assets with equity risk are not promised cash flows. Instead, the valuation is based on the *expected cash flows* on these assets over their lives. You need to consider two basic questions: the first relates to how you measure these cash flows, and the second to how to come up with expectations for these cash flows.

To estimate cash flows on an asset with equity risk, first consider the perspective of the equity investor in the asset. Assume that the equity investor borrowed some of the funds needed to buy the asset. The cash flows to the equity investor will therefore be the cash flows generated by the asset after all expenses, taxes, and after-debt payments. This cash flow is called the *cash flow to equity investors*. In a broader definition of cash flow, you can look at not just the equity investor in the asset but at the total cash flows generated by the asset for both the equity investor and the lenders. This cash flow, which is before debt payments but after operating expenses and taxes, is called the *cash flow to the firm* (where the firm is considered to include both debt and equity investors).

Note that since this is a risky asset, the cash flows are likely to vary across a broad range of outcomes, some good and some not so positive. To estimate the expected cash flow, we need to consider all possible outcomes in each period, weight them by their relative probabilities,[2] and arrive at an expected cash flow for that period.

Measuring Equity Risk and Estimating Risk-Adjusted Discount Rates. When we analyzed bonds with default risk, we noted that the interest rate has to be adjusted to reflect the default risk. This default-risk adjusted interest rate can be considered the *cost of debt* to the investor or business borrowing the money. When analyzing investments with equity risk, you have to make an adjustment to the riskless rate to arrive at a discount rate, but the adjustment must reflect the equity risk rather than the default risk. Furthermore, since there is no longer a promised interest payment, you can think of this rate as a risk-adjusted discount rate rather than an interest rate. This adjusted discount rate is the *cost of equity*.

We saw earlier that a firm can be viewed as a collection of assets, financed partly with debt and partly with equity. The composite cost of financing, which comes from both debt and equity, is a weighted average of the costs of debt and equity, with the weights depending upon how much of each financing is used. This cost is labeled the *cost of capital*.

If the cash flows that you are discounting are cash flows to equity investors, as defined in the previous section, the appropriate discount rate is the cost of equity. If the cash flows are prior to debt payments and therefore to the firm, the appropriate discount rate is the cost of capital.

VALUING AN ASSET WITH EQUITY RISK AND FINITE LIFE

Most assets acquired by firms have finite lives. At the end of that life, the assets are assumed to lose their operating capacity, though they might still preserve some value. To illustrate, assume that you buy an apartment building and plan to rent the apartments to earn income. The building will have a finite life, say, 30 to 40 years, at the end of which it will have to be torn down and a new building constructed, but the land will continue to have value.

You can value this building by using the cash flows that it will generate, prior to any debt payments, and discounting them at the composite cost of the financing used to buy the building, that is, the cost of capital. At the end of the expected life of the building, you estimate what the building (and the land it sits on) will be worth and discount this value back to the present, as well. In summary, the value of a finite life asset can be written as:

$$\text{Value of Finite – Life Asset} = \sum_{t=1}^{t=N} \frac{E(\text{Cash Flow on Asset}_t)}{(1 + k_c)^t} + \frac{\text{Value of Asset at End of Life}}{(1 + k_c)^N}$$

where k_c is the cost of capital.

This entire analysis can also be done from your perspective as the sole equity investor in this building. In this case, the cash flow is defined more narrowly as cash flows after debt payments, and the appropriate discount rate becomes the cost of equity. At the end of the building's life, you look at how much it will be worth but consider only the cash that will be left over after any remaining debt is paid off. Thus, the value of the equity investment in an asset with a fixed life of N years, say, an office building, can be written as:

$$\text{Value of Equity in Finite} - \text{Life Asset} = \sum_{t=1}^{t=N} \frac{E(\text{Cash Flow to Equity}_t)}{(1 + k_e)^t}$$

$$+ \frac{\text{Value of Equity in Asset at End of Life}}{(1 + k_e)^N}$$

where k_e is the rate of return that the equity investor in this asset would demand, given the riskiness of the cash flows, and the value of equity at the end of the asset's life is the value of the asset net of the debt outstanding on it.

Can you extend the life of the building by reinvesting more in maintaining it? Possibly. If you choose this course of action, however, the life of the building will be longer, but the cash flows to equity and to the firm each period have to be reduced[3] by the amount of the reinvestment needed for maintenance.

VALUING AN ASSET WITH AN INFINITE LIFE

When you value businesses and firms, as opposed to individual assets, you are often looking at entities that have no finite lives. If firms reinvest sufficient amounts in new assets each period, they could keep generating cash flows forever. In this section, we value assets that have infinite lives and uncertain cash flows.

EQUITY AND FIRM VALUATION

A firm, as defined here, includes both investments already made (call these *assets-in-place*) and investments yet to be made (call these *growth assets*). In addition, a firm can either borrow the funds it needs to make these investments, in which case it is using debt, or raise it from its owners, in the form of equity. Figure 2–4 summarizes this description of a firm in the form of a financial balance sheet.

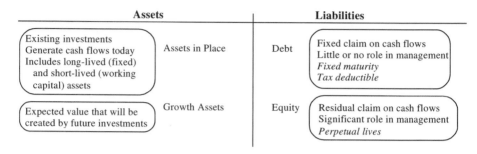

FIGURE 2–4
A Financial Balance Sheet

Note that while this summary does have some similarities with the accounting balance sheet, there are key differences. The most important one is that here you explicitly consider growth assets when you look at what a firm owns.

In the section on valuing assets with equity risk, we encountered the notions of cash flows to equity and cash flows to the firm. We saw that cash flows to equity are cash flows after debt payments, all expenses, and reinvestment needs have been met. In the context of a business, you can use the same definition to measure the cash flows to its equity investors. These cash flows, when discounted back at the cost of equity for the business, yield the value of the equity in the business, as illustrated in Figure 2–5.

Note that the definition of both cash flows and discount rates is consistent—they are both defined in terms of the equity investor in the business.

In an alternative approach, instead of valuing the equity stake in the asset or business, we can look at the value of the entire business. To do this, we look at the collective cash flows, not just to equity investors but also to lenders (or bondholders in the firm). The appropriate discount rate is the cost of capital, since it reflects both the cost of equity and the cost of debt. The process is illustrated in Figure 2–6.

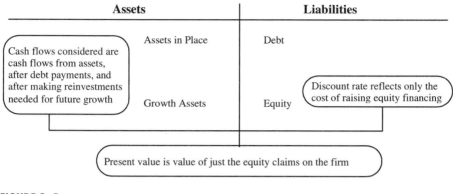

FIGURE 2–5
Equity Valuation

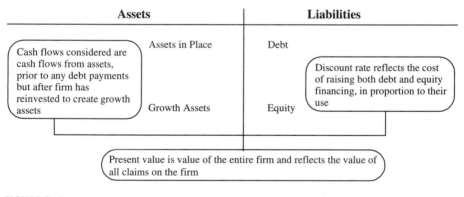

FIGURE 2–6
Firm Valuation

Note again that we are defining both cash flows and discount rates consistently, to reflect the fact that we are valuing not just the equity portion of the investment but the investment itself.

DIVIDENDS AND EQUITY VALUATION

When valuing equity investments in publicly traded companies, you could argue that the only cash flows investors in these investments get from the firm are dividends. Therefore, the value of the equity in these investments can be computed as the present value of expected dividend payments on the equity:

$$\text{Value of Equity (Only Dividends)} = \sum_{t=1}^{t=\infty} \frac{E(\text{Dividend}_t)}{(1+k_e)^t}$$

The mechanics are similar to those involved in pricing a bond, with dividend payments replacing coupon payments, and the cost of equity replacing the interest rate on the bond. The fact that equity in a publicly traded firm has an infinite life, however, indicates that you cannot arrive at closure on the valuation without making additional assumptions.

Stable (and Constant) Growth Scenario. One way in which you might be able to estimate the value of the equity in a firm is by assuming that the dividends, starting today, will grow at a constant rate forever. If you do that, you can estimate the value of the equity, using the present value formula for a perpetually growing cash flow. In fact, the value of the equity will be:

$$\text{Value of Equity (Dividends Growing at a Constant Rate Forever)} = \frac{E(\text{Dividend Next Period})}{(k_e - g_n)}$$

This model, called the *Gordon growth model*, is simple but limited, since it can value only companies that pay dividends, and only if these dividends are expected to grow at a constant rate forever. The reason this is a restrictive assumption is that no asset or firm's cash flows can grow forever at a rate higher than the growth rate of the economy. If it did, the firm would become the economy. Therefore, the constant growth rate is constrained to be less than or equal to the economy's growth rate. For valuations of firms in U.S. dollars, this puts an upper limit on the nominal growth rate of approximately 5%–6%.[4] This constraint also ensures that the growth rate used in the model will be less than the discount rate.

High-Growth Scenario. What happens if you have to value a stock whose dividends are growing at 15% a year? The solution is simple. You value the stock in two parts. In the first part, you estimate the expected dividends each period for as long as the growth rate of this firm's dividends remains higher than the growth rate of the economy, then sum up the present value of the dividends. In the second part, you assume that the growth rate in dividends will drop to a stable or constant rate forever sometime in the future. Once you make this assumption, you can apply the Gordon growth model to estimate the present value of all dividends in stable growth. This present value is called the *terminal price* and represents the expected value of the stock in the future, when the firm becomes a stable growth firm. The present value of this terminal price is added to the present value of the dividends to obtain the value of the stock today:

$$\text{Value of Equity with High-Growth Dividends} = \sum_{t=1}^{t=N} \frac{E(\text{Dividends}_t)}{(1 + k_e)^t} + \frac{\text{Terminal Price}_N}{(1 + k_e)^N}$$

where N is the number of years of high growth and the terminal price is based upon the assumption of stable growth beyond year N.

$$\text{Terminal Price} = \frac{E(\text{Dividend}_{N+1})}{(k_e - g_n)}$$

Limitations of Dividend Discount Models. The dividend discount model was the first of the discounted cash flow models used in practice. While it does elucidate key fundamental concepts about valuation, it also has serious limitations, especially in the context of technology firms. The biggest problem, contrary to popular opinion, is not that these firms do not pay dividends. Given the high growth and reinvestment needs exhibited by these firms, not paying dividends may be, in fact, what you would expect them to do. The problem is that they do not pay dividends or do not pay as much as they can in dividends even when they have the cash flows to do so.

Dividends are discretionary and are determined by managers. If managers have excess cash, they can choose to pay a dividend but they can also choose to hold the cash or buy back stock. In the United States, the option of buying back stock has become increasingly attractive to many firms. Figure 2–7 summarizes dividends paid and equity repurchased at U.S. corporations between 1989 and 1998.

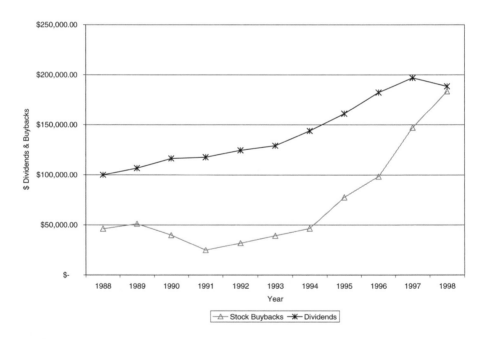

FIGURE 2–7
Stock Buybacks and Dividends: Aggregate for U.S. Firms — 1989–98 (*Source:* Compustat Database, 1998)

It is worth noting that while aggregate dividends at all U.S. firms have grown at a rate of about 7.29% a year over this 10-year period, stock buybacks have grown 16.53% a year. In another interesting shift, the proportion of cash returned to stockholders in the form of stock buybacks has climbed from 32% in 1989 to almost 50% in 1998.

The shift has been even more dramatic at technology firms, as is evidenced by two facts about them:

1. Of the 1,340 firms classified as technology firms by Morningstar in 1999, only 74 paid dividends. Of these, only 15 had dividend yields that exceeded 1%. Collectively, these firms paid out less than $2 billion in dividends in 1999.

2. In 1999, technology firms collectively bought back $21.2 billion, more than 10 times what they paid in dividends.

The net effect of using dividend discount models to value technology firms is a significant understatement in their value.

ILLUSTRATION 2.1

Valuing a Technology Stock with the Dividend Discount Model: Hewlett Packard

Hewlett Packard (HP) reported earnings per share of $3.00 in 1999 and paid out dividends of $0.60. Assume that HP's earnings will grow 16% a year for the next 10 years and that the dividend payout ratio (dividends as a percent of earnings) will remain at 20% for that period. Also assume that HP's cost of equity is 10.40% for that period. Table 2.2 summarizes the expected dividends per share for the next 10 years and the present value of these dividends.

After year 10, you expect Hewlett Packard's earnings to grow 6% a year and its dividend payout ratio to increase to 60%. Assuming that the cost of equity remains unchanged at 10.40%, you can estimate the price at the end of year 10 (terminal price):

Expected Earnings per share in year 11	$= EPS_{10} \ (1 + \text{growth rate in year } 11)$
	$= \$13.23 \ (1.06) = \$14.03$
Expected Dividends per share in year 11	$= EPS_{11} \ (\text{Payout Ratio}_{11})$
	$= \$14.03 \ (0.60) = \$8.42$
Terminal Price	$= DPS_{11} \ / \ (\text{Cost of equity}_{11} - \text{Growth rate}_{11})$
	$= \$8.42 \ / \ (.104 - .06) = \$191.30$

TABLE 2.2 Expected Dividends per Share

YEAR	EPS	DPS	PV OF DPS AT 10.40%
1	$3.48	$0.70	$0.63
2	$4.04	$0.81	$0.66
3	$4.68	$0.94	$0.70
4	$5.43	$1.09	$0.73
5	$6.30	$1.26	$0.77
6	$7.31	$1.46	$0.81
7	$8.48	$1.70	$0.85
8	$9.84	$1.97	$0.89
9	$11.41	$2.28	$0.94
10	$13.23	$2.65	$0.98
	PV of Dividends =		$7.96

The present value of this terminal price should be added on to the present value of the dividends during the first 10 years to yield a dividend discount model value for HP:

Value per share of HP $= \$7.96 + \$191.30 \ / \ 1.104^{10} = \$79.08$

Since HP was trading at $131 per share at the time of this valuation, the dividend discount model at least would suggest that HP is overvalued.

 ddmst.xls: This spreadsheet enables you to value a stable growth dividend paying stock, using a dividend discount model.

ddm2st.xls: This spreadsheet enables you to value a dividend paying stock, using a two-stage dividend discount model.

A Broader Measure of Cash Flows to Equity

To counter the problem of firms not paying out what they can afford to in dividends, you might consider a broader definition of cash flow, which you can call *free cash flow to equity*, defined as the cash left over after operating expenses, interest expenses, net debt cash flows, and reinvestment needs. *Net debt cash flows* refer to the difference between new debt issued and repayments of old debt. If the new debt issued exceeds debt repayments, the free cash flow to equity will be higher. In *reinvestment needs*, you include any investments that the firm has to make in long-term assets (such as land, buildings, equipment, and research, for a technology firm) and short-term assets (such as inventory and accounts receivable) to generate future growth:

Free Cash Flow to Equity (FCFE) = Net Income – Reinvestment Needs
– (Debt Repaid – New Debt Issued)

Think of this as potential dividends, or what the company could have paid out in dividend. To illustrate, in 1998, the Motorola free cash flow to equity using this definition was:

$$FCFE_{Motorola} = \text{Net Income} - \text{Reinvestment Needs}$$
$$- (\text{Debt Repaid} - \text{New Debt Issued})$$
$$= \$1,614 \text{ million} - \$1,876 \text{ million} - (8 - 246 \text{ million})$$
$$= -\$24 \text{ million}$$

Clearly, Motorola did not generate positive cash flows after reinvestment needs and net debt payments. Surprisingly, the firm did pay a dividend, albeit a small one. Any dividends paid by Motorola during 1998 had to be financed with existing cash balances, since the free cash flow to equity is negative.

Once the free cash flows to equity have been estimated, the process of estimating value parallels the dividend discount model. To value equity in a firm where the free cash flows to equity are growing at a constant rate forever, you use the present value equation to estimate the value of cash flows in perpetual growth:

$$\text{Value of Equity in Infinite} - \text{Life Asset} = \frac{E(FCFE_1)}{(k_e - g_n)}$$

All the constraints relating to the magnitude of the constant growth rate used, as discussed in the context of the dividend discount model, continue to apply here.

In the more general case, where free cash flows to equity are growing at a rate higher than the growth rate of the economy, the value of the equity can be estimated, again in two parts. The first part is the present value of the free cash flows to equity during the high-growth phase, and the second part is the present value of the terminal value of equity, estimated based on the assumption that the firm will reach stable growth sometime in the future:

Value of Equity with High-Growth FCFE =

$$\sum_{t=1}^{t=N} \frac{E(FCFE_t)}{(1+k_e)^t} + \frac{\text{Terminal Value of Equity}_N}{(1+k_e)^N}$$

With the FCFE approach, you have the flexibility you need to value equity in any type of business or publicly traded company.

ILLUSTRATION 2.2

Valuing Equity with FCFE: Hewlett Packard

Consider the case of Hewlett Packard. The last illustration valued HP with a dividend discount model but added the caveat that HP might not be paying out what it can afford to in dividends. HP had a net income in 1999 of $3,491 million, and reinvested about 50% of this net income. Assume that HP's reinvestment needs will continue to be 50% of earnings for the next 10 years (while it generates 16% growth in earnings each year) and that net debt issued will be 10% of the reinvestment. Table 2.3 summarizes the free cash flows to equity at the firm for this period and computes the present value of these cash flows at HP's cost of equity of 10.40%.

TABLE 2.3 Value of FCFE

Year	Net Income	Reinvestment	Net Debt Cash Flow	FCFE	PV of FCFE
1	$4,050	$2,025	$202	$2,227	$2,017
2	$4,697	$2,349	$235	$2,584	$2,120
3	$5,449	$2,725	$272	$2,997	$2,227
4	$6,321	$3,160	$316	$3,477	$2,340
5	$7,332	$3,666	$367	$4,033	$2,459
6	$8,505	$4,253	$425	$4,678	$2,584
7	$9,866	$4,933	$493	$5,426	$2,715
8	$11,445	$5,722	$572	$6,295	$2,852
9	$13,276	$6,638	$664	$7,302	$2,997
10	$15,400	$7,700	$770	$8,470	$3,149
PV of FCFE during high-growth phase					$25,461

Note that since more debt is issued than paid, net debt cash flows are positive and increase the free cash flows to equity each year. To estimate the terminal price, assume that net income will grow 6% a year forever after year 10. Since lower growth require less reinvestment, assume that the reinvestment rate after year 10 will be 40% of net income; net debt issued will remain 10% of reinvestment:

$FCFE_{11}$ = Net Income$_{11}$ − Reinvestment$_{11}$ − Net Debt Paid (Issued)$_{11}$
= $15,400 (1.06) − $15,400 (1.06) (0.40) − (−653) = $9,142 million

Terminal Price$_{10}$ = $FCFE_{11}$ / $(k_e − g)$ = $9,142 / (.104 − .06) = $207,764 million

The value of equity today can be computed as the sum of the present values of the free cash flows to equity during the next 10 years and the present value of the terminal value at the end of the 10th year:

Value of Equity Today = $25,461 million + $207,764 / $(1.104)^{10}$ = $102,708 million

On a free cash flow to equity basis, you would value the equity of Hewlett Packard at $102.708 billion. Dividing by the number of shares outstanding (997.231 million) yields a value per share:

Value per Share of HP = $102,708 / 997.231 = $102.99

The value per share is higher than the dividend discount model value of $79.08, but it is still lower than the market price of $131 per share.

FROM VALUING EQUITY TO VALUING THE FIRM

A firm is more than just its equity investors. It has other claimants, including bondholders and banks. When you value the firm, therefore, you consider cash flows to all of these claimholders. You can define the *free cash flow to the firm* as being the cash flow left over after operating expenses, taxes and reinvestment needs but before any debt payments (interest or principal payments):

Free Cash Flow to Firm (FCFF) =
After-Tax Operating Income − Reinvestment Needs

The two differences between FCFE and FCFF become clearer when you compare their definitions. The free cash flow to equity begins with net income, which is after interest expenses and taxes, whereas the free cash flow to the firm begins with after-tax operating income, which is before interest expenses.

Another difference is that the FCFE is after net debt cash flows, whereas the FCFF is before net debt cash flows.

What exactly does the free cash flow to the firm measure? On one hand, it measures the cash flows generated by the assets before any financing costs are considered and thus is a measure of operating cash flow. On the other hand, the free cash flow to the firm is the cash flow used to service all claim-holders' needs for cash—interest and principal to debt holders and dividends and stock buybacks to equity investors.

Once the free cash flows to the firm have been estimated, the process of computing value follows a familiar path. If valuing a firm or business with free cash flows growing at a constant rate forever, you can use the perpetual growth equation:

$$\text{Value of Firm with FCFF Growing at Constant Rate} = \frac{E(FCFF_t)}{(k_c - g_n)}$$

There are two key distinctions between this model and the constant-growth FCFE model used earlier. The first is that you consider cash flows before debt payments in this model, whereas you used cash flows after debt payments when valuing equity. The second is that you then discount these cash flows back at a composite cost of financing, that is, the cost of capital to arrive at the value of the firm, whereas you used the cost of equity as the discount rate when valuing equity.

To value firms where free cash flows to the firm are growing at a rate higher than that of the economy, you can modify this equation to consider the present value of the cash flows until the firm is in stable growth. To this present value, add the present value of the terminal value, which captures all cash flows in stable growth:

Value of High-Growth Business =

$$\sum_{t=1}^{t=N} \frac{E(FCFF_t)}{(1+k_c)^t} + \frac{\text{Terminal Value of Business}_N}{(1+k_c)^N}$$

ILLUSTRATION 2.3

Valuing an Asset with Stable Growth

Assume now that Hewlett Packard is interested in selling its printer division. Assume that the division reported cash flows before debt payments but after reinvestment needs of $400 million in 1999, and the cash flows are expected to grow 5% a year in the long term. The cost of capital for the division is 9%. The division can be valued as follows:

Value of Division = $400 (1.05) / (.09 − .05) = $10,500 million

ILLUSTRATION 2.4

Valuing a Firm in High Growth

Diebold is a technology firm that provides systems, software, and services to the financial services, education, and health care businesses. In 1999, the firm reported a free cash flow to the firm of $100 million. Assume that these free cash flows will grow at 15% a year for the next 5 years and at 5% thereafter. Diebold has a cost of capital of 11%. The value of Diebold as a firm can then be estimated as in Table 2.4:

TABLE 2.4 Value of Diebold

YEAR	EXPECTED FCFF	TERMINAL VALUE	PV OF CASH FLOW
1	$115.00		$103.60
2	$132.25		$107.34
3	$152.09		$111.21
4	$174.90		$115.21
5	$201.14	$3,519.88	$2,208.24
PV of Cash Flows =			$2,645.60

We estimate the terminal value by using the free cash flow to the firm in year six, the cost of capital of 11%, and the expected constant growth rate of 5%, as follows:

Terminal Value = $201.14 (1.05) / (.11 − .05) = $3,519.88 million

It is then discounted back to the present to get the value of the firm today, shown in Table 2.4 as $2,645.60 million.

Note that this is not the value of the equity of the firm. To get to the value of the equity, you need to subtract from $2,646 million the value of all nonequity claims in the firm. Diebold had debt outstanding of $138.25 million at the end of 1999. Subtracting this from the value of the firm would yield the value of equity at the firm:

Value of Equity at Diebold = $2,646 − $138 = $2,508 million

Dividing by the number of shares outstanding gives you the value per share:

Value per Share at Diebold = $2,508 million / 71.172 million = $37.17

The stock was trading at $29.625 at the time of this analysis (July 2000).

VALUING TECHNOLOGY STOCKS

The value of any asset is a function of the cash flows generated by that asset, the life of the asset, the expected growth in the cash flows, and the riskiness associated with the cash flows. If the value of technology firms is also determined by these same variables, what is different about them? From a conceptual standpoint, you can argue that there is very little that is different. From an estimation standpoint, however, a number of problems are, if not specific to technology firms, more serious when valuing these firms.

These estimation issues can be understood in the context of the four inputs that go into any firm valuation—cash flows, growth, discount rates, and asset life. We consider each of these issues briefly in this section. We build on each of these inputs separately in the next four chapters.

ESTIMATED CASH FLOW TO THE FIRM

The cash flow to the firm that you would like to estimate should be both after taxes and after all reinvestment needs have been met. Since a firm includes both debt and equity investors, the cash flow to the firm should be before interest and principal payments on debt.

The cash flow to the firm can be measured in two ways. One is to add up the cash flows to all of the different claimholders in the firm. Thus, the cash flows to equity investors (which take the form of dividends or stock buybacks) are added to the cash flows to debt holders (interest payments, net of the tax benefit, and net debt payments) to arrive at the cash flow. The other approach to estimating cash flow to the firm, which should yield equivalent results, is to estimate the cash flows to the firm prior to debt payments but after reinvestment needs have been met:

EBIT (1 – tax rate)
– (Capital Expenditures – Depreciation)
– Change in Noncash Working Capital
= Free Cash Flow to the Firm

The difference between capital expenditures and depreciation (net capital expenditures) and the increase in noncash working capital represents the reinvestments made by the firm to generate future or contemporaneous growth.

Another way of presenting the same equation is to cumulate the net capital expenditures and working capital change into one number and state it as a percentage of the after-tax operating income. This ratio of reinvestment to after-tax operating income is called the reinvestment rate, and the free cash flow to the firm can be written as:

Free Cash Flow to the Firm = EBIT (1 – t) (1 – Reinvestment Rate)

Note that the reinvestment rate can exceed 100%[5] if the firm has substantial reinvestment needs. If that occurs, the free cash flow to a firm will be negative even though after-tax operating income is positive.

What is unique about technology firms? First, some older technology firms and many newer technology firms have negative operating income, leading to negative free cash flows. Even among technology firms that have positive operating income, you sometimes see negative free cash flows, largely because of the prevalence of large reinvestment needs. While the presence of negative free cash flows, by itself, is not a problem for firm valuation, more of the value of these firms has to come from future cash flows and especially the terminal value. Second, significant problems are associated with how operating income and reinvestment is measured by accountants at technology firms. The biggest capital expenditure for most technology firms is in research and development, and this expense is treated as an operating expense for accounting purposes. This practice leads to a mismeasurement of both the operating income of the firm and its capital expenditures.

EXPECTED GROWTH

In valuation, it is the expected future cash flows that determine value. Although the definition of the cash flow, described in the last section, still holds, it is the forecasts of earnings, net capital expenditures, and working capital that will yield these cash flows. One of the most significant inputs into any valuation is the *expected growth rate* in operating income. While you could use past growth or consider analyst forecasts to make this estimate, the fundamentals that drive growth are simple. The expected growth in operating income is a product of a firm's *reinvestment rate*, that is, the proportion of the after-tax operating income that is invested in net capital expenditures and changes in noncash working capital, and the *quality of these reinvestments*, measured as the return on the capital invested. For a firm that has a steady and sustainable return on capital on its investments, the expected growth rate in operating income can be written as:

$$\text{Expected Growth}_{EBIT} = \text{Reinvestment Rate} \times \text{Return on Capital}$$

where

$$\text{Reinvestment Rate} = \frac{\text{Capital Expenditure} - \text{Depreciation} + \Delta\,\text{Noncash WC}}{\text{EBIT} (1 - \text{Tax Rate})}$$

Return on Capital = EBIT $(1 - t)$ / Capital Invested

Both measures should be forward looking, and the return on capital should represent the expected return on capital on future investments. That said, the return on capital is often based on the firm's return on capital on assets in place, where the book value of capital is assumed to measure the capital invested in these assets. Implicitly, you can assume then that the current accounting return on capital is a good measure of the true returns earned on assets in place and that this return is a good proxy for returns that will be made on future investments.

There are again reasons why this computation may not work for technology firms. The first reason is related to the treatment of research and development expenses as operating rather than capital expenses, leading to both reinvestment rates and returns on capital that do not reflect reality at technology firms. Second, the computation relating growth to reinvestment rates and returns on capital cannot be applied unadjusted to estimate growth at companies that are reporting operating losses (such as Amazon or Ariba) or at companies that have returns on capital that are expected to change over time. Since most technology firms fall into one or another of these exceptions, you have to develop variations that allow you to estimate growth at firms such as these.

DISCOUNT RATE

The expected cash flows need to be discounted back at a rate that reflects the cost of financing these assets. The cost of capital is a composite cost of financing that reflects the costs of both debt and equity and their relative weights in the financing structure:

$$\text{Cost of Capital} = k_{equity} \left(\text{Equity} / (\text{Debt+Equity}) \right)$$
$$+ k_{debt} \left(\text{Debt} / (\text{Debt} + \text{Equity}) \right)$$

where the cost of equity represents the rate of return required by equity investors in the firm, and the cost of debt measures the current cost of borrowing, adjusted for the tax benefits of borrowing. The weights on debt and equity must be market value weights.

The definition of cost of capital is no different for technology firms than it is for other firms, but there are three areas of difference. One is that many technology firms are disproportionately dependent upon equity for their financing, leading to costs of capital that are very close to their costs of equity.[6] When technology firms do borrow money, they tend to issue hybrid securities, such as convertible bonds, that share characteristics with debt and equity. The second difference is that the parameters of the cost of capital computation (the costs of equity and debt, as well as the debt ratio) can be expected to change over time as the firm becomes larger and more stable. This change will result in costs of capital that will be different from year to year. The third difference is that the estimation of the costs of equity and debt, which tend to depend on historical data, can be more difficult with technology firms, which often have short and volatile histories.

ASSET LIFE

Publicly traded firms do not have finite lives. Given that you cannot estimate cash flows forever, you can generally impose closure in valuation models by stopping your estimation of cash flows sometime in the future and then computing a terminal value that reflects all cash flows beyond that point. A number of different approaches exist for computing the terminal value, including the use of multiples. The approach that is most consistent with a discounted cash flow model is one where you assume that cash flows, beyond the terminal year, will grow at a constant rate forever, in which case the terminal value can be estimated as follows:

$$\text{Terminal Value}_n = \text{FCFF}_{n+1} / (\text{Cost of Capital}_{n+1} - g_n)$$

where the cost of capital and the growth rate in the model are sustainable forever. This fact, that they are constant forever, allows you to put some reasonable constraints on them. Since no firm can grow forever at a rate higher than the growth rate of the economy in which it operates, the stable growth rate cannot be greater than the overall growth rate of the economy. In the same vein, stable growth firms should be of average risk.

Thus, in every discounted cash flow valuation, you need to make two critical assumptions about stable growth. The first relates to when the firm that you are valuing will become a stable growth firm if it is not one already. The second relates to what the characteristics of the firm will be in stable growth, in terms of return on capital and cost of capital. These assumptions are both more difficult to make and more crucial to valuations when you are looking at technology firms.

There is also the very real possibility with a technology firm that the firm being valued might not survive to reach stable growth. If this happens, the terminal value in the discounted cash flow valuation will be the liquidation value of the assets of the firm, rather than the ongoing concern value estimated above.

BRINGING IT ALL TOGETHER

To value any firm, you begin by estimating how long high growth will last, how high the growth rate will be during that period, and what the cash flows will be during the period. You end by estimating a terminal value and discounting all of the cash flows, including the terminal value, back to the present to estimate the value of the firm. Figure 2–8 summarizes the process and the inputs in a discounted cash flow model.

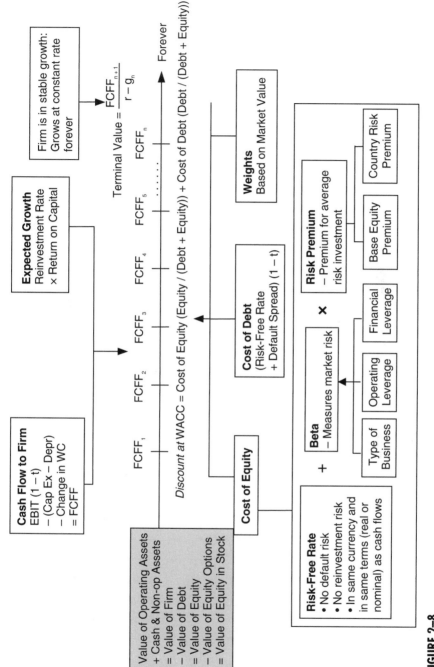

FIGURE 2-8
Discounted Cash Flow Valuation

SUMMARY

The value of an asset is the present value of the expected cash flows generated by it. This simple principle can be used to value any type of asset, ranging from one with guaranteed cash flows (riskless) to one with uncertain cash flows. The cash flow on an asset can be measured prior to debt payments (in which case it is categorized as a cash flow to the firm) or after debt payments (when it is called cash flow to equity). If the cash flows are prior to debt payments, that is, they are cash flows to the firm, they should be discounted at the cost of capital. If the cash flows are after debt payments, that is, they are cash flows to equity, they should be discounted at the cost of equity.

Firms are different from individual assets because their lives are not restricted. Consequently, you might need to compute the cash flows on firms forever in order to value them. Since this is an impossible task, you estimate a measure of value at the end of your forecast period. This value is called the terminal value and can account for a large portion of the value of the asset.

In summary, then, the value of a firm is a function of four variables: the cash flows from assets in place (existing investments), the expected growth in these cash flows, the length of the period over which the firm can sustain high growth, and the cost of capital. In the chapters to come, you consider each of these inputs with special emphasis on technology firms.

ENDNOTES

1. When you buy a corporate bond with a coupon rate of 8%, you are promised a payment of 8% of the face value of the bond each period, but the payment may be lower or nonexistent if the company defaults.

2. Note that in many cases, though we might not explicitly state probabilities and outcomes, we are implicitly doing so when we use expected cash flows.

3. By maintaining the building better, you might also be able to charge higher rents, which may provide an offsetting increase in the cash flows.

4. The nominal growth rate of the U.S. economy through the 1990s has been about 5%. The growth rate of the global economy, in nominal U.S. dollar terms, has been about 6% over that period.

5. In practical terms, this firm will have to raise external financing, from debt, equity, or both, to cover the excess reinvestment.

6. Startup technology firms can be the exceptions to this rule, often using substantial amounts of bank debt and hybrid securities to raise capital.

3

THE PRICE OF RISK: ESTIMATING DISCOUNT RATES

To value a firm, you need to estimate its costs of equity and capital. In this chapter, we first consider what each of these is supposed to measure, explore a simple model for the costs, and then examine the special problems associated with estimating each for technology firms.

The cost of equity is the rate of return that investors in a firm's equity expect to make on their investments. Since publicly traded firms usually have thousands of investors, the cost of equity is usually measured from the perspective of the marginal investors in the firm—the investors most likely to be trading on the firm's stock. The models used to estimate the cost of equity attempt to measure the risk added by an investment to the marginal investor's portfolio and usually require a riskless rate and an average market risk premium or premiums to arrive at the cost of equity.

The cost of debt is the current rate at which a firm can borrow, adjusted for any tax benefits associated with borrowing. Firms with higher default risk should have higher costs of debt than firms with lower default risk.

Technology firms present a particular challenge when it comes to estimating cost of equity. Conventional approaches to estimating equity risk that are based on stock prices flounder, given the limited and volatile price history exhibited by many of these firms. While more mature technology firms are predominantly financed with equity, some younger technology firms, especially startup ventures, do carry substantial amounts of debt. Attaching a cost of debt to the borrowings can become difficult because these firms are often not rated, lose money, and use hybrid securities like convertible bonds.

Cost of Equity

The cost of equity is the rate of return that investors in a firm's equity expect to make. In this section, we see why equity risk should be measured from the perspective of the marginal investor in a firm's equity, examine alternative models for measuring the cost of equity, and then consider how best to estimate the cost of equity for technology firms

Risk and Return Models

To estimate the cost of equity, you need to develop first a measure or measures of risk and then use those measures of risk to arrive at expected returns on equity investments. So, we begin with a short examination of the different risk and return models that are often used to estimate the cost of equity, and the common elements and differences across these models. We then look at how to use these models to estimate the cost of equity for technology firms.

Common Elements across Risk and Return Models.   There are several accepted risk and return models in finance, and they all share some common views about risk.

First, they all define risk in terms of variance in actual returns around an expected return; thus, an investment is riskless when the actual return is always equal to the expected return.

Second, they all argue that risk has to be measured from the perspective of the marginal investor in an asset and that this marginal investor is *well diversified*. Therefore, the argument goes, it is only the risk that an investment adds to a diversified portfolio that should be measured and compensated. In fact, it is this view of risk that leads risk models to break the risk in any investment into two components: a firm-specific component that measures risk that relates only to that investment or to a few investments like it, and a market component that contains risk that affects a large subset of or all investments. It is the latter risk that is not diversifiable and should be rewarded.

Competing Models. While all risk and return models agree on this fairly crucial distinction, they part ways when it comes to how to measure this market risk.

- The *capital asset pricing model*, with its assumptions that there are no transactions costs or private information, concludes that the marginal investor holds a portfolio that includes every traded asset in the market and that the risk of any investment is the risk added on to this "market portfolio." This risk is measured with a market beta (β_M), leading to an expected return of:

Expected Return = Riskfree Rate + β_M (Risk Premium on Market Portfolio)

  Thus, the cost of equity in the capital asset pricing model is a function of three inputs: the riskless rate, the risk premium on the market portfolio, and the beta of the equity investment being assessed. We discuss these in more detail later in this section.
- The *arbitrage pricing model*, which is built on the assumption that assets should be priced to prevent arbitrage, allows for multiple sources of market risk and uses

the betas relative to each of these sources to measure the expected return. Thus, the expected return is:

$$\text{Expected Return} = \text{Riskfree Rate} + \sum_{j=1}^{j=K} \beta_j (\text{Risk Premium}_j)$$

where

β_j = Beta of Investment Relative to Factor j

Risk Premium_j = Risk Premium for Factor j

In the arbitrage pricing model, the cost of equity is determined by the riskless rate, the risk premiums for each of the factors in the model, and the betas relative to each factor. The factors remain unnamed and are estimated with a statistical technique called factor analysis.

■ *Multifactor models*, which specify macro-economic variables as the market risk factors, take the same form as the arbitrage pricing model, with multiple betas and risk premiums:

$$\text{Expected Return} = \text{Riskfree Rate} + \sum_{j=1}^{j=K} \beta_j (\text{Risk Premium}_j)$$

where β_j is the beta of investment relative to macro-economic factor j and Risk Premium_j is Risk Premium for the macro-economic factor j. The cost of equity for a firm in a multifactor model depends on the riskless rate, the risk premiums for each of the macro-economic factors, and the betas for an investment, relative to each macro-economic factor.

■ *Regression models*, which relate the actual returns on stocks to observable and measurable firm characteristics such as market capitalization, are the final approach to estimating the costs of equity for firms. In this approach, the regression equation is first estimated from historical data and then used to obtain the costs of equity for individual firms.

Choice of a Model for Technology Firms. Given these choices, which, if any, of these models should you use to estimate the cost of equity for technology firms? The first, and perhaps most significant, problem in applying these models to valuing technology firms may lie in their perspective on risk. The assumption that the marginal investor in a stock, that is, the investor most likely to be trading on the stock, is a well-diversified entity may be a difficult one to sustain for technology firms for two reasons:

1.   Since most technology firms are young and the original owners continue to operate as top managers, the proportion of stock held by the top managers at these firms is much higher than it is in other firms. Larry Ellison at Oracle, Bill Gates at Microsoft, and Jeff Bezos at Amazon.com all continue to hold large percentages of their firms' stock.
2.   With the smaller technology firms, the marginal investor may be an individual who is not well diversified. In fact, the marginal investor may well be a day trader whose time horizon can be measured in minutes rather than years.

How would altering the marginal investors' characteristics change the way you measure risk? Instead of considering only the risk that cannot be diversified away (which is what the betas measure), you should be looking at total risk in investments if the investor is not diversified.

Should you, therefore, abandon traditional risk and return models when looking at technology firms? Not necessarily. Even though the largest holder of stock in many technology firms is the owner/founder, little trading occurs on this holding. In fact, in stocks like Oracle and Microsoft, the bulk of the trading is still done by institutional investors in the stock. This would indicate that the marginal investors, especially in the more liquid and widely traded technology stocks, are diversified institutional investors. When looking at less liquid technology stocks, held and traded primarily by individuals, you should be more cautious about using the conventional measures of risk.

If you do assume that it is, in fact, appropriate to value technology stocks by using the perspective of well-diversified investors, should you use the capital asset pricing model, the arbitrage pricing model, or the multifactor model? The capital asset pricing model may be the most widely used model in valuation practice, but it does contain some significant dangers for technology stocks, especially if the market betas are estimated in the conventional way.[1] Empirical tests of the model indicate that these betas underestimate the risk in small-capitalization stocks relative to large-capitalization stocks. In addition, stocks with high price-earnings ratios seem to earn lower returns than those predicted by the capital asset pricing model over long periods.

What are the alternatives? One is to use the arbitrage pricing or multifactor models. While these models have the potential to better capture the risk of investing in technology firms, they require even more historical data than does the capital asset pricing model. Another alternative is to abandon the conventional approach to estimating market betas in the capital asset pricing model and consider ways of adapting the estimation process to better measure the risk of technology stocks. The next section makes a case that the latter approach offers more promise.

ESTIMATION ISSUES

All risk and return models require three sets of inputs. The first is the risk-free rate, the second is the appropriate risk premium or premiums for the factor or factors in the model, and the third is the beta or betas of the investment being analyzed.

Riskless Rate. A riskless asset is one for which the investor knows the expected returns with certainty. Consequently, for an investment to be riskless over a specified time period (time horizon), two conditions must be met:

- There is *no default risk*, which generally implies that the security has to be issued by the government. Not all governments are viewed as default free, and this does create a practical problem in obtaining riskless rates in some markets.

■ There is *no uncertainty about reinvestment rates*, which implies that there are no cash flows prior to the end of your time horizon, since these cash flows have to be reinvested at rates that are unknown today.

Should you use a short-term or a long-term government bond rate as a riskless rate? The answer depends on when your cash flows come due. Assume, for instance, that you are analyzing a cash flow for five years and you need a five-year riskless rate. A six-month Treasury bill is not riskless for a five-year time horizon since there is reinvestment risk at the end of each six-month period. In fact, neither is a five-year government bond with coupons since the coupons have to be reinvested, at the rates prevailing at that time, every six months for the next five years. Only a five-year zero-coupon government bond fulfils these conditions—it has no default risk and there are no cash flows prior to the end of the fifth year.

Thus, the riskless rate is the rate on a zero-coupon government bond matching the time horizon of the cash flow being analyzed; here, since the only cash flow is the principal on the bond coming due at maturity, there is neither default nor reinvestment risk. In theory, this translates into using different riskless rates for each cash flow on an investment: the one-year zero-coupon rate for the cash flow in year 1, the two-year zero-coupon rate for the cash flow in year 2, and so on.

Matching each cash flow with a different riskless rate can be tedious, especially in the context of a valuation, where the cash flows are often spread over 10 years or more. A simpler, though less precise, solution will suffice. You could estimate the weighted average of when the cash flows come due by computing a duration for the cash flows in the valuation. In fact, extending a measure of duration often used in the context of bonds, you can estimate the duration of the cash flows in a valuation to be:

$$\text{Duration of Cash Flows} = \frac{\sum_{t=1}^{t=\infty} t \frac{CF_t}{(1+r)^t}}{\sum_{t=1} \frac{CF_t}{(1+r)^t}}$$

where CF_t is the cash flow in year t and r is the discount rate (cost of capital, if valuing a firm).

Once the duration of the cash flows has been estimated, you can then use a government bond with equivalent duration to derive a riskless rate. Since the cash flows on technology stocks tend to be weighted toward the later years (and are often negative in the earlier years), they will have a longer duration, and this would suggest that longer-term government bond rates should be used as riskless rates when you are valuing these stocks.

Risk Premium. The risk premium is clearly a significant input in all the asset pricing models. In the next subsections, we begin by examining the fundamental determinants of risk premiums and then look at practical approaches to estimating these premiums.

What the Risk Premium Measures

The risk premium measures the "extra return" that would be demanded by investors for shifting their money from a riskless investment to an average-risk investment. It should be a function of how risk-averse investors are and how risky they perceive stocks (and other risky investments) to be, relative to a riskless investment. Since each investor in a market is likely to have a different assessment of an acceptable premium, the premium is a weighted average of these individual premiums, where the weights are based on the wealth the investor brings to the market. Wealthier investors will have their risk premiums weighted more than those of investors with less wealth.

Estimating Risk Premiums

We look now at two ways to estimate the risk premium in the capital asset pricing model. One way is to look at the past and estimate the premium earned by risky investments (stocks) over riskless investments (government bonds); this is called the *historical premium*. The other way is to use the premium extracted by looking at how markets price risky assets today; this is called an *implied premium*.

Historical Risk Premiums

The most common approach to estimating the risk premium is to base it on historical data. In the arbitrage pricing model and multifactor models, the raw data on which the premiums are based is historical data on asset prices over very long time periods. In the Capital Asset Pricing Model (CAPM), the premium is estimated by an examination of the difference between average returns on stocks and average returns on riskless securities over an extended period of history.

In most cases, you follow these steps to find historical risk premiums. First, you define a time period for the estimation, which can range as far back as 1926 for U.S. data.[2] Then, you calculate the average returns on stocks and average returns on a riskless security over the period. Finally, you calculate the difference between the returns on stocks and the riskless return and use it as a risk premium to predict future returns. When you use historical premiums, you implicitly assume that the risk aversion of investors has not changed over time and that the relative riskiness of the risky portfolio (stocks) has not changed over time, either.

In calculating the average returns over past periods, you face a measurement question: Should you use arithmetic or geometric averages to compute the risk premium? The arithmetic mean is the average of the annual returns for the period under consideration, whereas the geometric mean is the compounded annual return over the same period. The following example demonstrates the difference.

YEAR	PRICE	RETURN
0	50	
1	100	100%
2	60	−40%

The arithmetic average return over the two years is 30%, but the geometric average is only 9.54% ($1.2^{0.5} - 1 = 1.0954$). Those who use the arithmetic average premium argue that it is much more consistent with the framework[3] of the CAPM and is a better predictor of the risk premium in the next period. The geometric mean is justified on the grounds that it takes into account compounding and that it is a better predictor of the average premium in the long term. There can be substantial differences in risk premiums based on the choices made at this stage, as illustrated in Table 3.1. The data in the table is based on historical data on stock, treasury bill, and treasury bond returns and provides estimates of historical risk premiums.

TABLE 3.1 Historical Risk Premiums for the U.S. Market

	STOCKS − TREASURY BILLS		STOCKS − TREASURY BONDS	
	ARITHMETIC	GEOMETRIC	ARITHMETIC	GEOMETRIC
1928–1999	8.73%	6.96%	7.63%	6.05%
1962–1999	6.97%	5.89%	6.06%	5.36%
1990–1999	13.29%	16.12%	10.97%	13.16%

(*Source:* Federal Reserve, *www.stls.frb.org/fred*, July 15, 2000)

As you can see, the historical premiums can vary widely depending on whether you go back to 1928, 1962, or 1990, whether you use T-bills or T-bonds as the riskless rate, and whether you use arithmetic or geometric average premiums.[4] Although it is impossible to prove one premium right and the others wrong, you are on safer ground using:

■ *Longer-term premiums*, since stock returns are volatile and shorter time periods can provide premiums with large standard errors. For instance, the premium extracted from 25 years of data will have a standard error[5] of about 4% to 5%.

■ *Long-term bond rates as riskless rates*, since your time horizons in financial analysis tend to be long term, and you use the Treasury bond rate as your riskless rate.

■ *Geometric average premiums*, since arithmetic average premiums overstate the expected returns over long periods.[6] The geometric mean yields lower premium estimates than does the arithmetic mean and provides a more appropriate estimate for longer time horizons.[7] On this issue, however, there is significant disagreement. Ibbotson Associates argues for the arithmetic average premium, noting that it is the best estimate of the premium for the next period. Indro and Lee (1997) compare arithmetic and geometric premiums, find them both wanting, and argue for a weighted average, with the weight on the geometric premium increasing with the time horizon.

These arguments would lead you closer to 6.05%, which is the geometric average premium for stocks over Treasury bonds from 1928 to 1999 if you use historical premiums. In using this premium, however, you are assuming that there are no trends in the risk premium and that investors today demand premiums similar to those that they used to demand two, four, or six decades ago. Given the changes that have occurred in the markets and in the investor base over the last century, you should have serious concerns about using this premium, especially in the context of valuation.

 histret.xls: A dataset on the Web summarizes historical returns on stocks, T-bonds, and T-bills going back to 1926.

Implied Equity Premiums

A second approach to estimating risk premiums does not require surveys or historical data but does assume that the overall market prices stocks correctly. Consider, for instance, a very simple valuation model for stocks:

$$\text{Value} = \frac{\text{Expected Dividends Next Period}}{(\text{Required Return on Equity} - \text{Expected Growth Rate})}$$

This is the present value of dividends growing at a constant rate forever, developed in Chapter 2, "Show Me the Money: The Fundamentals of Discounted Cash Flow Valuation." Three of the four inputs in this model can be estimated from publicly available information: the current level of the market (value), the expected dividends next period, and the expected growth rate in earnings and dividends in the long term. The only unknown is the required return on equity; when you solve for it, you get an implied expected return on stocks. Subtracting out the riskless rate yields an implied equity risk premium.

To illustrate the estimation of implied equity risk premiums, assume that the current level of the S&P 500 Index is 900. Assume also that the expected dividends on the index next year will be 2% of current stock prices (this is called the dividend yield) and that the expected growth rate in earnings and dividends in the long term is 7%. Solving for the required return on equity yields the following:

$$900 = (.02 \times 900) / (r - .07)$$

Solving for r,

$$r = (18 + 63) / 900 = 9\%$$

If the current riskless rate is 6%, this calculation yields a risk premium of 3%.

The advantage of this approach is that it is market driven and current and does not require any historical data. It is, however, bounded by whether the valuation model used is the right one and by whether the inputs to that model are available and reliable. For instance, in the above example, the use of dividends as the cash flow to equity investors and the assumption of constant growth might lead to an implied risk premium that is too low. Finally, the implied risk premium is based on the assumption that the market is correctly priced.

The contrast between the implied risk premium and the historical premiums is best illustrated by graphing the implied premiums in the S&P 500 going back to 1960 (see Figure 3–1).

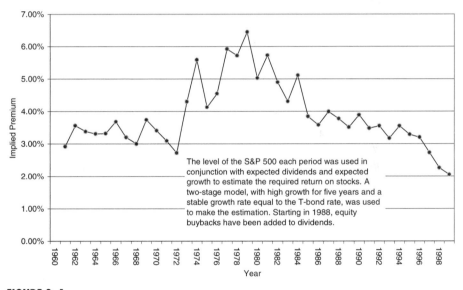

FIGURE 3–1
Implied Premium for U.S. Equity Market

Each year, we estimate expected dividends and expected growth[8] and use the level of the index at the end of the year to estimate implied equity premiums. Note that implied equity risk premiums are consistently lower than the historical premiums estimated in Table 3.1. The implied premium has also decreased over time.[9] At the beginning of 2000, for instance, the implied equity risk premium was about 2%, well below the historical premium of 6.05%.

 histimpl.xls: This dataset on the Web shows the inputs used to calculate the premium in each year for the U.S. market.

 implprem.xls: This spreadsheet enables you to esti- mate the implied equity premium in a market.

Risk Premiums to Use in Valuing Technology Stocks

When valuing technology stocks, what risk premium should you use to estimate the cost of equity? The choice between historical and implied premiums should not be based on what types of stocks you are valuing but on what you believe about markets. If you believe that markets are, on average, right, you should use implied equity risk premiums in all your valuations. If, on the other hand, you believe that mar- kets collectively can become under- or overvalued and that there is a tendency to revert to historical norms, you should use historical risk premiums. There are dangers associated with each approach.

If you decide to use historical risk premiums in valuation in periods such as the current one (when implied premiums are much lower than historical premiums), you will tend to find more stocks to be overvalued than undervalued. The rea- son is that large-risk premiums lead to higher discount rates (than those being assessed by the market currently) and lower present values. This effect is exacerbated for technology stocks, in general, and new technology stocks, in particular, because their payoffs in terms of cash flows occur far out in the future. If, on the other hand, you decide to use the implied equity risk premium and the market overall is overvalued, you will tend to overvalue stocks as well, and technology stocks more than others.

Is there an intermediate solution? Yes. The average implied equity-risk premium between 1970 and 1999 is approximately 4%. By using this premium, you are assuming that while markets might have been overvalued in some of these years and undervalued in others, it has been, on average, correct over this period.

Finally, why don't we use a technology stock risk premium to value technology stocks? In the standard models of risk and return that you will be applying, the risk premium is the premium that marginal investors demand for investing in the average-risk investment. Thus, it should remain the same for all assets. What will change across assets is your assessment of the risk of these assets (estimated as a beta or betas).

How a Country's Risk Affects Risk Premiums

Of the five companies that we will be valuing, Rediff.com poses a unique challenge. Rediff is an Internet portal directed at the Indian market. The sheer size of this market might be one of the more attractive parts of investment in Rediff; still, an investment in an emerging market might be exposed to additional risk that dies not exist, at least to a similar extent, for an investment in Yahoo! or Amazon. Should there be an additional risk premium added on to Rediff's cost of equity to reflect its emerging market status? Yes, and we should estimate it in two steps.

First, we derive a measure of India's country risk. To arrive at this measure, we begin with a country rating, which measures the default risk perceived in the country's bonds. The country rating for India in June 2000 was Ba2, and the default spread for Ba2-rated bonds over the U.S. Treasury bond was approximately 3%.[10] Second, we estimate an additional equity risk premium for India by measuring how much more volatile the Indian equity market is than its bond market. Using 1998-99 data, you could estimate the annualized standard deviation in the Sensex (Indian equity index) to be 31.82% and the annualized standard deviation in the Indian 10-year government bond to be 14.90%.[11] The country risk premium for India can then be estimated as follows:

Country Risk Premium for India

$$= \text{Default Spread for Country} \times \frac{\sigma_{Equity}}{\sigma_{Government\ Bond}}$$

$$= 3.00\% \times (31.82\% / 14.90\%) = 6.43\%$$

This determination is added to the risk premium of 4% estimated for a mature equity market, from the last part.[12]

How will this risk premium show up in Rediff's cost of equity? To make this judgment, we have to estimate Rediff's exposure to this risk and doing so requires an analysis of what it is that determines this risk and how best to measure it. In the next section, we turn to this measurement question.

Betas. The beta or betas that measure risk in models of risk in finance have two basic characteristics that you need to keep in mind during estimation. The first is that they measure the *risk added on to a diversified portfolio*, rather than total risk. Thus, it is entirely possible for an investment to be high risk in terms of individual risk but to be low risk in terms of market risk. The second characteristic that all betas share is that *they measure the relative risk* of an asset and, thus, are standardized around one. The market-capitalization weighted average beta across all investments, in the capital asset pricing model, should be equal to one. In any multifactor model, each beta should have the same property.

Keeping in mind these characteristics, you would like the beta you estimate for an asset to measure the risk added on by that asset to a diversified portfolio. This, of course, raises interesting followup questions. When you talk about diversified portfolios, are you referring to a portfolio diversified into just equity or should you include other asset classes? Should you look at diversifying only domestically or should you look globally? In the CAPM, for instance, with no transactions costs, the diversified portfolio includes all asset classes and is globally diversified. If there are transactions costs and barriers to global investment, the market portfolio may not include all asset classes or be as globally diversified. You can try an alternate route to answering these questions. In coming up with a diversified portfolio, you should take the perspective of the marginal investor in the market. The extent to which that marginal investor is diversified should determine the composition of the index to use in estimating betas.

Next, consider two approaches to estimating betas. The first is the regression approach, where historical stock returns are used to compute the beta of a stock. The other is the bottom-up approach, where you estimate the beta by breaking down a firm into individual businesses and estimating the betas of these businesses.

The Regression (or Top-Down) Approach

The textbook description of beta estimation is simple. You estimate beta for an asset by regressing the returns on any asset against returns on an index representing the market portfolio, over a reasonable time period, as shown in Figure 3–2.

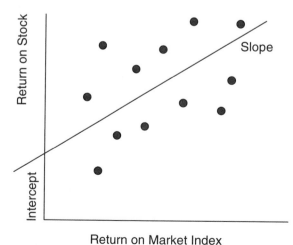

FIGURE 3–2

Regression of Returns on Stock against Return on Market Index

In the figure, the returns on the asset (R_j) represent the Y variable, and the returns on the market index (R_M) represent the X variable. Note that the regression equation that you obtain is as follows:

$$R_j = a + b\ R_M$$

The slope of the regression "b" is the beta because it measures the risk added on by that investment to the index used to capture the market portfolio. In addition, it also fulfils the requirement that it be standardized, since the weighted average of the slope coefficients estimated for all of the securities in the index will be one.

Although you can use the regression approach to estimate betas for technology firms, these betas are likely to be affected by three problems that, while not unique to these firms, are exaggerated in their case.

The Problem of Estimation Choices for Betas

The regression betas will vary widely depending on how the regression is set up and run. Consider the case of Cisco. You could estimate Cisco's beta relative to the S&P 500, the index most widely used by beta estimation services in the United States, and get the regression shown in Figure 3–3.

This regression uses monthly returns over 76 months to arrive at this estimate. Alternatively, you could have estimated Cisco's beta relative to the index of the exchange on which it is traded—the NASDAQ. The regression output is shown in Figure 3–4.

Note how different the betas are with the two indices: 1.09 with the NASDAQ versus 1.39 with the S&P 500. Which one is the right index? In the capital asset pricing model, the index that comes closer to the "market portfolio," which contains all traded assets in proportion to their market value, would be the better index. From that perspective, the S&P 500 would be the better choice since it includes the 500 largest market capitalization firms in the United States. But, you could legitimately

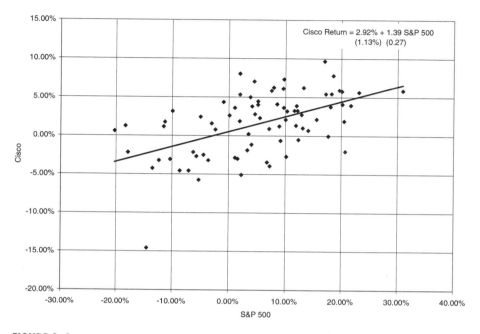

FIGURE 3–3
Beta Estimate for Cisco: S&P 500 (*Source: www.standardandpoors.com,* June 15, 2000, McGraw Hill)

have estimated Cisco's beta against other indices such as the Wilshire 5000 (which includes far more U.S. stocks) or the Morgan Stanley Capital Index (which has a better claim as an index that represents a global market portfolio). The betas would have been very different from the betas estimated above.

The choice of index is but one of the many choices that can affect the beta estimate. There are at least two others. One is the period over which you estimate the beta. Approximately six years of history were used in the two beta estimates above, but there is no consensus on this, with some services using only two years of history. Another choice is the return interval used to estimate returns. Monthly returns were used in the two estimates above, but daily, weekly, quarterly, or annual returns could also have been used. Table 3.2 reports the beta estimate for Cisco, relative to the S&P 500, as a function of these choices.

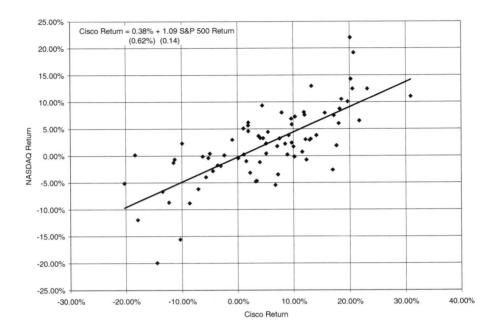

FIGURE 3–4
Beta Estimate for Cisco: NASDAQ (*Source: www.standardandpoors.com,* June 15, 2000, McGraw Hill)

TABLE 3.2 Beta Estimates for Cisco versus S&P 500

	DAILY	WEEKLY	MONTHLY	QUARTERLY
2 years	1.72	1.74	1.82	2.70
5 years	1.63	1.70	1.45	1.78

(*Source: www.standardandpoors.com,* June 15, 2000, McGraw Hill)

It should be troubling, from the perspective of valuation, that the regression technique can yield beta estimates ranging from 1.45 to 2.70.

The Problem of Noise

The beta estimate from the regression is noisy, and the range that emerges for the beta is large. Figure 3–5 reports the beta estimate for Amazon.com. Since it has been traded only since 1997, three years of monthly returns were used to make this estimate.

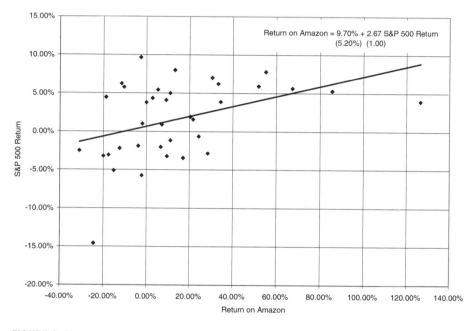

FIGURE 3–5

Beta Estimate for Amazon.com (*Source: www.amazon.com,* June 1, 2000, Amazon Corp.)

The beta estimate for Amazon of 2.67 comes with a standard error of 1.00. If you assume that the beta estimate is normally distributed, this would imply that the true beta for Amazon would lie between 1.67 (2.67 – one standard error) and 3.67 (2.67 + one standard error) with 67% confidence. While beta estimates for all firms come with standard errors, they tend to be much larger for technology firms, partly because of their limited histories and partly because of the volatility of their stock prices.

In fact, the beta estimate for Ariba has to be based on less than one year of data. Rediff.com, as an initial public offering, represents the limiting case for this problem since it has no public history. Its beta cannot be estimated with the regression approach.

The Problem of Firms Changing over Time

Even if a stock does not dominate the index and the regression beta has a low standard error, there is a final problem with regression beta estimates: they are based on historical data, and firms change over time. Technology firms change more than most because the technology evolves, revenues grow exponentially, and the firm's basic product mix often changes. In addition, these firms often acquire other firms to grow. Thus, the regression reflects the firm's characteristics, on average, over the period of the estimation rather than the firm as it exists today. Again, this problem is obvious with both Amazon and Cisco. Amazon, over the four years of its history, has seen its revenues increase from $16 million in 1996 to $1.6 billion in 1999. Clearly, it was a very different firm in 1999 than it was in 1996.

Bottom-Up Betas

The beta of a firm might be estimated from a regression, but it is determined by fundamental decisions that a firm takes on where to invest, what type of cost structure it plans to maintain, and how much debt it takes on. The alternative approach to beta estimation considers these fundamentals and is the bottom-up approach to beta estimation. To understand this approach, we first consider the fundamentals that determine betas and then provide a framework for estimating bottom-up betas.

Determinants of Betas

The beta of a firm is determined by three variables: (1) the type of business(es) the firm is in, (2) the degree of operating leverage in the firm, and (3) the firm's financial leverage. While much of the discussion in this section is couched in terms of CAPM betas, the same analysis can be applied to the betas estimated in the APM and the multifactor model as well.

1. *Type of Business*
   Since betas measure the risk of a firm relative to a market index, the more sensitive a business is to market conditions, the higher its beta. Thus, other things

remaining equal, cyclical firms can be expected to have higher betas than noncyclical firms. To illustrates companies involved in housing and automobiles, two sectors of the economy that are very sensitive to economic conditions, will have higher betas than those of companies that are in food processing and tobacco, which are relatively insensitive to business cycles.

Building on this point, you can see that the degree to which a product's purchase is discretionary affects the beta of the firm manufacturing the product. "Discretionary" refers to the capacity of customers of the firm to delay, defer, or not buy the product or service if their income drops. Technology firms that produce products that are nondiscretionary to their customers should have lower betas than those of technology firms that produce discretionary products. For instance, you would expect a firm that manufactures expensive add-ons for computers to have a higher beta than a firm that manufactures computers, and a firm that produces computer games to have a higher beta than a firm that produces virus protection programs.

There is also a link between a firm's growth potential and the discretionary nature of its products. If a significant portion of a firm's value comes from expected future growth, you would expect it to have a higher beta than that of a firm that gets most of its value from existing assets. The reason is that a high-growth firm has to attract new customers to its products or persuade existing customers to use more of its products, and the extent to which either occurs may depend on how well customers are doing.

2. *Degree of Operating Leverage*
   The degree of operating leverage is a function of the cost structure of a firm and is usually defined in terms of the relationship between fixed costs and total costs. A firm that has high operating leverage (i.e., high fixed costs relative to total costs) will also have higher variability in earnings before interest and taxes (EBIT) than would a firm producing a similar product with low

operating leverage. Other things remaining equal, the higher variance in operating income will lead to a higher beta for the firm with high operating leverage.

While operating leverage affects betas, it is difficult to measure the operating leverage of a firm, at least from the outside, since fixed and variable costs are often aggregated in income statements. It is possible to get an approximate measure of the operating leverage of a firm by looking at changes in operating income as a function of changes in sales:

Degree of Operating leverage = % Change in Operating Profit / % Change in Sales

For firms with high operating leverage, operating income should change more than proportionately when sales change.

What is the relevance for technology firms? Many new technology firms have significant fixed costs associated with setting up infrastructure and developing new products. Once these costs have been incurred, however, the variable costs are often low. America Online, for instance, faces very little additional costs when it adds a new subscriber, having used its resources to develop a communication network in prior years. For firms like Cisco and Microsoft, research and development expenses can be viewed as fixed costs, since the failure to do research can be disastrous for future growth. These high fixed costs should lead to higher betas for technology firms. Furthermore, since economies of scale are associated with size, you would expect smaller technology firms to have much higher betas than larger technology firms.

3. *Degree of Financial Leverage*
   Other things remaining equal, an increase in financial leverage will increase the equity beta of a firm. Intuitively, the obligated payments on debt increase the variance in net income, with higher leverage increasing

income during good times and decreasing income during economic downturns. If all of the firm's risks are borne by the stockholders (i.e., the beta of debt is zero)[13] and debt has a tax benefit to the firm, then

$$\beta_L = \beta_u \ (1 + (1 - t) \ (D / E))$$

where β_L is the levered beta for equity in the firm; β_u is the unlevered beta of the firm (i.e., the beta of the firm without any debt); t is the corporate tax rate; and D/E is the debt/equity ratio.

The unlevered beta of a firm is determined by the types of businesses in which it operates and its operating leverage. Thus, the equity beta of a company is determined both by the riskiness of the business it operates in and by the amount of financial leverage risk it has taken on.

Technology firms tend to be lightly levered. Thus, very seldom can debt be fingered as the culprit when a firm has a high beta. Given the high risk inherent in their underlying businesses, technology firms often have high unlevered betas. Borrowing money will only exaggerate the impact of leverage and push the betas of these firms to even higher levels.

 lexbeta.xls: This spreadsheet enables you to estimate the unlevered beta for a firm and compute the betas as a function of the leverage of the firm.

Estimating Bottom-Up Betas

Breaking down betas into their business, operating leverage, and financial leverage components provides you with an alternative way of estimating betas, where you do not need past prices to estimate the firm's beta.

To develop this alternative approach, we need to introduce an additional feature that betas possess and that proves invaluable. The beta of two assets put together is a weighted average of the individual asset betas, with the weights based on market value. Consequently, the beta for a firm is a weighted average of the betas of all of the different businesses the firm is in. Thus, the bottom-up beta for a firm can be estimated as follows.

1. *Identify the business or businesses* that make up the firm.
2. *Estimate the unlevered beta(s) for the business or businesses that the firm is involved in.*

    The simplest approach uses these unlevered betas directly, without adjusting for any differences between the firm being analyzed and the average firm in the sector. When you follow this approach, you implicitly assume that all firms in a sector have the same operating leverage. Given that smaller firms tend to have a greater proportion of fixed costs than those of larger firms, a more discriminating approach requires that you do one of the following:

    a. Assume that market capitalization and operating leverage are correlated, and use the *unlevered beta of firms with similar market capitalization* in estimating the unlevered beta.
    b. Calculate the *operating leverage of the division or firm being analyzed, and compare it to the operating leverage of comparable firms*. If the firm being analyzed has a higher proportion of fixed costs than the comparable firms, the unlevered beta should be adjusted upward (downward).

To calculate the unlevered beta for the firm, *take a weighted average of the unlevered betas*, using the estimated values of the different businesses that the firm is involved in. If the values are not available, use a reasonable proxy such as operating income or revenues.

3. *Calculate the leverage for the firm,* using market values if available. If not, use the target leverage specified by the management of the firm or industry-typical debt ratios.

4. *Estimate the levered beta* for the firm (and each of its businesses) using the unlevered beta from step 3 and the leverage from step 4.

Advantages of Bottom-Up Betas

This approach provides much better beta estimates for firms for three reasons.

The first is that you estimate the unlevered betas, by sector, by averaging across regression betas. While regression betas have large standard errors, averaging across regression betas reduces the noise in the estimate. In fact, the standard error of the average beta can be approximated as follows:

$$\text{Standard Error}_{\text{Average Beta}} = \frac{\text{Average Standard Error}_{\text{Beta Estimate}}}{\sqrt{n}}$$

where n is the number of firms in the sector.

To illustrate, consider the software sector. The average standard error for beta estimates in this sector is 0.50, and 225 firms are in the sector. The standard error of the average beta estimate can then be estimated as follows:

$$\text{Standard Error}_{\text{Average Software Beta}} = \frac{\text{Average Standard Error}_{\text{Beta Estimate}}}{\sqrt{n}}$$

$$= \frac{0.50}{\sqrt{225}} = 0.03$$

The second advantage of the bottom-up approach is that the beta estimates reflect the firm as it exists today, since the estimate is based on current weightings for different businesses. In fact, expected changes in business mix can be reflected in beta estimates quite easily with bottom-up betas.

The final advantage is that the levered beta is computed from the current financial leverage of the firm, rather than from the average leverage over the period of the regression. Thus, the beta can be estimated more accurately for firms that have changed their debt/equity ratio in recent periods.

 betas.xls: This dataset on the Web has updated betas and unlevered betas, by business sector, in the United States.

ILLUSTRATION 3.1

Estimating Bottom-Up Betas

The betas for the firms in the analysis can be estimated with the bottom-up approach and the average betas for the sectors in which each of the firms operates.

1. Bottom-Up Beta for Cisco

To estimate Cisco's bottom-up beta, assume that Cisco is in a single business (telecomm services) and that the firms in Table 3.3 are comparable firms.[14]

The average levered beta for the comparable firms is 1.43. The debt-to-equity ratio is computed for the comparable firms, using the cumulated market value of equity ($8821,54) and the cumulated market value of debt ($13,909) of the firms.[15] This average value is less affected by extreme values for the debt-to-equity ratio that individual firms may possess. The unlevered beta can then be estimated, using an average tax rate of 30.56%, as follows:[16]

Unlevered Beta = 1.43 / (1+ (1 − 0.3056) × (13909 / 882154)) = 1.412

TABLE 3.3 Bottom-Up Beta for Cisco

COMPANY NAME	BETA	MARKET CAP $ (MIL)	TOTAL DEBT $ (MIL)
3Com Corp.	1.35	16,620.70	45.00
ADC Telecom.	1.40	21,498.00	46.20
Alcatel ADR	0.90	336,934.70	4,793.90
Ciena Corp.	1.70	18,395.90	—
Comverse Technology	1.45	13,499.20	301.10
E-TEK Dynamics		15,517.00	28.90
JDS Uniphase	1.60	65,566.00	—
Lucent Technologies	1.30	201,173.20	7,026.00
Nortel Networks	1.40	164,284.30	1,665.00
Tellabs, Inc.	1.75	28,664.50	2.80
Average	1.43		

(*Source:* Value Line, June 2000 CD-ROM)

This beta is affected by the fact that these firms have cash on their balance sheets and cash has a beta of zero. The proportion of firm value (market value of equity plus debt) that was cash is computed to be 1.41%, and an unlevered beta for the business is estimated as follows:[17]

$$\text{Unlevered Beta (Cleansed of Cash)} = \text{Unlevered Beta} / (1 - \text{Cash} / \text{Firm Value})$$
$$= 1.412 / (1 - .0141) = 1.43$$

To estimate Cisco's bottom-up beta, we use Cisco market values of equity and debt:

Market Value of Equity = \$64.88/share × 6890 million = \$446,989 million
Estimated Market Value of Debt = \$0
Bottom-Up Beta for Cisco = 1.43

Note that this will be the beta that we use to value Cisco's operating assets. The cash is viewed as a separate asset that is added on to the value of the operating assets.

2. Bottom-Up Betas for Ariba, Amazon.com, and Rediff.com

Ariba and Amazon.com are considered Internet firms, but they operate in businesses where they compete with more conventional firms (brick and mortar, so to speak). For instance, Amazon.com can be considered a specialty retailer that delivers its products online, just as Ariba can be considered a firm that provides business services that operates on the Internet. To estimate Ariba and Amazon.com's betas, therefore, you can look at two groups of comparable firms. First, you can look at Internet firms as a group and estimate the betas for firms that offer business services online (for Ariba) and for Internet retailers (for Amazon). Second, you can estimate the betas of firms in the businesses in which Ariba and Amazon.com operate—business services and specialty retailing. Table 3.4 summarizes the estimates of the unlevered betas for each group.

TABLE 3.4 Unlevered Beta Estimates for Sectors

IN BUSINESS	ARIBA	AMAZON.COM
Internet firms	1.78	1.61
Brick and mortar	1.18	1.01

(*Source:* Value Line, June 2000 CD-ROM)

To value these firms, we assume that Ariba and Amazon are currently viewed by investors as Internet firms first and business service or retail firms second and the betas for Internet firms are used as their betas for the next five years. As both firms become larger, the fact that they deliver their products and services online will become secondary and their primary businesses will come to the fore. Consequently, the betas will be moved toward those of conventional firms after year five.[18] Since Amazon does have debt outstanding, the levered beta for the next five years is estimated to be 1.74, based on its market value of equity (at the time of the analysis) of $17.24 billion and the market value of debt of $1.345 billion.

Amazon's levered beta = 1.61 (1 + (1 − .00) (1.345 / 17.24)) = 1.74

A zero-percent tax rate is used, since Amazon is losing money and has considerable net operating losses to carry forward. As Amazon starts making money, this tax rate will change to reflect the marginal rate.

For Rediff.com, we face a tougher decision. The firm operates an Internet portal and, thus, would not have existed prior to the online boom, but it does make its money in conventional ways—from other firms advertising on its site. Portals try to attract customers by providing content or services (such as search engines) for free, and they charge for advertising based on the number of visitors they attract. Fundamentally, therefore, they do not differ from newspapers and magazines, which base their advertising rates on circulation and readership. As with Ariba and Amazon, we begin by using the average beta for Internet portals that are publicly traded as the beta for Rediff.com; the average beta of these firms was 1.90. We then move the beta of Rediff.com toward the average for publishing and newspaper firms as the firm matures; the average beta for these firms was 1.07. There is the real possibility that Rediff could evolve into a different kind of online business, becoming an online exchange or expanding into online retailing. Since all of these businesses currently have high betas (1.7 − 1.9), it should not make a significant difference in the near-term cost of equity.

3. Bottom-Up Beta for Motorola

Unlike Cisco, Ariba, and Amazon.com, Motorola operates in two different businesses: telecomm equipment and semiconductors. Since the beta for Motorola is a weighted average of the betas of these two businesses, you first have to compute the weights to attach to each business. In theory, the weights should be market value weights, but the divisions are not traded. You have three choices. You could use the operating income that Motorola reports for each business to weight them. This approach has intuitive appeal, but it can lead to negative weights for any business that is currently generating negative operation income. Alternatively, you could use the revenues generated by each business to weight them. This approach is simple and the weights are always positive, but you are implicitly assuming that the margins are equal across businesses. In the third approach, you estimate the revenues in each business first and then multiply them by the average value/sales ratio prevalent in publicly traded firms in that business to estimate an approximate value for each business. We use the values from Table 3.5 to weight the businesses. The unlevered betas of other firms in each of the two businesses are used to compute Motorola's beta.

We can then estimate the equity beta by using the current financial leverage for Motorola as a firm. Combining the market value of equity of $73.306 billion and the value of debt of $5.426 billion and using a 35% tax rate for the firm, we arrive at the current beta for Motorola.

Equity Beta for Motorola = $1.1563 (1 + (1 − .35)(5.426 / 73.306)) = 1.212$

TABLE 3.5 Motorola: Bottom-Up Beta

SEGMENT	REVENUES	VALUE/SALES	ESTIMATED VALUE	PROPORTION	UNLEVERED BETA
Telecom Equipment	$28,472.00	6.69	$190,478	71.76%	1.09
Semiconductors	$7,370.00	10.17	$74,953	28.24%	1.32
Motorola	$35,842.00	Bottom-Up Unlevered Beta =			1.1563

(*Source:* Motorola 10-K, *www.motorola.com*, June 1, 2000, Motorola Corp.)

Estimating the Cost of Equity. Having estimated the riskless rate, the risk premium(s), and the beta(s), you can now estimate the expected return from investing in equity at any firm. In the CAPM, this expected return can be written as:

Expected Return = Riskless Rate + Beta × Expected Risk Premium

where the riskless rate would be the rate on a long-term government bond, the beta would be either the historical, fundamental, or accounting betas described above, and the risk premium would be either the historical premium or an implied premium.

In the arbitrage pricing and multifactor model, the expected return would be written as follows:

$$\text{Expected Return} = \text{Riskless Rate} + \sum_{j-1}^{j=n} \beta_j \times \text{Risk Premium}_j$$

where the riskless rate is the long-term government bond rate, β_j is the beta relative to factor j, estimated from historical data or fundamentals, and Risk Premium$_j$ is the risk premium relative to factor j, estimated from historical data.

The expected return on an equity investment in a firm, given its risk, has implications for both equity investors in the firm and the managers of the firm. For equity investors, it is the rate they need to earn to be compensated for the risk they have taken in investing in the equity of the firm. If, after analyzing an investment, they conclude they cannot make this return, they would not buy this investment; alternatively, if they decide they can make a higher return, they would make the investment. For managers in the firm, the return that investors need to make to break even on their equity investments becomes the return they have to try to deliver to these investors. In other words, this is the cost of equity to the firm.

ILLUSTRATION 3.2

Estimating the Cost of Equity

In the following analysis, we estimate the cost of equity for the firms we are valuing, using the CAPM. In doing so, we use the bottom-up betas since they reflect best the true riskiness of these firms. Table 3.6 summarizes these estimates.

TABLE 3.6 Cost of Equity Calculation (for Next Five Years)

	AMAZON	ARIBA	CISCO	MOTOROLA	REDIFF
Bottom-up unlevered beta	1.61	1.78	1.43	1.1563	1.90
Bottom-up beta	1.74	1.78	1.43	1.212	1.90
Riskless rate	6.00%	6.00%	6.00%	6.00%	6.00%
Risk premium	0.00%	4.00%	4.00%	4.00%	10.43%
Cost of equity	12.94%	13.12%	11.72%	10.85%	25.82%

Note that the riskless rate and risk premium are the same for each of the first four firms. The only input that varies across these firms is the beta, with the higher beta stocks having higher costs of equity than the lower beta firms. The risk premium for Rediff.com is higher because it includes the country risk premium of 6.43% for India, leading to a much higher cost of equity for the firm. The cost of equity is estimated in U.S. dollars to reflect the fact that the cash flows are estimated in U.S. dollars.[19]

Risk, Cost of Equity, and Private Firms. Implicit in the use of beta as a measure of risk is the assumption that the marginal investor in equity is a well-diversified investor. While this is a defensible assumption when analyzing publicly traded firms, it becomes much more difficult to sustain for private firms. The owner of a private firm generally has the bulk of his or her wealth invested in the business. Consequently, he or she cares about the total risk in the business, rather than just the market risk.

There are three ways of estimating the cost of equity for a private firm with undiversified owners:

1. Assume that the business is run with the near-term objective of selling to a large publicly traded firm, or making an initial public offering; this is often the case with young technology firms. In such a case, it is reasonable to use the market beta and cost of equity that comes from it.

2. Add a premium to the cost of equity to reflect the higher risk created by the owner's inability to diversify. (This way of estimating may help explain the high returns some venture capitalists demand on their equity investments in fledgling businesses.)

3. Adjust the beta to reflect total risk rather than market risk. This adjustment is a relatively simple one, since the R squared of the regression measures the proportion of the risk that is market risk.

$$\text{Total Beta} = \text{Market Beta} / \sqrt{R^2}$$

In the case of Rediff.com, where the market beta is 1.90 and the average R^2 of the comparable publicly traded firms is 16%, this approach would lead to a total beta estimate of 4.75, resulting in a cost of equity of 55.54% for Rediff.com as a private firm. However, the cost of equity you use to value the initial public offering is based on the market beta, since the potential investors in the initial public offering are likely to be well diversified.

What if you were a venture capitalist analyzing an equity investment in a private firm? The cost of equity you would use will fall somewhere between the cost of equity that you estimate based on the market beta and the cost of equity you obtain from a total beta, depending on how diversified the venture capitalist is. Most venture capitalists are diversified across firms in a sector, that is, they are sector focused, but not diversified across sectors. Consequently, their costs of equity will be higher than those estimated with a market beta.

FROM COST OF EQUITY TO COST OF CAPITAL

Equity, albeit an important and indispensable ingredient of the financing mix for every business, is but one ingredient. Many businesses finance some or much of their operations by using debt or some security that is a combination of equity and debt. The costs of these sources of financing are generally different from the cost of equity, and the cost of financing for a firm should reflect their costs as well, in proportion to their use in the financing mix. Intuitively, the *cost of capital* is the weighted average of the costs of the different components of capital used by a firm to fund its operations.

Estimating the cost of capital for a technology firm is complicated by three factors:

■ These firms are disproportionately dependent on equity for capital. In fact, some of these firms are entirely financed with equity.

■ The firms that use public debt tend to use hybrid securities, such as convertible bonds, to raise funds.

■ Smaller technology firms have bank borrowings and are often not rated by the ratings agencies.

In this section, we consider first how best to estimate the cost of debt for technology firms and how to deal with hybrid securities in cost of capital calculations.

CALCULATING THE COST OF DEBT

The *cost of debt* measures the current cost to the firm of borrowing funds to finance projects. In general terms, it is determined by the following variables:

1. *The current level of interest rates:* As the level of interest rates increases, the cost of debt for firms will also increase.

2. *The default risk of the company:* As the default risk of a firm increases, the cost of borrowing money will also increase.

3. *The tax advantage associated with debt:* Since interest is tax deductible, the after-tax cost of debt is a function of the tax rate. The tax benefit that accrues from paying interest makes the after-tax cost of debt lower than the pre-tax cost. Furthermore, this benefit increases as the tax rate increases.

After-Tax Cost of Debt = Pre-Tax Cost of Debt (1 – Tax Rate)

Estimating the Default Risk and Default Spread of a Firm. The simplest scenario for estimating the cost of debt occurs when a firm has long-term bonds outstanding that are widely traded. The market price of the bond, in conjunction with its coupon and maturity, can serve to compute a yield you use as the cost of debt. For instance, this approach works for a firm like AT&T that has dozens of outstanding bonds that are liquid and traded frequently.

Many firms have bonds outstanding that do not trade on a regular basis. Since these firms are usually rated, you can estimate their costs of debt by using their ratings and associated default spreads.

Some companies choose not to get rated. Many smaller firms and most private businesses fall into this category. While ratings agencies have sprung up in many emerging markets, there are still a number of markets where companies are not rated on the basis of default risk. When no rating is available to estimate the cost of debt, there are two alternatives:

- *Recent borrowing history:* Many firms that are not rated still borrow money from banks and other financial institutions. By looking at the most recent borrowings made by a firm, you can get a sense of the types of default spreads being charged the firm and use these spreads to come up with a cost of debt.
- *Estimate a synthetic rating:* An alternative is to play the role of a ratings agency and assign a rating to a firm based on its financial ratios; this rating is called a *synthetic rating*. To make this assessment, you begin with rated firms and examine the financial characteristics shared by firms within each ratings class. To illustrate, Table 3.7 lists the range of interest coverage ratios for riskier nonfinancial service firms in each S&P ratings class.[20]

Now consider Motorola. It has an interest coverage ratio of 10.54. Based on this ratio, you would assess a "synthetic rating" of AA for the firm. This approach can be expanded to allow for multiple ratios and qualitative variables, as well.

Once you have a bond rating for a firm, you can estimate the cost of borrowing by adding a default spread, based on the rating, to the riskless rate. Allowing for a default spread of 0.50% for AA rated firms and a riskless rate of 6%, you estimate a pre-tax cost of debt of 6.50% for Motorola.

While this approach works reasonably well for firms that have established income streams, for young firms it can be difficult to get a good synthetic rating based on current operating income. The ratings of these firms reflect expectations about the future, and the operating income can usually be expected to change dramatically over the next few years. In these cases, an estimated synthetic rating can be based on the expected interest coverage ratio over the next few years, rather than the current interest coverage ratio.

TABLE 3.7 Interest Coverage Ratios and Ratings

INTEREST COVERAGE RATIO	RATING
> 12.5	AAA
9.50–12.50	AA
7.50–9.50	A+
6.00–7.50	A
4.50–6.00	A–
3.50–4.50	BBB
3.00–3.50	BB
2.50–3.00	B+
2.00–2.50	B
1.50–2.00	B–
1.25–1.50	CCC
0.80–1.25	CC
0.50–0.80	C
< 0.65	D

(*Source:* Compustat Database, 1998)

ILLUSTRATION 3.3

Estimating the Cost of Debt for Amazon

Amazon.com has $1,480.66 billion in debt outstanding. While this is a relatively small amount of debt, given that Amazon's market value of equity is $17.236 billion, it is still surprising since Amazon reported an operating loss of $276 million in 1999. To estimate the cost of debt for Amazon, you could use its current bond rating of B, assigned to it by Standard and Poor. Alternatively, you could estimate the interest coverage ratio for the firm and compute a synthetic rating. With a negative operating income, the interest coverage ratio will be negative, yielding a synthetic rating of D.

How do you reconcile the two ratings (B from the ratings agency and D from the synthetic rating), and which one should you use in your analysis? The ratings agencies are clearly assuming that Amazon's operating income in future years will be higher and, thus, would justify their higher rating. To estimate an equivalent synthetic rating, we use the projections of operating income that we have for Amazon for the next three years and compute an average interest coverage ratio based on the average operating income and current interest expense:[21]

Average operating income (next 3 years) = $270 million

Interest expenses (current) = $84.57 million

Interest coverage ratio = 270 / 84.57 = 3.19

Synthetic rating = BB

Default spread for BB-rated bonds = 2.00%

Pre-tax cost of debt for Amazon.com = Riskless Rate + Default spread = 6% + 2% = 8%

After-tax cost of debt for Amazon.com = 8% (since firm does not pay taxes currently)

The cost of debt for Amazon will change over time for two reasons. One aspect is that Amazon will start paying taxes in three years and the interest expense will yield a tax savings. The other aspect is that Amazon will become a larger, more stable firm over the next few years, leading to better ratings and lower default spreads. Table 3.8 summarizes the cost of debt estimates for Amazon over the next 10 years.

TABLE 3.8 Pre-Tax and After-Tax Cost of Debt: Amazon

YEAR	COST OF DEBT	TAX RATE	AFTER-TAX COST OF DEBT
1	8.00%	0.00%	8.00%
2	8.00%	0.00%	8.00%
3	8.00%	18.40%	6.53%
4	8.00%	35.00%	5.20%
5	8.00%	35.00%	5.20%

(continued)

TABLE 3.8 *(Continued)*

YEAR	COST OF DEBT	TAX RATE	AFTER-TAX COST OF DEBT
6	7.80%	35.00%	5.07%
7	7.75%	35.00%	5.04%
8	7.67%	35.00%	4.98%
9	7.50%	35.00%	4.88%
10	7.00%	35.00%	4.55%

Note that the after-tax cost of debt declines from 8% in year 1 of the analysis to 4.55% in year 10.[22]

 ratings.xls: This spreadsheet enables you to estimate the synthetic rating and cost of debt for any firm.

CALCULATING THE COST OF HYBRID SECURITIES

While debt and equity represent the fundamental financing choices available for firms, some types of financing share characteristics with both debt and equity. These are called *hybrid securities*. In this section, we consider how best to estimate the costs of two such securities: preferred stock and convertible stock.

Preferred Stock. *Preferred stock* shares some of the characteristics of debt—the preferred dividend is prespecified at the time of the issue and is paid out before common dividend—and some of the characteristics of equity: the payments of preferred dividend are not tax deductible. Preferred stock is generally issued in perpetuity and the cost of preferred stock can be written as follows:

k_{ps} = Preferred Dividend per Share / Market Price per Preferred Share

This approach assumes the dividend is constant in dollar terms forever and that the preferred stock has no special features (convertibility, callability, etc.). If such special features exist, they will have to be valued separately to estimate the cost of preferred stock. In terms of risk, preferred stock is safer than common equity because preferred dividends are paid before dividends on common equity. It is, however, riskier than debt since interest payments are made prior to preferred dividend payments. Consequently, on a pre-tax basis, it should command a higher cost than debt and a lower cost than equity.

Convertible Bonds. A *convertible bond* is a bond that can be converted into equity at the option of the bondholder. A convertible bond can be viewed as a combination of a straight bond (debt) and a conversion option (equity). Technology firms are heavy users of convertible debt, for two reasons:

1. The conversion option on the bond increases its price and reduces the coupon rate on the bond. This allows firms with low operating cash flows to service debt payments.
2. The high volatility in stock prices that characterizes many technology firms works in their favor by increasing the value of conversion options on convertible bonds.

What is the cost of a convertible bond? The simplest approach to analyzing a convertible bond is to break it down into debt and equity components and treat the components separately. There are two ways in which to accomplish this breakdown:

- Use an option pricing model to value the conversion option, which is treated as equity. The difference between the price of the convertible bond and the conversion option value is then treated as debt.
- Value the convertible bond as if it were a straight bond, using the stated coupon rate and maturity for the valuation. This value is treated as debt. The difference between the convertible bond price and this value is the value of the conversion option and is treated as equity.

ILLUSTRATION 3.4

Breaking Down a Convertible Bond into Debt and Equity Components: Amazon Inc.

In 1999, Amazon Inc. issued convertible bonds with a coupon rate of 4.75% and a 10-year maturity. Since the firm was losing money, it was rated CCC+ by S&P at the time of the issue and would have had to pay 11% if it had issued straight bonds at the same time. The bonds were issued at a price that was 98% of par, and the total par value of the convertible bond issue was $1.25 billion. Each convertible bond (with a face value of $1,000) can be broken down into straight bond and conversion option components.

Straight Bond Component = Value of a Straight 4.75% Coupon Bond Due in 10 Years with an 11% Interest Rate = $636 (Assuming Semiannual Coupons)

Conversion Option = $980 − $636 = $344

The straight bond component of $636 is treated as debt and has the same cost as the rest of debt. The conversion option of $344 is treated as equity, with the same cost of equity as other equity issued by the firm. For the entire bond issue of $1.25 billion, the value of debt is $795 million and the value of equity is $430 million.

CALCULATING THE WEIGHTS OF DEBT AND EQUITY COMPONENTS

The weights assigned to equity and debt in calculating the weighted average cost of capital must be based on market value, not book value. This is so because the cost of capital measures the cost of issuing securities—stocks as well as bonds—to finance projects, and these securities are issued at market value, not at book value.

There are three standard arguments against using market value, and none of them are convincing.

First, some financial managers argue that book value is more reliable than market value because it is not as volatile. While it is true that book value does not change as much as market value, this is more a reflection of book value's weakness than its strength, since the true value of the firm changes over time as both firm-specific and market information is revealed. Market value, with its volatility, is still a much better reflection of true value than is book value.[23]

Second, the defenders of book value also suggest that using book value rather than market value is a more conservative approach to estimating debt ratios. If the market value debt ratios are lower than book value debt ratios, as they generally are, the cost of capital calculated with book value ratios will be lower than those calculated with market value ratios, making them less conservative estimates, not more. To illustrate this point, consider Amazon. The firm's market value of equity of $17.26 billion and the market value of debt of $1.345 billion yield a market debt ratio of 7.81%. In contrast, using Amazon's book values for equity ($266.28 million) and debt ($1,480.66 million) results in a book debt ratio of 84.76%. The cost of capital can be calculated as follows:

With market value debt ratios: 12.94% (.9219) + 8% (.0781) = 12.56%

With book value debt ratios: 12.94% (.1524) + 8% (.8476) = 8.75%

Third, it is claimed that lenders will not lend on the basis of market value, but this claim again seems to be based more on perception than fact. Any homeowner who has taken a second mortgage on a house that has appreciated in value knows that lenders do lend on the basis of market value. It is true, however, that the greater the perceived volatility in the market value of an asset, the lower the borrowing potential on that asset.

There is one important point to be made about market values. Market prices for equity can change a great deal from period to period for technology firms. Amazon's market value of equity would have been $33 billion if this analysis had been done three months earlier, and the debt ratio would have been lower. The effect on the cost of capital will be muted, however, because technology firms tend to have small amounts of debt on their balance sheets. Even Amazon, which has a lot of debt for a new technology firm, has only seen its debt ratio increase from 4% to 7.81%, even as its equity market value dropped by 50%. With a cost of equity of 12.94% and a cost of debt of 8%, the cost of capital has changed from 12.74% to 12.56% as the debt ratio has increased.[24]

Estimating the Market Values of Equity and Debt. The market value of equity is generally the number of shares outstanding times the current stock price. If there other equity claims in the firm such as warrants and management option, these should also be valued and added to the value of the equity in the firm.

The market value of debt is usually more difficult to obtain directly, since very few firms have all their debt in the form of outstanding bonds trading in the market. Many firms have nontraded debt, such as bank debt, which is specified in book value terms, but not market value terms. A simple way to convert book value debt into market value debt is to treat the entire debt on the books as one coupon bond, with a coupon set equal to the interest expenses on all the debt and the maturity set equal to the face-value weighted average maturity of the debt, and then to value this coupon bond at the current cost of debt for the company. Thus, the market value of $1 billion in debt, with interest expenses of $60 million and a maturity of six years, when the current cost of debt is 7.5%, can be estimated as follows:

$$\text{Estimated Market Value of Debt} = 60\left[\frac{1 - \dfrac{1}{(1.075)^6}}{0.075}\right] + \frac{1,000}{(1.075)^6} = \$930$$

While this will yield a market value for the debt in the balance sheet, it still ignores other commitments that a firm has made that should be categorized as debt. The most important of these is operating leases. When a lease is classified as an operating lease, the lease expenses are treated as operating expenses and the operating lease does not show up as part of the debt of the firm. When a lease is classified as a capital lease, the present value of the lease expenses is treated as debt, and interest is imputed on this amount and shown in the income statement. You could make the argument that in an operating lease, the lease payments are just as much a commitment as are lease expenses in a capital lease or interest payments on debt. Converting operating lease expenses into a debt equivalent is straightforward. The operating lease commitments in future years, which are revealed in the footnotes to the financial statements for U.S. firms, should be discounted back at a rate that reflects their status as unsecured and fairly risky debt. As an approximation, using the firm's current pretax cost of borrowing as the discount rate yields a good estimate of the value of operating leases.

ILLUSTRATION 3.5

Difference between Market Value and Book Value Debt Ratios

Table 3.9 contrasts the book values of debt and equity with the market values for Cisco, Motorola, Amazon, and Ariba. Rediff has no debt on its books. For the four publicly traded firms, we estimate the market value of equity by using the current market price and the number of shares outstanding. For Rediff.com, we use the book value of equity, but the absence of debt makes the debt ratio zero. Cisco has no conventional debt, but Motorola, Amazon, and Ariba do have debt on their books. All of these firms except for Motorola also have operating lease commitments, and these commitments are treated as debt.

We estimate the market value of debt by using the book value of debt, the interest expense on the debt, the average maturity of the debt, and the pre-tax cost of debt for each firm. For Motorola, the book value of debt is $5,593 million, the interest expense on the debt is $305 million, the average maturity of the debt is 3.26 years, and the pre-tax cost of debt is 6.50%. The estimated market value is as follows:

$$\text{Estimated MV of Motorola Debt} = \left[\frac{1 - \dfrac{1}{(1.065)^{3.26}}}{0.065} \right] + \frac{5,593}{(1.065)^{3.26}} = \$5,426 \text{ million}$$

TABLE 3.9 Comparison of Book Value and Market Value Debt Ratios

	AMAZON	ARIBA	CISCO	MOTOROLA	REDIFF.COM
BV of Debt	1481	1.47	0	5,593	0
BV of Equity	266	122.18	11,722	16,828	0.29
BV D/ (D+E)	84.76%	1.19%	0%	24.95%	0%
MV of Equity	17,237	17,832	446,989	73,706	NA
MV of Debt	1345	1.47	0	5,426	0
PV: Leases	114	26.1	827	0	0
MV D/ (D+E)	7.81%	0.15%	0.18%	6.86%	0%

Since Motorola has no operating lease commitments, the estimated market value of Motorola's debt is $5,426 million.

Ariba has a small amount of conventional debt ($1.47 million) on its balance sheet, which is at market value. To this amount, we add the present value of operating lease commitments that Ariba has over the next five years, with the cost of debt of 9.25% used as the discount rate. Table 3.10 presents the debt value of operating leases.

TABLE 3.10 Debt Value of Operating Leases: Ariba

YEAR	LEASE COMMITMENT	PRESENT VALUE AT 9.25%
1	$5.10	$4.67
2	$5.20	$4.35
3	$5.29	$4.06
4	$5.40	$3.79
5	$5.42	$3.49
6 and beyond[a]	$9.78	$5.75
Total present value =		$26.10 million

[a] *The 10-K reports on the cumulated value of operating leases after year six. In this case, we have assumed that the entire payment is in year six. If the amount had been larger, we would have treated it as an annuity over multiple years for computing the present value.*

The cumulative market value of debt for Ariba is $27.57 million. We estimate the market values of debt and operating leases for Amazon and Cisco by a similar approach.

 wacccalc.xls: This spreadsheet enables you to convert book values of debt into market values.

ESTIMATING THE COST OF CAPITAL

Since a firm can raise its money from three sources—equity, debt, and preferred stock—the cost of capital is defined as the weighted average of each of these costs. Thus, if E, D, and PS are the market values of equity, debt, and preferred stock, respectively, the cost of capital can be written as follows:

$$\text{Cost of Capital} = k_e\ (E\ /\ (D + E + PS)) + k_d\ (D\ /\ (D + E + PS)) + k_{ps}\ (PS\ /\ (D + E + PS))$$

ILLUSTRATION 3.6

Estimating Cost of Capital

Concluding the analysis in this chapter, we estimate the costs of capital for each of the five firms that we will be valuing, as summarized in Table 3.11.

Note that the costs of capital are close to the costs of equity for all of the firms and almost identical to them for three. The reason is that equity dominates the capital structures for all of the firms, especially the youngest — Ariba and Rediff.com.

TABLE 3.11 Cost of Capital Calculation

	AMAZON	ARIBA	CISCO	MOTOROLA	REDIFF.COM
Cost of Equity	12.94%	13.12%	11.72%	10.85%	25.82%
Equity/ (Debt + Equity)	92.19%	99.85%	99.82%	93.14%	100.00%
Cost of Debt	8.00%	9.25%	4.03%	4.23%	10.00%
Debt/ (Debt + Equity)	7.81%	0.15%	0.18%	6.86%	0%
Cost of Capital	12.56%	13.11%	11.71%	10.39%	25.82%

SUMMARY

The costs of equity and capital are fundamental inputs in discounted cash flow valuation, and the estimation problems can be far greater when you look at technology firms. In this chapter, we considered the estimation issues and suggested solutions to some of the more common shortcomings.

Risk and return models for estimating the cost of equity begin with the premise that the marginal investor is well diversified and is therefore concerned only about the risk an investment adds to a diversified portfolio. This added risk is measured differently in different models, ranging from a market beta in the capital asset pricing model to proxies such as market capitalization in proxy models. This view of risk is justified for technology firms, even though many of them continue to be closely held and run by their founders—institutional investors, who tend to be well diversified, tend to dominate trading in these stocks. The standard procedures for estimating risk parameters, however, have to be modified substantially both because of these firms' limited and volatile price histories and because of the changes that these firms can go through in short periods. Bottom-up betas, based on the businesses in which the firms operate, are an alternative to regression betas and usually have lower standard error and better reflect the firm's current standing. In addition, the cost of equity should be estimated by use of implied, rather than historical premiums, and should be based on long-term riskless rates, rather than short-term ones.

When technology firms borrow money, they often use hybrid securities such as convertible bonds. They are also often unrated, leaving you with the task of estimating cost of debt on the basis of one or two years of history.

As a final point, it is worth noting that the costs of debt and equity, the weights on each, and the resulting cost of capital will change over time for all firms, but especially so for young, high-growth firms. Consequently, we need to not only estimate the current cost of capital but forecast how the costs of debt, equity, and capital will change as the firm grows larger and more stable.

ENDNOTES

1. The conventional approach, described in the next section, estimates the beta for a stock by running a regression of stock returns against a market index.

2. The most widely used database, from Ibbotson Associates, has returns going back to 1926. Jeremy Siegel, at Wharton, recently presented data going back to the early 1800s.

3. The CAPM is built on the premise of expected returns being averages and risk being measured with variance. Since the variance is estimated around the arithmetic average and not the geometric average, it may seem logical to stay with arithmetic averages to estimate risk premiums.

4. Booth (1999) examines both nominal and real equity risk premiums from 1871 to 1997. Despite nominal equity returns having clearly changed over time, Booth concludes that the real equity return has been about 9% over that period. He suggests adding the expected inflation rate to this number to estimate the expected return on equity.

5. Assuming that returns in individual years are independent, you can calculate the standard error of a 25-year estimate by dividing the annual standard deviation in stock prices in the U.S. (about 25%) by the square root of the number of years $(\sqrt{25} = 5)$, yielding a standard error of 5% (25% / 5) in the estimate.

6. When you look at markets like the United States that have survived for 70 years without significant breaks, you are looking at the exception. To provide a contrast, consider the other stock markets in which one could have invested in 1926; many of these markets did not survive, and an investor would have lost much of his or her wealth.

7. Part of the reason for the large difference between arithmetic and geometric premium is the serial correlation in stock returns—good years have tended to be followed by bad years, and vice versa.

8. From 1980 on, analyst projections of growth as the input on growth were used. Earlier, forecasts of expected growth based on growth in the previous five years were used. Since growth is often too high for a stable growth model, we used a two-stage model.

9. Pettit (1999) provides several reasons why equity risk premiums today are lower than they have been historically and argues for a 5% risk premium.

10. India does not have any dollar-denominated bonds that are traded. The dollar-denominated bonds issued by other Ba2-rated countries were used to estimate the spread over the U.S. Treasury bond rate.

11. Weekly returns over 100 weeks ending July 7, 2000, were used to make both estimates.

12. For a more extensive discussion of country risk premiums, see my paper on estimating risk premiums on my Web site: http://www.stern.nyu.edu/~adamodar/New_Home_Page/
   papers.html

13. If debt has market risk (i.e., its beta is greater than zero), this formula can be modified to take it into account. If the beta of debt is β_D, the beta of equity can be written as:

$$\beta_L = \beta_u (1 + (1 - t)(D / E)) - \beta_D (D / E)$$

14. The categorization of comparable firms from Morningstar.com is used to develop this list.

15. There are two measurement alternatives. One is to compute the unlevered beta for each firm and to average the unlevered betas. The other is to compute the debt-to-equity ratio for each firm and take the average debt-to-equity ratio.

16. The average effective tax rate for the comparable firms of 30.56% is used to estimate the unlevered beta.

17. I do this because cash balances can be different for different firms in the same business.

18. You adjust betas from year 6 through 10 to move them from Internet levels to conventional levels.

19. You can convert the dollar cost of equity into an Indian rupee cost of equity fairly easily by taking into account the difference in inflation rates in the two countries. For instance, using expected inflation rates of 6% for India and 3% in the United States, you can estimate the rupee cost of equity for Rediff.com as follows:
Cost of equity (in Rs) =
$(1 + \$ \text{ Cost of equity}) (1 + \text{Inflation rate}_{\text{India}}) /$
$(1 + \text{Inflation rate}_{\text{U.S.}}) - 1 = 1.2582 (1.06 / 1.03) - 1 = 29.49\%$

20. This table was developed in early 1999 by listing all rated firms with market capitalization lower than $2 billion, listing their interest coverage ratios, and then sorting firms on the basis of their bond ratings. The ranges were adjusted to eliminate outliers and to prevent overlapping ranges.

21. This projected interest coverage ratio can be estimated using projected interest expenses as well. This is, however, difficult to do unless we assume that interest expenses grow at the same rate as revenues or capital.

22. The tax rate is explained in fuller detail in Chapter 5, "Looking Forward: Estimating Growth."

23. Some analysts argue that stock prices are much more volatile than the underlying true value. Even if this argument is justified (and it has not conclusively been shown to be so), the difference between market value and true value is likely to be much smaller than the difference between book value and true value.

24. The effect would be even smaller if you adjusted the beta for the higher debt-to-equity ratio that Amazon has after the drop in market value of equity.

4

CASH IS KING:
ESTIMATING
CASH FLOWS

The value of an asset comes from its capacity to generate cash flows. When valuing a firm, these cash flows should be estimated after taxes, prior to debt payments, and after reinvestment needs. There are thus three basic steps to estimating these cash flows. The first is to estimate the operating income generated by a firm on its existing assets and investments. Although you can obtain an estimate of this from the income statement, you must substantially adjust the accounting income for technology firms to yield a true operating income. The second step is to estimate the portion of this operating income that would go toward taxes. In this chapter, we investigate the difference between effective and marginal taxes at this stage, as well as the effects of substantial net operating losses carried forward. The third step is to develop a measure of how much a firm is reinvesting for future growth. While this reinvestment will be divided into reinvestment in tangible and long-lived assets (net capital expenditures) and short-term assets (working capital), we will again use a much broader definition of reinvestment to include investments in R&D and acquisitions as part of capital expenditures.

DEFINING THE CASH FLOW TO THE FIRM

In Chapter 2, "Show Me the Money: The Fundamentals of Discounted Cash Flow Valuation," the cash flow to the firm was defined as the cash flow before debt payments, but after taxes and reinvestment needs. It was defined to be:

Earnings Before Interest and Taxes (1 – Tax Rate)
– (Capital Expenditures – Depreciation)
– Change in Noncash Working Capital
= Free Cash Flow to the Firm

In this section, we take a closer look at each of these items, with an emphasis on technology firms. We begin by defining earnings before interest and taxes (operating income), then examine the tax rate to use to measure the after-tax operating income, and conclude with a discussion of a firm's reinvestments, both in net capital expenditures and working capital.

OPERATING EARNINGS (EBIT)

A key input to the free cash flow to the firm is the operating income. The income statement for a firm provides a measure of the operating income of the firm in the form of the earnings before interest and taxes (EBIT). For most technology firms, there are two important considerations in using this measure. One is to obtain as updated an estimate as possible, given how much these firms change over time. The other is that reported earnings at these firms may bear little resemblance to true earnings because of limitations in accounting rules and standards.

UPDATED EARNINGS

Firms reveal their earnings in their financial statements and annual reports to stockholders. Annual reports are released only at the end of a firm's financial year, but you are often required to value firms all through the year. Consequently, the last annual report that is available for a firm being valued can contain information that is sometimes six or nine months old. In the case of firms that are changing rapidly over time, it is dangerous to base value estimates on information that is this old. Instead, we should use more recent information. Since firms in the United States are required to file quarterly reports with the SEC (10-Qs), and to reveal these reports to the public, you can obtain a more recent estimate of key items in the financial statements by aggregating the numbers over the most recent four quarters. The estimates of revenues and earnings that emerge from this exercise are called *trailing 12-month* revenues and earnings and can be very different from the values for the same variables in the last annual report.

There is a price paid for the updating. Unfortunately, not all items in the annual report are revealed in the quarterly reports. You have to either use the numbers in the last annual report (which does lead to inconsistent inputs) or estimate their values at the end of the last quarter (which leads to estimation error). For example, firms usually do not reveal details about options outstanding (issued to managers and employees) in quarterly reports, but they do reveal them in annual reports. Since we need to value these options, we can use the options outstanding as of the last annual report or assume that the options outstanding today have changed to reflect changes in the other variables. (For instance, if revenues have doubled, the options have doubled as well.)

For technology firms, and especially young technology firms, it is critical that you stay with the most updated numbers you can find, even if these numbers are estimates. These firms are often growing exponentially, and using numbers from the last financial year will lead you to misvalue them. For larger firms that are not changing dramatically from period to period, on the other hand, the gains from updating may be outweighed by the costs of incomplete information.

ILLUSTRATION 4.1

Updated Earnings for Technology Firms

Amazon and Motorola have financial years that end in December, making their last annual reports (10-Ks) the final reports available prior to their valuation. Ariba's financial year ends in September. Consequently, when Ariba was valued in June 2000, the last 10-K was as of September 1999 and several months old, and the firm had released two quarterly reports (10-Qs), one in December 1999 and one in March 2000. To illustrate how much the fundamental inputs to the valuation have changed in the six months, Table 4.1 compares the information in the last 10-K to the trailing 12-month information in the latest 10-Q for revenues, operating income, and net income.

TABLE 4.1 Trailing 12-Month versus 10-K (in Thousands): Ariba

	SIX MONTHS, ENDING MARCH 2000	SIX MONTHS, ENDING MARCH 1999	ANNUAL SEPTEMBER 1999	TRAILING 12-MONTH
Revenues	$63,521	$16,338	$45,372	$92,555
EBIT	–$140,604	–$8,315	–$31,421	–$163,710
R&D	$11,567	$3,849	$11,620	$19,338
Net Income	–$136,274	–$8,128	–$29,300	–$157,446

The trailing 12-month revenues are twice the revenues reported in the latest 10-K, and the firm's operating loss and net loss have both increased more than fivefold. Ariba in March 2000 was a very different firm from Ariba in September 1999. Note that these are not the only three inputs that have changed. The number of shares outstanding in the firm has changed dramatically as well, from 35.03 million shares in September 1999 to 179.24 million shares in the latest 10-Q (March 2000) to 235.8 million shares in June 2000. The most recent number of shares outstanding will be used in the valuation.

For Rediff.com, the filings made by the firm with the Securities and Exchange Commission, just prior to its initial public offering, were used. These filings included financial statements on the last four quarters, ending March 2000. The trailing 4-quarter data on revenues, operating income, and other expenses are used as the basis for projections in the valuation.

Cisco's financial year ends in July, making its last 10-K the most dated of the five firms being analyzed. In Table 4.2, Cisco's trailing 12-month (through December 1999) revenues, earnings, R&D, and net income are compared to the numbers from the last 10-K.

TABLE 4.2 Trailing 12-Month versus 10-K (in Millions): Cisco

	ANNUAL JULY 1999 (LAST 10-K)	TRAILING 12-MONTH
Revenues	$12,154	$14,555
EBIT	$3,455	$3,911
R&D	$1,594	$1,705
Net Income	$2,051	$2,560

Note that the differences, though large, are not as dramatically different as they are for Ariba. The importance of updating information is clearly much greater for younger firms than it is for more mature firms.

ADJUSTMENTS TO OPERATING EARNINGS

The reported operating earnings at technology firms are misleading for three reasons. The first is the treatment of research and development expenses as an operating expense, when, in fact, it is the single most critical component of capital expenditures at many of these firms. The second and lesser adjustment is for operating lease expenses, a financing expense that is treated in financial statements as an operating expense. The third factor to consider is the effect of the phenomenon of "managed earnings" at these firms. Technology firms sometimes use accounting techniques to post earnings that beat analyst estimates, resulting in misleading measures of earnings.

Capitalizing R&D Expenses. A significant shortcoming of accounting statements is the way in which they treat research and development expenses. Under the rationale that the products of research are too uncertain and difficult to quantify, accounting standards have generally required that all R&D expenses are to be expensed in the period in which they occur. This requirement has several consequences, but one of the most profound is that the value of the assets created by research does not show up on the balance sheet as part of the total assets of the firm. This, in turn, creates ripple effects for the measurement of capital and profitability ratios for the firm.

Research expenses, notwithstanding the uncertainty about future benefits, should be capitalized. To capitalize and value research assets, you make an assumption about how long it takes for research and development to be converted, on average, into commercial products. This period is called the *amortizable life* of these assets. This life will vary across firms and reflect the length of time before a commercial product emerges from the research. To illustrate, research and development expenses at a pharmaceutical company should have fairly long amortizable lives since the approval process for new drugs is long. In contrast, research and development expenses at a software firm, where products tend to emerge from research much more quickly, should be amortized over a shorter period.

Once the amortizable life of research and development expenses has been estimated, the next step is to collect data on R&D expenses over past years, ranging over the amortizable life of the research asset. Thus, if the research asset has an amortizable life of five years, the R&D expenses in each of the five years prior to the current one have to be obtained. For simplicity, we can assume that the amortization is uniform over time leading to the following estimate of the residual value of the research asset today:

$$\text{Value of the Research Asset} = \sum_{t=-(n-1)}^{t=0} R\&D_t \frac{(n+t)}{n}$$

Thus, in the case of the research asset with a five-year life, you cumulate one-fifth of the R&D expenses from four years ago, two-fifths of the R&D expenses from three years ago, three-fifths of the R&D expenses from two years ago, four-fifths of the R&D expenses from last year, and this year's entire R&D expense to arrive at the *value of the research asset*.

Finally, we adjust the operating income to reflect the capitalization of R&D expenses. First, we add back the R&D expenses that were subtracted to arrive at the operating income, reflecting their recategorization as capital expenses. Next, we treat the amortization of the research asset the same way that depreciation is and net it out to arrive at the adjusted operating income:

Adjusted Operating Income =
Operating Income + R&D Expenses – Amortization of Research Asset

The adjusted operating income will generally increase for firms that have R&D expenses that are growing over time.

R&Dconv.xls: This spreadsheet enables you to convert R&D expenses from operating to capital expenses.

ILLUSTRATION 4.2

Capitalizing R&D Expenses: Cisco, Motorola, and Ariba

Of the five firms that are being analyzed, three — Cisco, Motorola, and Ariba — have significant research and development expenses, which are currently being treated as operating expenses. To get a reasonable measure of operating earnings at these firms, you must convert these expenses into capital expenses.

The first step in this conversion is determining an amortizable life for R&D expenses. How long do you (or the firm) expect it to take for research to pay off? Table 4.3 reports on the amortizable lives used for each of the three companies in the analysis that have significant R&D expenses and the justification for amortization.

TABLE 4.3 Amortizable Lives for Research and Development Expenses

COMPANY	AMORTIZABLE LIFE	JUSTIFICATION
Ariba	3 years	Technology is evolving rapidly, and payoff from R&D is likely to be quick.
Cisco	5 years	The firm has a mix of research. Some projects will pay off quickly; some will take longer.
Motorola	5 years	The firm has a mix of research. Some projects will pay off quickly; some will take longer.

Amazon and Rediff.com do not have significant R&D expenses, which is not surprising given their businesses.

The second step in the analysis is collecting research and development expenses from prior years, where the number of years of historical data is a function of the amortizable life. Table 4.4 provides this information for each of the firms.

TABLE 4.4 Historical R&D Expenses (in Millions)

	ARIBA	CISCO	MOTOROLA
Current year	$19.34	$1,594.00	$3,438.00
-1	$11.62	$1,026.00	$2,893.00
-2	$4.50	$698.00	$2,748.00
-3	$1.90	$399.00	$2,394.00
-4		$211.00	$2,197.00
-5		$89.00	$1,860.00

For Ariba, the current year's information reflects the R&D in the trailing 12 months; for Motorola and Cisco, the R&D is from the most recent financial year.

The portion of the expenses in prior years that would have been amortized already and the amortization this year from each of these expenses is considered. To make estimation simpler, these expenses are amortized linearly over time; with a five-year life, 20% is amortized each year. This technique allows you to estimate the value of the research asset created at each of these firms and to amortize R&D expenses in the current year. The procedure is illustrated for Cisco in Table 4.5.

TABLE 4.5 Value of Research Asset: Cisco

YEAR	R&D EXPENSE	UNAMORTIZED AT THE END OF THE YEAR		AMORTIZATION THIS YEAR
Current	$1,594.00	100.00%	$1,594.00	
-1	$1,026.00	80.00%	$820.80	$205.20
-2	$698.00	60.00%	$418.80	$139.60
-3	$399.00	40.00%	$159.60	$79.80
-4	$211.00	20.00%	$42.20	$42.20
-5	$89.00	0.00%	$—	$17.80
Value of the research asset =			$3,035.40	
Amortization this year =				$484.60

The value of the research asset and the amortization in the current year are estimated and reported in Table 4.6 for Ariba and Motorola.

The final step in the process is the adjustment of the operating income to reflect the capitalization of research and development expenses. We make the adjustment by adding back R&D expenses to the operating income (to reflect its reclassification as a capital expense) and subtracting the amortization of the research asset, estimated in the last step. Table 4.6 summarizes the adjusted operating income for each of the three firms.

Note that Cisco and Motorola have adjusted operating incomes that exceed their reported operating incomes by about a billion dollars each.

TABLE 4.6 Adjusted Operating Income

	ARIBA	CISCO	MOTOROLA
Value of research asset =	$28.59	$3,035.40	$8,798.20
Amortization: R&D asset =	$6.01	$484.60	$2,418.40
EBIT	$(163.70)	$3,455.00	$3,216.00
+ Current year's R&D	$19.34	$1,594.00	$3,438.00
− R&D amortization	$6.01	$484.60	$2,418.40
Adjusted EBIT	$(150.37)	$4,564.40	$4,235.60

Capitalizing Other Operating Expenses. Although R&D expenses are the most prominent example of capital expenses being treated as operating expenses, there are other operating expenses that arguably should also be treated as capital expenses. Consumer product companies such as Gillette and Coca Cola could argue that a portion of advertising expenses should be treated as capital expenses since advertisements are designed to augment brand name value. For many new technology firms, including e-tailers such as Amazon.com, the biggest operating expense item is selling, general, and administrative expenses (SG&A). These firms could argue that a portion of these expenses should be treated as capital expenses since they are designed to increase brand name awareness and bring in new customers. America Online, for instance, used this argument to justify capitalizing the expenses associated with the free trial CDs that it bundled with magazines in the United States.

While this argument has some merit, you should remain wary about using it to justify capitalizing these expenses. For an operating expense to be capitalized, there should be substantial evidence that the benefits from the expense accrue over multiple periods. Does a customer who is enticed to buy from Amazon, based on an advertisement or promotion, continue as a customer for the long term? There are some analysts who claim that this is indeed the case, and they attribute significant value added to each new customer.[1] It would be logical, under those circumstances, to capitalize these expenses with a procedure similar to that used to capitalize R&D expenses:

- Determine the period over which the benefits from the operating expense (such as SG&A) will flow.
- Estimate the value of the asset (similar to the research asset) created by these expenses. If the expenses are SG&A expenses, this would be the SG&A asset.
- Adjust the operating income for the expense and the amortization of the created asset:

Adjusted Operating Income =
Operating Income + SG&A Expenses for the Current Period
– Amortization of SG&A Asset

ILLUSTRATION 4.3

Should You Capitalize SG&A Expense?
Amazon & Rediff.com

Consider SG&A expenses at Amazon and Rediff.com. To judge whether or not you should capitalize this expense, you need to get a sense of what these expenses are and how long the benefits accruing from these expenses last. For instance, assume that an Amazon promotion (the expense of which would be included in SG&A) attracts a new customer to the Web site; assume also that customers, once they try Amazon, continue, on average, to be customers for three years. You would then use a three-year amortizable life for SG&A expenses and capitalize them the same way you capitalized R&D: by collecting historical information on SG&A expenses, amortizing them each year, estimating the value of the selling asset, and then adjusting operating income.

We decided that selling, general, and administrative expenses should continue to be treated as operating expenses and not capitalized for Amazon for two reasons. First, retail customers are difficult to retain, especially online, and Amazon faces serious competition not only from B&N.com and Borders.com but also from traditional retailers, like Wal-Mart, setting up their online operations. Consequently, the customers that Amazon might attract with its advertising or sales promotions are unlikely to stay for an extended period just because of the initial inducements. Second, as the company has become larger, its selling, general, and administrative expenses seem increasingly directed toward generating revenues in current periods rather than future periods.

For Rediff.com, SG&A expenses were capitalized for three reasons. First, its business as an Internet portal will allow it to retain customers it attracts with its advertising and sales promotions for an extended period. Second, the fact that Rediff serves the Indian market (and is thus less likely to face competition from global giants[2]) and the small size of the company does provide it with the potential at least for a large and longer-term payoff from selling expenses. Finally, Rediff could very well use the investments in SG&A as a gateway to enter into other businesses in the future. A three-year amortization period was used for these expenses. Table 4.7 summarizes the estimates of the asset created by capitalizing SG&A expenses and the amortization on that asset.

TABLE 4.7 Capitalizing SG&A Expenses: Rediff.com (in Thousands)

YEAR	SG&A EXPENSE	UNAMORTIZED PORTION		AMORTIZATION THIS YEAR
Current	$5,276.00	1.00	$5,276.00	
-1	$1,550.00	0.67	$1,033.33	$727.67
-2	$0.00	0.33	$0.00	$0.00
-3	$0.00	0.00	$0.00	$0.00
Value of SG&A Asset =			$6,309.33	
Amortization of SG&A Asset This Year =				$516.67

Note that Rediff has been in existence only two years and there are no SG&A expenses from two and three years ago.

The reported operating loss at Rediff.com of −$6.915 million can now be adjusted for the capitalization of SG&A expenses (shown in thousands):

Reported EBIT	= −$6,915
+ SG&A expenses in current financial year	= $5,276
− Amortization of SG&A asset	= $517
Adjusted EBIT	= −$2,156

Converting Operating Leases into Debt. The second adjustment is for financing expenses that accountants treat as operating expenses. The most significant example is operating lease expenses, which are treated as operating expenses, in contrast to capital leases, which are presented as debt. In Chapter 3, "The Price of Risk: Estimating Discount Rates," we noted that there is no distinction between the two from the financial standpoint and that operating leases should be converted into debt.

In Chapter 3, the basic approach for converting operating leases into debt was presented. Future operating lease commitments are discounted back at the firm's pre-tax cost of debt. The present value of the operating lease commitments is then added to the conventional debt of the firm to arrive at the total debt outstanding.

Once operating leases are recategorized as debt, the operating incomes can be adjusted in two steps. First, the operating lease expense is added back to the operating income, since it is a financial expense. Next, the depreciation on the leased asset is subtracted to arrive at adjusted operating income:

Adjusted Operating Income =
Operating Income + Operating Lease Expenses
– Depreciation on Leased Asset

If you assume that the depreciation on the leased asset approximates the principal portion of the debt being repaid, you can calculate the adjusted operating income by adding back the imputed interest expense on the debt value of the operating lease expense:

Adjusted Operating Income =
Operating Income + Debt Value of Operating Lease Expense
× Interest Rate on Debt

ILLUSTRATION 4.4

Adjusting Operating Income for Operating Leases

Amazon, Ariba, and Cisco all have operating leases on which they provide more details in their financial statements. The present value of operating leases is reported in Table 4.8 for each of the firms, using the pre-tax cost of borrowing for each firm as the discount rate and converting into annuities the lump sum that these firms report in their financial statements.

TABLE 4.8 Debt Value of Operating Leases

| Year | AMAZON PRE-TAX COST OF DEBT = 8.0% | | ARIBA PRE-TAX COST OF DEBT = 9.25% | | CISCO PRE-TAX COST OF DEBT = 6.2% | |
	Commitment	Present Value	Commitment	Present Value	Commitment	Present Value
1	$68.30	$63.24	$5.10	$4.67	$156.00	$146.89
2	$39.40	$33.78	$5.20	$4.35	$143.00	$126.79
3	$20.50	$16.27	$5.29	$4.06	$122.00	$101.86
4	$1.00	$0.74	$5.40	$3.79	$109.00	$85.69
5	$ —	$ —	$5.42	$3.49	$97.00	$71.80
6+	$ —	$ —	$9.78	$5.75	$448.00	$294.39
Debt Value of Leases =		$114.03		$26.10		$827.43

The operating lease expenses after year five for Cisco are treated as an annuity.[3] The present value of operating leases is treated as the equivalent of debt and is added to the conventional debt of the firm.

Finally, you adjust the operating income for the imputed interest expense on the debt value of operating leases. Table 4.9 summarizes the net effect of this adjustment for each of the three firms that have operating leases.

These imputed interest expenses will be added to the stated operating income to arrive at adjusted operating income estimates for each of these firms.

TABLE 4.9 Imputed Interest Expense on Operating Leases

	AMAZON	ARIBA	CISCO
Debt value of operating leases	$114.33	$26.10	$827.40
Pre-tax cost of debt	8.00%	9.25%	6.20%
Imputed interest expenses on operating lease debt	$9.15	$2.41	$51.30

Oplease.xls: This spreadsheet enables you to convert operating lease expenses into debt.

Handling Managed Earnings: Consequences and Adjustments.   Technology firms have become particularly adept at meeting and beating analyst estimates of earnings each quarter. While beating earnings estimates can be viewed as a positive development, some technology firms adopt questionable accounting techniques to accomplish this objective. When valuing these firms, you have to correct operating income for these accounting manipulations to arrive at the correct operating income.

The Phenomenon of Managed Earnings

In the 1990s, firms like Microsoft and Intel set the pattern for technology firms. In fact, Microsoft beat analyst estimates of earnings in 39 of the 40 quarters during the decade, and Intel posted a record almost as impressive. As the market values of these firms rose, other technology firms followed in their footsteps in trying to deliver earnings that were higher than analyst estimates by at least a few pennies. The evidence is overwhelming that the phenomenon is spreading. For an unprecedented 18 quarters in a row, from 1996 to 2000, more firms beat consensus earnings estimates than missed them.[4] In another indication of the management of earnings, the gap between the earnings reported by firms to the Internal Revenue Service and that reported to equity investors has been growing over the last decade.

Given that these analyst estimates are expectations, what does this gap tell you? One possibility is that analysts consistently underestimate earnings and never learn from their mistakes. While this is a possibility, it seems extremely unlikely to persist over an entire decade. Another possibility is that technology firms particularly have far more discretion in how they measure and report earnings and are using this discretion to beat estimates. In particular, the treatment of research expenses as operating expenses gives these firms an advantage when it comes to managing earnings.

Does managing earnings really increase a firm's stock price? It might be possible to beat analysts quarter after quarter, but are markets as gullible? They are not, and the advent of *whispered earnings estimates* is in reaction to the consistent delivery of earnings that are above expectations. What are whispered earnings? They are implicit earnings estimates that firms like Intel and Microsoft have to beat to surprise the market, and these estimates are usually a few cents higher than analyst estimates. For instance, on April 10, 1997, Intel reported earnings per share of $2.10 per share, higher than analyst estimates of $2.06 per share, but saw its stock price drop five points because the whispered earnings estimate had been $2.15. In other words, markets had built into expectations the amount by which Intel had beaten earnings estimates historically.

Why Firms Manage Earnings

Firms generally manage earnings because they believe that they will be rewarded by markets for delivering earnings that are smoother and come in consistently above analyst estimates. As evidence, they point to the success of firms like Microsoft and Intel and to the brutal punishment meted out, especially at technology firms, to those who do not meet these expectations.

Many financial managers also seem to believe that investors take earnings numbers at face value, and these managers work at delivering bottom lines that reflect this belief. This may explain why any attempts by the Financial Accounting

Standards Board (FASB) to change the way earnings are measured are fought with vigor, even when the changes make sense. For instance, any attempts by FASB to value the options granted by these firms to their managers at a fair value and charging them against earnings or to change the way mergers are accounted for have been consistently opposed by technology firms.

It may also be in the best interests of the managers of firms to manage earnings. Managers know that they are more likely to be fired when earnings drop significantly, relative to prior periods. Furthermore, there are firms where managerial compensation is still built around profit targets, and meeting these targets can lead to lucrative bonuses.

Techniques for Managing Earnings

How do firms manage earnings? One aspect of good earnings management is the care and nurturing of analyst expectations, a practice that Microsoft perfected during the 1990s. Executives at the firm monitored analyst estimates of earnings and stepped in to lower expectations when they believed that the estimates were too high.[5] Several other techniques are used, and we consider some of the most common in this section. Not all the techniques are hurtful to the firm, and some may indeed be considered prudent management.

1. *Planning ahead*: Firms can plan investments and asset sales to keep earnings rising smoothly.

2. *Recognizing revenues*: Firms have some leeway when revenues have to be recognized. For example, Microsoft, in 1995, adopted an extremely conservative approach to accounting for revenues from its sale of Windows 95 and chose not to show large chunks of revenues that they were entitled (though not obligated) to show.[6] In fact, the firm had accumulated $1.1 billion in unearned revenues by the end of 1996 that it could borrow against to supplement earnings in a weaker quarter.

3. *Booking revenues early*: In an opposite phenomenon, firms sometimes ship products during the final days of a weak quarter to distributors and retailers and record

the revenues. Consider the case of MicroStrategy, a technology firm that went public in 1998. In the last two quarters of 1999, the firm reported revenue growth of 20% and 27%, respectively, but much of that growth was attributable to large deals announced just days after each quarter ended, with some revenues attributed to the just-ended quarter.[7] In a more elaborate variant of this strategy, two technology firms, both of which need to boost revenues, can enter into a transaction that swaps revenues.

4. *Capitalizing operating expenses*: Just as with revenue recognition, firms are given some discretion in classifying expenses as operating or capital expenses, especially for items like software R&D. AOL's practice of capitalizing and writing off the cost of the CDs and disks it provided with magazines, for instance, allowed it to report positive earnings through much of the late 1990s.

5. *Writing off restructuring*: A major restructuring charge can result in lower income in the current period, but it provides two benefits to the firm taking it. Since operating earnings are reported both before and after the restructuring charge, it allows the firm to separate the expense from operations. It also makes beating earnings easier in future quarters.

   To see how restructuring can boost earnings, consider the case of IBM. By writing off old plants and equipment in the year they are closed, IBM was able to drop depreciation expenses to 5% of revenue in 1996 from an average of 7% in 1990–94. The difference, in 1996 revenue, was $1.64 billion, or 18% of the company's $9.02 billion in pre-tax profit last year.

   Technology firms have been particularly adept at writing off a large portion of acquisition costs as in-process R&D to register increases in earnings in subsequent quarters. Lev and Deng (1997)[8] studied 389 firms that wrote off in-process R&D between 1990 and 1996;[9] these write-offs amounted, on average, to 72% of the purchase price on these acquisitions and increased the acquiring firm's earnings 22% in the fourth quarter after the acquisition.

6. *Using reserves*: Firms are allowed to build up reserves for bad debts, product returns, and other potential losses. Some firms are conservative in their estimates in good years and use the excess reserves that they have built up during these years to smooth out earnings in other years.

7. *Reporting income from investments*: Firms with substantial holdings of marketable securities or investments in other firms often have these investments recorded on their books at values well below their market values. Thus, liquidating these investments can result in large capital gains that can boost income in the period. Technology firms such as Intel have used this route to beat earnings estimates.

Adjustments to Operating Income. To the extent that firms manage earnings, you have to be cautious about using the current year's earnings as a base for projections. In particular:

■ Any expense (or income) that is truly a one-time expense (or income) should be removed from the operating income and should not be used in forecasting future operating income. While this would seem to indicate that all extraordinary charges should be expunged from operating income, there are some extraordinary charges that seem to occur at regular intervals, say, once every four or five years. Such expenses should be viewed as irregular rather than extraordinary expenses and should be built into forecasts. The easiest way to build in irregular expenses is to annualize the expense. Put simply, annualizing would mean taking one-fifth of any expense that occurs once every five years and computing the income based on this apportioned expense.

■ We would skeptically view revenue growth that is being sustained by questionable accounting practices. It is very likely that this growth is not sustainable and will be reversed in future periods.

■ Smoothing earnings, by itself, is not a problem as long as it is not viewed as an indicator of the risk (or lack of it) in the firm. Firms with smooth earnings can have very volatile operations.

ILLUSTRATION 4.5

Estimating Operating Income for Firms

In Table 4.10, the estimates of earnings before interest and taxes are reported for Amazon, Ariba, Cisco, Motorola, and Rediff.com. The two adjustments are for R&D (or SG&A) expenditures and operating leases, described in the earlier sections. We also correct the operating income for any one-time losses or income.

TABLE 4.10 Adjusted Operating Income Estimates (in Millions)

	AMAZON	ARIBA	CISCO	MOTOROLA	REDIFF.COM
EBIT	$(276.00)	$(163.70)	$3,455.00	$2,364.00	$(6.92)
+ Extraordinary Losses (Gains)	$ —	$ —	$ —	$852.00	0
+ Current year's R&D or SG&A	$ —	$19.34	$1,594.00	$3,438.00	$5.28
– R&D or SG&A Amortization	$ —	$6.01	$484.60	$2,418.40	$0.52
EBIT Adjusted for R&D and SG&A	$(276.00)	$(150.37)	$4,564.40	$4,235.60	$(2.16)
+ Interest Expense on Operating Lease Debt	$9.15	$2.41	$51.30	$ —	0
EBIT Adjusted for R&D and Operating Leases	$(266.85)	$(147.96)	$4,615.70	$4,235.60	$(2.16)

Motorola operating income was adjusted for two one-time items: the firm reported $1.932 billion in special charges related to its Iridium project and $1.18 billion in one-time gains. The net loss of $852 million reduced operating income and was added back to arrive at the adjusted operating income.

THE TAX EFFECT

To compute the after-tax operating income, you multiply the earnings before interest and taxes by an estimated tax rate. This simple procedure can be complicated by three issues that often arise when you look at technology firms. The first issue is the wide differences you observe between effective and marginal tax rates for these firms and the choice you face between the two in valuation. The second issue arises usually with new technology firms and is caused by the large losses they often report, leading to large net operating losses that are carried forward and can save taxes in future years. The third issue arises from the capitalizing of research and development expenses. The fact that R&D expenditures can be expensed immediately leads to much higher tax benefits for the firm.

EFFECTIVE VERSUS MARGINAL TAX RATE

You are faced with a choice of several different tax rates. The most widely reported tax rate in financial statements is the *effective tax rate*, which is computed from the reported income statement as follows:

Effective Tax Rate = Taxes Due / Taxable Income

The second choice on tax rates is the *marginal tax rate*, which is the tax rate the firm faces on its last dollar of income. This rate depends on the tax code and reflects the amount that firms must pay as taxes on their marginal income. In the United States, for instance, the federal corporate tax rate on marginal income is 35%; with the addition of state and local taxes, most firms face a marginal corporate tax rate of 40% or higher.

Given that most of the taxable income of publicly traded firms is at the highest marginal tax bracket, why would a firm's effective tax rate be different from its marginal tax rate? There are at least three reasons.

1. Many firms, at least in the United States, follow different accounting standards for tax and for reporting purposes. For instance, firms often use straight line depreciation for reporting purposes and accelerated depreciation for tax purposes. As a consequence, the reported taxable income is significantly higher than the taxable income on which taxes are based.[10]

2. Firms sometimes use tax credits to reduce the taxes they pay. These credits, in turn, can reduce the effective tax rate below the marginal tax rate.

3. Finally, firms can sometimes defer taxes on income to future periods. If firms defer taxes, the taxes paid in the current period will be at a rate lower than the marginal tax rate. In a later period, however, when the firm pays the deferred taxes, the effective tax rate will be higher than the marginal tax rate.

In valuing a firm, should you use the marginal or the effective tax rates? If the same tax rate has to be applied to earnings every period, the safer choice is the marginal tax rate because none of the three reasons noted above can be sustained in perpetuity. As new capital expenditures taper off, the difference between reported and tax income will narrow; tax credits are seldom perpetual, and firms eventually do have to pay their deferred taxes. There is no reason, however, why the tax rates used to compute the after-tax cash flows cannot change over time. Thus, in valuing a firm with an effective tax rate of 24% in the current period and a marginal tax rate of 35%, you can estimate the first year's cash flows by using the effective tax rate of 24% and then increase the tax rate to 35% over time. It is critical that the tax rate used in perpetuity to compute the terminal value be the marginal tax rate.

taxrate.xls: A dataset on the Web summarizes average effective tax rates, by industry group, in the United States for the most recent quarter.

THE EFFECT OF NET OPERATING LOSSES

For firms with large net operating losses carried forward or continuing operating losses, we must change tax rates over time. In the early years, these firms will have a zero tax rate, as losses carried forward offset income. As the net operating losses decrease, the tax rates will climb toward the marginal tax rate. As the tax rates used to estimate the after-tax operating income change, the rates used to compute the after-tax cost of debt in the cost of capital computation also need to change. Thus, for a firm with net operating losses carried forward, the tax rate used for both the computation of after-tax operating income and cost of capital will be zero during the years when the losses shelter income.

ILLUSTRATION 4.6

Effective and Marginal Tax Rates for Firms

In Table 4.11, the effective and estimated marginal tax rates are listed for the five companies that you are valuing.

TABLE 4.11 Effective and Marginal Tax Rate, 1999

	AMAZON	ARIBA	CISCO	MOTOROLA	REDIFF.COM
Taxable income	−643.2	−136	3316	1283	−6.9
Taxes paid	0	0	1220	392	0
Effective tax rate	0.00%	0.00%	36.79%	30.55%	0.00%
Marginal tax rate	0.00%	0.00%	35.00%	35%	0%

Three of the five firms that we are analyzing pay no taxes, since they report negative taxable income. Based upon their 1999 annual reports, Cisco and Motorola report effective tax rates of 36.79% and 30.55%, respectively. In valuing both firms, we use the 35% federal marginal tax rate, though it is possible that state and local taxes could make the marginal tax rate higher.

For Amazon and Ariba, we will continue to use a 0% tax rate as long as the firms continue to lose money. In fact, the net operating losses that they have already accumulated and will continue to accumulate in future years will shelter the income they make in the first year or two they are profitable. When they do begin paying taxes, we will use the 35% marginal tax rate for them as well. We use a similar procedure for Rediff.com, but with the 38.5% marginal tax rate that applies to Indian firms.[11] Table 4.12 lists the tax rates for Amazon, Ariba, and Rediff.com for the next 10 years.

TABLE 4.12 Expected Tax Rates

	AMAZON	ARIBA	REDIFF.COM
1	0.00%	0.00%	0.00%
2	0.00%	0.00%	0.00%
3	18.40%	0.00%	0.00%
4	35.00%	0.00%	0.00%
5	35.00%	19.98%	21.13%
6	35.00%	35.00%	38.50%
7	35.00%	35.00%	38.50%
8	35.00%	35.00%	38.50%
9	35.00%	35.00%	38.50%
10	35.00%	35.00%	38.50%

The tax rate remains 0% as long as the firms are losing money or have net operating losses to shelter their income, and increases to the marginal rates in the years in which they do not. The transition year for each of the firms is the year in which the net operating losses shelter some but not all income, resulting in a tax rate greater than 0% but less than the marginal tax rate. The details of the income that are forecast to arrive at these tax rates are considered in the next chapter.

THE TAX BENEFITS OF R&D EXPENSING

In an earlier section, we argued that R&D expenses should be capitalized. If you decide to capitalize such expenses, you might be missing a tax benefit. Firms are allowed to deduct their entire R&D expense for tax purposes. In contrast, they are allowed to deduct only the depreciation on their capital expenses. To capture the tax benefit, therefore, you would add the tax savings on the difference between the entire R&D expense and the amortized amount of the research asset to the after-tax operating income of the firm:

Additional Tax Benefit $_{\text{R&D Expensing}}$ =
(R&D – Amortization of Research Asset) × Tax Rate

You need to make a similar adjustment for any other operating expense that you choose to capitalize.

ILLUSTRATION 4.7

Tax Benefit from Expensing

The tax benefit derived from the expensing of R&D and SG&A expenses is measured in Table 4.13.

TABLE 4.13 Tax Benefit from Expensing of R&D and SG&A Expenses

	AMAZON	ARIBA	CISCO	MOTOROLA	REDIFF.COM
R&D expense	$ —	$19.34	$1,594.00	$3,438.00	$ —
SG&A expense	$ —	$ —	$ —	$—	$5.28
Total	$ —	$19.34	$1,594.00	$3,438.00	$5.28
Tax benefit	$ —	$ —	$557.90	$1,203.30	$ —
Amortization of R&D	$ —	$6.01	$484.60	$2,418.40	$ —
Amortization of SG&A	$ —	$ —	$ —	$ —	$0.52
Total	$ —	$6.01	$484.60	$2,418.40	$0.52
Tax benefit	$ —	$ —	$169.61	$846.44	$ —
Differential tax benefit	$ —	$ —	$388.29	$356.86	$ —

Thus, Cisco derives a tax benefit of $388 million because it can expense R&D expenses rather than capitalize them. Note that Rediff.com and Ariba, which do not pay taxes, derive no marginal tax benefit right now but will do so in future years.

REINVESTMENT NEEDS

The cash flow to the firm is computed after reinvestments. Two components go into estimating reinvestment. The first is *net capital expenditures*, which is the difference between capital expenditures and depreciation. The other is *investments in noncash working capital*. With technology firms, again, these numbers can be difficult to estimate.

NET CAPITAL EXPENDITURES

While capital expenditures and depreciation can easily be obtained for the current year for any firm in the United States,[12] they should be used with the following cautions when estimating the net capital expenditures.

- Firms seldom have smooth capital expenditure streams. Firms can go through periods when capital expenditures are very high (as is the case when a new product is introduced or a new plant is built), followed by periods of relatively light capital expenditures. Consequently, when estimating the capital expenditures to use for forecasting future cash flows, you should look at capital expenditures over time and normalize them by taking an average, or you should look at industry norms.
- As mentioned in the discussion of operating income, research and development expenses are really capital expenditures. Consequently, R&D expenses need to be treated as capital expenditures, and the research asset that is created as a consequence needs to be amortized, with the amortization showing up as part of depreciation.
- In estimating capital expenditures, you should not distinguish between internal investments (which are usually categorized as capital expenditures in cash flow

statements) and external investments (which are acquisitions). The capital expenditures of a firm, therefore, need to include acquisitions. Since firms seldom make acquisitions every year and since each acquisition has a different price tag, the point about normalizing capital expenditures applies even more strongly to this item. The capital expenditure projections for a firm that makes an acquisition of $100 million approximately every five years should therefore include about $20 million, adjusted for inflation, every year. We would also add that all acquisitions, whether they are financed with stock or cash, should be considered.[13]

■ Finally, the capitalizing of operating leases has consequences for capital expenditures. The operating lease expense has to be added to capital expenditures and the depreciation of the operating lease asset has to be added to other depreciation.

ILLUSTRATION 4.8

Estimating Net Capital Expenditures

A detailed discussion of how net capital expenditures were estimated for Cisco and shorter summaries of the estimates for the other firms is presented here. In the process, we will consider many of the issues raised in the preceding section.

To estimate net capital expenditures for Cisco, we begin with the estimates of capital expenditure ($584 million) and depreciation ($486 million) in the 10-K. Based on these numbers, we would have concluded that Cisco's net capital expenditures in 1999 were $98 million.

The first adjustment we make to this number is to incorporate the effect of research and development expenses that were capitalized earlier in this chapter. You do that by adding back the R&D expenses in the most recent financial year ($1,594 million) and subtracting the amortization of the research asset ($485 million).

The second adjustment is to bring in the effect of acquisitions that Cisco made during the last financial year. Table 4.14 summarizes the acquisitions made during the year and the price paid on these acquisitions.

TABLE 4.14 Cisco's Acquisitions: 1999 Financial Year (in Millions)

ACQUIRED	METHOD OF ACQUISITION	PRICE PAID
GeoTel	Pooling	$1,344
Fibex	Pooling	318
Sentient	Pooling	103
American Internet Corporation	Purchase	58
Summa Four	Purchase	129
Clarity Wireless	Purchase	153
Selsius Systems	Purchase	134
PipeLinks	Purchase	118
Amteva Technologies	Purchase	159
		$2,516

Note that both purchase and pooling transactions are included and that the sum total of these acquisitions is added to net capital expenditures in 1999. We are assuming, given Cisco's track record, that its acquisitions in 1999 are not unusual and reflect Cisco's reinvestment policy. The amortization associated with these acquisitions is already included as part of depreciation by the firm.[14] Table 4.15 summarizes the final net capital expenditures for Cisco, as well as similar adjustments for the other firms that you are valuing.

The adjusted net capital expenditures include capitalized R&D expenses (for Ariba, Cisco, and Motorola), capitalized SG&A expenses (for Rediff.com) and acquisitions (for Cisco). In addition, operating leases are considered part of capital expenditures. These numbers are better reflections of how much these firms are reinvesting in their businesses.

TABLE 4.15 Net Capital Expenditures

	AMAZON	ARIBA	CISCO	MOTOROLA	REDIFF.COM
Capital Expenditures	$275.00	$61.87	$584.00	$2,684.00	$1.75
– Depreciation	$67.42	$1.42	$486.00	$2,182.00	$0.23
Net Cap Ex (from Financials)	$207.58	$60.45	$98.00	$502.00	$1.52
+ R&D Expenditures	$ —	$19.34	$1,594.00	$3,438.00	$ —
– Amortization of R&D	$ —	$6.01	$484.60	$2,418.40	$ —
+ SG&A Expenditures	$ —	$ —	$ —	$ —	$5.28
– Amortization of SG&A	$ —	$ —	$ —	$ —	$0.52
+ Acquisitions	$ —	$ —	$2,516.00	$ —	$ —
+ Operating lease expense	$43.00	$3.62	$121.00	$0.00	$ —
– Depreciation on leased asset	$22.81	$4.35	$103.43	$0.00	$ —
Adjusted Net Cap Ex	$207.58	$73.78	$3,740.97	$1,521.60	$6.28

capex.xls: A dataset on the Web summarizes capital expenditures, as a percent of revenues and firm value, by industry group, in the United States for the most recent quarter.

NONCASH WORKING CAPITAL INVESTMENTS

The second component of reinvestment is the cash that needs to be set aside for working capital needs. Working capital needs are defined as noncash working capital, and the cash flow effect is the period-to-period change in this number; increases represent cash outflows, decreases are cash inflows. While some analysts include operating cash sometimes in working capital estimates, as long as cash earns a fair return (in the form of interest), it should not be included in computing cash flows.

Again, while you can estimate the noncash working capital change fairly simply for any year by using financial statements, you must use this estimate with caution. Changes in noncash working capital are unstable, with big increases in some years followed by big decreases in the following years. To ensure that the projections are not the result of an unusual base year, you should tie the changes in working capital to expected changes in revenues or costs of goods sold at the firm over time. The noncash working capital as a percent of revenues is used, in conjunction with expected revenue changes each period, to estimate projected changes in noncash working capital over time. You can obtain the noncash working capital as a percent of revenues by looking at the firm's history or at industry standards. As a final point: noncash working capital can be negative, which can translate into positive cash flows from working capital as revenue increases. It is prudent, when this occurs, to set noncash working capital needs to zero.[15]

ILLUSTRATION 4.9

Estimating Noncash Working Capital Needs

The noncash working capital investment varies widely across the five firms that you are valuing. The noncash working capital items and their values are summarized in Table 4.16 and presented as a percent of revenue for each firm.

The noncash working capital is negative at three of the five firms that you are analyzing: Ariba, Cisco, and, surprisingly (for a retail firm), Amazon. Since noncash working capital can be volatile over time and three of these firms are young firms, two other statistics are reported. The first is the average noncash working capital as a percent of revenues over the last three years for all of the firms except Rediff. The average continues to be negative for Amazon, Ariba, and Cisco and is slightly higher than the current working capital number at Motorola. The average noncash working capital as a percent of revenues for other firms in the industry are also reported in the table: specialty retailers for Amazon, business service providers for Ariba, Internet portals for Rediff.com, telecom equipment for Cisco, and semiconductors and telecom equipment for Motorola. For Amazon and Ariba, the noncash working capital as a percent of revenues is much higher for the industries than for the firms, reflecting the larger size and relative maturity of the comparable firms in the group.

TABLE 4.16 Noncash Working Capital Investments

	AMAZON	ARIBA	CISCO	MOTOROLA	REDIFF.COM
Revenues	$1,640.00	$92.56	$12,154.00	$30,931.00	$1,906.00
Accounts receivable	220.65	5.16	1,242.00	5,125.00	827.00
Inventory & other current assets	85.34	2.74	1,357.00	7,334.00	0
Accounts payable	463.03	3.85	361.00	3,015.00	334.00
Other current liabilities	261.59	42.53	2,642.00	6,897.00	0
Noncash working capital	−418.63	−38.48	−404.00	2,547.00	493.00
Percent of revenues	−25.53%	−41.57%	−3.32%	8.23%	25.87%
Change from last year	$(308.55)	$(32.99)	$(700.00)	$(829.00)	$493.00
Average over last 3 years	−15.16%	−23.33%	-3.16%	8.91%	NMF
Average for industry	8.71%	6.35%	-2.71%	7.04%	4.33%

When valuing these companies, we will have to make an assumption about noncash working capital to estimate free cash flows to the firm. For Motorola to estimate cash flows, it is assumed that the current ratio of working capital to revenues (8.23%) will be maintained. For Amazon, the noncash working capital will be set at 3% of revenues, higher than the firm's current levels but lower than the industry average. There is some merit to the argument that Internet retailers will be able to maintain a lower inventory than do traditional retailers, but it is unlikely that suppliers will continue to fund operations (as they are doing now, with a negative working capital). For Ariba, noncash working capital is set at 5% of revenues, slightly lower than the industry average but much higher than the current number. For Rediff.com, the current noncash working capital proportion of 50.7% is adjusted down to 10%, higher than the average for the industry and reflecting the greater difficulties that the firm will face in the Indian market.

 wcdata.xls: A dataset on the Web summarizes noncash working capital needs, by industry group, in the United States for the most recent quarter.

ILLUSTRATION 4.10

Estimating Free Cash Flow to Firm

Now that we have estimates of the operating income, the tax rate, the net capital expenditures and changes in the noncash working capital, we are in a position to estimate the free cash flows to the firms in the most recent period. Table 4.17 reports the free cash flows to the firm for all five firms.

TABLE 4.17 Free Cash Flows to Firm in Most Recent Period (in Millions)

	AMAZON	ARIBA	CISCO	MOTOROLA	REDIFF.COM
EBIT	$(266.85)	$(147.96)	$4,615.70	$4,235.60	$(2.16)
Tax Rate	0.00%	0.00%	35.00%	35.00%	0.00%
EBIT (1 – t)	$(266.85)	$(147.96)	$3,000.20	$2,753.14	$(2.16)
+ Tax Benefit of Expensing	$ —	$ —	$388.29	$356.86	$ —
– Net Capital Expenditures	$207.58	$73.78	$3,740.97	$1,521.60	$6.28
– Change in Noncash Working Capital	$(308.55)	$(32.99)	$(700.00)	$(829.00)	$0.49
FCFF	$(165.88)	$(188.75)	$347.52	$2,417.40	$(8.93)

Of the five firms that you are valuing, three had negative free cash flows to the firm in the most recent period. These three—Amazon, Ariba, and Rediff—all had negative operating income. The challenge we will face in the coming chapters is estimating these cash flows in future years.

SUMMARY

When valuing a firm, the cash flows that are discounted should be after taxes and reinvestment needs but before debt payments. In this chapter, we considered some of the challenges in developing this number for technology firms. The cash flow estimation process begins with the operating income, that is, the income that the firm generated from its operations. To arrive at an estimate of this number, you make three adjustments to the operating income that you see in financial statements.

The first is for research and development expenses, which are categorized as operating expenses by accountants but should be treated as capital expenses. In fact, any operating expense that generates benefits over multiple periods should be treated similarly.

The second adjustment is the conversion of operating lease expenses from operating expenses to financial expenses.

The third is the cleansing of the operating income of one-time or extraordinary gains or losses.

Since the operating income tends to change fairly dramatically from period to period for young firms, you should use the most updated information that you can get on these firms.

To state this operating income in after-tax terms, you need a tax rate. Firms generally state their effective tax rates in their financial statements, but these effective tax rates can be different from marginal tax rates. The tax rate used should converge on the marginal tax rate in future periods, although the effective tax rate can be used to arrive at the after-tax operating income in the current period. For firms that are losing money and not paying taxes, the net operating losses that they are accumulating will protect some of their future income from taxation.

The reinvestment that firms make in their own operations is then considered in two parts. The first part is the net capital expenditure of the firm, that is, the difference between capital expenditures (a cash outflow) and depreciation (effectively, a cash inflow). In this net capital expenditure, you include the capitalized operating expenses (such as R&D) and acquisitions. The second part relates to investments in noncash working capital, mainly inventory and accounts receivable. Increases in noncash working capital represent cash outflows to the firm; decreases represent cash inflows. Noncash working capital at most firms tends to be volatile and may need to be smoothed out when you are forecasting future cash flows.

ENDNOTES

1. As an example, *Smart Money* magazine noted that Jamie Kiggen, an equity research analyst at Donaldson, Lufkin, and Jenrette valued an Amazon customer at $2,400 in an equity research report in 1999. This value was based on the assumption that the customer would continue to buy from Amazon.com and on an expected profit margin from such sales.

2. Rediff offers the portal in Indian languages. Yahoo! or a similar company would therefore have to go to considerable effort to match it.

3. The expenses are treated as a three-year annuity, reflecting the average annual operating lease expenses over the first five years—about $145 million. Dividing the lump-sum payment in year six by this average yields three years.

4. This information was derived from I/B/E/S estimates.

5. Microsoft preserved its credibility with analysts by also letting them know when their estimates were too low. Firms that are consistently pessimistic in their analyst presentations lose their credibility and, consequently, their effectiveness in managing earnings.

6. Firms that bought Windows 95 in 1995 also bought the right to upgrades and support in 1996 and 1997. Microsoft could have shown these as revenues in 1995.

7. *Forbes* magazine carried an article on March 6, 2000, on MicroStrategy. In that article, it was described how MicroStrategy and NCR had entered into a licensing and technology agreement for $52.5 million in revenues and how MicroStrategy then booked $17.5 million of this revenue in the quarter that had ended four days before.

8. B. Lev and Z. Deng, (unpublished paper) 1997, The Valuation of Acquired R&D, Accounting Department, New York University.

9. Only three firms wrote off in-process R&D during the prior decade (1980–89).

10. Since the effective tax rate is based on the taxes paid (which come from the tax statement) and the reported income, the effective tax rate will be lower than the marginal tax rate for firms that change accounting methods to inflate reported earnings.

11. The marginal tax rate for firms in India is 35% with a 10% surcharge, leading to a tax rate of 38.5%.

12. It is actually surprisingly difficult to obtain the capital expenditure numbers even for large, publicly traded firms in some markets outside the United States. Accounting standards in these markets often allow firms to lump investments together and report them in the aggregate.

13. Even though there is no direct cash flow from a stock acquisition, there is an indirect one. The firm could have issued the stock to the public and used that cash on the acquisition.

14. It is only the tax-deductible amortization that really matters. To the extent that amortization is not tax deductible, you would look at the EBIT before the amortization and not consider it while estimating net capital expenditures.

15. While it is entirely possible that firms can generate positive cash flows from working capital decreasing for short periods, it is dangerous to assume that this situation can occur forever.

5

LOOKING
FORWARD:
ESTIMATING
GROWTH

The value of a firm is the present value of expected future cash flows generated by the firm. The most critical input in valuation, especially for high-growth firms, is the growth rate to use to forecast future revenues and earnings. In this chapter, we consider how best to estimate these growth rates for technology firms, especially those with low revenues and negative earnings.

There are three basic ways of estimating growth for any firm. One way is to look at the growth in a firm's past earnings, that is, its historical growth rate. While this can be a useful input when valuing stable firms, there are both dangers and limitations in using this growth rate for high-growth firms, especially technology firms. The historical growth rate can often not be estimated, and even if it can, it cannot be relied on as an estimate of expected future growth.

A second way of estimating growth is to trust the equity research analysts that follow the firm to correctly estimate growth for the firm and to use that growth rate in valuation. Although technology firms are widely followed by analysts, the quality of growth estimates, especially over longer periods, is poor. Relying on these growth estimates in a valuation can lead to erroneous and inconsistent estimates of value.

A third method is to estimate the growth from a firm's fundamentals. A firm's growth ultimately is determined by how much is reinvested into new assets and the quality of these investments, with investments widely defined to include acquisitions, building up distribution channels, or even expanding marketing capabilities. By estimating these inputs, you are, in a sense, estimating a firm's fundamental growth rate. While the determinants of fundamental growth remain the same for all firms, estimating these inputs for technology firms can pose special challenges. Where, you might ask, are the subjective elements that go into estimating growth: the quality of management, changing market dynamics, the possibility that firms may change their business mixes? In a sense, they are in every valuation input. When you estimate expected future margins and returns, any views that you might have about how a firm is likely to change in the future should find its way into these estimates.

THE IMPORTANCE OF GROWTH

Growth is a critical component of value in all valuations, and it represents a large portion of value at technology firms and almost all of the value at the new technology firms. In fact, this is the reason why many investors and private equity investors are attracted to technology firms in the first place. Thus, growth is both the calling card and the primary determinant of value at these firms.

In this section, we view the value of a firm as the sum of the values of its existing investments and its expected growth potential. We then look at a series of statistics that measure the importance of growth assets at technology firms.

GROWTH ASSETS AND ASSETS IN PLACE

A firm can be valuable because it owns assets that generate cash flows now or because it is expected to acquire such assets in the future. The first group of assets are categorized as assets in place and the second as growth assets. Figure 5–1 presents a financial balance sheet for a firm.

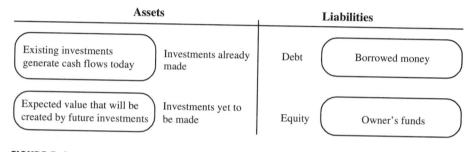

FIGURE 5–1
A Financial View of a Firm

Note that an accounting balance sheet can be very different from a financial balance sheet, since accounting for growth assets tends to be both conservative and inconsistent.

For technology firms, accounting balance sheets do a poor job of summarizing the values of the assets of the firm. They often completely ignore the largest component of value, which is future growth, and do not measure well the value of assets in place because R&D expenses are not treated as capital expenses.

GROWTH ASSETS AT TECHNOLOGY FIRMS

For technology firms, a large proportion of the value comes from growth assets. These growth assets can include new projects or investments on the part of the firm, or, as is the case with Cisco, acquisitions of other firms. For firms like Rediff.com, almost all of the value is from growth assets. Thus, while growth is a critical input in most valuations, it should receive an even greater emphasis when you look at technology firms.

You can use a number of measures to illustrate how much more important growth assets are to technology firms than they are to other firms. One is to compare the market value of the firm, which is the market measure of the value of assets at firms, to the book value of capital invested in the firm, which is the accounting measure of the same value. Figure 5–2 compares the market value of equity to book value at the five firms that we are analyzing.

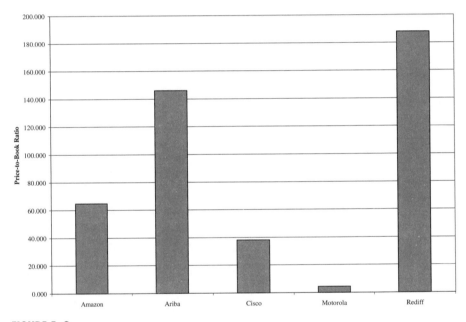

FIGURE 5–2
Price-to-Book Ratio

Note that the price-to-book-value ratio is smallest for Motorola and largest for Rediff.com, a result that is consistent with the categorization of these firms in terms of where they stand in the life cycle.

HISTORICAL GROWTH

When estimating the expected growth for a firm, you generally begin by looking at the firm's history. How rapidly have the firm's operations, as measured by revenues or earnings, grown in the recent past? While past growth is not always a good indicator of future growth, it does convey information that can be valuable in making estimates for the future. In this section, we begin by looking at measurement issues that arise when estimating past growth, especially for young technology firms, and then consider how past growth can be used in projections.

ESTIMATING HISTORICAL GROWTH

Given a firm's earnings history, estimating historical growth rates may seem like a simple exercise, but several measurement problems can arise. In particular, the average growth rates can be different, depending on how the average is estimated and whether you allow for compounding in the growth over time. Estimating growth rates can also be complicated by the presence of negative earnings in the past or in the current period.

Arithmetic versus Geometric Averages. The average growth rate can vary depending on whether it is an arithmetic average or a geometric average. The arithmetic average is the simple average of past growth rates, whereas the geometric mean takes into account the compounding that occurs from period to period:

$$\text{Arithmetic Average} = \frac{\sum\limits_{t=-n}^{t} g_t}{n}$$

where g_t = Growth Rate in Year t = $(\text{Earnings}_t / \text{Earnings}_{t-1}) - 1$

$$\text{Geometric Average} = \left[\frac{\text{Earnings}_0}{\text{Earnings}_{-n}}\right]^{(1/n)} - 1$$

where Earnings_t = Earnings in Year t

The two estimates can be very different, especially for firms with volatile earnings. The geometric average is a much more accurate measure of true growth in past earnings, especially when year-to-year growth has been erratic.

In fact, the point about arithmetic and geometric growth rates also applies to revenues, though the difference between the two growth rates tends to be smaller for revenues than for earnings. For technology firms, the caveats about using arithmetic growth carry even more weight.

ILLUSTRATION 5.1

Differences between Arithmetic and Geometric Averages: Motorola

Table 5.1 reports on the revenues, EBITDA, and EBIT for Motorola for each year from 1994 to 1999. The arithmetic and geometric average growth rates in each series are reported at the bottom of the table.

TABLE 5.1 Arithmetic and Geometric Average Growth Rates: Motorola

	REVENUES	% CHANGE	EBITDA	% CHANGE	EBIT	% CHANGE
1994	$22,245		$4,151		$2,604	
1995	$27,037	21.54	$4,850	16.84	$2,931	12.56
1996	$27,973	3.46	$4,268	–12.00	$1,960	–33.13
1997	$29,794	6.51	$4,276	0.19	$1,947	–0.66
1998	$29,398	–1.33	$3,019	–29.40	$822	–57.78
1999	$30,931	5.21	$5,398	78.80	$3,216	291.24
Arithmetic average		7.08		10.89		42.45
Geometric average		6.82		5.39		4.31
Standard deviation		8.61		41.56		141.78

$$\text{Geometric Average} = (\text{Earnings}_{1999} / \text{Earnings}_{1994})^{1/5} - 1$$

The arithmetic average growth rate is lower than the geometric average growth rate for all three items. The difference is much larger with operating income (EBIT), however, than it is with revenues and EBITDA because the operating income is the most volatile of the three numbers, with a standard deviation in year-to-year changes of almost 142%. From a comparison of the operating income in 1994 and 1999, it is also quite clear that the geometric averages are much better indicators of true growth. Motorola's earnings grew only marginally during the period, as reflected in its geometric average growth rate, which is 4.31%, but not in its arithmetic average growth rate, which indicates much faster growth.

Negative Earnings. Measures of historical growth are distorted by the presence of negative earnings numbers. The percentage change in earnings on a year-by-year basis is defined as:

% Change in Earnings in Period t = $(\text{Earnings}_t - \text{Earnings}_{t-1}) / \text{Earnings}_{t-1}$

If the earnings in the last period (Earnings_{t-1}) are negative, this calculation yields a meaningless number. This status extends into the calculation of the geometric mean. If the earnings in the initial time period are negative or zero, the geometric mean cannot be estimated.

Although there are ways of estimating growth even when earnings are negative,[1] the resulting growth rates are not very useful indicators of past growth. It is best to view the past growth as not meaningful in those cases.

ILLUSTRATION 5.2

Negative Earnings

The problems with estimating earnings growth when earnings are negative are obvious for three of the five firms in the sample that have negative earnings. Amazon's operating earnings (EBIT) went from −$62 million in 1998 to −$276 million in 1999. Clearly, the firm's earnings deteriorated, but estimating a standard earnings growth rate would lead us to the following growth rate:

Earnings Growth for Amazon in 1999 = $(-276 - (-62)) / -62 = 3.4516$ or 345.16%

You run into similar problems with both Ariba and Rediff.com.

Even with Motorola, which has had positive earnings for much of the last decade, the negative earnings issue arises when you look at net income and earnings per share over the last five years. Table 5.2 reports on both numbers from 1994 to 1999.

TABLE 5.2 Net Income and EPS: Motorola

	NET INCOME	EPS
1994	$1,560.00	$0.88
1995	$1,781.00	$0.98
1996	$1,154.00	$0.65
1997	$1,180.00	$0.66
1998	$(962.00)	$(0.54)
1999	$817.00	$0.45

The negative net income (and earnings per share) numbers in 1998 make the estimation of a growth rate in 1999 problematic. For instance, the earnings per share increased from −$0.54 to $0.45, but the growth rate, estimated using the conventional equation, would be:

Earnings Growth Rate in 1999 = ($0.45 − (−$0.54)) / (−$0.54) = −183.33%

This growth rate, a negative number, makes no sense given the improvement in earnings during the year. There are two fixes to this problem. One is to replace the actual earnings per share in the denominator with the absolute value:

Earnings Growth Rate in 1999$_{absolute value}$ = ($0.45 − (−$0.54)) / ($0.54) = 83.33%

The other is to use the higher of the earnings per share from the two years yielding:

Earnings Growth Rate in 1999$_{higher value}$ = ($0.45 − (−$0.54)) / ($0.45) = 120.00%

The growth rate is now positive, as you would expect it to be, but the values for the growth rates themselves are not very useful for making estimates for the future.

THE USEFULNESS OF HISTORICAL GROWTH

Is the growth rate in the past a good indicator of growth in the future? Not necessarily, especially for technology firms. In this section, we consider how well historical growth predicts future growth for all firms and why the changing size and volatile businesses of technology firms can undercut growth projections.

Higgledy-Piggledy Growth. Past growth rates are useful in forecasting future growth, but they have considerable noise associated with them. In a study of the relationship between past growth rates and future growth rates, Little (1960) coined the term *higgledy-piggledy growth* because he found little evidence that firms that grew fast in one period continued to grow fast in the next period. In the process of running a series of correlations between growth rates in consecutive periods of different length, he frequently found negative correlations between growth rates in the two periods, and the average correlation across the two periods was close to zero (0.02).

The growth rates at technology firms tend to be even more volatile than growth rates at other firms in the market. The correlation between growth rates in earnings in consecutive time periods (five-year, three-year, and one-year) for technology firms relative to the rest of the market is reported in Figure 5–3.

While the correlations tend to be higher across the board for one-year growth rates than for three-year or five-year growth rates in earnings, they are also consistently lower for technology firms than they are for the rest of the market. This would suggest that you should be more cautious about using past growth, especially in earnings, for forecasting future growth.

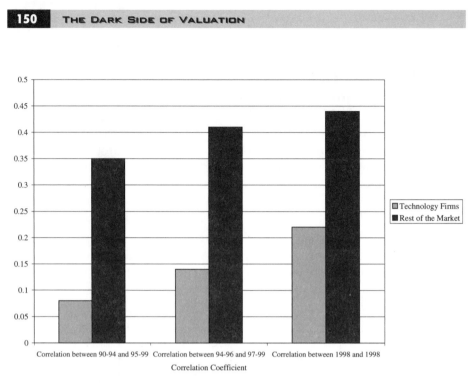

FIGURE 5-3
Correlations in Historical Growth in EPS (*Source:* Compustat Database, 1998)

Revenue Growth versus Earnings Growth. In general, revenue growth tends to be more persistent and predictable than earnings growth because accounting choices have a far smaller effect on revenues than they do on earnings. While this is true for all firms, it is particularly true for technology firms, which have discretion on when and how much to spend on research and can shift earnings from one period to another much more easily than they can shift revenues. Figure 5–4 compares the correlations in revenue and earnings growth over one-year, three-year, and five-year periods at technology firms.

Revenue growth correlates more consistently over time than does earnings growth. The implication is that historical growth in revenues is a far more useful number when it comes to forecasting than is historical growth in earnings.

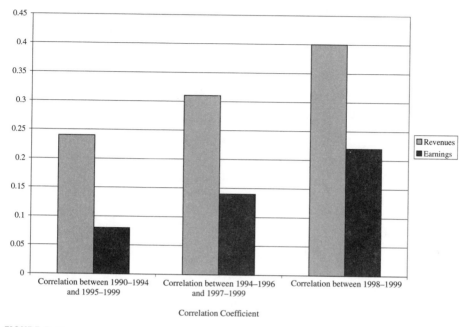

FIGURE 5–4

Correlations in Revenue and Earnings Growth: Technology Firms (*Source:* Compustat Database, 1998)

The Effects of Firm Size. Since the growth rate is stated in percentage terms, the role of size has to be weighed in the analysis. It is easier for a firm with $10 million in earnings to generate a 50% growth rate than it is for a firm with $500 million in earnings. Since it becomes harder for firms to sustain high growth rates as they become larger, past growth rates for firms that have grown dramatically in size may be difficult to sustain in the future. While this is a problem in analysis of all firms, it is a particular problem with technology firms. The fundamentals at these firms, in terms of management, products, and underlying markets, may not have changed, but it will still be difficult to maintain historical growth rates as the firms double or triple in size.

The true test for a small technology firm lies in how well it handles growth. Some firms, such as Cisco, Oracle, and even Amazon, have been able to continue to deliver their products and services efficiently as they have grown. In other words, they have been able to scale up successfully. Other firms, especially new technology firms, have had much more difficulty replicating their success as they become larger. In analyzing small technology firms, therefore, it is important that you look at plans to increase growth, and it is even more critical that you examine the systems in place to handle this growth.

ILLUSTRATION 5.3

Cisco: Earnings Growth and Size of the Firm

In Table 5.3, Cisco's evolution from a firm with $28 million in revenues and net income of about $4 million in 1989 to revenues in excess of $12 billion and net income of $2.096 billion in 1999 is reported.

TABLE 5.3　Revenues, Operating Earnings, and Net Income: Cisco

YEAR	REVENUES	% CHANGE	EBIT	% CHANGE	NET INCOME	% CHANGE
1989	$28		$7		$4	
1990	$70	152.28	$21	216.42	$14	232.54
1991	$183	162.51	$66	209.44	$43	210.72
1992	$340	85.40	$129	95.48	$84	95.39
1993	$649	91.10	$264	103.70	$172	103.77
1994	$1,243	91.51	$488	85.20	$315	83.18
1995	$2,233	79.62	$794	62.69	$457	45.08
1996	$4,096	83.46	$1,416	78.31	$913	99.78
1997	$6,440	57.23	$2,135	50.78	$1,049	14.90
1998	$8,488	31.80	$2,704	26.65	$1,355	29.17
1999	$12,154	43.19	$3,455	27.77	$2,096	54.69
Arithmetic avg. =		87.81		95.64		96.92
Geometric avg. =		83.78		86.57		86.22

Although this table presents the results of a phenomenally successful decade for Cisco, it does suggest three reasons why you should be cautious about assuming that the firm will continue to grow at a similar rate in the future. First, the growth rates have been tapering off as the firm becomes larger on all three measures. Second, if you assume that Cisco will maintain its historic growth (estimated with the geometric average) over the last decade for the next five years, the revenue and earnings growth that the firm will have to post will be unsustainable. For instance, if operating income grows at 86.57% for the next five years, Cisco's operating income in five years will be $78 billion. Third, Cisco's growth has come primarily from acquisitions of small firms with promising technologies that Cisco has commercially developed with its capabilities. In 1999, for instance, Cisco acquired 15 firms; these acquisitions accounted for almost 80% of their reinvestment that year. If you assume that Cisco will continue to grow at historical rates, you are assuming that the number of acquisitions will also grow at the same rate. Thus, Cisco would have to acquire almost 80 firms five years from now to maintain historical growth.

HISTORICAL GROWTH AT TECHNOLOGY FIRMS

The presence of negative earnings, volatile growth rates over time, and the rapid changes that technology firms go through over time make historical growth rates unreliable indicators of future growth for these firms. Notwithstanding this, you can still find ways to incorporate information from historical growth into estimates of future growth if you follow these general guidelines:

- Focus on revenue growth, rather than earnings growth, to get a measure of both the pace of growth and the momentum that can be carried forward into future years. Revenue growth is less volatile than earnings growth and is much less likely to be swayed by accounting adjustments and choices.

- Rather than look at average growth over the last few years, look at growth each year. This figure can provide information on how the growth is changing as the firm becomes larger and can help you make projections for the future.

■ Use historical growth rates as the basis for projections only in the near future (next year or two), since technologies can change rapidly and undercut future estimates.

■ Consider historical growth in the overall market and in other firms that are serving it. This information can help you decide what the growth rates of the firm you are valuing will converge on over time.

ILLUSTRATION 5.4

Historical Growth Information

Having examined the issues related to how growth rates are estimated, the difficulties created by negative earnings, and the effects of changing firm size on growth rates, you can now see a summation in Table 5.4 of historical growth at the five firms that you are valuing.

TABLE 5.4 Historical Growth Estimates: Growth Rates over Last Two and Five Years—Annualized Geometric Averages

	AMAZON	ARIBA	CISCO	MOTOROLA	REDIFF
Revenue Growth Rates (%)					
Last year	168.85	442.70	43.19	5.21	124.71
Last 2 years	232.88	672.64	37.38	1.89	NA
Last 5 years	NA	NA	57.78	6.82	NA
Operating Income Growth Rates (%)					
Last year	NA	NA	27.77	291.24	NA
Last 2 years	NA	NA	27.21	28.52	NA
Last 5 years	NA	NA	47.91	4.31	NA
Net Income Growth Rates (%)					
Last year	NA	NA	54.69	NA	NA
Last 2 years	NA	NA	41.35	−16.79	NA
Last 5 years	NA	NA	46.09	−12.13	NA

The most striking feature of the table is the number of estimates that cannot be obtained, either because the firm is too young or because earnings are negative. We consider historical revenue growth when making forecasts for each of these firms, but we do not use historical growth in earnings for any of them.

histgr.xls: A dataset on the Web summarizes historical growth rates in earnings and revenues, by industry group, for the United States.

ANALYST ESTIMATES OF GROWTH

Many technology firms are heavily followed by equity research analysts, who make projections of earnings growth for these firms, sometimes for periods of up to five years. How useful are these estimates of expected growth from analysts and how, if at all, can they be used in valuing technology firms? In this section, we consider the process that analysts follow to estimate expected growth and examine why such growth rates may not be appropriate when valuing technology firms.

NUMBER OF ANALYSTS FOLLOWING TECHNOLOGY FIRMS

For several reasons, the number of equity research analysts that follow technology firms is disproportionately large when compared to the number that follow firms in other sectors. The first reason is that the need for equity research may be greatest in these firms since the values of these firms can shift dramatically with new information on both current investments and future prospects. Another reason for the attention is that institutional investors have increased their holdings of technology firms and analysts tend to follow suit.

The number of analysts, at least on the sell side, following the five firms that we are analyzing is reported in Figure 5–5, categorized by whether they have buy, hold, or sell recommendations on each of the firms.

Rediff has only two analysts following it; the other firms have more than 20 analysts each following them. The analysts are generally much more positive (buy recommendations) than negative (hold recommendations). It is worth noting that not one of the 126 analysts following these five firms has a sell recommendation out. Note also that the graph in Figure 5–5 understates the number of analysts following these firms since it not only ignores buy-side analysts but also analysts in markets outside the United States.[2]

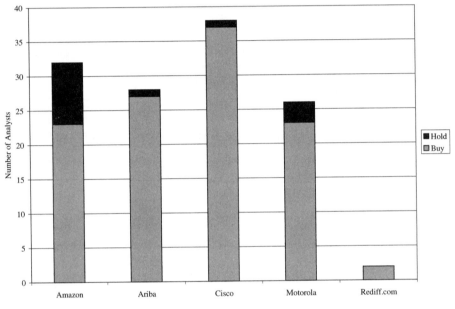

FIGURE 5–5
Analyst Following (*Source:* Morningstar, *www.morningstar.com,* June 7, 2000, Morningstar, Inc.)

THE QUALITY OF EARNINGS FORECASTS

If firms are followed by a large number of analysts and these analysts are indeed better informed than the rest of the market, then the forecasts of growth that emerge from analysts should be better than estimates based on either historical growth or other publicly available information. But is this presumption justified? Are analyst forecasts of growth superior to other forecasts?

The general consensus from studies that have looked at short-term forecasts (one quarter ahead to four quarters ahead) of earnings is that analysts provide better forecasts of earnings than do models that depend purely on historical data. The mean relative absolute error, which measures the absolute difference between the actual earnings and the forecast for the next quarter, in percentage terms, is smaller for analyst forecasts than it is for forecasts based on historical data. Two studies shed further light on the value of analysts' forecasts.

Crichfield, Dyckman, and Lakonishok (1978) examine the relative accuracy of forecasts in the Earnings Forecaster, a publication from Standard & Poor's that summarizes forecasts of earnings from more than 50 investment firms. They measure the squared forecast errors by month of the year and compute the ratio of analyst forecast error to the forecast error from time-series models of earnings. They find that the time-series models actually outperform analyst forecasts from April until August, but underperform them from September through January. They hypothesize that this is because more firm-specific information is available to analysts during the latter part of the year.

The other study, by O'Brien (1988), compares consensus analyst forecasts from the Institutions Brokers Estimate System (I/B/E/S) with time-series forecasts from one quarter ahead to four quarters ahead. The analyst forecasts outperform the time-series model for one-quarter ahead and two-quarter ahead forecasts, do as well as the time-series model for three-quarter ahead forecasts, and do worse than the time-series model for four-quarter ahead forecasts. Thus, the advantage gained by analysts from firm-specific information seems to deteriorate as the time horizon for forecasting is extended.

In valuation, the focus is more on long-term growth rates in earnings than on next quarter's earnings. There is little evidence to suggest that analysts provide superior forecasts of earnings when the forecasts are over three or five years. An early study by Cragg and Malkiel compared long-term forecasts by five investment management firms in 1962 and 1963 with actual growth over the following three years to conclude that analysts were poor long-term forecasters. This view is contested by Vander Weide and Carleton (1988), who find that the consensus prediction of five-year growth in the I/B/E/S is superior to historically oriented growth measures in predicting future growth. There is an intuitive basis for arguing that analyst predictions of growth rates must be better than those of models based on time-series or other historical data simply because they use more information. The evidence indicates, however, that this superiority in forecasting is surprisingly small for long-term forecasts and that past growth rates play a significant role in determining analyst forecasts.

There is one final consideration. Analysts generally forecast earnings per share, and most services report these estimates. When valuing a firm, you often need forecasts of operating income, and the growth in earnings per share will not be equal to the growth in operating income. In general, the growth rate in operating income should be lower than the growth rate in earnings per share.[3] Thus, even if you decide to use analyst forecasts, you will have to adjust them down to reflect the need to forecast operating income growth.

ILLUSTRATION 5.5

Analyst Estimates of Growth

All five of the firms that we are valuing are followed by analysts, and Table 5.5 provides consensus estimates (median) of earnings and earnings growth, both in the short and long term on each of these firms.

TABLE 5.5 Analyst Estimates of Earnings

	AMAZON	ARIBA	CISCO	MOTOROLA	REDIFF.COM
EPS: 2000	$(1.39)	$(0.23)	$0.53	$1.05	$(0.43)
EPS: 2001	$(0.80)	$(0.11)	$0.70	$1.41	$0.10
EPS: Expected 5-year growth rate	NA	NA	32.19%	22.93%	NA

There is considerable disagreement on the expected earnings growth rate even at Cisco and Motorola and a wide range of estimates on earnings per share in the next two years at the other firms. For the three firms with negative earnings, the estimated growth rate over the next five years is not reported.

THE FUNDAMENTAL DETERMINANTS OF GROWTH

With both historical and analyst estimates, growth is an exogenous variable that affects value but is divorced from the operating details of the firm. The soundest way of incorporating growth into value is to make it endogenous, that is, to make it a function of how much a firm reinvests for future growth and the quality of its reinvestment.

We consider three scenarios and examine how to estimate growth in each. The first scenario is for a firm earning a high return on capital that it expects to sustain over time. The second is for a firm earning a positive return on capital that is expected to increase over time. The third is the most general scenario, for a firm that expects operating margins to change over time, sometimes from negative values to positive levels.

SCENARIO: STABLE RETURN ON CAPITAL

When a firm has a stable return on capital, its expected growth in operating income is a product of the reinvestment rate, that is, the proportion of the after-tax operating income that is invested in net capital expenditures and noncash working capital, and the quality of these reinvestments, measured as the return on the capital invested.

$$\text{Expected Growth}_{\text{EBIT}} = \text{Reinvestment Rate} \times \text{Return on Capital}$$

where

Reinvestment Rate =

$$\frac{\text{Capital Expenditure} - \text{Depreciation} + \Delta\text{Noncash WC}}{\text{EBIT}(1 - \text{Tax Rate})}$$

Return on Capital = EBIT $(1 - t)$ / Capital Invested

In making these estimates, we use the adjusted operating income and reinvestment values computed in Chapter 4, "Cash is King: Estimating Cash Flows." Both measures should be forward looking, and the return on capital should represent the expected return on capital on future investments. In the rest of this section, we consider how best to estimate the reinvestment rate and the return on capital.

Reinvestment Rate. The reinvestment rate measures how much a firm is plowing back to generate future growth. The reinvestment rate is often measured by looking at the most recent financial statements for the firm. Although this is a good place to start, it is not necessarily the best estimate of the future reinvestment rate. A firm's reinvestment rate can ebb and flow, especially in firms that invest in relatively few large projects or acquisitions. For these firms, looking at an average reinvestment rate over time may be a better measure of the future. In addition, as firms grow and mature, their reinvestment needs (and rates) tend to decrease. For firms that have expanded significantly over the last few years, the historical reinvestment rate is likely to be higher than the expected future reinvestment rate. For these firms, industry averages for reinvestment rates may provide a better indication of the future than using numbers from the past. Finally, it is important that you continue treating R&D expenses and operating lease expenses consistently. The R&D expenses, in particular, need to be categorized as part of capital expenditures for purposes of measuring the reinvestment rate.

Return on Capital. The return on capital is often based on the firm's return on capital on existing investments, where the book value of capital is assumed to measure the capital invested. Implicitly, you assume that the current accounting return on capital is a good measure of the true returns earned on existing investments and that this return is a good proxy for returns that will be made on future investments. This assumption, of course, is open to question for the following reasons:

■ The book value of capital might not be a good measure of the capital invested in existing investments, since it reflects the historical cost of these assets and accounting decisions on depreciation. When the book value understates the capital invested, the return on capital will be overstated; when book value overstates the capital invested, the return on capital will be understated. This problem is exacerbated if the book value of capital is not adjusted to reflect the value of the research asset or the capital value of operating leases.

■ The operating income, like the book value of capital, is an accounting measure of the earnings made by a firm during a period. All the problems in using unadjusted operating income described in Chapter 4 continue to apply.

■ Even if the operating income and book value of capital are measured correctly, the return on capital on existing investments may not be equal to the marginal return on capital that the firm expects to make on new investments, especially as you go further into the future.

Given these concerns, you should consider not only a firm's current return on capital, but any trends in this return, as well as the industry average return on capital. If the current return on capital for a firm is significantly higher than the industry average, the forecasted return on capital should be set lower than the current return to reflect the erosion that is likely to occur as competition responds.

Finally, any firm that earns a return on capital greater than its cost of capital is earning an excess return. The excess returns are the result of a firm's competitive advantages or barriers to entry into the industry. High excess returns locked in for very long periods imply that this firm has a permanent competitive advantage.

ILLUSTRATION 5.6

Measuring the Reinvestment Rate, Return on Capital, and Expected Growth Rate: Cisco and Motorola

We will use the most recent year's financial statements to estimate Cisco's and Motorola's reinvestment rates and returns on capital for the year. In Chapter 4, we estimated the reinvestments made by the firms and included both R&D expenses and acquisitions in the estimate. Table 5.6 summarizes the estimate of reinvestment both in dollar terms and as a percent of the after-tax operating income at each of the firms.

TABLE 5.6 Estimating the Reinvestment Rates: Most Recent Financial Year

	Cisco	Motorola
Net capital expenditures	$3,740.97	$1,521.60
Change in noncash working capital	$(700.00)	$(829.00)
Reinvestment	$3,040.97	$692.60
Adjusted EBIT	$4,615.70	$4,235.60
Adjusted EBIT $(1 - t)$	$3,388.49	$3,110.00
Reinvestment rate	89.74%	22.27%

Cisco reinvested almost 90% of its after-tax operating income, and Motorola reinvested about a quarter of its after-tax operating income.

The reinvestment rate is a volatile number and often shifts significantly from year to year. In Table 5.7, we compare the reinvestment rate in the most recent year to the average reinvestment rate over the last three years and the industry-average reinvestment rate. We also compute the reinvestment rate for the most recent year with the change in working capital normalized.[4]

Both Cisco and Motorola have lower reinvestment rates in the current year than they have had in the last three years and higher reinvestment rates than comparable firms.

TABLE 5.7 Reinvestment Rate: Historical Averages and Industry Averages

	CISCO (%)	MOTOROLA (%)
Reinvestment rate	89.74	22.27
Reinvestment rate (with normalized working capital)	106.81	52.99
Average reinvestment rate (last 3 years)	113.16	71.33
Industry average reinvestment rate	79.29	42.93

We also estimate the return on capital at Cisco and Motorola in the most recent financial year and, in Table 5.8, compare it to the industry averages and the average over the last three years.

TABLE 5.8 Returns on Capital: Cisco and Motorola

	CISCO	MOTOROLA
Unadjusted		
EBIT(1 – t)	$2,245.75	2090.4
Book value of debt	$0.00	5542
Book value of equity	7191	12222
Capital invested	$7,191.00	$17,764.00
Return on capital	31.23%	11.77%
Adjusted for Operating Leases and R&D		
EBIT(1 – t)	$3,388.49	$3,110.00
Book value of debt	$827.43	$5,542.00
Book value of equity	$9,117.00	$20,000.60
Capital invested	$9,944.43	$25,542.60
Return on capital	34.07%	12.18%
Average: last 3 years	38.15%	8.12%
Industry average	18.34%	22.27%

Cisco earned a return on capital that was significantly higher than the returns earned by comparable firms, reflecting both its technological edge and its superior management.

Motorola, on the other hand, earned a return on capital that was lower than the industry average, though it was higher than what Motorola has earned over the last three years.

Table 5.9 reports estimates for the reinvestment rate and return on capital at Cisco and Motorola, and the expected growth rate that emerges from these estimates.

TABLE 5.9 Expected Growth Rate Estimates

	CISCO (%)	MOTOROLA (%)
A. Last Year's Estimates		
Reinvestment rate	89.23	22.27
ROC	34.07	12.18
Expected growth rate	30.40	2.71
B. Last Year's Estimates: With Normalized WC		
Reinvestment rate	106.81	52.99
ROC	34.07	12.18
Expected growth rate	36.39	6.45
C. Average over Last 3 Years		
Reinvestment rate	113.16	71.33
ROC	38.15	8.12
Expected growth rate	43.17	5.79
D. Industry Averages		
Reinvestment rate	79.29	42.93
ROC	18.34	22.27
Expected growth rate	14.54	9.56

Clearly, the estimates of expected growth are a function of what you assume about future investments. For the valuation, we assume that the current return on capital and reinvestment rate (with normalized working capital) will be sustained for the foreseeable future for Cisco, since the firm is in a growing market and has a surplus of investment opportunities. Cisco's reinvestment rate of 106.81% and return on capital of 34.07% yields an expected growth rate of 36.39% in operating income for the firm. Note that almost two-thirds of this growth comes from Cisco's acquisitions, reflecting both the volume of these acquisitions (in the reinvestment rate) and Cisco's success with this strategy (in the return on capital).

For Motorola, it is assumed that the reinvestment rate will remain at the most recent year's levels (with normalized working capital) but return on capital will be moved toward the industry average (halfway between Motorola's return on capital and the industry average). The changing return on capital over time will affect earnings growth; in the next section, we consider how best to estimate this growth.

---

 fundgrEB.xls: A dataset on the Web summarizes reinvestment rates and return on capital, by industry group, in the United States for the most recent quarter.

SCENARIO: POSITIVE AND CHANGING RETURN ON CAPITAL

The analysis in the last section is based on the assumption that the return on capital remains stable over time. If the return on capital changes over time, then the expected growth rate for the firm will have a second component, which will increase the growth rate if the return on capital increases and will decrease the growth rate if the return on capital decreases.

Expected Growth Rate =
$ROC_t \times$ Reinvestment Rate $+ (ROC_t - ROC_{t-1}) / ROC_{t-1}$

For example, a firm that sees its return on capital improve from 10% to 11% while maintaining a reinvestment rate of 40% will have an expected growth rate of:

Expected Growth Rate $= .11 \times .40 + (.11 - .10) / .10 = 14.40\%$

In effect, the improvement in the return on capital increases the earnings on existing assets, and this improvement translates into an additional growth of 10% for the firm.

Marginal and Average Returns on Capital. So far, we have looked at the return on capital as the measure that determines return. In reality, however, there are two measures of returns on capital. One is the return earned by a firm collectively on all of its investments, which we define as the average return on capital. The other is the return earned by a firm on just the new investments it makes in a year, which is the marginal return on capital.

Changes in the marginal return on capital do not create a second-order effect, and the value of the firm is a product of the marginal return on capital and the reinvestment rate. Changes in the average return on capital, however, will result in the additional impact on growth chronicled above.

Candidates for Changing Average Return on Capital. What types of firms are likely to see their return on capital change over time? One category would include firms with poor returns on capital that improve their operating efficiency and margins and, consequently, their return on capital. In these firms, the expected growth rate will be much higher than the product of the reinvestment rate and the return on capital. In fact, since the return on capital on these firms is usually low before the turnaround, small changes in the return on capital translate into big changes in the growth rate. Thus, an increase in the return on capital on existing assets of 1% to 2% doubles the earnings (resulting in a growth rate of 100%).

The other category would include firms that have very high returns on capital on their existing investments but are likely to see these returns slip, not only on new investments but on existing investments, as competition enters the business. Here, the change will push down expected growth.

ILLUSTRATION 5.7

Estimating Expected Growth with Changing Return on Capital

In the previous illustration, we estimated a reinvestment rate of 52.99% for Motorola and a current return on capital of 12.18%. We also assumed that Motorola's return on capital will increase toward the industry average of 22.27% as the firm sheds the residue of its ill-fated Iridium investment and returns to its roots.

Assume that Motorola's return on capital will increase from 12.18% to 17.22% over the next five years.[5] For simplicity, also assume that the change occurs linearly over the next five years. The expected growth rate in operating income each year for the next five years can then be estimated as follows:[6]

Expected Growth Rate

$= ROC_{current} \times \text{Reinvestment Rate}_{current} + \{[1 + (ROC_{In\ 5\ years} - ROC_{Current}) / ROC_{Current}]^{1/5} - 1\}$

$= .1218 \times .5299 + \{[1 + (.1722 - .1218) / .1218]^{1/5} - 1\}$

$= .1363 \text{ or } 13.63\%$

The improvement in return on capital over the next five years will result in a higher growth rate in operating earnings at Motorola over that period.

 chgrowth.xls: This spreadsheet enables you to estimate the expected growth rate in operating income for a firm where the return on capital is expected to change over time.

SCENARIO: NEGATIVE RETURN ON CAPITAL

The third and most difficult scenario for estimating growth is the case of a firm that is losing money and experiencing a negative return on capital. Since the firm is losing money, the reinvestment rate is also likely to be negative. To estimate growth in these firms, we move up the income statement and first project growth in revenues. Next, we use the firm's expected operating margin in future years to estimate the operating income in those years. If the expected margin in future years is positive, the expected operating income will also turn positive, allowing us to apply traditional valuation approaches in valuing these firms. We also estimate, by linking revenues to the capital invested in the firm, how much the firm must reinvest to generate revenue growth.

Growth in Revenues.   Many high-growth firms, while reporting losses, also show large increases in revenues from period to period. The first step in forecasting cash flows is forecasting revenues in future years, usually by forecasting a growth rate in revenues each period. In making these estimates, keep in mind these five points:

- The rate of growth in revenues will decrease as the firm's revenues increase. Thus, a 10-fold increase in revenues is entirely feasible for a firm with revenues of $2 million but unlikely for a firm with revenues of $2 billion.

- Compounded growth rates in revenues over time can seem low, but appearances are deceptive. A compounded growth rate in revenues of 40% over 10 years will result in, roughly, a 40-fold increase in revenues over the period.

- Although growth rates in revenues may be the mechanism that you use to forecast future revenues, you do have to keep track of the dollar revenues to ensure that they are reasonable, given the size of the overall market in which the firm operates. If a firm's projected revenues 10 years out would give the firm a 90% or 100% share (or greater) of the overall market in a competitive marketplace, you clearly should reassess the revenue growth rate.

- Assumptions about revenue growth and operating margins must be internally consistent. Firms can post higher growth rates in revenues by adopting more aggressive pricing strategies, but the higher revenue growth will then be accompanied by lower margins.

- In coming up with an estimate of revenue growth of the firm you are valuing, you will make a number of subjective judgments about the nature of competition, the capacity of the firm to handle the revenue growth, and the marketing capabilities of the firm.

ILLUSTRATION 5.8

Estimating Revenues at Amazon, Ariba, and Rediff.com

We begin by estimating the expected growth in revenues at Amazon, Ariba, and Rediff.com. In Table 5.10, the expected revenue growth rates are reported at each of these firms.

TABLE 5.10 Revenue Growth Rates: Amazon, Ariba, and Rediff.com

YEAR	AMAZON (%)	ARIBA (%)	REDIFF.COM (%)
1	120.00	400.00	500.00
2	90.00	200.00	300.00
3	75.00	150.00	200.00
4	50.00	100.00	125.00
5	30.00	75.00	100.00
6	25.20	60.00	75.00
7	20.40	40.00	50.00
8	15.60	20.00	25.00
9	10.80	10.00	15.00
10	5.00	5.00	5.00
Compounded growth rate	40.00	82.39	104.57

We based our estimates of growth in the initial years on the growth in revenues over the last year and used higher growth rates for Ariba and Rediff since they have lower revenues than Amazon. As a check, also examine, in Table 5.11, how much the revenues at each of these firms would be in 10 years and how the revenues would compare with those of the largest firms in the businesses in which they operate today.

If your projections of revenue growth are borne out, Amazon will have a significant but not overwhelming share of the retail market by the 10th year. Implicitly, we are assuming a number of favorable trends in Amazon's favor: a substantial growth in the overall online retailing market, a strengthening of Amazon's brand name thereby allowing it to keep ahead of competition, and successful partnerships with other online ventures to boost revenues.

TABLE 5.11 Revenue Comparison

	AMAZON	ARIBA	REDIFF.COM
Current revenues	$1,640	$93	$2
Revenues in 10 years	$47,425	$37,717	$2,569
Comparable firms			
Largest firm	The Gap ($12,090)	EDS ($18,730)	Yahoo! ($589)
	Walmart ($173,281)		

With our projections of growth, Ariba, on the other hand, will be significantly larger than the largest firms in its peer group. However, its target market is a huge one and if Ariba succeeds in opening up the market, the growth rate is attainable. Here again, we are assuming that Ariba has a good chance of winning the technology battle with competitors like Commerce One and that conventional firms will in fact expand their use of online ventures for business services.

Finally, Yahoo!, the Internet portal with the largest revenues, is still a very young firm with revenues of only $589 million. Rediff.com, with projected growth, will be almost five times larger in 10 years. Again, you are assuming that there will continue to be exponential growth in the overall Indian market that will make this projection feasible. You are also assuming that Rediff will be able to tap into other revenue sources and perhaps even other businesses to generate this growth.

Operating Margin Forecasts. Before considering how best to estimate the operating margins, let us begin with an assessment of where many high-growth firms, early in the life cycle, stand when the valuation begins. They usually have low revenues and negative operating margins. If revenue growth translates low revenues into high revenues and operating margins stay negative, these firms will not only be worth nothing but are unlikely to survive. For firms to be valuable, the higher revenues eventually have to deliver positive earnings. In a valuation model, this translates into positive operating margins in the future. A key input in valuing a high-growth firm, then, is the operating margin you would expect it to have as it matures.

In estimating this margin, you should begin by looking at the business that the firm is in. Many new firms claim to be pioneers in their businesses, and some believe that they have no competitors; it is more likely, however, that they are the first to find a new way of delivering a product or service that before was delivered through other channels. For example, Amazon might have been one of the first firms to sell books online, but Barnes and Noble and Borders preceded them as book retailers. In fact, one can consider online retailers as logical successors to catalog retailers such as L.L.Bean or Lillian Vernon. Similarly, Yahoo! might have been one of the first (and most successful) Internet portals, but they are following the lead of newspapers that have used content and features to attract readers and used their readership to attract advertising. Using the average operating margin of competitors in the business may strike some as conservative. After all, they would point out, Amazon can hold less inventory than Borders and does not have the burden of carrying the operating leases that Barnes and Noble does (on its stores); Amazon should, therefore, be more efficient about generating its revenues. This may be true but it is unlikely that the operating margins for Internet retailers can be persistently higher than their brick-and-mortar counterparts. If they were, you would expect to see a migration of traditional retailers to online retailing and increased competition among online retailers on price and products, thus driving the margin down.

Although the margin for the business in which a firm operates provides a target value, you need to confront two other estimation issues. Given that the operating margins in the early stages of the life cycle are negative, you first have to consider how the margin will improve from current levels to the target values. Generally, the improvements in margins will be greatest in the earlier years (at least in percentage terms) and then taper off as the firm approaches maturity. The second issue is one that arises over revenue growth. Firms may be able to post higher revenue growth with lower margins, but the trade-off has to be considered. While firms generally want both higher revenue growth and higher margins, the margin and revenue growth assumptions have to be consistent.

ILLUSTRATION 5.9

Estimating Operating Margins

To estimate the operating margins for Amazon, Ariba, and Rediff.com, we begin by estimating the operating margins of the businesses in which each firm engages. In Table 5.12, we define these businesses and estimate the target operating margins.

TABLE 5.12 Target Operating Margins

	AMAZON	ARIBA	REDIFF.COM
Business	Specialty Retailing	Business Services/ Software	Internet Portals
Pre-tax operating margin	9.32%	16.36%	40.00%

The pre-tax operating margin[7] for Internet portals is estimated prior to selling, and general and administrative expenses to be consistent with our treatment of these expenses as capital expenses for Rediff.com.

The firms are all losing money currently and have negative operating margins. We assume that the firms will move toward their target margins, with greater marginal improvements[8] in the earlier years and smaller ones in the later years. Table 5.13 summarizes the expected operating margins over time for all three firms.

TABLE 5.13 Expected Operating Margins

YEAR	AMAZON (%)	ARIBA (%)	REDIFF.COM (%)
Current	–16.27	–159.84	–113.10
1	–3.48	–71.74	–36.55
2	2.92	–27.69	1.73
3	6.12	–5.67	20.86
4	7.72	5.35	30.43
5	8.52	10.85	35.22
6	8.92	13.61	37.61
7	9.12	14.98	38.80

(continued)

TABLE 5.13 *(Continued)*

YEAR	AMAZON (%)	ARIBA (%)	REDIFF.COM (%)
8	9.22	15.67	39.40
9	9.27	16.02	39.70
10	9.30	16.19	39.85
Terminal year	9.32	16.36	40.00

Since we estimated revenue growth in the last section and the margins in this one, we can now estimate the pre-tax operating income at each of the firms over the next 10 years, as in Table 5.14.

TABLE 5.14 Expected Operating Income

YEAR	AMAZON	ARIBA	REDIFF.COM
1	$(587)	$(740)	$(13)
2	$(238)	$(996)	$(17)
3	$351	$(961)	$2
4	$1,101	$(393)	$64
5	$1,806	$650	$188
6	$2,495	$2,110	$381
7	$3,146	$3,703	$610
8	$3,718	$4,893	$786
9	$4,164	$5,629	$918
10	$4,396	$6,041	$971

As the margins move toward target levels and revenues grow, the operating income at each of the three firms also increases.

Sales-to-Capital Ratio. High revenue growth is clearly a desirable objective, especially when linked with positive operating margins in future years. Firms do, however, have to invest to generate both revenue growth and positive operating margins in future years. This investment can take traditional forms (plant and equipment), but it should also include acquisitions of other firms, partnerships, investments in distribution and marketing capabilities, and research and development.

To link revenue growth with reinvestment needs, we look at the revenues that every dollar of invested capital generates. This ratio, called the sales-to-capital ratio, enables us to estimate how much additional investment the firm has to make to generate the projected revenue growth. This investment can be in internal projects, acquisitions, or working capital. To estimate the reinvestment needs in any year, then, we divide the revenue growth that we have projected (in dollar terms) by the sales-to-capital ratio. Thus, if we expect revenues to grow by $1 billion and we use a sales-to-capital ratio of 2.5, we would estimate a reinvestment need for this firm of $400 million ($1 billion divided by 2.5). Lower sales-to-capital ratios increase reinvestment needs (and reduce cash flows), whereas higher sales-to-capital ratios decrease reinvestment needs (and increase cash flows).

To estimate the sales-to-capital ratio, we look at both a firm's past and the business in which it operates. To measure this ratio historically, we look at changes in revenue each year and divide it by the reinvestment made that year. We also look at the average ratio of sales to book capital invested in the business in which the firm operates.

Should the reinvestment occur in the same year that the revenue grows? The answer will depend on the firm that you are valuing and the business it is in. For software firms like Ariba, where there is little or no lag between reinvestment and payoff, the reinvestment and revenue growth can be contemporaneous. For manufacturing firms or firms with heavy infrastructure investments, there will be a lag between reinvestment and revenue growth. The answer will also depend on how a firm reinvests. Firms that grow through acquisition of established firms with revenues will see revenue growth right after the reinvestment. Firms that grow through internal investment will see a longer lag.

Linking operating margins to reinvestment needs is much more difficult to do, since a firm's capacity to earn operating income and sustain high returns comes from the competitive advantages that it acquires, partly through internal investment and partly through acquisitions. Firms that adopt a two-track strategy in investing, where one track focuses on generating higher revenues and the other on building up competitive strengths, should have higher operating margins and values than firms that concentrate only on revenue growth.

Link to Return on Capital. One of the dangers that you face when using a sales-to-capital ratio to generate reinvestment needs is that you might underestimate or overestimate your reinvestment needs. You can keep tabs on whether this misjudgment is happening and correct it by also estimating the after-tax return on capital on the firm each year through the analysis. To estimate the return on capital in a future year, you use the estimated after-tax operating income in that year and divide it by the total capital invested in that firm in that year. The former number comes from your estimates of revenue growth and operating margins, and you can estimated the latter by aggregating the reinvestments made by the firm all the way through the future year. For instance, a firm that has $500 million in capital invested today and is required to reinvest $300 million next year and $400 million the year after will have capital invested of $1.2 billion at the end of the second year.

For firms losing money today, the return on capital will be a negative number when the estimation begins but will improve as margins improve. If the sales-to-capital ratio is set too high, the return on capital in the later years will be too high; if it is set too low, the return on capital will be too low. Too low or high relative to what, you ask? Two comparisons are worth making. The first is to the average return on capital for mature firms in the business in which the firm operates— mature retailers, in the case of Amazon. The second is to the firm's own cost of capital. A projected return on capital of 40% for a firm with a cost of capital of 10% in a sector where returns on capital hover around 15% is an indicator that the firm is investing too little for the projected revenue growth and operating margins. Decreasing the sales-to-capital ratio until the return on capital converges on 15% would be prudent.

ILLUSTRATION 5.10

Estimated Sales-to-Capital Ratios

To estimate how much Amazon, Ariba, and Rediff.com have to invest to generate the expected revenue growth, we estimate, in Table 5.15, the firm's current sales-to-capital ratio, its marginal sales-to-capital ratio in the last year, and the average sales-to-capital ratio for the business area in which each operates.

TABLE 5.15 Sales-to-Capital Ratio Estimates

	AMAZON	ARIBA	REDIFF.COM
Firm's sales to capital	0.94	0.75	NA
Marginal sales to capital: most recent year	2.86	2.88	NA
Industry average sales to capital	3.18	2.33	0.70
Sales-to-capital ratio used in valuation	3.02	2.50	1.00

We used a sales-to-capital ratio of 3.02 for Amazon and 2.50 for Ariba, approximately midway through their marginal sales-to-capital ratio from last year and the industry average. For Rediff, the industry average reflects the average sales-to-capital ratio for Internet portals, and you set the sales-to-capital ratio at a slightly higher number.

Based on these estimates of the sales-to-capital ratio for each firm, we can now estimate, in Table 5.16, how much each firm will have to reinvest each year for the next 10 years.

For all three firms, we have assumed that reinvestment pays off in revenue growth in the same year. If we had introduced a lag, the reinvestment would have led revenue growth by that period.

As a final check, we estimate, in Table 5.17, the return on capital each year for the next 10 years for all three firms.

TABLE 5.16 Estimated Reinvestment Needs

	AMAZON		ARIBA		REDIFF.COM	
Year	Increase in Revenue	Reinvestment	Increase in Revenue	Reinvestment	Increase in Revenue	Reinvestment
1	$1,968	$652	$370	$148	$9.53	$9.53
2	$3,247	$1,075	$926	$370	$34.31	$34.31
3	$5,141	$1,702	$2,083	$833	$91.49	$91.49
4	$5,998	$1,986	$3,471	$1,388	$171.54	$171.54
5	$5,398	$1,788	$5,207	$2,083	$308.77	$308.77
6	$5,895	$1,952	$7,289	$2,916	$463.16	$463.16
7	$5,975	$1,978	$7,775	$3,110	$540.35	$540.35
8	$5,501	$1,822	$5,443	$2,177	$405.26	$405.26
9	$4,403	$1,458	$3,266	$1,306	$303.95	$303.95
10	$2,258	$748	$1,796	$718	$116.51	$116.51

TABLE 5.17 Estimated Return on Capital

YEAR	AMAZON (%)	ARIBA (%)	REDIFF.COM (%)
1	−7.18	−218.10	−73.69
2	8.35	−128.01	5.19
3	17.25	−29.33	38.21
4	17.45	24.69	40.98
5	18.09	36.49	42.79
6	18.97	34.56	40.23
7	19.17	33.59	35.67
8	18.97	30.24	30.22
9	18.51	28.38	28.03
10	17.73	27.40	25.69
Industry average	16.94	23.96	35.25

The returns on capital at all three firms converge to sustainable levels, at least relative to industry averages, by the terminal year. This suggests that our estimates of sales to capital ratios are reasonable.

margins.xls: This dataset on the Web summarizes operating margins, by industry, for the United States.

THE QUALITATIVE ASPECTS OF GROWTH

The emphasis on quantitative elements—return on capital and reinvestment rates for profitable firms, and margins, revenue growth, and sales to capital ratios for unprofitable firms—may strike some as skewed. After all, growth is determined by a number of subjective factors: the quality of management, the strength of a firm's marketing, its capacity to form partnerships with other firms, and the management's strategic vision, among many others. Where, you might ask, is there room in the growth equations that have been presented in this chapter for these factors?

The answer is that qualitative factors matter and they all ultimately have to show up in one or more of the quantitative inputs that determine growth. Consider the following:

- The quality of management plays a significant role in the returns on capital that you assume firms can earn on their new investments and in how long they can sustain these returns. Thus, the fact that John Chambers is CEO is one reason why Cisco's return on capital is allowed to remain at 34% and why it is assumed that Cisco will continue to be successful in its path of growing through acquisitions.
- The marketing strengths of a firm and its choice of marketing strategy are reflected in the operating margins and turnover ratios that you assume for firms. Thus, it takes faith in Amazon's capacity to market its products

effectively to assume a high turnover ratio (a sales-to-capital ratio of 3) and a high target margin (9.32%). In fact, you can consider various marketing strategies, which trade off lower margins for higher turnover ratios, and consider the implications for value. The brand name of a firm's products and the strength of its distribution system also affect these estimates.

- Defining reinvestment broadly to include acquisitions, research and development, and investments in marketing and distribution enables you to consider different ways in which firms can grow. Cisco's reinvestment and growth come from acquisitions, Amazon's from investments in distribution and partnerships with other firms, Motorola's and Ariba's from investments in technology and research, and Rediff's from investment in marketing. The effectiveness of these reinvestment strategies is captured in the return on capital that you assume for the future, with Cisco assumed to be the most effective (with the highest return on capital) and Motorola the least effective (with the lowest return on capital).

- The strength of the competition that firms face is in the background but it does determine how high the excess returns (return on capital – cost of capital) will be and how quickly they will slide. Thus, you are assuming that Cisco will continue to dominate its competitors over the next decade when you assume that the firm's excess returns will remain at current levels for that period.

Thus, every qualitative factor is quantified and the growth implications are considered. What if you cannot quantify the effects? If you cannot, you should remain skeptical about whether these factors truly affect value. What about those qualitative factors that do not affect the return on capital, margin, or reinvestment rate? At the risk of sounding dogmatic, these factors cannot affect value.

Why is it necessary to impose this quantitative structure on growth estimate? One of the biggest dangers in valuing technology firms is that story-telling can be used to justify growth rates that are neither reasonable nor sustainable. Thus, you might be told that Amazon will grow 60% a year because the online retailing market is huge and that Cisco will grow 50% a year because it has great management. While there is truth in these stories, a consideration of how these qualitative views translate into the quantitative elements of growth is an essential step toward consistent valuations.

Can different investors consider the same qualitative factors and come to different conclusions about the implications for returns on capital, margins, and reinvestment rates, and, consequently, on growth? Absolutely. In fact, you would expect differences in opinion about the future and different estimates of value. The payoff to knowing a firm (and the sector in which it operates) better than other investors is that your estimates of growth and value will be better than theirs. Unfortunately, this does not guarantee that your investment returns will be higher than theirs.

THE QUESTION OF DETAIL

In estimating revenues and cash flows for the future, you are often faced with the question of how much detail should go into these projections. For instance, should you try to break Amazon's expected revenues into revenues from books, revenues from CDs, revenues from electronics, and so on? Should Cisco's operating expenses be considered as individual expense items?

While more detail may seem to be the path to more precise values, it is not necessarily so. There are two points worth making in this regard. The first is that estimating individual details (revenues from CDs, for example) is more difficult than estimating aggregates. Thus, a more detailed projection may actually result in more erroneous valuations. The second point is that the details are likely to get murkier the further into the future you go with your projections.

All too often, analysts lose sight of the big picture as they delve further and further into the details. The big assumptions (about revenue growth and margins) get mixed in with small ones (the number of accounts receivable days in five years) and the valuation suffers. The bottom line then is that you should delve into only those details that make a difference to your valuation and avoid those details that do not.

SUMMARY

Growth is the key input in every valuation, and there are three sources for estimation growth rates. One is the past, though both estimating and using historical growth rates can be difficult for technology firms, with their volatile and sometimes negative earnings. The second is analyst estimates of growth. Though analysts can be privy to information that is not available to the rest of the market, this information does not result in growth rates that are superior to historical growth estimates. Furthermore, the analyst emphasis on earnings per share growth can be a problem in forecasting operating income. The third and soundest way of estimating growth is to base it on a firm's fundamentals.

We considered three approaches to estimating fundamental growth. In the first, we considered a firm with a sustainable reinvestment rate and return and capital and argued that growth is the product of the two for this firm. In the second approach, we considered a firm with a changing return on capital and noted that there will be an additional component of growth for this firm. If the return on capital improves, growth will be higher, whereas if it drops, growth will be lower. The third approach, designed for firms with changing margins, began with forecasted revenues and then used estimated margins to arrive at operating income each year. We maintain consistency by requiring that the firm reinvest a sufficient amount to create the revenue growth each year.

ENDNOTES

1. Damodaran, A., *Investment Valuation*. John Wiley & Sons: New York, NY. 1994.

2. Sell-side analysts work for brokerage houses and investment banks, and their research is offered to clients of these firms as a

service. In contrast, buy-side analysts work for institutional investors, and their research is generally proprietary.

3. This is because earnings per share will reflect the effects of financial leverage while operating earnings will not.

4. To normalize working capital, you compute the working capital as a percent of revenues at the firm at the end of the most recent year and multiply it by the revenue change in the most recent year to estimate the change in noncash working capital.

5. Note that 17.22% is exactly halfway between the current return on capital and the industry average (22.27%).

6. You are allowing for a compounded growth rate over time. Thus, if earnings are expected to grow 25% over three years, you estimate the expected growth rate each year to be:

Expected Growth Rate Each Year = $(1.25)^{1/3} - 1$

7. We use the operating margin prior to selling expenses at Yahoo! to get the estimate.

8. The margin each year is computed as follows:
(Margin This Year + Target Margin) / 2

6 ESTIMATING FIRM VALUE

In the last chapter, we examined the determinants of expected growth. Firms that reinvest substantial portions of their earnings and earn high returns on these investments should be able to grow at high rates. But for how long? In this chapter, we discuss closure to firm valuation by considering this question. As a firm grows, it becomes more difficult for it to maintain high growth, and it eventually will grow at a rate less than or equal to the growth rate of the economy in which it operates. This growth rate, labeled stable growth, can be sustained in perpetuity, allowing us to estimate the value of all cash flows beyond that point as a terminal value.

The key question in this chapter is the estimation of when and how this transition to stable growth will occur for the firm that you are valuing. Will the growth rate drop abruptly at a point in time to a stable growth rate, or will it occur more gradually over time? To answer these questions, we look at a firm's size (relative to the market that it serves), its current growth rate, and its competitive advantages.

In the second part of the chapter, we examine how to incorporate the value of cash, marketable securities, and other nonoperating assets into the value of the firm. Cross-holdings in other companies can pose problems in valuation, partly because of the way these holdings are reflected in accounting statements.

CLOSURE IN VALUATION

In theory, at least, publicly traded firms can have infinite lives. Since you cannot estimate cash flows forever, you generally impose closure in discounted cash flow valuation by stopping your estimation of cash flows sometime in the future and then computing a terminal value that reflects the value of the firm at that point:

$$\text{Value of a Firm} = \sum_{t=1}^{t=n} \frac{CF_t}{(1+k_c)^t} + \frac{\text{Terminal Value}_n}{(1+k_c)^n}$$

You can find the terminal value in one of three ways. One method is to apply a multiple to estimate the value in the terminal year. The second is to assume a liquidation of the firm's assets in the terminal year and estimate what others would pay for the assets that the firm has accumulated at that point. The third is to assume that the cash flows of the firm will grow at a constant rate forever—a stable growth rate. With stable growth, you can estimate the terminal value by using a perpetual growth model.

MULTIPLE APPROACH

In this approach, we estimate the value of a firm in a future year by applying a multiple to the firm's earnings or revenues in that year. For instance, a firm with expected revenues of

$6 billion 10 years from now will have an estimated terminal value in that year of $12 billion if a value-to-sales multiple of 2 is used. While this approach has the virtue of simplicity, the multiple has a huge effect on the final firm value, and where it is obtained can be critical. If, as is common, the multiple is estimated by looking at how comparable firms in the business today are priced by the market, the valuation becomes a relative valuation rather than a discounted cash flow valuation. If the multiple is estimated with fundamentals, it converges on the stable growth model, described in the next section.

All in all, using multiples to estimate terminal value, when those multiples are estimated from comparable firms, results in a dangerous mix of relative and discounted cash flow valuation. Although there are advantages to relative valuation—and you will consider these in a later chapter—a discounted cash flow valuation should provide you with an estimate of intrinsic value, not relative value. Consequently, the only consistent way of estimating terminal value in a discounted cash flow model is to use either a liquidation value or a stable growth model.

LIQUIDATION VALUE

In some valuations, you can assume that the firm will cease operations at a point in time in the future and sell the assets it has accumulated to the highest bidders. The estimate that emerges is called a liquidation value. The liquidation value can be estimated in two ways. One is to base it on the book value of the assets, adjusted for any inflation during the period. Thus, if the book value of assets 10 years from now is expected to be $2 billion, the average age of the assets at that point is five years, and the expected inflation rate is 3%, then the expected liquidation value can be estimated as:[1]

Expected Liquidation Value
$$= \text{Book Value of Assets}_{\text{Term yr}} (1+ \text{inflation rate})^{\text{Average age of assets}}$$
$$= \$2 \text{ billion } (1.03)^5 = \$2.319 \text{ billion}$$

The limitation of this approach is that it is based on accounting book value and does not reflect the earning power of the assets.

The alternative approach is to base the estimate of the value on the earning power of the assets. To make this estimate, you would first have to estimate the expected cash flows from the assets and then discount these cash flows back to the present, using an appropriate discount rate. In the example above, for instance, if you assumed that the assets in question could be expected to generate $400 million in after-tax cash flows for 15 years (after the terminal year) and the cost of capital was 10%, your estimate of the expected liquidation value would be

Expected Liquidation Value

$$= \$400 \text{ million } \frac{\left(1 - \dfrac{1}{(1.10)^{15}}\right)}{0.10}$$

$$= \$3.042 \text{ billion}$$

STABLE GROWTH MODEL

In the liquidation value approach, you are assuming that your firm has a finite life and that it will be liquidated at the end of that life. Firms, however, can reinvest some of their cash flows back into new assets and extend their lives. If you assume that cash flows, beyond the terminal year, will grow at a constant rate forever, the terminal value can be estimated as follows:

Terminal Value$_n$
= Free Cash Flow to Firm$_{n+1}$ / (Cost of Capital$_{n+1}$ – g$_n$)

where the cost of capital and the growth rate in the model are sustainable forever. It is this fact, that is, they are constant forever, that allows you to put some reasonable constraints on the growth rate. Since no firm can grow forever at a rate higher than the growth rate of the economy in which it operates, the constant growth rate cannot be greater than the overall growth rate of the economy. This constant growth rate is called a *stable growth rate*. In fact, constraining the stable growth rate to be less than or equal to the growth rate of the economy will also ensure that the growth rate will always be less than the cost of capital.[2]

While this approach to estimating terminal value is widely practiced, many are not aware of the fact that the stable growth rate can be a negative number. If this is the case, the firm will become smaller each year and eventually disappear. This allows us to estimate the terminal value for firms that we do not expect to survive forever.

Key Assumptions About Stable Growth. In every discounted cash flow valuation, you need to make three critical assumptions about stable growth. The first relates to when the firm that you are valuing will become a stable growth firm if it is not one already. The second assumption relates to what the characteristics of the firm will be in stable growth, in terms of return on capital and cost of capital. The final assumption relates to how the firm that you are valuing will make the transition from high growth to stable growth.

Length of the High-Growth Period

The question of how long a firm will be able to sustain high growth is perhaps one of the more difficult questions to answer in a valuation, but two points are worth making. The first is that it is not a question of whether firms will hit the stable growth wall, but when. All firms ultimately become stable growth firms, in the best case, because high growth makes a firm larger and the firm's size will eventually become a barrier to further high growth. In the worst case scenario, firms may not survive and will be liquidated. The second point is that high growth in valuation, or at least high growth that creates value,[3] comes from firms earning high returns on their marginal investments. In other words, increased value comes from firms having a return on capital that is well in excess of the cost of capital. Thus, when you assume that a firm will experience high growth for the next five or 10 years, you are also implicitly assuming that it will earn excess returns (over and above the cost of capital) during that period. In a competitive market, these excess returns will eventually draw in new competitors, and the excess returns will disappear.

You should look at three factors when considering how long a firm will be able to maintain high growth:

1. *Size of the firm*: Smaller firms are much more likely to earn excess returns and maintain these excess returns than otherwise similar larger firms. The reason is that they have more room to grow and a larger potential market. Ariba and Amazon are small firms in large markets and should have the potential for high growth (at least in revenues) over long periods. The same can be said about Rediff.com. When looking at the size of the firm, you should look not only at its current market share but also at the potential growth in the total market for its products or services. Cisco may have a large market share of its current market, but it may be able to grow in spite of this because the entire market is growing rapidly.

2. *Existing growth rate and excess returns:* Momentum does matter when it comes to projecting growth. Firms that have been reporting rapidly growing revenues are more likely to see revenues grow rapidly, at least in the near future. Firms that are earning high returns on capital and high excess returns in the current period are likely to sustain these excess returns for the next few years.

3. *Magnitude and sustainability of competitive advantages*: This is perhaps the most critical determinant of the length of the high-growth period. If there are significant barriers to entry and sustainable competitive advantages, firms can maintain high growth for longer periods. If, on the other hand, there are no or minor barriers to entry or if the firm's existing competitive advantages are fading, you should be far more conservative about allowing for long growth periods. The qual-

ity of existing management also influences growth. Some top managers[4] have the capacity to make the strategic choices that increase competitive advantages and create new ones.

ILLUSTRATION 6.1

Length of High-Growth Period

To examine how long high growth will last at each of the five firms, you assess their standings on each of the above characteristics in Table 6.1.

TABLE 6.1   Assessment of Length of High-Growth Period

	FIRM SIZE/ MARKET SIZE	CURRENT GROWTH/ COMPETITIVE ADVANTAGES	LENGTH OF HIGH-GROWTH PERIOD
Amazon	Firm has a very small market share of a very large market (specialty retailing). There is ample potential for growth (at least in revenues).	Firm is losing money currently but has a first-mover advantage as one of the first e-tailers. Amazon also has a small technological edge in the processing of online orders.	10 years
Ariba	Firm has small revenues in a small and fast-growing market (if you define the market as B2B commerce). However, the potential market is huge.	Ariba is losing money but it is in a technological battle for this market. If Ariba's technology wins, it could earn excess returns for an extended period.	10 years
Cisco	Firm has a large market share of a fast-growing market.	Firm has a technological edge on its rivals and a knack of succeeding with its acquisition strategy. Firm is earning significant excess returns now.	12 years

(continued)

TABLE 6.1 *(Continued)*

	FIRM SIZE/ MARKET SIZE	CURRENT GROWTH/ COMPETITIVE ADVANTAGES	LENGTH OF HIGH-GROWTH PERIOD
Motorola	Firm has a small market share of a growth market that is maturing (semiconductors) and a significant market share of a growing market (telecommunication equipment).	Motorola's research has provided it with technological advantages as well as patents. It is not the technological leader in any of its markets, though. Firm has anemic returns currently.	5 years
Rediff.com	Has a small market share of a small market (Indian Internet users) that could grow exponentially.	Local language capabilities give its portals an advantage over foreign competitors.	10 years

There is clearly a strong subjective component to making a judgment on how long high growth will last. Much of what was said in Chapter 5, "Looking Forward: Estimating Growth," about the interrelationships between qualitative variables and growth has relevance for this discussion as well.

Characteristics of a Stable-Growth Firm

As firms move from high growth to stable growth, you need to give them the characteristics of stable-growth firms. A firm in stable growth is different from that same firm in high growth in a number of dimensions. For instance:

- High-growth firms tend to be *more exposed to market risk* (and have higher betas) than do stable-growth firms. Thus, although it might be reasonable to assume a beta of 1.8 in high growth, it is important that the beta be lowered, if not to 1, at least toward 1 in stable growth.[5]

- High-growth firms tend to have *high returns on capital and earn excess returns*. In stable growth, it becomes much more difficult to sustain excess returns. Some analysts believe that the only assumption consistent with stable growth is to assume no excess returns; the return on capital is set equal to the cost of capital.

Although, in principle, excess returns in perpetuity are not feasible, it is difficult in practice to assume that firms will suddenly lose the capacity to earn excess returns. Since entire industries often earn excess returns over long periods, assuming a firm's return on capital will move toward its industry average in stable growth will yield more reasonable estimates of value.[6]

■ High-growth firms tend to *use less debt* than do stable growth firms. As firms mature, their debt capacity increases. You cannot answer the question whether the debt ratio for a firm should be moved toward a more sustainable level in stable growth without looking at the incumbent managers' views on debt and how much power stockholders have in these firms. If managers are willing to change their debt ratios and stockholders retain some power, it is reasonable to assume that the debt ratio will move to a higher level in stable growth; if not, it is safer to leave the debt ratio at existing levels.

■ Finally, stable-growth firms tend to reinvest less than high-growth firms. In fact, you can estimate how much a stable-growth firm will need to reinvest, using the relationship developed in Chapter 5 between growth rates, reinvestment needs, and returns on capital.

$$\frac{\text{Reinvestment Rate}}{\text{in Stable Growth}} = \text{Stable Growth Rate} / ROC_n$$

where the ROC_n is the return on capital that the firm can sustain in stable growth. This reinvestment rate can then be used to generate the free cash flow to the firm in the first year of stable growth.

Linking the reinvestment rate to the stable growth rate also makes the valuation less sensitive to assumptions about stable growth. Increasing the stable growth rate while holding all else constant can dramatically increase value, but changing the reinvestment rate as the growth rate changes will create an offsetting effect. The gains from increasing the growth rate will be partially or completely offset by the loss in cash flows because of the higher reinvestment rate. Whether value increases or decreases as the stable growth rate increases will entirely depend on what you assume about excess returns. If the return on capital is higher than the cost of capital in the stable growth period, increasing the stable growth rate will increase value. *If the return on capital is equal to the stable growth rate, increasing the stable growth rate will have no effect on value.* This can be proved quite easily:

$$\text{Terminal Value} = \frac{\text{EBIT}_{n+1}(1-t)(1-\text{Reinvestment Rate})}{\text{Cost of Capital}_n - \text{Stable Growth Rate}}$$

Substituting in the stable growth rate as a function of the reinvestment rate, from above, you get:

Terminal Value =

$$\frac{\text{EBIT}_{n+1}(1-t)(1-\text{Reinvestment Rate})}{\text{Cost of Capital}_n - (\text{Reinvestment Rate} \times \text{Return on Capital})}$$

Setting the return on capital equal to the cost of capital, you arrive at:

Terminal Value =

$$\frac{\text{EBIT}_{n+1}(1-t)(1-\text{Reinvestment Rate})}{\text{Cost of Capital}_n - (\text{Reinvestment Rate} \times \text{Cost on Capital})}$$

Simplifying, the terminal value can be stated as:

$$\text{Terminal Value}_{\text{ROC = WACC}} = \frac{\text{EBIT}_{n+1}(1-t)}{\text{Cost of Capital}_n}$$

Note that the growth rate drops out of the formulation.

ILLUSTRATION 6.2

Stable Growth Inputs

In Chapter 5, reinvestment rates were calculated for the five firms that are being valued, and in Chapter 4, "Cash is King: Estimating Cash Flows," the costs of capital were esti-mated. We revisit these estimates and revise them for the firms in their stable growth periods, in Table 6.2.

The betas for all of the firms are adjusted down toward 1. For Amazon, the average beta of stable specialty retailers (1.10) is used as the stable period beta. For Cisco and Motor-ola, we move the beta to the average for the market since the sectors to which they belong are still in high growth and have higher betas. For Ariba and Rediff, a stable beta of 1.20 is used to reflect the fact that even in stable growth, these firms are likely to be riskier than the average firm in the market. The debt ratio for four of the firms is adjusted upward, moving Amazon's up to the average for the specialty retailing sector (15%) and Ariba and Rediff to a debt ratio (10%) that is sustainable given their operating incomes in 10 years. Cisco's debt ratio is also moved up to 10% in stable growth,[7] but Motorola's debt ratio is left at its current levels. The firm has had the capacity to borrow money for the last few years but has not used it, reflecting management's aversion to debt.

For all of the firms, a stable growth rate of 5% is used. Even though Rediff is an Indian Internet portal, the valuation is in U.S. dollars and the stable growth rate is therefore set at the same level as the other firms that we are valuing.[8] The reinvestment rate in stable growth is estimated according to the following equation:

Reinvestment Rate = Expected Growth Rate / Return on Capital

Note that the reinvestment rate is lower for firms with higher returns on capital in stable growth. To estimate the return on capital in stable growth, the industry average for spe-cialty retailers (16.96%) is used for Amazon and the average of comparable firms (16.52%) is used for Cisco. For Motorola, the return on capital in stable growth is left unchanged from the high-growth phase level of 17.22%, which was estimated as the midpoint between the firm's current return on capital and the industry average. For Ariba, the return on capital is moved to 20% in stable growth, which is slightly lower than the current industry average of 23.96%.[9] Finally, for Rediff.com, a return on capital of 25% is used, based on the estimate of operating income and capital invested in the firm in 10 years.[10]

TABLE 6.2 Stable Growth Estimates

	AMAZON		ARIBA		CISCO		MOTOROLA		REDIFF.COM	
	High Growth	Stable Growth	High Growth	Stable Growth	High Growth	Stable Growth	High Growth	Stable Growth	High Growth	Stable Growth
Beta	1.74	1.10	1.78	1.20	1.43	1.00	1.21	1.00	1.90	1.20
Cost of equity	12.94%	10.40%	13.12%	10.80%	11.72%	10.00%	10.85%	10.00%	25.82%	18.52%
After-tax cost of debt	8.00%	4.55%	9.25%	4.55%	4.03%	4.03%	4.23%	4.23%	10.00%	4.31%
Debt ratio	7.81%	15.00%	0.15%	10.00%	0.18%	10.00%	6.86%	6.86%	0.00%	20.00%
Cost of capital	12.56%	9.52%	13.11%	10.18%	11.71%	9.40%	10.39%	9.60%	25.82%	15.67%
Return on capital	-7.18%	16.94%	-218.1%	20.00%	34.07%	16.52%	17.22%	17.22%	-73.69%	25.00%
Reinvestment rate	NMF	29.52%	NMF	25.00%	106.8%	30.27%	52.99%	29.04%	NMF	20.00%
Expected growth rate	NMF	5.00%	NMF	5.00%	36.39%	5.00%	13.22%	5.00%	NMF	5.00%

For all of the firms, it is worth noting that, by setting the return on capital above the cost of capital, we are assuming that excess returns continue in perpetuity. This assumption is potentially troublesome, but the competitive advantages that these firms have built up historically or will build up over the high-growth phase will not disappear in an instant. The excess returns will fade over time, but moving them to or toward industry averages in stable growth seems like a reasonable compromise.

 eva.xls: This dataset on the Web summarizes the returns on capital, costs of capital, and excess returns, by industry group, for firms in the United States.

The Transition to Stable Growth. Once you have decided that a firm will be in stable growth at a point in time in the future, you then consider how the firm will change as it approaches stable growth. There are three distinct scenarios. In the first, the firm will maintain its high growth rate for a period of time and then become a stable-growth firm abruptly; this is a two-stage model. In the second scenario, the firm will maintain its high-growth rate for a period and then experience a transition period where its characteristics change gradually toward stable growth levels; this is a three-stage model. In the third scenario, the firm's characteristics change each year from the initial period to the stable growth period; this can be considered an n-stage model.

Which of these three scenarios you choose depends on the firm being valued. Since the firm goes in one year from high growth to stable growth in the two-stage model, this model is more appropriate for firms with moderate growth rates, where the shift will not be too dramatic. For firms with very high growth rates in operating income, a transition phase allows for a gradual adjustment, not just of growth rates but also of risk characteristics, returns on capital, and reinvestment rates toward stable growth levels. For very young firms or for firms with negative operating margins, allowing for changes in each year (in an n-stage model) is prudent.

ILLUSTRATION 6.3

Choosing a Growth Pattern

For Motorola, the high growth rate during the next five years is mostly due to the improvement expected in the return on capital. Without the adjustment, the growth rate would have been 6.45%; with the improvement, it is 13.63%. Once the return improvements end, the firm will be close to stable growth. Consequently, we will use a two-stage model and assume that stable growth begins after year five.

For Cisco, the estimated growth rate is 36.39% as a consequence of its phenomenal reinvestment rate (106.81%) and its high return on capital (34.07%). The firm is expected to maintain its current reinvestment rate and return on capital for the next few years, although the return on capital will be difficult to sustain as the firm becomes larger and competition increases. As a result, the growth period of 12 years is divided into a high-growth phase (six years) and a transition phase (six years). During the transition phase, the beta, debt ratio, reinvestment rate, and growth rates of the firm adjust toward stable growth levels. In practical terms, we are assuming that Cisco will maintain its current acquisition pace for the next six years, and that both the pace and the returns will begin slowing down after year six. Table 6.3 summarizes the values of each in years seven through 12.

Note that the adjustment over the transition period is linear, making estimation more straightforward.

For Amazon, Ariba, and Rediff.com, the operating margins, reinvestment rates, and returns on capital change each year during the high-growth period. The betas, debt ratios, and costs of capital change only in the second half of the high-growth period for each of these firms.

TABLE 6.3 Cisco's Transition to Stable Growth

	YEAR						
	1–6	7	8	9	10	11	12
Expected growth	36.39%	31.16%	25.93%	20.70%	15.46%	10.23%	5.00%
Reinvestment rate	106.81%	94.05%	81.29%	68.54%	55.78%	43.02%	30.27%
Beta	1.43	1.36	1.29	1.22	1.14	1.07	1.00
Debt ratio	0.18%	1.81%	3.45%	5.09%	6.73%	8.36%	10.00%
Cost of capital	11.71%	11.32%	10.94%	10.55%	10.17%	9.79%	9.40%

VALUING OPERATING ASSETS

Now that we have estimated the basic inputs to the discounted cash flow valuation model—the discount rates, cash flows, high-growth period, and characteristics in stable growth—we are in a position to value the operating assets in these firms. In summary, the value of the operating assets of a firm should be the present value of the expected cash flows to the firm, discounted at the cost of capital, added to the present value of the terminal value estimated as described in the last section.

 fcffginzu.xls: This spreadsheet enables you to value the operating assets of a firm, allowing for a high-growth phase and a transition phase.

ILLUSTRATION 6.4

Valuation of Amazon.com's Operating Assets

The assumptions about Amazon are summarized and presented in Table 6.4.

The details of these assumptions were discussed throughout the last three chapters. Using these inputs, we generate the expected cash flows and costs of capital for Amazon in Table 6.5.

To compute the value of Amazon at the end of the high-growth period, we use the expected cash flow to the firm in the terminal year (year 11), the cost of capital in that year, and the stable growth rate:

Terminal Value for Amazon (in Year 10) = $2,126 / (.0952 − .05) = $47,016 million

The value of Amazon's operating assets is the sum of the present values of the cash flows during the high-growth phase and the present value of the terminal value:[11]

PV of FCFF during high-growth phase = $(1,760) million
PV of Terminal Value = $47,016 / 2.9888 = $15,731 million
Value of Operating Assets for Amazon = $13,971 million

TABLE 6.4 Assumptions for Valuing Amazon

INPUT	ASSUMPTIONS
Revenue growth	Compounded average growth rate over next 10 years = 40%. Growth rate decreases from 120% next year to 5% in year 10.
Operating margin	Operating margin improves from current level of −16.27% to a target margin of 9.32% (which is the average for specialty retailers) in year 10.
Reinvestment needs	The estimated reinvestment each year is based on the assumption that the sales-to-capital ratio will be 3.02; for every dollar of additional capital invested, there will be $3.02 in additional sales.
Beta	The beta of the firm is 1.74 for the first five years and decreases gradually to a stable period beta of 1.10. (The risk-free rate is 6%, and the market risk premium is 4%.)
Debt ratio	The debt ratio for the next five years remains at current levels (7.81%) and increases gradually to 15% by year 10.

TABLE 6.5 Expected Cash Flows and Discount Rates: Amazon (in Millions)

	Base	1	2	3	4	5	6	7	8	9	10	Terminal Year
Revenue Growth		120.00%	90.00%	75.00%	50.00%	30.00%	25.20%	20.40%	15.60%	10.80%	5.00%	5%
Revenues	$1,640	$3,608	$6,855	$11,997	$17,995	$23,393	$29,288	$35,263	$40,764	$45,167	$47,425	$49,797
Operating Margin	-16.27%	-3.48%	2.92%	6.12%	7.72%	8.52%	8.92%	9.12%	9.22%	9.27%	9.30%	9.32%
EBIT	-$267	-$125	$200	$734	$1,389	$1,993	$2,613	$3,216	$3,758	$4,187	$4,408	$4,641
Taxes	$0	$0	$0	$135	$486	$698	$914	$1,126	$1,315	$1,465	$1,543	$1,624
EBIT(1-t)	-$267	-$125	$200	$599	$903	$1,296	$1,698	$2,090	$2,443	$2,722	$2,865	$3,017
+ Depreciation	$67	$101	$131	$165	$198	$229	$254	$267	$280	$294	$309	$324
- Capital Exp.	$275	$694	$1,109	$1,713	$2,004	$1,855	$2,029	$2,066	$1,936	$1,620	$989	$1,143
- Chg WC	-$309	$59	$97	$154	$180	$162	$177	$179	$165	$132	$68	$71
FCFF	-$166	-$777	-$875	-$1,103	-$1,083	-$492	-$254	$112	$621	$1,264	$2,118	$2,126
NOL	$423	$549	$348	$0	$0	$0	$0	$0	$0	$0	$0	$0
Tax Rate	0.00%	0.00%	0.00%	18.40%	35.00%	35.00%	35.00%	35.00%	35.00%	35.00%	35.00%	35.00%
Debt Ratio	7.81%	7.81%	7.81%	7.81%	7.81%	7.81%	9.24%	9.60%	10.20%	11.40%	15.00%	15.00%
Beta	1.74	1.74	1.74	1.74	1.74	1.74	1.61	1.48	1.35	1.23	1.10	1.10
Cost of Equity	12.94%	12.94%	12.94%	12.94%	12.94%	12.94%	12.43%	11.93%	11.42%	10.91%	10.40%	10.40%
Cost of Debt	8.00%	8.00%	8.00%	8.00%	8.00%	8.00%	7.80%	7.75%	7.67%	7.50%	7.00%	7.00%
After-Tax Cost of Debt	8.00%	8.00%	8.00%	6.53%	5.20%	5.20%	5.07%	5.04%	4.98%	4.88%	4.55%	4.55%
Cost of Capital	12.56%	12.56%	12.56%	12.44%	12.34%	12.34%	11.75%	11.26%	10.76%	10.22%	9.52%	9.52%
Cumulative WACC		1.1256	1.2669	1.4245	1.6003	1.7977	2.0090	2.2353	2.4759	2.7289	2.9887	
Present Value of FCFF		$(690)	$(691)	$(774)	$(677)	$(274)	$(126)	$50	$251	$463	$708	

Reinvestment = (Capital Exp - Depreciation + Change in WC)

199

ILLUSTRATION 6.5

Valuation of Ariba's Operating Assets

The assumptions underlying the Ariba valuation are summarized in Table 6.6.

TABLE 6.6 Assumptions for Valuing Ariba

INPUT	ASSUMPTIONS
Revenue growth	Compounded average growth rate over next 10 years = 82.39%. Growth rate decreases from 400% next year to 5% in year 10.
Operating margin	Operating margin improves from current level of –160% to a target margin of 16.36% (which is the average for comparable firms) in year 10.
Reinvestment needs	The estimated reinvestment each year is based on the assumption that the sales to capital ratio will be 2.50; for every dollar of additional capital invested, there will be $2.50 in additional sales.
Beta	The beta of the firm is 1.78 for the first five years and decreases gradually to a stable period beta of 1.20. (The risk-free rate is 6%, and the market risk premium is 4%.)
Debt ratio	The debt ratio for the next five years remains at current levels (0.15%) and increases gradually to 10% by year 10.

The expected cash flows and costs of capital for Ariba are summarized in Table 6.7.

The value of Ariba when high growth ends in 10 years is estimated from the free cash flow to the firm in the terminal year (year 11) and the stable growth rate:

Terminal Value for Ariba (in Year 10) = $3,159 / (.1018 – .05) = $61,034 million

The value of Ariba's operating assets is the sum of the present values of the cash flows during the high-growth phase and the present value of the terminal value estimated above:

PV of FCFF During High-Growth Phase = $(1,367)
PV of Terminal Value = $61,034 / 3.1816 = $19,184
Value of Operating Assets for Ariba = $17,816

TABLE 6.7 Expected Cash Flows and Discount Rates at Ariba (in Millions)

	Base	1	2	3	4	5	6	7	8	9	10	Terminal Year
Revenue Growth Rate		400.00%	200.00%	150.00%	100.00%	75.00%	60.00%	40.00%	20.00%	10.00%	5.00%	5%
Revenues	$93	$463	$1,388	$3,471	$6,942	$12,149	$19,438	$27,213	$32,655	$35,921	$37,717	$39,603
Operating Margin	−160%	−71.74%	−27.69%	−5.67%	5.35%	10.85%	13.61%	14.98%	15.67%	16.02%	16.19%	16.36%
EBIT	−$148	−$332	−$384	−$197	$371	$1,319	$2,645	$4,077	$5,118	$5,753	$6,106	$6,479
Taxes	$0	$0	$0	$0	$0	$263	$926	$1,427	$1,791	$2,014	$2,137	$2,268
EBIT(1 − t)	−$148	−$332	−$384	−$197	$371	$1,055	$1,719	$2,650	$3,326	$3,739	$3,969	$4,211
+ Depreciation	$7	$15	$26	$42	$58	$70	$77	$81	$85	$89	$93	$98
− Capital Exp.	$81	$144	$350	$770	$1,273	$1,892	$2,628	$2,802	$1,990	$1,232	$722	$1,057
− Chg WC	−$33	$19	$46	$104	$174	$260	$364	$389	$272	$163	$90	$94
FCFF	−$189	−$480	−$755	−$1,030	−$1,017	−$1,027	−$1,196	−$460	$1,149	$2,433	$3,250	$3,159
NOL	$24	$356	$741	$937	$566	$0	$0	$0	$0	$0	$0	$0
Tax Rate	0.00%	0.00%	0.00%	0.00%	0.00%	19.98%	35.00%	35.00%	35.00%	35.00%	35.00%	35.00%
Debt Ratio	0.15%	0.15%	0.15%	0.15%	0.15%	0.15%	2.12%	2.62%	3.44%	5.08%	10.00%	10.00%
Beta	1.78	1.78	1.78	1.78	1.78	1.78	1.66	1.55	1.43	1.32	1.20	1.20
Cost of Equity	13.12%	13.12%	13.12%	13.12%	13.12%	13.12%	12.66%	12.19%	11.73%	11.26%	10.80%	10.80%
Cost of Debt	9.25%	9.25%	9.25%	9.25%	9.25%	9.25%	8.80%	8.69%	8.50%	8.13%	7.00%	7.00%
After-Tax Cost of Debt	9.25%	9.25%	9.25%	9.25%	9.25%	7.40%	5.72%	5.65%	5.53%	5.28%	4.55%	4.55%
Cost of Capital	13.11%	13.11%	13.11%	13.11%	13.11%	13.11%	12.51%	12.02%	11.51%	10.96%	10.18%	10.18%
Cumulative WACC		1.1311	1.2795	1.4473	1.6371	1.8517	2.0833	2.3338	2.6025	2.8877	3.1816	
Present Value of FCFF		−$424.46	−$589.85	−$711.47	−$621.35	−$554.86	−$574.32	−$196.99	$441.67	$842.62	$1,021.58	

201

ILLUSTRATION 6.6

Valuation of Cisco's Operating Assets

The inputs in the Cisco valuation are summarized in Table 6.8.

TABLE 6.8 Assumptions for Valuing Cisco

	HIGH GROWTH	TRANSITION	FOREVER
Length of period	6 years	6 years	Past year 12
Growth rate	36.39%	Decreases linearly from 36.39% to 5%	5.00%
Debt ratio	0.18%	Increases linearly from 0.18% to 10%	10.00%
Beta	1.43	Decreases linearly from 1.43 to 1.00	1.00
Pre-tax cost of debt	6.20%	6.20%	6.20%
Tax rate	35.00%	35.00%	35.00%
Return on capital	34.07%	Decreases from 34.07% to 16.52%	16.52%
Reinvestment rate	106.81%	Decreases from 106.81% to 30.27%	30.27%

A risk-free rate of 6% and a market risk premium of 4% are used in the valuation. The expected cash flows and costs of capital are summarized in Table 6.9.

Cisco's terminal value at the end of year 12, when high growth ends, is estimated from the free cash flows to the firm in the terminal year (year 13), the cost of capital in that year, and the stable growth rate:

Free Cash Flow to $Firm_{13}$ = After-Tax Operating $Income_{13}$ $(1-$ Reinvestment $Rate_{Stable})$
$$= \$61,028 \ (1 - .3027) = \$42,557 \text{ million}$$
Terminal Value for Cisco (in Year 12) = $\$42,557 \ / \ (.094 - .05) = \$966,545$

The value of Cisco's operating assets is the sum of the present values of the cash flows during the high-growth phase and the present value of the terminal value estimated above:

Present Value of FCFF in High-Growth Phase = $34,779 million
Present Value of Terminal Value of Firm = $966,545 / 3.5104 = $275,336 million
Value of Operating Assets of the Firm = $310,115 million

TABLE 6.9 Expected Cash Flows and Discount Rates at Cisco (in Millions)

	CURRENT	1	2	3	4	5	6	7	8	9	10	11	12
Expected Growth		36.39%	36.39%	36.39%	36.39%	36.39%	36.39%	31.16%	25.93%	20.70%	15.46%	10.23%	5.00%
Cumulated Growth		136.39%	186.03%	253.73%	346.08%	472.03%	643.81%	844.43%	1063.38%	1283.47%	1481.95%	1633.59%	1715.27%
Reinvestment Rate		106.81%	106.81%	106.81%	106.81%	106.81%	106.81%	94.05%	81.29%	68.54%	55.78%	43.02%	30.27%
EBIT(1 − t)	$3,388	$4,622	$6,304	$8,598	$11,727	$15,995	$21,816	$28,614	$36,033	$43,490	$50,216	$55,354	$58,122
− Net Cap Ex	$3,741	$4,638	$6,325	$8,628	$11,767	$16,050	$21,891	$25,265	$27,496	$28,001	$26,382	$22,571	$16,921
− Chg Wk Cap	($122)	$299	$407	$555	$758	$1,033	$1,409	$1,646	$1,796	$1,806	$1,628	$1,244	$670
FCFF	($231)	($315)	($429)	($585)	($798)	($1,089)	($1,485)	$1,703	$6,741	$13,684	$22,206	$31,539	$40,530
Cost of Capital		11.71%	11.71%	11.71%	11.71%	11.71%	11.71%	11.32%	10.94%	10.55%	10.17%	9.79%	9.40%
Cumulated WACC		1.1171	1.2478	1.3939	1.5571	1.7394	1.9430	2.1630	2.3996	2.6529	2.9227	3.2087	3.5104
Present Value		($282)	($344)	($420)	($513)	($626)	($764)	$787	$2,809	$5,158	$7,598	$9,829	$11,546

203

ILLUSTRATION 6.7

Valuation of Motorola's Operating Assets

To value Motorola, we make the assumptions summarized in Table 6.10.

TABLE 6.10 Assumptions for Valuing Motorola

	HIGH-GROWTH PERIOD	STABLE-GROWTH PHASE
Length of high-growth period	5	Forever
Growth rate	13.63%	5.00%
Debt ratio	6.86%	6.86%
Beta used for stock	1.21	1.00
Cost of debt	6.50%	6.50%
Tax rate	35.00%	35.00%
Return on capital	Improves from 12.18% to 17.22%	17.22%
Reinvestment rate	52.99%	29.04%

A risk-free rate of 6% and a market risk premium of 4% are used in the valuation. The expected cash flows and costs of capital over the high-growth period are summarized in Table 6.11.

Motorola's value in year five is estimated from the free cash flows to the firm in year six, the cost of capital in that year, and the stable growth rate:

Free Cash Flow to Firm$_6$ = After-Tax Operating Income$_6$ $(1-$ Reinvestment Rate$_{Stable})$
  = $6,075 (1 − .2904) = $4,311 million
Terminal Value for Motorola (in Year 5) = $4,311 / (.096 − .05) = $93,641 million

The value of Motorola's operating assets is the sum of the present values of the cash flows during the high-growth phase and the present value of the terminal value estimated above:

Present Value of FCFF in High-Growth Phase = $7,980
Present Value of Terminal Value of Firm = $93,641 / 1.6394 = $58,159
Value of Operating Assets of the Firm = $66,139

TABLE 6.11 Expected Cash Flows and Discount Rates: Motorola (in Millions)

	CURRENT	1	2	3	4	5
Expected Growth		13.63%	13.63%	13.63%	13.63%	13.63%
Reinvestment Rate		52.99%	52.99%	52.99%	52.99%	52.99%
EBIT × (1 − t)	$3,110.00	$3,533.89	$4,015.56	$4,562.88	$5,184.80	$5,891.49
− Net Cap Ex	$1,521.60	$1,525.28	$1,733.17	$1,969.40	$2,237.83	$2,542.85
− Chg. Wk Cap	$126.23	$347.16	$394.47	$448.24	$509.34	$578.76
FCFF	$1,462.17	$1,661.46	$1,887.92	$2,145.24	$2,437.63	$2,769.88
Cost of Capital		10.39%	10.39%	10.39%	10.39%	10.39%
Present Value		$1,505.05	$1,549.19	$1,594.62	$1,641.38	$1,689.52

ILLUSTRATION 6.8

Valuation of Rediff's Operating Assets

The assumptions for valuing Rediff.com are summarized in Table 6.12.

TABLE 6.12 Assumptions for Valuing Rediff.com

INPUT	ASSUMPTIONS
Revenue growth	Compounded average growth rate over next 10 years = 104.57%. Growth rate decreases from 500% next year to 5% in year 10.
Operating margin	Operating margin improves from current level of −113% to a target margin of 40.00% (which is the average for comparable firms) in year 10.
Reinvestment needs	The estimated reinvestment each year is based on the assumption that the sales-to-capital ratio will be 1.00; for every dollar of additional capital invested, there will be $1.00 in additional sales.
Beta	The beta of the firm is 1.90 for the first five years, and decreases gradually to a stable period beta of 1.20. The risk-free rate is 6% (since the valuation is in US$). To estimate the risk premium, add a mature market premium of 4% to a country risk premium for India of 6.43% to yield a total risk premium of 10.43%.
Debt ratio	The debt ratio for the next five years remains at current levels (0%) and increases gradually to 20% by year 10.

The expected cash flows and costs of capital are summarized in Table 6.13. Implicit in these estimates is the assumption that Rediff.com will remain an Internet portal for the bulk of this period. If, in fact, Rediff chooses a different route (business mix), the estimates will have to change, as will the value.

Rediff's value at the end of its high-growth period (10 years) is estimated from the cash flows in the terminal year (year 11), the cost of capital in that year, and the stable growth rate:

Terminal Value (in '000s) for Rediff (in Year 10) = $505,602 / (.1567 − .05) = $4,736,851

The value of Rediff's operating assets is the sum of the present values of the cash flows during the high-growth phase and the present value of the terminal value estimated above:

PV of FCFF During High-Growth Phase = $(140,793)
PV of Terminal Value = $4,736,851 / 7.8479 = $603,585
Value of Operating Assets of the Firm = $462,792

TABLE 6.13 Expected Cash Flows and Discount Rates: Rediff.com (in Thousands)

	BASE	1	2	3	4	5	6	7	8	9	10	TERMINAL YEAR
Revenue Growth		500.00%	300.00%	200.00%	125.00%	100.00%	75.00%	50.00%	25.00%	15.00%	5.00%	5%
Revenues	$1,906	$11,436	$45,744	$137,232	$308,772	$617,544	$1,080,702	$1,621,053	$2,026,316	$2,330,264	$2,446,777	$2,569,116
Operating Margin	-113.1%	-36.55%	1.73%	20.86%	30.43%	35.22%	37.61%	38.80%	39.40%	39.70%	39.85%	40.00%
EBIT	-$2,156	-$4,180	$789	$28,630	$93,963	$217,472	$406,429	$629,032	$798,408	$925,137	$975,053	$1,027,646
Taxes	$0	$0	$0	$9,714	$36,176	$83,727	$156,475	$242,177	$307,387	$356,178	$375,395	$395,644
EBIT(1 – t)	-$2,156	-$4,180	$789	$18,916	$57,787	$133,745	$249,954	$386,855	$491,021	$568,960	$599,657	$632,002
+ Depr	$746	$1,678	$3,356	$5,872	$8,808	$11,010	$12,662	$13,295	$13,960	$14,658	$15,390	$16,160
– Cap Ex	$7,026	$10,731	$35,948	$92,786	$171,771	$304,344	$452,662	$526,628	$398,960	$303,408	$126,078	$136,444
– Chg WC	$496	$477	$1,715	$4,574	$8,577	$15,439	$23,158	$27,018	$20,263	$15,197	$5,826	$6,117
FCFF	-$8,932	-$13,710	-$33,519	-$72,572	-$113,753	-$175,027	-$213,204	-$153,496	$85,758	$265,012	$483,144	$505,602
NOL	$9	$4,188	$3,399	$0	$0	$0	$0	$0	$0	$0	$0	$0
Tax Rate	0.00%	0.00%	0.00%	33.93%	38.50%	38.50%	38.50%	38.50%	38.50%	38.50%	38.50%	38.50%
Debt Ratio	0.00%	0.00%	0.00%	0.00%	0.00%	0.00%	4.00%	5.00%	6.67%	10.00%	20.00%	20.00%
Beta	1.90	1.90	1.90	1.90	1.90	1.90	1.76	1.62	1.48	1.34	1.20	1.20
Cost of Equity	25.82%	25.82%	25.82%	25.82%	25.82%	25.82%	24.36%	22.90%	21.44%	19.98%	18.52%	18.52%
Cost of Debt	10.00%	10.00%	10.00%	10.00%	10.00%	10.00%	9.40%	9.25%	9.00%	8.50%	7.00%	7.00%
After-Tax Cost of Debt	10.00%	10.00%	10.00%	6.61%	6.15%	6.15%	5.78%	5.69%	5.54%	5.23%	4.31%	4.31%
Cost of Capital	25.82%	25.82%	25.82%	25.82%	25.82%	25.82%	23.61%	22.04%	20.38%	18.50%	15.67%	15.67%
Cumulative WACC		1.2582	1.5830	1.9917	2.5059	3.1528	3.8973	4.7561	5.7252	6.7845	7.8479	
Present Value of FCFF		-$10,897	-$21,174	-$36,438	-$45,395	-$55,515	-$54,706	-$32,273	$14,979	$39,062	$61,564	

THE SURVIVAL ISSUE

Implicit in the use of a terminal value in discounted cash flow valuation is the assumption that the value of a firm comes from it being a going concern with a perpetual life. For many risky firms, there is the very real possibility that they might not be in existence in five or 10 years, with volatile earnings and shifting technology. Should the valuation reflect this chance of failure, and if so, how can the likelihood that a firm will not survive be built into a valuation?

LIFE CYCLE AND FIRM SURVIVAL

There is a link between a firm's stage in the life cycle and the firm's survival. Young firms with negative earnings and cash flows can run into serious cash flow problems and end up being acquired at bargain basement prices by firms with more resources. Why are new technology firms more exposed to this problem? The negative cash flows from operations, when combined with significant reinvestment needs, can result in rapid depletion of cash reserves. When financial markets are accessible and additional equity can be raised at will, raising more funds to meet these funding needs is not a problem. However, when stock prices drop and access to markets becomes more limited, these firms can be in trouble.

A widely used measure of the potential for a cash flow problem for firms with negative earnings is the cash-burn ratio, which is estimated as the cash balance of the firm divided by its earnings before interest, taxes, and depreciation (EBITDA).

Cash Burn Ratio = Cash Balance / EBITDA

Thus, a firm with a cash balance of $1 billion and EBITDA of $-$1.5 billion will burn through its cash balance in eight months.

LIKELIHOOD OF FAILURE AND VALUATION

One view of survival is that the expected cash flows that you use in a valuation reflect cash flows over a wide range of scenarios from very good to abysmal and the probabilities of the scenarios occurring. Thus, the expected value already has built into it the likelihood that the firm will not survive. Any market risk associated with survival or failure is assumed to be incorporated into the cost of capital. Firms with a high likelihood of failure will therefore have higher discount rates and lower present values. Therefore, there is no need to adjust this value down any further to reflect survival.

Another view of survival is that discounted cash flow valuations tend to have an optimistic bias and that the likelihood that the firm will not survive is not considered adequately in the value. With this view, the discounted cash flow value that emerges from the analysis in the prior section overstates the value of operating assets and has to be adjusted to reflect the likelihood that the firm will not survive to deliver its terminal value or even the positive cash flows that you have forecast in future years.

Value: Discounted (or Not) for Survival. For firms like Cisco and Motorola that have substantial assets in place and relatively small probabilities of distress, attaching an extra discount for nonsurvival is double-counting risk.

For firms like Ariba and Rediff.com, the decision depends on whether expected cash flows incorporate the probability that these firms may not make it past the first few years. If they do, the valuation already reflects the likelihood that the firms will not survive past the first few years. If they do not, you do have to discount the value for the likelihood that the firm will not survive the near future. One way to estimate this discount is to use the cash-burn ratio, described earlier, to estimate a probability of failure and adjust the operating asset value for this probability:

Adjusted Value =
DCF Value of Operating Assets (1 – Probability of Distress)
+ Distressed Sale Value (Probability of Distress)

For a firm with a discounted cash flow value of $1 billion on its assets, a distress sale value of $500 million and a 20% probability of default, the adjusted value would be $900 million:

Adjusted Value = $1,000 (.8) + $500 (.2) = $900 million

Two points are worth noting here. It is not the failure to survive per se that causes the loss of value but the fact that the distressed sale value is at a discount on the true value. The second point is that this approach revolves around estimating the probability of failure. This probability is difficult to estimate because it will depend on both the magnitude of the cash reserves of the firm (relative to its cash needs) and the state of the market. In buoyant equity markets, even firms with little or no cash can survive because they can access markets for more funds. Under more negative market conditions, even firms with significant cash balances may find themselves under threat.

There will be no discount for failure for any of the firms being valued in this book, for two reasons. One is that we are using expected cash flows that adequately reflect the likelihood of failure. The other reason is that each of these firms has a valuable enough niche in the market, that even in the event of failure, other firms will be interested in buying their assets at a fair value.

CASH AND NONOPERATING ASSETS

The operating income is the income from operating assets, and the cost of capital measures the cost of financing these assets. When the operating cash flows are discounted to the present, you have valued the operating assets of the firm. Firms, however, often have significant amounts of cash and marketable securities on their books, as well as holdings in other firms and nonoperating assets. The value of these assets should be added to the value of the operating assets to arrive at firm value. Some analysts prefer to consider the income from cash and marketable securities in their cash flows and adjust the discount rate[12] to reflect the safety of these assets. When done right, this approach should yield the same firm value.

CASH AND MARKETABLE SECURITIES

Firms often hold substantial amounts in cash and other marketable securities. When valuing firms, you should add the value of these holdings to the value of the other operating assets to arrive at the firm value. In this section, we first consider how to deal with cash and near-cash investments (such as government securities) and then consider holdings of more risky marketable securities.

Cash and Near-Cash Investments. Investments in short-term government securities or commercial paper, which can be converted into cash quickly and with very low cost, are considered near-cash investments. When valuing a firm, you add the value of cash balances and near-cash investments to the value of operating assets.

There is, however, one consideration that may affect how cash is treated. If a firm needs cash for its operations—an operating cash balance—you should consider such cash part of working capital requirements rather than a source of additional value. Any cash and near-cash investments that exceed the operating cash requirements can then be added to the value of operating assets. How much cash does a firm need for its operations? The answer depends on both the firm and the economy in which the firm operates. A small retail firm in an emerging market, where cash transactions are more common than credit card transactions, may require an operating cash balance that is substantial. In contrast, a manufacturing firm in a developed market may not need any operating cash. In fact, if the cash held by a firm is interest bearing and the interest earned on the cash reflects a fair rate of return,[13] you would not consider that cash to be part of working capital. Instead, you would add it to the value of operating assets to value the firm.

Other Marketable Securities. Marketable securities can include corporate bonds, with default risk embedded in them, and traded equities, which have equity risk associated with them. As the marketable securities held by a firm become more risky, the choices on how to deal with them become more complex. You have three ways of accounting for marketable securities:

- The simplest and most direct approach is to estimate the current market value of these marketable securities and add the value to the value of operating assets. For firms valued as going-concerns with a large number of holdings of marketable securities, this may be the only practical option.

- The second approach is to estimate the current market value of the marketable securities and net out the effect of capital gains taxes that may be due if those securities were sold today. This capital gains tax bite depends on how much was paid for these assets at the time of the purchase and the value today. This is the best way of estimating value when valuing a firm for liquidation.

- The third and most difficult way of incorporating the value of marketable securities into firm value is to value the firms that issued these securities and estimate the value of these securities. This approach tends to work best for firms that have relatively few, but large, holdings in other publicly traded firms.

ILLUSTRATION 6.9

Cash and Marketable Securities

Each of the five firms that we are valuing holds cash and near-cash investments. In addition, Cisco, Motorola, and Amazon own stock in other publicly traded firms. Table 6.14 summarizes these holdings at each of the five firms.

Note that the current market value of the securities owned by the firms is used and that the capital gains taxes have not been netted out in these holdings, since these firms are being valued on a going concerns basis.

TABLE 6.14 Cash, Near-Cash Investments, and Marketable Securities

	AMAZON	ARIBA	CISCO	MOTOROLA	REDIFF
Cash & near-cash investments	$117	$50	$827	$3,345	$12
Other marketable securities	$589	$48	$1,189	$699	$—
Total	$706	$98	$2,016	$4,044	$12

HOLDINGS IN OTHER FIRMS

In this category, we consider a broader category of nonoperating assets, where we look at holdings in other companies, public as well as private. We begin by looking at the differences in accounting treatment of different holdings and how this treatment can affect the way the holdings are reported in financial statements.

Accounting Treatment. The way in which holdings in other firms are shown in accounting statements depends on how the investment is categorized and the motive behind the investment. In general, an investment in another firm can be categorized as a minority, passive investment; a minority, active investment; or a majority, active investment. The accounting rules vary depending on the categorization.

Minority, Passive Investments

If the securities or assets owned in another firm represent less than 20% of the overall ownership of that firm, then the investment is generally treated as a minority, passive investment. These investments have an acquisition value, which represents the price the firm originally paid for the securities, and, often, a market value. Accounting principles require that these assets be subcategorized into one of three groups: investments that will be held to maturity, investments that are available for sale, and trading investments. The accounting principles vary for each.

- For investments that will be held to maturity, the valuation is at historical cost or book value, and interest or dividends from this investment are shown in the income statement.
- For investments that are available for sale, the valuation is at market value, but the unrealized gains or losses are shown as part of the equity in the balance sheet and not in the income statement. Thus, unrealized losses reduce the book value of the equity in the firm, and unrealized gains increase the book value of equity.
- For trading investments, the valuation is at market value and the unrealized gains and losses are shown in the income statement.

Firms are allowed an element of discretion in the way they classify investments and, through this choice, in the way they value these assets. This classification ensures that firms such as investment banks, whose assets are primarily securities held in other firms for purposes of trading, revalue the bulk of these assets at market levels each period. This practice, called *marking-to-market*, provides one of the few instances in which market value trumps book value in accounting statements.

Minority, Active Investments

If the securities or assets owned in another firm represent between 20% and 50% of the overall ownership of that firm, then an investment is treated as a minority, active investment. While these investments have an initial acquisition value, a proportional share of subsequent profits and losses is used for adjustment of the acquisition cost. That share is based on the ownership proportion and on the net income and losses made by the firm in which the investment was made. In addition, the dividends received from the investment reduce the acquisition cost. This approach to valuing investments is called the *equity approach*.

The market value of these investments is not considered until the investment is liquidated, at which point the gain or loss from the sale, relative to the adjusted acquisition cost, is shown as part of the earnings in that period.

Majority, Active Investments

If the securities or assets owned in another firm represent more than 50% of the overall ownership of that firm, then an investment is treated as a majority active investment.[14] In this case, the investment is no longer shown as a financial investment but is instead replaced by the assets and liabilities of the firm in which the investment was made. This approach leads to a consolidation of the balance sheets of the two firms, where the assets and liabilities of the two firms are merged and presented as one balance sheet. The share of the subsidiary that is owned by other investors is shown as a minority interest on the liability side of the balance sheet. A similar consolidation occurs in the other financial statements of the firm as well, with the statement of cash flows reflecting the cumulated cash inflows and outflows of the combined firm. This approach is in contrast to the equity approach, used for minority active investments, in which only the dividends received on the investment are shown as a cash inflow in the cash flow statement.

Here again, the market value of this investment is not considered until the ownership stake is liquidated. At that point, the difference between the market price and the net value of the equity stake in the firm is treated as a gain or loss for the period.

Valuing Cross-Holdings in Other Firms. Given that the holdings in other firms can be accounted for in three different ways, how do you deal with each in valuation?

1. If the holdings are treated as minority, passive investments and the investments are reported in the balance sheet at the original cost or book value, you would value the firm in which these investments are held and consider the proportion of the value that comes from the holding. For instance, assume that a firm owns 20% of another firm that has an estimated value of $500 million. The estimated value of this holding is $100 million.

2. If the holdings are minority, passive investments and the investments are recorded at market value, you have one of two choices. You can assume that the market is correct and use the assessed market value of these cross-held assets to value the firm. Alternatively, you can value the companies in which the investments have been made and add the estimated value of the holdings to the value of operating assets.

3. If the holdings are minority, active interests, you need to value the firms in which these investments are held and add the proportion of that value to the value of the operating assets of the firm.

4. If the holdings are majority, active interests, the income statements are consolidated. If you value a firm based on the operating income in the consolidated statement, you are valuing the parent company and the subsidiary together.[15] If the parent company owns less than 100% of the subsidiary, you would need to subtract out from your estimate of value the portion of the subsidiary that does not belong to the parent. While many analysts claim to accomplish this by subtracting the minority interest that is shown in the parent company, this minority interest is in book value terms and will generally not reflect the market value ownership. To be precise, if the subsidiary is valued at $2 billion and the parent company owns only 60%, you would need to subtract out 40% of $2 billion ($800 million) to get your estimate of value.

OTHER NONOPERATING ASSETS

Firms can have other nonoperating assets, but they are likely to be of less importance than those listed above. In particular, firms can have unutilized assets that do not generate cash flows and have book values that bear little resemblance to market values. An example would be prime real estate holdings that have appreciated significantly in value since the firm acquired them but produce little if any cash flows. An open question also remains about overfunded pension plans. Do the excess funds belong to stockholders, and if so, how do you incorporate the effect into value?

Unutilized Assets. The strength of discounted cash flow models is that they base their estimate of the value of assets on expected cash flows that these assets generate. In some cases, however, this can lead to assets of substantial value being ignored in the final valuation. For instance, assume that a firm owns a plot of land that has not been developed and that the book value of the land reflects its original acquisition price. The land has significant market value but does not generate any cash flow for the firm yet. If a conscious effort is not made to bring the expected cash flows from developing the land into the valuation, the value of the land will be left out of the final estimate.

How do you reflect the value of such assets in firm value? An inventory of all such assets (or at least the most valuable ones) is a first step, followed up by estimates of market value for each of the assets. You obtain these estimates by looking at what the assets would fetch in the market today or by projecting the cash flows that could be generated if the assets were developed and then discounting the cash flows at the appropriate discount rate.

The problem with incorporating unutilized assets into firm value is an informational one. Firms do not reveal their unutilized assets as part of their financial statements. While it may sometimes be possible to find out about such assets as investors or analysts, it is far more likely that the assets will be uncovered only when you have access to information about what the firm owns and uses.

Pension Fund Assets. Firms with defined pension liabilities sometimes accumulate pension fund assets in excess of these liabilities. While the excess does belong to stockholders, they usually face a tax liability if they claim it. The conservative rule in dealing with overfunded pension plans would be to assume that the social and tax costs of reclaiming the excess funds are so large that few firms would ever even attempt to do it. The more realistic approach would be to add the after-tax portion of the excess funds into the valuation. Thus, a firm with $4 billion in pension fund assets and $3 billion in pension liabilities would show $0.5 billion as the added value; the tax rate that firms usually face for withdrawing pension fund assets in the U.S. is 50%.

ILLUSTRATION 6.10

Value of Other Nonoperating Assets

Amazon has holdings, reported below, in several firms with whom it has strategic partnerships.

Company	% Ownership
Della.com	21.9%
drugstore.com	26.7%
Gear.com	49.0%
HomeGrocer.com	28.0%
Kozmo.com	21.7%
Naxon Corporation	61.0%
Pets.com	48.4%

Amazon uses the equity method to record its ownership in these firms, which are shown as investments on the balance sheet, with a value of $226.73 million. This estimate, however, reflects the book values of Amazon's investments in these firms, not the market value. Since three of these firms are publicly traded, Amazon's share of the market value is used for these firms, and book value is used for the nontraded firms.[16]

The value of other nonoperating assets at the five firms that we are valuing are reported in Table 6.15.

TABLE 6.15 Cash and Nonoperating Assets

	AMAZON	ARIBA	CISCO	MOTOROLA	REDIFF.COM
Majority active interests	$ —	$—	$ —	$ —	$ —
Minority active interests	$ —	$—	$ —	$ —	$ —
Minority passive interests	$371	$54	$7,032	$5,200[a]	$ —

(continued)

TABLE 6.15 *(Continued)*

	AMAZON	ARIBA	CISCO	MOTOROLA	REDIFF.COM
Unutilized assets	$—	$—	$—	$—	$—
Pension fund overfunding	$—	$—	$—	$—	$—
Total	$371	$54	$7,032	$5,200	$—

a. Motorola's holdings represent 16% of Nextel.

We should note that while there is no mention of unutilized assets in the financial statements, there might well be such assets at each of these firms.

 cash.xls: A dataset on the Web summarizes the value of cash and marketable securities, by industry group, in the United States for the most recent quarter.

FIRM VALUE AND EQUITY VALUE

Once you have estimates of the values of the operating assets, cash and marketable securities, and the other nonoperating assets owned by a firm, you can estimate the value of the firm as the sum of the three components.

To get the value of the equity from the firm value, you subtract the nonequity claims on the firm. Nonequity claims would include debt and preferred stock, though the latter are often treated as equity in financial statements. What debt should you subtract? The debt that you considered in computing the cost of capital will be the debt that you should be netting out from firm value to get to the value of equity. To be consistent, therefore, you should consider both interest-bearing liabilities and leases (in present value terms) to be debt and use the estimated market value for both.

If the firm you are valuing has preferred stock, you would use the market value of the stock (if it is traded) or estimate a market value[17] (if it is not) and deduct it from firm value to get to the value of common equity.

ILLUSTRATION 6.11

Firm Value and Equity Value

The values of the five firms and the estimated values of equity in these firms are summarized in Table 6.16.

TABLE 6.16 Firm and Equity Values

	AMAZON	ARIBA	CISCO	MOTOROLA	REDIFF.COM
Value of Operating Assets	$13,971	$17,816	$310,115	$66,139	$463
+ Cash, Near Cash & Marketable Securities	$706	$98	$2,016	$4,044	$12
+ Value of Operating Assets	$371	$54	$7,032	$5,200	$0
Firm Value	$15,048	$17,968	$319,163	$74,253	$474
– Debt	$1,459	$28	$827	$5,426	$0
– Preferred Stock	$0	$0	$0	$0	$0
Value of Equity	$13,589	$17,941	$318,336	$69,957	$474

The firm value incorporates both the operating and nonoperating assets owned by these firms.

SUMMARY

The value of a firm is the present value of its expected cash flows over its life. Since firms have infinite lives, you apply closure to a valuation by estimating cash flows for a period and then estimating a value for the firm at the end of the period—a terminal value. Many analysts estimate the terminal value by using a multiple of earnings or revenues in the final estimation year. If you assume that firms have infinite lives, an approach that is more consistent with discounted cash flow valuation is to assume that the cash flows of the firm will grow at a constant rate forever beyond a point in time. When the firm that you are valuing will approach this growth rate, which you label a stable growth rate, is a key part of any discounted cash flow valuation. Small firms that are growing fast and have significant competitive advantages should be able to grow at high rates for much longer periods than larger and more mature firms without these competitive advantages. If you do not want to assume an infinite life for a firm, you can estimate a liquidation value, based on what others will pay for the assets that the firm has accumulated during the high-growth phase.

Once the terminal values and operating cash flows have been estimated, they are discounted back to the present to yield the value of the operating assets of the firm. To this value, you add the value of cash, near-cash investments, and marketable securities, as well as the value of holdings in other firms to arrive at the value of the firm. Subtracting out the value of nonequity claims yields the value of equity in the firm.

ENDNOTES

1. This is the estimate of asset value 10 years from now.

2. The cost of capital includes a nominal riskless rate, which should reflect both expected inflation in the economy and real growth. Thus, if the nominal growth rate of the economy is 5% in the long term, the long-term nominal riskless rate should be at least that number.

3. Growth without excess returns will make a firm larger but not more valuable.

4. Jack Welch at GE and Robert Goizueta at Coca Cola are good examples of CEOs who made a profound difference in the growth of their firms.

5. As a rule of thumb, betas above 1.2 or below 0.8 are inconsistent with stable-growth firms. Two-thirds of all U.S. firms have betas that fall within this range.

6. Industries also go through life cycles. The industry average will therefore also change over time.

7. The optimal debt ratio for Cisco currently is 10%. The details of the calculation will be provided in a later chapter.

8. An argument can be made that real growth in India will be higher in the long term than for the rest of the world. If we subscribed to this argument, we would use a slightly higher expected growth rate.

9. As the industry itself matures, we would expect to see the return on capital drift down.

10. While this may seem high, it has to reflect the fact that operating income was defined as income before selling expenses and that a significant portion of the capital will be capitalized selling expenses. In addition, we also use a much higher cost of capital for Rediff because of the country risk premium associated with India.

11. You compute the present value by using the compounded cost of capital over time. For example, the compounded cost of capital in year 6 = (1.1256)(1.1256)(1.1244)(1.1234)(1.1234)(1.1175) = 2.0090.

12. When a firm has cash and marketable securities, the unlevered beta must be adjusted downward to reflect the safety of these assets.

13. Note that if the cash is invested in riskless assets such as Treasury bills, the riskless rate is a fair rate of return.

14. Firms have evaded the requirements of consolidation by keeping their share of ownership in other firms below 50%.

15. If the parent and subsidiary are in different businesses, with different risk levels, you would need to use a cost of capital that reflects these differences (a weighted average of two different costs of capital).

16. An alternative approach is to apply the price-to-book-value ratio for the sector to which these companies belong and multiply the book value by this ratio. The result will yield an estimated market value. If the holdings are large, relative to the company being valued, this is a more effective tactic for capturing the value of these holdings.

17. Estimating market value for preferred stock is relatively simple. Preferred stock generally is perpetual, and the estimated market value of the preferred stock is therefore:

Value of Preferred Stock =
Preferred Dividend / Cost of Preferred Stock

The cost of preferred stock should be higher than the pre-tax cost of debt, since debt has a prior claim on the cash flows and assets of the firm.

7

MANAGEMENT OPTIONS, CONTROL, AND LIQUIDITY

$\square$nce you have valued the equity in a firm, it may appear to be a relatively simple exercise to estimate the value per share. All it seems you need to do is divide the value of the equity by the number of shares outstanding. But, in the case of technology firms, even this simple exercise can become complicated by the presence of management and employee options. In this chapter, we begin by considering the magnitude of this option overhang on valuation and then consider ways of incorporating the effect into the value per share.

We also consider two other issues that may be of relevance, especially when valuing smaller technology firms or private businesses. The first issue is the concentration of shares in the hands of the owner/managers of these firms and the consequences for stockholder power and control. This effect is intensified when a firm has shares with different voting rights.

The second issue is the effect of illiquidity. When investors in a firm's stock or equity cannot easily liquidate their positions, the lack of liquidity can affect value. This can become an issue, not only when you are valuing private firms, but also when valuing small publicly traded firms with relatively few shares traded.

MANAGEMENT AND EMPLOYEE OPTIONS

Firms use options to reward managers as well as other employees. These options have two effects on value per share. One is created by options that have already been granted. These options reduce the value of equity per share, since a portion of the existing equity in the firm has to be set aside to meet these eventual option exercises. The other is the likelihood that these firms will continue to use options to reward employees or to compensate them. These expected option grants reduce the portion of the expected future cash flows that accrue to existing stockholders.

THE MAGNITUDE OF THE OPTION OVERHANG

The use of options in management compensation packages is not new to technology firms. Many firms in the 1970s and 1980s initiated option-based compensation packages to induce top managers to think like stockholders in their decision making. What is different about technology firms? One difference is that management contracts at these firms are much more heavily weighted toward options than are those at other firms. The second difference is that the paucity of cash at these firms has meant that options are granted not just to top managers but to employees all through the organization, making the total option grants much larger. The third difference is that some of the smaller firms have used options to meet operating expenses and to pay for supplies.

Figure 7–1 summarizes the number of options outstanding as a percent of outstanding stock at technology firms and compares them to options outstanding at nontechnology firms.

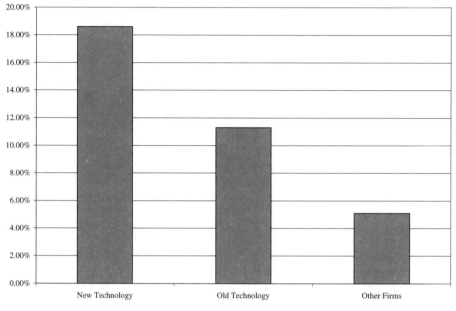

FIGURE 7–1
Options as Percent of Outstanding Stock (*Source:* Morningstar, *www.morningstar.com*, June 7, 2000, Morningstar, Inc.)

As Figure 7–1 makes clear, the overhang is larger for younger new technology firms. In Figure 7–2, the number of options as a percent of outstanding stock at Amazon, Ariba, Cisco, Motorola, and Rediff.com are reported.

Rediff.com has no options outstanding, but the other four firms have options outstanding. Amazon, in particular, has options on 80.34 million shares, representing more than 22% of the actual shares outstanding at the firm (351.77 million). Motorola, reflecting its status as an older and more mature firm, has far fewer options outstanding, relative to the number of outstanding shares.

Firms that use employee options usually restrict when and whether these options can be exercised. It is standard, for instance, that the options granted to an employee cannot be exercised until they are *vested*. For vesting to occur, the employee usually has to remain for a period that is specified in a contract. Firms do this to keep employee turnover low, but the practice also has implications for option valuation, as we examine later. Firms that issue options do not face any tax consequences in the year in which they make the issue. When the options are exercised, however, firms are allowed to treat the difference between the stock price and the exercise price as an employee expense. This tax deductibility also has implications for option value.

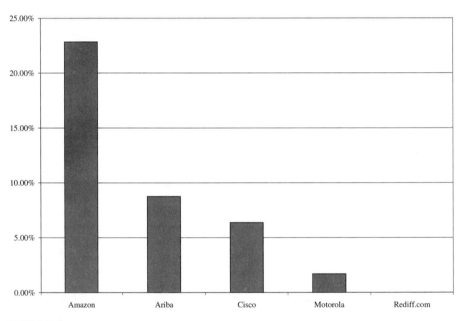

FIGURE 7–2
Options Outstanding as Percent Shares Outstanding

ILLUSTRATION 7.1

Options Outstanding

Table 7.1 summarizes the number of options outstanding at each of the firms that we are valuing, with the average exercise price and maturity of the options, as well as the percent of the options that are vested in each firm.

TABLE 7.1 Options Outstanding

	AMAZON	ARIBA	CISCO	MOTOROLA	REDIFF.COM
Number of options outstanding	80.34	20.675	439.00	36.98	0
Average exercise price	$27.76	$6.77	$22.52	$46.00	NA
Average maturity	9.00	9.31	6.80	6.20	NA
% vested	58%	61%	71%	75%	NA

While Amazon has far more options outstanding as a percent of the outstanding stock, Ariba's options have a much lower exercise price, on average. In fact, Ariba's stock price of $75 at the time of this analysis was almost eight times the average exercise price of $6.77. The average maturity of the options at all of these firms is also in excess of six years for Cisco and Motorola, and in excess of nine years for Amazon and Ariba.[1] The combination of a low exercise price and long maturity make the options issued by these firms very valuable. Fewer of Amazon and Ariba's options are vested, reflecting the fact that these are younger firms which have granted more of these options recently.

OPTIONS IN EXISTENCE

Given the large number of options outstanding at many technology firms, your first task is to consider ways in which you can incorporate their effect into value per share. The section begins by presenting the argument for why these outstanding options matter when computing value per share and then considers four ways in which you can incorporate their effect on value.

Why Options Affect Value per Share. Why do existing options affect value per share? Note that not all options do. In fact, options issued and listed by the options exchanges have no effect on the value per share of the firms on which they are issued. The options issued by firms do have an effect on value per share, since there is a chance that they will be exercised in the near or far future. Given that these options offer the right to individuals to buy stock at a fixed price, they will be exercised only if the stock price rises above that exercise price. When they are exercised, the firm has two choices, both of which have negative consequences for existing stockholders. The firm can issue additional shares to cover the option exercise. But this increases the number of shares outstanding and reduces the value per share to existing stockholders.[2] Alternatively, the firm can use cash flows from operations to buy back shares in the open market and use these shares to meet the option exercise. This approach reduces the cash flows available to current equity investors in future periods and makes their equity less valuable today.

Ways of Incorporating Existing Options into Value. Four approaches are used to incorporate the effect of options that are already outstanding into the value per share. However, the first three approaches can lead to misleading estimates of value.

1. **Use fully diluted number of shares to estimate per-share value.** The simplest way to incorporate the effect of outstanding options on value per share is to divide the value of equity by the number of shares that will be outstanding if all options are exercised today—the fully diluted number of shares. While this approach has the virtue of simplicity, it will lead to too low an estimate of value per share for two reasons:

   ■ It considers all options outstanding, not just ones that are in the money and vested. To be fair, there are variants of this approach where the shares outstanding are adjusted to reflect only in-the-money and vested options.

   ■ It does not incorporate the expected proceeds from exercise, which will comprise a cash inflow to the firm.

   Finally, this approach does not build in the time premium on the options into the valuation either.

ILLUSTRATION 7.2

Fully Diluted Approach to Estimating Value per Share

To apply the fully diluted approach to estimate the per-share value, use the equity values estimated in Chapter 6, "Estimating Firm Value," for each firm in conjunction with the number of shares outstanding, including those underlying the options. Table 7.2 summarizes the value per share derived from this approach.

TABLE 7.2 Fully Diluted Approach to Estimating Value per Share

	AMAZON	ARIBA	CISCO	MOTOROLA	REDIFF.COM
Value of equity	$13,589	$17,941	$318,336	$69,957	$474
Primary shares	351.77	235.8	6890	2152	24.9
Fully diluted shares	432.11	256.475	7329	2188.98	24.9
Value per share (primary)	$38.63	$76.08	$46.20	$32.51	$19.05
Value per share (fully diluted)	$31.45	$69.95	$43.44	$31.96	$19.05

The value per share from the fully diluted approach is significantly lower than the value per share from the primary shares outstanding. This value, however, ignores both the proceeds from the exercise of the options as well as the time value inherent in the options.

2. **Estimate expected option exercises in the future and build in expected dilution.** In this approach, you forecast when in the future the options will be exercised and build in the expected cash outflows associated with the exercise, by assuming that the firm will buy back stock to cover the exercise. The biggest limitation of this approach is that it requires estimates of what the stock price will be in the future and when options will be exercised on the stock. Given that your

objective is to examine whether the price today is correct, forecasting future prices to estimate the current value per share seems circular. In general, this approach is neither practical nor particularly useful for reasonable estimates of value.

3. **Adjust for outstanding options, but add proceeds to equity.** This approach, called the Treasury Stock approach, is a variant of the fully diluted approach. Here, the number of shares is adjusted to reflect options that are outstanding, but the expected proceeds from the exercise (exercise price × number of options) are added to the value of equity. The limitations of this approach are that, like the fully diluted approach, it does not consider the time premium on the options and there is no effective way of dealing with vesting. Generally, this approach, by underestimating the value of options granted, will overestimate the value of equity per share.

   The biggest advantage of this approach is that it does not require a value per share (or stock price) to incorporate the option value into per-share value. As you will see with the last (and recommended) approach, a circularity is created when the stock price is input into the estimation of value per share.

ILLUSTRATION 7.3

Treasury Stock Approach

In Table 7.3, we estimate the value per share by using the treasury stock approach for Amazon, Ariba, Cisco, Motorola, and Rediff.com.

Note that the value per share from this approach is higher than the value per share from the fully diluted approach for each of the companies with options outstanding. The difference is greatest for Amazon because the options have a higher exercise price, relative to the current stock price. The estimated value per share still ignores the time value of the options.

TABLE 7.3 Value of Equity per Share: Treasury Stock Approach

	AMAZON	ARIBA	CISCO	MOTOROLA	REDIFF.COM
Number of options outstanding	80.34	20.675	439	36.98	0
Average exercise price	$27.76	$6.77	$22.52	$46.00	$0.00
Proceeds from exercise	$2,229.84	$139.97	$9,886.28	$1,701.08	$0.00
Value of equity	$13,588.61	$17,940.64	$318,335.78	$69,956.97	$474.37
+ Proceeds from exercise	$2,229.84	$139.97	$9,886.28	$1,701.08	$0.00
Total value	$15,818.45	$18,080.61	$328,222.06	$71,658.05	$474.37
Fully diluted number of shares	432.11	256.475	7329	2188.98	24.9
Value per share	$36.61	$70.50	$44.78	$32.74	$19.05

4. **Value options by using an option pricing model.** The correct approach to dealing with options is to estimate the value of the options today, given today's value per share and the time premium on the option. Once this value has been estimated, it is subtracted from the equity value and divided by the number of shares outstanding to arrive at value per share.

Value of Equity per Share = (Value of Equity – Value of Options Outstanding) / Primary Number of Shares Outstanding

In valuing these options, however, you confront four measurement issues.

a. **Vesting.** Not all of the options outstanding are vested, and some of the nonvested options might never be exercised.

b. **Stock price.** The stock price to use in valuing these options is debatable. The value per share is an input to the process as well as the output of the process.

c. **Taxation.** Since firms are allowed to deduct a portion of the expense associated with option exercises, there may be a potential tax savings when the options are exercised.

d. **Nontraded firms.** Key inputs to the option pricing model, including the stock price and the variance, cannot be obtained for private firms or firms on the verge of a public offering, like Rediff.com. The options must nevertheless be valued.

These options are discussed in more detail below.

a. Dealing with vesting: Recall that firms granting employee options usually require that the employee receiving the options stay with the firm for a specified period, for the option to be vested. Consequently, when you examine the options outstanding at a firm, you are looking at a mix of vested and nonvested options. The nonvested options should be worth less than the vested options, but the probability of vesting will depend on how in-the-money the options are and the period left for an employee to vest. While there have been attempts[3] to develop option pricing models that allow for the possibility that employees may leave a firm before vesting and forfeit the value of their options, the likelihood of such an occurrence when a manager's holdings are substantial should be small. Carpenter (1998) developed a simple extension of the standard option pricing model to allow for early exercise and forfeiture and used it to value executive options.

b. Arriving at a stock price to use: The answer to which stock price to use may seem obvious. Since the stock is traded and you can obtain a stock price, it would seem that you should be using the current stock price to value options. However, you are valuing these options to arrive at a value per share that you will then compare to the market price to decide whether a stock is under- or overvalued. Thus, it seems inconsistent to use the current market price to arrive at the value of the options and then use this option value to estimate an entirely different value per share.

There is a solution. You can value the options by using the estimated value per share. Doing so creates circular reasoning in your valuation. In other words, you need the option value to estimate value per share and value per share to estimate the option value. We would recommend that the value per share be initially estimated by the treasury stock approach and that you then converge on the proper value per share by iterating.[4]

There is another related issue. When options are exercised, they increase the number of shares outstanding, and by doing so, they can have an effect on the stock price. In conventional option pricing models, the exercise of the option does not affect the stock price. These models must be adapted to allow for the dilutive effect of option exercise. We examine how option-pricing models can be modified to allow for dilution in Chapter 11, "Real Options in Valuation."

c. Taxation: When options are exercised, the firm can deduct the difference between the stock price at the time and the exercise price as an employee expense, for tax purposes. This potential tax benefit reduces the drain on value created by having options outstanding. One way in which you could estimate the tax benefit is to multiply the difference between the stock price today and the exercise price by the tax rate; clearly, this would make sense only if the options are in-the-money. Although this approach does not allow for the expected price appreciation over time, it has the benefit of simplicity. An alternative way of estimating the tax benefit is to compute the after-tax value of the options:

After-Tax Value of Options = Value from Option Pricing Model (1 – Tax Rate)

This approach is also straightforward and allows you to consider the tax benefits from option exercise in valuation. One of the advantages of this approach is that you can use it to consider the potential tax benefit even when options are out-of-the-money.

d. Nontraded firms: A couple of key inputs to the option pricing model—the current price per share and the variance in stock prices—cannot be obtained if a firm is not publicly traded. There are two choices in this case. One is to revert to the treasury stock approach to estimate the value of the options outstanding and abandon the option pricing models. The other choice is to stay with the option pricing models and to estimate the value per share from the discounted cash flow model. The variance of similar firms that are publicly traded can be used to estimate the value of the options.

ILLUSTRATION 7.4

Option Value Approach

In Table 7.4, we begin by estimating the value of the options outstanding, using a modified option pricing model that allows for dilution.[5] To estimate the value of the options, we first estimate the standard deviation in stock prices[6] over the previous two years. Weekly returns are used to make the estimate, and the estimate is annualized.[7] All options, vested as well as nonvested, are valued and there is no adjustment for nonvesting.

In estimating the after-tax value of the options at Amazon and Ariba, we have used their prospective marginal tax rate of 35%. If the options are exercised prior to these firms reaching their marginal tax rates, the tax benefit is lower since the expenses are carried forward and offset against income in future periods.

You can now calculate the value per share by subtracting the value of the options outstanding from the value of equity and dividing by the primary number of shares outstanding, as in Table 7.5.

The inconsistency referred to earlier is clear when you compare the value per share estimated in Table 7.5 to the price per share used in Table 7.4 to estimate the value of the options. For instance, Amazon's value per share is $32.33, whereas the price per share used in the option valuation is $49. If you choose to iterate, you would revalue the options by using the estimated value of $32.33, which would lower the value of the options and increase the value per share, leading to a second iteration and a third one, and so on. The values converge to yield a consistent estimate. The consistent estimates of value are provided in Table 7.6.

For Motorola and Ariba, the difference in value from iterating is negligible, since the value per share that we estimated for the firms is close to the current stock price. For Cisco, the value of the options drops by almost 40%, but the overall effect on value is muted because the number of options outstanding as a percent of outstanding stock is small. The difference in values is greatest at Amazon, for two reasons. First, the value per share was significantly lower than the current price at the time of the valuation. Second, Amazon had the highest value for options outstanding as a percent of stock outstanding.

TABLE 7.4 Estimated Value of Options Outstanding

OPTION PRICING MODEL	AMAZON	ARIBA	CISCO	MOTOROLA	REDIFF.COM
Number of options outstanding	80.34	20.675	439	36.98	0
Average exercise price	$27.76	$6.77	$22.52	$46.00	$0.00
Estimated standard deviation (volatility)	85%	80%	40%	34%	80%
Stock price at time of analysis	$49.00	$75.63	$64.88	$34.25	$10.00
Value per option	$42.44	$72.92	$50.13	$11.75	$8.68
Value of options outstanding	$3,409.67	$1,508.00	$22,008.00	$435.00	$0.00
Tax rate	35.00%	35.00%	35.00%	35.00%	38.50%
After-tax value of options outstanding	$2,216	$980.00	$14,305.00	$283.00	$0.00

TABLE 7.5 Value of Equity per Share

	AMAZON	ARIBA	CISCO	MOTOROLA	REDIFF.COM
Value of equity	$13,588.61	$17,940.64	$318,335.78	$69,956.97	$474.37
– Value of options outstanding	$2,216.00	$980.00	$14,305.00	$283.00	$0.00
Value of equity in shares outstanding	$11,372.32	$16,960.71	$304,030.58	$69,674.46	$474.37
Primary shares outstanding	351.77	235.8	6890	2152	24.9
Value per share	$32.33	$71.93	$44.13	$32.38	$19.05

TABLE 7.6 Consistent Estimates of Value per Share

	AMAZON	ARIBA	CISCO	MOTOROLA	REDIFF.COM
Value of options (with current stock price)	$2,216.00	$980.00	$14,305.00	$282.51	$0.00
Value per share	$32.33	$71.93	$44.13	$32.38	$19.05
Value of options (with iterated value)	$1,500.00	$933.00	$8,861.00	$282.51	$0.00
Value per share	$34.37	$72.13	$44.92	$32.38	$19.05

FUTURE OPTION GRANTS

While incorporating options that are already outstanding is fairly straightforward, incorporating the effects of future option grants is much more complicated. In this section, we examine the argument for why these option issues affect value and discuss how to incorporate these effects into value.

Why Future Options Issues Affect Value. Just as outstanding options represent potential dilution or cash outflows to existing equity investors, expected option grants in the future will affect value per share by increasing the number of shares outstanding in future periods. The simplest way of thinking about this expected dilution is to consider the terminal value in the discounted cash flow model. As constructed in the last chapter, the terminal value is discounted to the present and divided by the shares outstanding today to arrive at the value per share. However, expected option issues in the future will increase the number of shares outstanding in the terminal year and therefore reduce the portion of the terminal value that belongs to existing equity investors.

Ways of Incorporating Effect into Value per Share. It is much more difficult to incorporate the effect of expected option issues into value than existing options outstanding. The reason is that you have to forecast not only how many options will be issued by a firm in future periods but also what the terms of these options will be. While this forecasting may be possible for a couple of periods with proprietary information (the firm lets you know how much it plans to issue and at what terms), it will become more difficult in circumstances beyond that point. Below, we consider a way in which to obtain an estimate of the option value and look at two ways of dealing with this estimate, once obtained.

Estimate Option Value as an Operating or Capital Expense. You can estimate the value of options that will be granted in future periods as a percentage of revenues or operating income. By doing so, you avoid the need to estimate the number and terms of future option issues. Estimation will also become easier because you can draw on the firm's own history (by looking at the value of option grants in previous years as a proportion of revenues) and the experiences of more mature firms in the sector. Generally, as firms become larger, the value of options granted as a percent of revenues should become smaller.

Having estimated the value of expected future option issues, you are left with another choice. You can consider this value each period as an operating expense and compute the operating income after the expense. You are assuming, then, that option issues form part of annual compensation. Alternatively, you can treat this value as a capital expense and amortize it over multiple periods. While the cash flow in each period is unaffected by this distinction, it has consequences for the return on capital and reinvestment rates that you measure for a firm.

It is important that you do not double-count future option issues. The current operating expenses of the firm already include the expenses associated with option exercises in the current period. The operating margins and returns on capital that you might derive by looking at industry averages reflect the effects of option exercise in the current period for the firms in the industry. If the effect on operating income of option exercise in the current period is less than the expected value of new option issues, you have to allow for an additional expense associated with option issues. Conversely, if a disproportionately large number of options were exercised in the last period, you have to reduce the operating expenses to allow for the fact that the expected effect of option issues in future periods will be smaller.

ILLUSTRATION 7.5

Valuing with Expected Option Issues

In all of the valuations you have seen so far, the current operating income and the industry averages were key inputs. The current operating income was used to compute the current return on capital, margin, and reinvestment rate for the firm. The industry average margins or returns on capital were used to estimate the stable growth inputs.

The current operating income reflects the effects of options exercised over the last period but not the effect of new options issued. To the extent that the latter is greater (or lower) than the former, the operating income, margins, and returns on capital have been over-stated (or understated). To illustrate the adjustment, we consider the number of options issued and the number exercised at Amazon and Cisco during the last year, summarized in Table 7.7, and the exercise prices of each.

TABLE 7.7 Options Issued and Exercised: Amazon and Cisco

	AMAZON			CISCO		
	Number	Exercise Price	Value	Number	Exercise Price	Value
Options granted	31.739	$63.60	$1,273	107	$49.58	$4,589
Options canceled	11.281	$3.86	—	10	$24.66	$0
Options exercised	16.125	$19.70	$472	93	$6.85	$5,396
Effect on operating income			–$809			+$807

The values of the option grants are estimated with the option pricing model,[8] whereas the value of the options exercised is the exercise value—the difference between the stock price and the exercise price. For Amazon, the value of the options granted was signifi-cantly higher than the value of the exercised options. Consequently, its operating loss would have been even greater (by $809 million) than was estimated in Chapter 4 if the difference between the exercise value and the new options granted is considered an addi-tional employee expense. For Cisco, on the other hand, the value of the options exercised exceeded the value of the options granted. The difference between the two (of $807 mil-lion) should be added to operating income to arrive at the corrected operating income. Similar adjustments can be made to the operating income at Ariba and Motorola; Ariba's operating income would have been $246 million lower with the adjustment, and Motor-ola's would have increased by $14 million.

The industry-average returns on capital and margins are more difficult to adjust. You would have to make the adjustment described above to every firm in the industry and compute returns on capital and margins after the adjustment. For simplicity, the value of options exercised is assumed to be equal to the value of options issued in the current period for the industry.

Table 7.8 reports on the adjustment to current operating income and the final values per share that emerge as a result of this adjustment.

TABLE 7.8 Values per Share with Option Adjustment to Current Operating Income

	AMAZON	ARIBA	CISCO	MOTOROLA
Unadjusted operating income	$(276.00)	$(163.70)	$3,455.00	$3,216.00
Value per share (no option adjustment)	$32.33	$71.93	$44.13	$32.38
Adjusted operating income	$(1,076.29)	$(409.00)	$4,262.00	$3,230.00
Value (option grant adjustment)	$26.62	$58.80	$53.04	$32.48

The effect of the adjustment is trivial at Motorola. The value per share is lower than the original estimates at Amazon and Ariba, reflecting the drain on value per share that options will continue to be in future years. The value per share is higher at Cisco because of the increase in operating income created by the adjustment.

Estimate Expected Stock Price Dilution from Option Issues. The other way of dealing with expected option grants in the future is to build in the expected dilution that will result from these option issues. To do so, you have to make a simplifying assumption. For instance, you could assume that options issued will represent a fixed percent of the outstanding stock each period and base this estimate on the firm's history or on the experience of more mature firms in the sector. Generally, this approach is more complicated than the first one and does not lead to a more precise estimate of value. Clearly, it would be inappropriate to do both: show option issues as an expense and allow for the dilution that will occur from the issue. That double-counts the same cost.

warrants.xls: This spreadsheet enables you to value the options outstanding in a firm, allowing for the dilution effect.

VALUE OF CONTROL

When you divide the value of the equity by the number of shares outstanding, you assume that the shares all have the same voting rights. If different classes of shares have different voting rights, the value of equity per share has to reflect these differences, with the shares with more voting rights having higher value. Note, though, that the total value of equity is still unchanged. To illustrate, assume that the value of equity in a firm is $500 million and that 50 million shares are outstanding; 25 million of these shares have voting rights and 25 million do not. Furthermore, assume that the voting shares will have a value 10% higher than the nonvoting shares. To estimate the value per share:

Value per Nonvoting Share = $500 million / (25 million × 1.10 + 25 million)

= $500 million / 52.5 million = $9.52

Value per Voting Share = $9.52 (1.10) = $10.48

The key issue that you face in valuation, then, is determining the discount to apply for nonvoting shares or, alternatively, the premium to attach to voting shares.

VOTING SHARES VERSUS NONVOTING SHARES

What premium should be assigned to the voting shares? You have two choices. One is to look at studies that empirically examine the size of the premium for voting rights and to assign this premium to all voting shares. Lease, McConnell, and Mikkelson (1983) examined 26 firms that had two classes of common stock outstanding, and they concluded that the voting shares traded at a premium relative to nonvoting shares.[9] The premium, on average, amounted to 5.44%, and the voting shares sold at a higher price in 88% of the months for which data were available.

The other choice is to be more discriminating and vary the premium depending on the firm. Voting rights have value because they give shareholders a say in the management of the firm. To the extent that voting shares can make a difference—by removing incumbent management, forcing management to change policy, or selling to a hostile bidder in a takeover—their price will reflect the possibility of a change in the way the firm is run.[10] Nonvoting shareholders, on the other hand, do not participate in these decisions.

VALUING CONTROL

If the value of control arises from the capacity to change the way a firm is run, it should be a function of how well or badly the firm is run. If the firm is well run, the potential gain from restructuring is negligible, and the difference in values between voting and nonvoting shares should be negligible as well. If the firm is managed badly, the potential gain from restructuring is significant, and voting shares should sell at a significant premium over nonvoting shares.

One way to value control is to value the firm under existing management and policies and then revalue it, assuming that the firm is optimally run. The difference between the two values is the value of control:

Value of Control = Value of Firm Optimally Run
                    − Status Quo Valuation of Firm

The key to estimating this value is to come up with the parameters that you would use to value the firm, optimally run. This issue is revisited in Chapter 12, "Value Enhancement."

CONTROL IN PRIVATE BUSINESSES

The issue of control also comes up when you are valuing private businesses, especially when the stake in the business that is being valued is less than a controlling one. For instance, a 49% stake in a private business may sell at a considerable discount on a 51% stake because the latter provides control whereas the former does not. You can estimate the discount, using the same approach that you developed for valuing control, by valuing the private business under the status quo and then again as an optimally managed business. The discount should be larger with a 49% stake in a poorly managed private business than it would be with a well-managed one.

VALUE OF LIQUIDITY

Once a firm has been valued, should there be a discount for illiquidity if the stake in the firm, whether it takes the form of publicly traded shares or a partnership, cannot be easily sold? Illiquidity falls in a continuum, and even publicly traded firms vary in terms of how liquid their holdings are. The illiquidity discount tends to be most significant when private businesses are up for sale. In practice, the estimation of liquidity discounts seems arbitrary, with discounts of 25% to 30% being most commonly used in practice.

DETERMINANTS OF ILLIQUIDITY DISCOUNT

The illiquidity discount should vary from firm to firm and should depend on the following factors:

- *Size of the business*: As a percent of value, the discount should be smaller for larger firms; a 30% discount may be reasonable for a million-dollar firm, but not for a billion-dollar firm.
- *Type of assets owned by the firm*: Firms with more liquid assets should be assigned lower liquidity discounts, since assets can be sold to raise cash. Thus, the discount should be lower for a private business with real estate and marketable securities as assets than for one with factories and equipment.

■ *Health and cash flows of the business*: Stable businesses that generate large annual cash flows should see their value discounted less than high-growth businesses where operating cash flows are either low or negative.

QUANTIFYING THE LIQUIDITY DISCOUNT

There are two ways of quantifying the liquidity discount. One way is to use the results of studies that have looked at restricted stock. Restricted securities are securities issued by a company, but not registered with the SEC, that can be sold through private placements to investors. These securities cannot be sold for a two-year holding period, and limited amounts can be sold after that. These restricted stocks trade at discounts ranging from 25% to 40%, because they cannot be traded. Silber, in 1991, related the discount to observable characteristics of the firms issuing the stock:

Ln(Price of Restricted Stock ÷ Price of Unrestricted Stock) =
4.33 + 0.036 Ln(Revenues)
– 0.142 (Restricted Block as a Percent of Total Stock Outstanding)
+ 0.174 (DERN) + 0.332 (DCUST)

where DERN = 1 if earnings were positive and zero if not, and DCUST = 1 if the investor with whom the stock was placed had a customer relationship with the firm and 0 if not.

The other, and potentially more promising, route is to extend the research on the magnitude of the bid-ask spread. Note that the spread, which measures the difference between the price at which one can buy a stock or sell it in an instant, is a measure of the liquidity discount for publicly traded stocks. Studies of the spread have noted that it tends to be larger for smaller, more volatile, and lower-priced stocks. You could look at private firms as very small, nontraded stocks and estimate a "spread" which would also be the liquidity discount.

While you would expect the illiquidity discounts to be larger at privately owned technology firms, the discounts will be tempered by the option that these firms have to go to the market. In 1999 and early 2000, for instance, when investors were attaching huge market values to Internet-based firms, investors in privately held online ventures may have been willing to settle for little or no discount because of this potential.

LIQUIDITY DISCOUNTS AT PUBLICLY TRADED FIRMS

Some publicly traded stocks are lightly traded, and the number of shares available for trade (often referred to as the float) is small relative to the total number of shares outstanding.[11] Investors who want to quickly sell their stock in these companies often have a price impact when they sell, and the impact will increase with the size of the holding.

Investors with longer time horizons and a lesser need to quickly convert their holdings into cash have a smaller problem associated with illiquidity than do investors with shorter time horizons and a greater need for cash. Investors should consider the possibility that they will need to convert their holdings into cash quickly when they look at lightly traded stocks as potential investments and should therefore require much larger discounts on value before they take large positions. Assume, for instance, that an investor is looking at Rediff.com, a stock that was valued at $19.05 per share. The stock would be underpriced if it were trading at $17, but it might not be underpriced enough for a short-term investor to take a large position in it. In contrast, a long-term investor may find the stock an attractive buy at that price.

ILLUSTRATION 7.6

Float and Bid-Ask Spreads

In Table 7.9, the trading volume, float, and bid-ask spreads are reported for Amazon, Ariba, Cisco, Motorola, and Rediff.com.

Although the bid-ask spreads are between 1/16 and 1/8 for all of the firms, the spread is a much larger percentage of the stock price for Rediff, which is trading at about $10 per share, than it is for Cisco or Ariba. In addition, only about 20% of the shares outstanding are available for trading at Rediff and only about a third of the shares at Amazon are traded.

TABLE 7.9 Liquidity Measures: Amazon, Ariba, Cisco, Motorola, and Rediff

	AMAZON	ARIBA	CISCO	MOTOROLA	REDIFF
Number of shares	351.77	235.80	6,890.00	2,152.00	24.90
Trading volume	8.22	6.19	42.87	14.1	NA
Float	138.80	134.70	6880.00	1940.00	4.60
Bid-ask spread	$0.0625	$0.1250	$0.0625	$0.0625	$0.125

SUMMARY

The existence of options and the possibility of future option grants makes getting from equity value to value per share a complicated exercise. To deal with options outstanding at the time of the valuation, there are four approaches.

The simplest is to estimate the value per share by dividing the value of equity by the fully diluted number of shares outstanding. This approach ignores both the expected proceeds from exercising the options and the time value of the options.

The second approach of forecasting expected option exercises in the future and estimating the effect on value per share is not only tedious but unlikely to work.

In the treasury stock approach, you add the expected proceeds from option exercise to the value of equity and then divide by the fully diluted number of shares outstanding. While this approach does consider the expected proceeds from exercise, it still ignores the option time premium.

In the final and preferred approach, you value the options by using an option pricing model and subtract the value from the value of equity. The resulting estimate is divided by the primary shares outstanding to arrive at the value of equity per share.

Usually, the current price of the stock is used in option pricing models, but the value per share estimated from the discounted cash flow valuation can be substituted to arrive at a more consistent estimate. To deal with expected option grants in the future, you must dissect the current operating income to consider the effect that option exercises in the current period had on operating expenses. If the options granted during the period had more value than the option expense resulting from exercise of options granted in prior periods, the current operating income has to be adjusted down to reflect the difference. Industry-average margins and returns on capital will also have to be adjusted for the same reason.

Once the value per share of equity has been estimated, that value may need to be adjusted for differences in voting rights. Shares with disproportionately high voting rights will sell at a premium relative to shares with low or no voting rights. The difference will be larger for firms that are badly managed and smaller for well-managed firms. When valuing a private firm, you may also need to discount the estimated value of equity to reflect the lack of liquidity in the shares. In fact, even publicly traded firms can face a discount if the shares that are traded are illiquid.

ENDNOTES

1. Employee options usually have 10-year lives at the time of issue.

2. This circumstance would be dilution in the true sense of the word, rather than the term that is used to describe any increase in the number of shares outstanding. The reason there is dilution is that the additional shares are issued only to the option holders at a price below the current price. In contrast, the dilution that occurs in a rights issue where every stockholder gets the right to buy additional shares at a lower price is value neutral. The shares will trade at a lower price, but everyone will have more shares outstanding.

3. Cuny and Jorion (1995) examine the valuation of options when there is the possibility of forfeiture.

4. The value per share, obtained with the treasury stock approach, will become the stock price in the option pricing model. The option value that results from using this price is used to compute a new value per share, that value is fed back into the option pricing model, and so on.

5. We use the Black-Scholes model, adjusted to reflect dilution.

6. The variance estimate is actually on the natural log of the stock prices, so you can cling to at least the possibility of a normal distribution. Neither stock prices nor stock returns can be normally distributed because prices cannot fall below zero and returns cannot be lower than –100%.

7. All of the inputs to the Black-Scholes model have to be in annual terms. To annualize a weekly variance, you multiply by 52.

8. To value these options, the standard deviations reported earlier and 10-year lives are used. The maturities of the options granted were obtained from the 10-Ks.

9. The two classes of stock received the same dividend.

10. In some cases, the rights of nonvoting stockholders are protected in the specific instance of a takeover by forcing the bidder to buy the nonvoting shares as well.

11. The float is estimated by subtracting out from the shares outstanding, shares that are owned by insiders, 5% owners, and rule 144 shares. (Rule 144 refers to restricted stock that cannot be traded.)

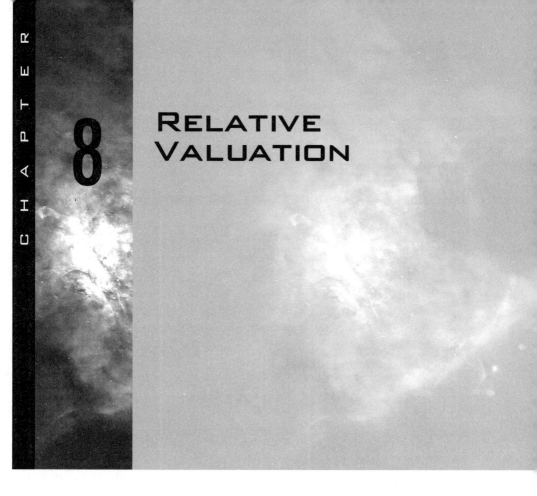

8

RELATIVE VALUATION

In discounted cash flow valuation, the objective is to find the value of assets, given their cash flow, growth, and risk characteristics. In relative valuation, the objective is to value assets, based on how similar assets are currently priced in the market. While multiples are easy to use and intuitive, they are also easy to misuse. Consequently, a series of tests are developed in this chapter that can be used to ensure that multiples are correctly used.

There are two components to relative valuation. The first is that prices have to be standardized, usually by converting them into multiples of earnings, book values, or sales, to value assets on a relative basis. The second is to find similar firms, which is difficult to do since no two firms are identical and firms in the same business can still differ on risk, growth potential, and cash flows. The question of how to control for these differences, when comparing a multiple across several firms, becomes key.

USE OF RELATIVE VALUATION

The use of relative valuation is widespread. Most equity research reports and many acquisition valuations are based on a multiple such as a price-to-sales ratio or the Value to EBITDA multiple and a group of comparable firms. In fact, firms in the same business as the firm being valued are called comparable, though as we see later in this chapter, that designation is not always true. In this section, we first consider the reasons for the popularity of relative valuation, then discuss some potential pitfalls.

REASONS FOR POPULARITY

Why is relative valuation so widely used? There are several reasons. First, a valuation based on a multiple and comparable firms can be completed with far fewer assumptions and far more quickly than a discounted cash flow valuation. Second, a relative valuation is simpler to understand and easier to present to clients and customers than a discounted cash flow valuation. Finally, a relative valuation is much more likely to reflect the current mood of the market, since it is an attempt to measure relative and not intrinsic value. Thus, in a market where all Internet stocks see their prices bid up, relative valuation is likely to yield higher values for these stocks than discounted cash flow valuations. In fact, relative valuations will generally yield values that are closer to the market price than discounted cash flow valuations. This is particularly important for those whose job it is to make judgments on relative value, and who are themselves judged on a relative basis. Consider, for instance, managers of technology mutual funds. These managers will be judged by how their funds do relative to other technology funds. Consequently, they will be rewarded if they pick technology stocks that are undervalued relative to other technology stocks, even if the entire sector is overvalued.

POTENTIAL PITFALLS

The strengths of relative valuation are also its weaknesses. First, the ease with which a relative valuation can be compiled, pulling together a multiple and a group of comparable firms, can also result in inconsistent estimates of value where key variables such as risk, growth, or cash flow potential are ignored. Second, the fact that multiples reflect the market mood also implies that using relative valuation to estimate the value of an asset can result in values that are too high, when the market is overvaluing comparable firms, or too low, when it is undervaluing these firms. Third, while there is scope for bias in any type of valuation, the lack of transparency regarding the underlying assumptions in relative valuations makes them particularly vulnerable to manipulation. A biased analyst who is allowed to choose the multiple on which the valuation is based and to pick the comparable firms can essentially ensure that almost any value can be justified.

STANDARDIZED VALUES AND MULTIPLES

The price of a stock is a function both of the value of the equity in a company and the number of shares outstanding in the firm. Thus, a stock split that doubles the number of units will approximately halve the stock price. Since stock prices are determined by the number of units of equity in a firm, stock prices cannot be compared across different firms. To compare the values of "similar" firms in the market, you need to standardize the values in some way. Values can be standardized relative to the earnings firms generate, to the book value or replacement value of the firms themselves, to the revenues that firms generate, or to measures that are specific to firms in a sector.

EARNINGS MULTIPLES

One of the more intuitive ways to think of the value of any asset is as a multiple of the earnings that assets generate. When buying a stock, one commonly looks at the price paid as a multiple of the earnings per share generated by the company. This price-earnings ratio can be estimated by current earnings per share, which is called a trailing PE, or an expected earnings per share in the next year, called a forward PE.

When buying a business, as opposed to just the equity in the business, one commonly examines the value of the firm as a multiple of the operating income or the earnings before interest, taxes, depreciation, and amortization (EBITDA). To a buyer of the equity or the firm, a lower multiple is better than a higher one, but these multiples will be affected by the growth potential and risk of the business being acquired.

BOOK VALUE OR REPLACEMENT VALUE MULTIPLES

Markets provide one estimate of the value of a business; accountants often provide a very different estimate of the same business. The accounting estimate of book value is determined by accounting rules and is heavily influenced by the original price paid for assets and any accounting adjustments (such as depreciation) made since. Investors often look at the relationship between the price they pay for a stock and the book value of equity (or net worth) as a measure of how over- or undervalued a stock is; the price-to-book-value ratio that emerges can vary widely across industries, depending again on the growth potential and the quality of the investments in each. When valuing businesses, you estimate this ratio by using the value of the firm and the book value of all capital (rather than just the equity). For those who believe that book value is not a good measure of the true value of the assets, an alternative is to use the replacement cost of the assets; the ratio of the value of the firm to replacement cost is called *Tobin's Q*.

REVENUE MULTIPLES

Both earnings and book value are accounting measures and are determined by accounting rules and principles. An alternative approach, which is far less affected by accounting choices, is to use the ratio of the value of an asset to the revenues it generates. For equity investors, this ratio is the price-sales ratio (PS), where the market value per share is divided by the revenues generated per share. For firm value, this ratio can be modified as the value-sales ratio (VS), where the numerator becomes the total value of the firm. This ratio, again, varies widely across sectors, largely as a function of the profit margins in each. The advantage of using revenue multiples, however, is that it becomes far easier to compare firms in different markets, with different accounting systems at work, than it is to compare earnings or book value multiples.

SECTOR-SPECIFIC MULTIPLES

Although earnings, book value, and revenue multiples are multiples that can be computed for firms in any sector and across the entire market, some multiples are specific to a sector. For instance, when Internet firms first appeared on the market in the late 1990s, they had negative earnings and negligible revenues and book values. Analysts looking for a multiple to value these firms divided the market value of each of these firms by the number of hits generated by that firm's Web site. Firms with a low market value per customer hit were viewed as more undervalued. More recently, e-tailers have been judged by the market value of equity per customer in the firms.

While there are conditions under which sector-specific multiples can be justified, and you look at a few in Chapter 10, "Other Multiples," they are dangerous for two reasons. First, since they cannot be computed for other sectors or for the entire market, sector-specific multiples can result in persistent over- or undervaluations of sectors relative to the rest of the market. Thus, investors who would never consider paying 80 times revenues for a firm might not have the same qualms about paying $2,000 for every page hit (on the Web site), largely because they have no sense of what high, low, or average is on this measure. Second, it is far more difficult to relate sector-specific multiples to fundamentals, which is an essential ingredient to using multiples well. For instance, does a visitor to a company's Web site translate into higher revenues and profits? The answer will not only vary from company to company but will also be difficult to estimate looking forward.

THE FOUR BASIC STEPS TO USING MULTIPLES

Multiples are easy to use and easy to misuse. There are four basic steps to using multiples wisely and for detecting misuse in the hands of others. The first step is to ensure that the multiple is defined consistently and that it is measured uniformly across the firms being compared. The second step is to be aware of the cross-sectional distribution of the multiple, not only across firms in the sector being analyzed but also across the entire market. The third step is to analyze the multiple and understand not only what fundamentals determine the multiple but also how changes in these fundamentals translate into changes in the multiple. The final step is finding the right firms to use for comparison and controlling for differences that may persist across these firms.

DEFINITIONAL TESTS

Even the simplest multiples can be defined differently by different analysts. Consider, for instance, the price-earnings ratio (PE). Most analysts define it to be the market price divided by the earnings per share, but that is where the consensus ends. There are a number of variants on the PE ratio. The current price is conventionally used in the numerator, but some analysts use the average price over the last six months or a year. The earnings per share in the denominator can be the earnings per share from the most recent financial year (yielding the current PE), the last four quarters of earnings (yielding the trailing PE), and expected earnings per share in the next financial year (resulting in a forward PE). In addition, calculation of earnings per share can be based on primary shares outstanding or fully diluted shares and can include or exclude extraordinary items. Figure 8–1 provides the PE ratios for Cisco using each of these measures.

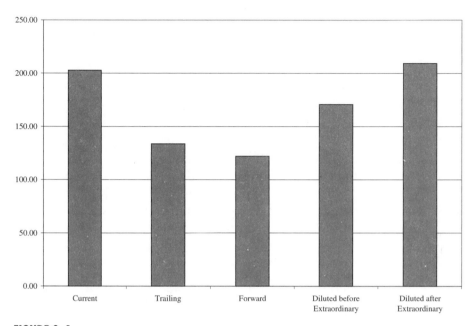

FIGURE 8–1
Estimate of Cisco's PE Ratio

Not only can these variants on earnings yield vastly differ-ent values for the price-earnings ratio, but the one that gets used by analysts depends on their biases. For instance, in peri-ods of rising earnings, the forward PE yields consistently lower values than the trailing PE, which, in turn, is lower than the current PE. A bullish analyst will tend to use the forward PE to make the case that the stock is trading at a low multiple of earnings, whereas a bearish analyst will focus on the current PE to make the case that the multiple is too high. The first step when discussing a valuation based on a multiple is to ensure that everyone in the discussion is using the same definition for that multiple.

Consistency. Every multiple has a numerator and a denominator. The numerator can be either an equity value (such as market price or value of equity) or a firm value (such as enterprise value, which is the sum of the values of debt and equity, net of cash). The denominator can be an equity measure (such as earnings per share, net income, or book value of equity) or a firm measure (such as operating income, EBITDA, or book value of capital).

One of the key tests to run on a multiple is to examine whether the numerator and denominator are defined consistently. *If the numerator for a multiple is an equity value, then the denominator should be an equity value as well. If the numerator is a firm value, then the denominator should be a firm value as well.* To illustrate, the price-earnings ratio is a consistently defined multiple, since the numerator is the price per share (which is an equity value) and the denominator is earnings per share (which is also an equity value). The Enterprise value to EBITDA multiple is also a consistently defined multiple, since the numerator and denominator are both firm value measures.

Are any multiples in use inconsistently defined? Consider the price-to-EBITDA multiple, a multiple that has acquired adherents in the last few years among analysts. The numerator in this multiple is an equity value, and the denominator is a measure of earnings to the firm. The analysts who use this multiple will probably argue that the inconsistency does not matter since the multiple is computed the same way for all of the comparable firms; but they would be wrong. If some firms on the list have no debt and others carry significant amounts of debt, the latter will look cheap on a price-to-EBITDA basis, when in fact they might be overpriced or correctly priced.

Uniformity. In relative valuation, the multiple is computed for all of the firms in a group and then compared across these firms for judgments on which firms are overpriced and which are underpriced. For this comparison to have any merit, the multiple must be defined uniformly across all of the firms in the group. Thus, if the trailing PE is used for one firm, it must be used for all of the others. In fact, one of the problems with using the current PE to compare firms in a group is that different firms can have different fiscal-year ends. This can lead to some firms having their prices divided by earnings from July 1999 to June 2000, with other firms having their prices divided by earnings from January 1999 to December 1999.

While the differences can be minor in mature sectors, where earnings do not make quantum jumps over six months, they can be large in high-growth sectors.

With both earnings and book value measures, there is another component to be concerned about: the accounting standards used to estimate earnings and book values. Differences in accounting standards can result in very different earnings and book value numbers for similar firms. This makes it very difficult to compare multiples across firms in different markets, with different accounting standards. Even within the United States, comparisons of earnings multiples can be thrown off when some firms use different accounting rules (on depreciation and expensing) for reporting purposes and tax purposes, and other firms do not.[1]

DESCRIPTIONAL TESTS

When using a multiple, it is always useful to have a sense of what a high value, a low value, or a typical value for that multiple is in the market. In other words, knowing the distributional characteristics of a multiple is a key part of using that multiple to identify under- or overvalued firms. In addition, you need to understand the effects of outliers on averages and to unearth any biases introduced in the process of estimating multiples.

Distributional Characteristics. Many analysts who use multiples have a sector focus and have a good sense of how different firms in their sector rank on specific multiples. What is often lacking, however, is a sense of how the multiple is distributed across the entire market. Why, you might ask, should a software analyst care about price-earnings ratios of utility stocks? Because both software and utility stocks are competing for the same investment dollar, they must, in a sense, play by the same rules. Furthermore, an awareness of how multiples vary across sectors can be very useful in detecting over- or undervaluation of the sector you are analyzing.

What are the distributional characteristics that matter? The standard statistics—the *average* and the *standard deviation*—are where you should start, but they represent the beginning of the exploration. The fact that multiples such as the price-earnings ratio can never be less than zero and are unconstrained in terms of maximum results in distributions for these multiples that are skewed toward the positive values. Consequently, the average values for these multiples will be higher than *median* values,[2] and the latter are much more representative of the typical firm in the group. While the maximum and minimum values are usually of limited use, the percentile values (10th percentile, 25th percentile, 75th percentile, 90th percentile...) can be useful in judging what a high or low value for the multiple in the group is.

Outliers and Averages. As noted earlier, multiples are unconstrained on the upper end, and firms can have price-earnings ratios of 500 or 2,000 or even 10,000. This can occur not only because of high stock prices but also because earnings at firms can sometime drop to a few cents. These outliers will result in averages that are not representative of the sample. In most cases, services that compute and report average values for multiples either throw out these outliers when computing the averages or constrain the multiples to be less than or equal to a fixed number. For instance, any firm that has a price-earnings ratio greater than 500 may be given a price-earnings ratio of 500.

When using averages obtained from a service, it is important that you know how the service dealt with outliers in computing the averages. In fact, the sensitivity of the estimated average to outliers is another reason for looking at the median values for multiples.

Biases in Estimating Multiples. With every multiple, there are firms for which the multiple cannot be computed. Consider again the price-earnings ratio. When the earnings per share are negative, the price-earnings ratio for a firm is not meaningful and is usually not reported. When looking at the average price-earnings ratio across a group of firms, you will see that the firms with negative earnings will all drop out of the sample because the price-earnings ratio cannot be computed. Why should this matter when the sample is large? The fact that the firms that are taken out of the sample are the firms losing money creates a bias in the selection process. In fact, the average PE ratio for the group will be biased because of the elimination of these firms.

There are three solutions to this problem. The first is to be aware of the bias and build it into the analysis. In practical terms, this will mean adjusting the average PE to reflect the elimination of the money-losing firms. The second is to aggregate the market value of equity and net income (or loss) for all of the firms in the group, including the money-losing ones, and compute the price-earnings ratio with the aggregated values. Figure 8–2 summarizes the average PE ratio, the median PE ratio, and the PE ratio based on aggregated earnings for specialty retailers.

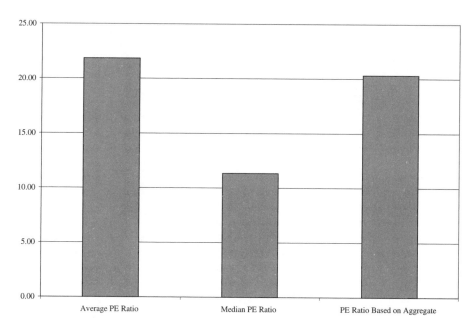

FIGURE 8–2
PE Ratio for Specialty Retailers

Note that the median PE ratio is much lower than the average PE ratio. Furthermore, the PE ratio based on the aggregate values of market value of equity and net income is lower than the average across firms where PE ratios could be computed. The third choice is to use a multiple that can be computed for all of the firms in the group. The inverse of the price-earnings ratio, which is called the earnings yield, can be computed for all firms, including those losing money.

ANALYTICAL TESTS

In discussing why analysts were so fond of using multiples, it was argued that relative valuations require fewer assumptions than discounted cash flow valuations. While this is technically true, it is only true on the surface. In reality, you make just as many assumptions when you do a relative valuation as you make in a discounted cash flow valuation. The difference is that the assumptions in a relative valuation are implicit and unstated, whereas those in discounted cash flow valuation are explicit. The two primary questions that you need to answer before using a multiple are these: What are the fundamentals that determine at what multiple a firm should trade? How do changes in the fundamentals affect the multiple?

Determinants. In the introduction to discounted cash flow valuation, we observed that the value of a firm is a function of three variables: its capacity to generate cash flows, the expected growth in these cash flows, and the uncertainty associated with these cash flows. Every multiple, whether it is of earnings, revenues, or book value, is a function of the same three variables—risk, growth, and cash flow generating potential. Intuitively, then, firms with higher growth rates, less risk, and greater cash flow generating potential should trade at higher multiples than firms with lower growth, higher risk, and less cash flow potential.

The specific measures of growth, risk, and cash flow generating potential that are used will vary from multiple to multiple. To look under the hood, so to speak, of equity and firm value multiples, you can go back to fairly simple discounted cash flow models for equity and firm value and use them to derive the multiples.

In the simplest discounted cash flow model for equity, which is a stable growth dividend discount model, the value of equity is:

$$\text{Value of Equity} = P_0 = \frac{DPS_1}{k_e - g_n}$$

where DPS_1 is the expected dividend in the next year, k_e is the cost of equity, and g_n is the expected stable growth rate. Dividing both sides by the earnings, you obtain the discounted cash flow equation specifying the PE ratio for a stable growth firm:

$$\frac{P_0}{EPS_0} = PE = \frac{\text{Payout Ratio} \times (1 + g_n)}{k_e - g_n}$$

Dividing both sides by the book value of equity, you can estimate the price-book value ratio for a stable growth firm:

$$\frac{P_0}{BV_0} = PBV = \frac{ROE \times \text{Payout Ratio} \times (1 + g_n)}{k_e - g_n}$$

where ROE is the return on equity. Dividing by the sales per share, you can estimate the price-sales ratio for a stable growth firm as a function of its profit margin, payout ratio, profit margin, and expected growth.

$$\frac{P_0}{Sales_0} = PS = \frac{\text{Net Profit Margin} \times \text{Payout Ratio} \times (1 + g_n)}{k_e - g_n}$$

You can do a similar analysis to derive the firm value multiples. The value of a firm in stable growth can be written as:

$$\text{Value of Firm} = V_0 = \frac{FCFF_1}{k_c - g_n}$$

Dividing both sides by the expected free cash flow to the firm yields the Value/FCFF multiple for a stable growth firm:

$$\frac{V_0}{FCFF_1} = \frac{1}{k_c - g_n}$$

Since the free cash flow of the firm is the after-tax operating income netted against the net capital expenditures and working capital needs of the firm, the multiples of EBIT, after-tax EBIT, and EBITDA can also be estimated similarly.

The point of this analysis is not to suggest that you go back to using discounted cash flow valuation but to understand the variables that may cause these multiples to vary across firms in the same sector. If you ignore these variables, you might conclude that a stock with a PE of 8 is cheaper than one with a PE of 12, when the true reason may be that the latter has higher expected growth; or you might decide that a stock with a P/BV ratio of 0.7 is cheaper than one with a P/BV ratio of 1.5, when the true reason may be that the latter has a much higher return on equity.

Relationship. Knowing the fundamentals that determine a multiple is a useful first step, but understanding how the multiple changes as the fundamentals change is just as critical to using the multiple. To illustrate, knowing that higher-growth firms have higher PE ratios is not a sufficient insight if you are called on to analyze whether a firm with a growth rate that is twice as high as the average growth rate for the sector should have a PE ratio that is 1.5 times, 1.8 times, or 2 times the average price-earnings ratio for the sector. To make this judgment, you need to know how the PE ratio changes as the growth rate changes.

A surprisingly large number of analyses are based on the assumption of a linear relationship between multiples and fundamentals. For instance, the PEG ratio, which is the ratio of the PE to the expected growth rate of a firm and is widely used to analyze high-growth firms, implicitly assumes that PE ratios and expected growth rates are linearly related.

One of the advantages of deriving the multiples from a discounted cash flow model, as was done in the last section, is that you can analyze the relationship between each fundamental variable and the multiple by keeping everything else constant and changing the value of that variable. When you do this, you will find very few linear relationships in valuation.

Companion Variable. Although the variables that determine a multiple can be extracted from a discounted cash flow model and although the relationship between each variable and the multiple can be developed by holding all else constant and asking what-if questions, one variable dominates when it comes to explaining each multiple. This variable, called the *companion variable*, can usually be identified by examination of how multiples differ across firms in a sector or across the entire market. In the next two chapters, the companion variables for the most widely used multiples from the price-earnings ratio to the value-to-sales multiples are identified and then used in analysis.

APPLICATION TESTS

When multiples are used, they tend to be used in conjunction with comparable firms to determine the value of a firm or its equity. But what is a comparable firm? The conventional practice is to look at firms within the same industry or business as comparable firms, but this method is not necessarily always the correct or the best way of identifying these firms. No matter how carefully you choose comparable firms, differences will remain between the firm you are valuing and the comparable firms. Figuring out how to control for these differences is a significant part of relative valuation.

What Is a Comparable Firm? A comparable firm is one with cash flows, growth potential, and risk similar to the firm being valued. It would be ideal if you could value a firm by looking at how an exactly identical firm—in terms of risk, growth, and cash flows—is priced. Nowhere in this definition is there a component that relates to the industry or sector to which a firm belongs. Thus, a telecommunications firm can be compared to a software firm if the two are identical in terms of cash flows, growth, and risk. In most analyses, however, analysts define comparable firms to be other firms in the firm's business or businesses. If there are enough firms in the industry to allow for it, this list is pruned further according to other criteria; for instance, only firms of similar size may be considered. The implicit assumption being made here is that firms in the same sector have similar risk, growth, and cash flow profiles and therefore can be compared with much more legitimacy.

This approach becomes more difficult to apply when there are relatively few firms in a sector. In most markets outside the United States, the number of publicly traded firms in a particular sector, especially in a narrowly defined sector, is small. It is also difficult to define firms in the same sector as comparable firms if differences in risk, growth, and cash flow profiles across firms within a sector are large. Thus, hundreds of computer software companies are listed in the United States, but the differences across these firms are also large. The trade-off is therefore a simple one. Defining an industry more broadly increases the number of comparable firms, but it also results in a more diverse group of companies.

There are alternatives to the conventional practice of defining comparable firms. One is to look for firms that are *similar in terms of valuation fundamentals*. For instance, to estimate the value of a firm with a beta of 1.2, an expected growth rate in earnings per share of 20%, and a return on equity of 40%,[3] you would find other firms across the entire market with similar characteristics.[4] The other alternative is to *consider all firms in the market* as comparable firms and to control for differences on the fundamentals across these firms, using statistical techniques such as multiple regressions.

Controlling for Differences Across Firms. No matter how carefully you construct your list of comparable firms, you will end up with firms that are different from the firm you are valuing. The differences may be small on some variables and large on others, and you will have to control for these differences in a relative valuation. Next, we'll discuss three ways of controlling for these differences.

Subjective Adjustments

Relative valuation begins with two choices: the multiple used in the analysis and the group of firms that comprises the comparable firms. The multiple is calculated for each of the comparable firms, and the average is computed. To evaluate an individual firm, you then compare the multiple it trades at to the average computed; if they are significantly different, you make a subjective judgment about whether the firm's individual characteristics (growth, risk, or cash flows) can explain the difference. Thus, a firm may have a PE ratio of 22 in a sector where the average PE is only 15, but you may conclude that this difference can be justified because the firm has higher growth potential than the average firm in the industry. If, in your judgment, the difference on the multiple cannot be explained by the fundamentals, the firm will be viewed as overvalued (if its multiple is higher than the average) or undervalued (if its multiple is lower than the average).

Modified Multiples

In this approach, you modify the multiple to take into account the most important variable determining it—the companion variable. Thus, the PE ratio is divided by the expected growth rate in EPS for a company to determine a growth-adjusted PE ratio or the PEG ratio. Similarly, the PBV ratio is divided by the ROE to find a *value ratio*, and the price-sales ratio is divided by the net margin. These modified ratios are then compared across companies in a sector. The implicit assumption you make is that these firms are comparable on all measures of value other than the one being controlled for. In addition, you are assuming that the relationship between the multiples and fundamentals is linear.

ILLUSTRATION 8.1

Comparing PE Ratios and Growth Rates Across Firms

Table 8.1 summarizes the PE ratios and expected growth rates in EPS over the next five years, based on consensus estimates from analysts, for the firms that are categorized as comparable to Cisco because they are in a similar business.

TABLE 8.1 Data Networking Firms

COMPANY NAME	BETA	PE	PROJECTED GROWTH	PEG
3Com Corp.	1.35	37.20	11.00%	3.38
ADC Telecom.	1.4	78.17	24.00%	3.26
Alcatel ADR	0.9	51.50	24.00%	2.15
Ciena Corp.	1.7	94.51	27.50%	3.44
Cisco	1.4	133.76	35.20%	3.80
Comverse Technology	1.45	70.42	28.88%	2.44
E-TEK Dynamics	1.85	295.56	55.00%	5.37
JDS Uniphase	1.6	296.28	65.00%	4.56
Lucent Technologies	1.3	54.28	24.00%	2.26
Nortel Networks	1.4	104.18	25.50%	4.09
Tellabs, Inc.	1.75	52.57	22.00%	2.39
Average		115.31	30.64%	3.38

(*Source:* Value Line, June 2000 CD-ROM)

Is Cisco under- or overvalued on a relative basis? A simple view of multiples would lead you to conclude that it is slightly overvalued because its PE ratio of 133.76 is higher than the average for the industry.

In making this comparison, you assume that Cisco has a growth rate similar to the average for the sector. One way of bringing growth into the comparison is to compute the PEG ratio, which is reported in the last column. Based on the average PEG ratio of 3.38 for the sector and the estimated growth rate for Cisco, you obtain the following value for the PE ratio for Cisco:

PE Ratio = $3.38 \times 35.2 = 119.06$

Based on this adjusted PE, Cisco remains overvalued at its current PE ratio of 133.76. While this may seem like an easy adjustment to resolve the problem of differences across firms, the conclusion holds only if these firms are of equivalent risk. Implicitly, this approach assumes a linear relationship between growth rates and PE.

Sector Regressions

When firms differ on more than one variable, it becomes difficult to modify the multiples to account for the differences across firms. You can run regressions of the multiples against the variables and then use these regressions to find predicted values for each firm. This approach works reasonably well when the number of comparable firms is large and the relationship between the multiple and the variables is stable. When these conditions do not hold, a few outliers can cause the coefficients to change dramatically and make the predictions much less reliable.

ILLUSTRATION 8.2

Revisiting the Cisco Analysis: Sector Regression

The price-earnings ratio is a function of the expected growth rate, risk, and the payout ratio. None of the firms in Cisco's comparable firm list pays significant dividends, but they differ in terms of risk. Table 8.2 summarizes the price-earnings ratios, betas, and expected growth rates for the firms on the list.

Since these firms differ on both risk and expected growth, you would run a regression of PE ratios on both variables:

$$PE = 35.08 - 65.73 \text{ Beta} + 573.10 \text{ Expected Growth} \qquad R^2 = 93.63\%$$
$$\quad (0.56) \quad (1.67) \qquad (11.93)$$

The numbers in parentheses are t-statistics and suggest that the relationships between PE ratios and the variables in the regression are statistically significant. R^2 indicates the percentage of the differences in PE ratios that is explained by the independent variables. Finally, the regression[5] itself can be used to get predicted PE ratios for the companies in the list. Thus, the predicted PE ratio for Cisco, based on its beta of 1.40 and the expected growth rate of 35.2%, would be:

Predicted PE_{Cisco} = 35.08 − 65.73 (1.40) + 573.10 (.352) = 144.79

Since the actual PE ratio for Cisco was 133.76, this result would suggest that the stock is undervalued by roughly 7.60%.

TABLE 8.2 Data Networking Firms

COMPANY NAME	PE	BETA	PROJECTED GROWTH
3Com Corp.	37.20	1.35	11.00%
ADC Telecom.	78.17	1.4	24.00%
Alcatel ADR	51.50	1.8	24.00%
Ciena Corp.	94.51	1.7	27.50%
Cisco	133.76	1.4	35.20%
Comverse Technology	70.42	1.45	28.88%
E-TEK Dynamics	295.56	1.25	55.00%
JDS Uniphase	296.28	1.6	65.00%
Lucent Technologies	54.28	1.3	24.00%
Nortel Networks	104.18	1.4	25.50%
Tellabs, Inc.	52.57	1.75	22.00%

(*Source:* Value Line, June 2000 CD-ROM)

Market Regression

Searching for comparable firms within the sector in which a firm operates is fairly restrictive, especially when relatively few firms are in the sector or when a firm operates in more than one sector. Since the definition of a comparable firm is not one that is in the same business but one that has the same growth, risk, and cash flow characteristics as the firm being analyzed, you need not restrict your choice of comparable firms to those in the same industry. The regression introduced in the previous section controls for differences on those variables that you believe cause multiples to vary across firms.

Based on the variables that determine each multiple, you should be able to regress PE, PBV, and PS ratios against the variables that should affect them:

Price Earnings = f (Growth, Payout Ratios, Risk)

Price to Book Value = f (Growth, Payout Ratios, Risk, ROE)

Price to Sales = f (Growth, Payout Ratios, Risk, Margin)

It is, however, possible that the proxies that you use for risk (beta), growth (expected growth rate), and cash flow (payout) may be imperfect and that the relationship may not be linear. To deal with these limitations, you can add more variables to the regression—for example, the size of the firm may operate as a proxy for risk—and use transformations of the variables to allow for nonlinear relationships.

The first advantage of this approach over the "subjective" comparison across firms in the same sector, described in the previous section, is that it does quantify, based on actual market data, the degree to which higher growth or risk should affect the multiples. It is true that these estimates can be noisy, but noise is a reflection of the reality that many analysts choose not to face when they make subjective judgments. Second, by looking at all firms in the market, you make more meaningful comparisons of firms that operate in industries with relatively few firms. Third, this approach enables you to examine whether all firms in an industry are under- or over-valued, by estimating their values relative to other firms in the market.

Reconciling Relative and Discounted Cash Flow Valuations

The two approaches to valuation—discounted cash flow valuation and relative valuation—will generally yield different estimates of value for the same firm. Furthermore, even within relative valuation, you can arrive at different estimates of value, depending on which multiple you use and on what firms you based the relative valuation.

The differences in value between discounted cash flow valuation and relative valuation come from different views of market efficiency or, put more precisely, market inefficiency. In discounted cash flow valuation, you assume that markets make mistakes, that they correct these mistakes over time, and that these mistakes can often occur across entire sectors or even the entire market. In relative valuation, you assume that while markets make mistakes on individual stocks, they are correct on average. In other words, when you value Cisco relative to comparable companies, you are assuming that the market has priced these companies correctly, on average, even though it might have made mistakes in the pricing of each of them individually. Thus, a stock may be overvalued on a discounted cash flow basis but undervalued on a relative basis if the firms used in the relative valuation are all overpriced by the market. The reverse would occur if an entire sector or market are underpriced.

SUMMARY

In relative valuation, you estimate the value of an asset by looking at how similar assets are priced. To make this comparison, you begin by converting prices into multiples—standardizing prices—and then comparing these multiples across firms that you define as comparable. Prices can be standardized according to earnings, book value, revenue, or sector-specific variables.

The allure of multiples remains their simplicity; there are four steps in using them soundly. First, you must define the multiple consistently and measure it uniformly across the firms being compared. Second, you need to have a sense of how the multiple varies across firms in the market. In other words, you need to know what a high value, a low value, and a typical value are for the multiple in question. Third, you need to identify the fundamental variables that determine each multiple and how changes in these fundamentals affect the value of the multiple. Finally, you need to find truly comparable firms and adjust for differences between the firms on fundamental characteristics.

In the next chapter, we take a closer look at earnings multiples, and in Chapter 10, we look at other multiples.

ENDNOTES

1. Firms that adopt different rules for reporting and tax purposes generally report higher earnings to their stockholders than they do to the tax authorities. When they are compared on a price-earnings basis to firms that do not maintain different reporting and tax books, they will look cheaper (lower PE).

2. With the median, half of all firms in the group fall below this value and half lie above.

3. The return on equity of 40% becomes a proxy for cash flow potential. With a 20% growth rate and a 40% return on equity, this firm will be able to return half of its earnings to its stockholders in the form of dividends or stock buybacks.

4. Finding these firms manually may become tedious when your universe includes 10,000 stocks. You could draw on statistical techniques such as cluster analysis to find similar firms.

5. Both approaches assume that the relationship between a multiple and the variables driving value are linear. Since this is not always true, you might have to run nonlinear versions of these regressions.

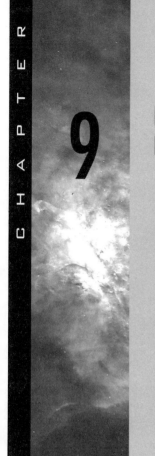

9

EARNINGS MULTIPLES

Earnings multiples remain the most commonly used measures of relative value. In this chapter, we begin with a detailed examination of the price-earnings ratio and then consider a variant that is often used for technology firms—the price earnings to growth ratio (PEG). We also look at value multiples and, in particular, the value to EBITDA multiple and other variants of earnings multiples in the second part of the chapter. We use the four-step process described in Chapter 8, "Relative Valuation," to look at each of these multiples.

PRICE-EARNINGS RATIO (PE)

The price-earnings multiple (PE) is the most widely used and misused of all multiples. Its simplicity makes it an attractive choice in applications ranging from pricing initial public offerings to equity research, but its relationship to a firm's financial fundamentals is often ignored, leading to significant errors in applications. This chapter provides some insight into the determinants of price-earnings ratios and how best to use them in valuation.

DEFINITIONS OF PE RATIO

The price-earnings ratio is the ratio of the market price per share to the earnings per share:

PE = Market Price per Share / Earnings per Share

The PE ratio is consistently defined: the numerator is the value of equity per share and the denominator measures earnings per share, which is a measure of equity earnings. The biggest problem with PE ratios is the variations on earnings per share used in computing the multiple. In Chapter 8, we saw that PE ratios could be computed with current earnings per share, trailing earnings per share, forward earnings per share, fully diluted earnings per share, and primary earnings per share. With technology firms, the PE ratio can be very different, depending on which measure of earnings per share is used. This difference can be explained by two factors:

- *The high growth in earnings per share at these firms*: Forward earnings per share can be substantially higher than trailing earnings per share, which, in turn, can be significantly different from current earnings per share.
- *Management options*: Since technology firms tend to have far more employee options outstanding, relative to the number of shares, the differences between diluted and primary earnings per share tend to be large.

When the PE ratios of technology firms are compared, it is difficult to ensure that the earnings per share are uniformly estimated across the firms, for the following reasons:

- Technology firms often grow by acquiring other firms, and they do not account for acquisitions the same way.

Some do only stock-based acquisitions and use only pooling, others use a mixture of pooling and purchase accounting, and still others use purchase accounting and write all or a portion of the goodwill as in-process R&D. These different approaches lead to different measures of earnings per share and different PE ratios.

■ Using diluted earnings per share in estimating PE ratios might bring the shares that are covered by management options into the multiple, but they treat options that are deep in-the-money or only slightly in-the-money as equivalent.

■ The expensing of R&D gives firms a way of shifting earnings from period to period and penalizes those firms that are spending more on research and development.

Technology firms that account for acquisitions with pooling and do not invest in R&D can have much lower PE ratios than do technology firms that use purchase accounting in acquisitions and invest substantial amounts in R&D.

CROSS-SECTIONAL DISTRIBUTION OF PE RATIOS

A critical step in using PE ratios is to understand how the multiple varies across firms in the sector and the market. In this section, we first examine the distribution of PE ratios across the entire market, then examine PE ratios in the technology sector.

Market Distribution. Figure 9–1 presents the distribution of PE ratios for U.S. stocks in July 2000. The current PE, trailing PE, and forward PE ratios are summarized in the figure.

Table 9.1 presents summary statistics on all three measures of the price-earnings ratio, starting with the mean and the standard deviation and including the median, 10th, and 90th percentile values. For computation of the mean, the PE ratio is set at 200 if it is greater than 200, to prevent outliers from having too large an influence on the summary statistics.[1]

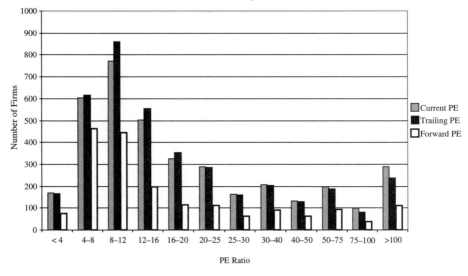

U.S. Stocks: July 2000

FIGURE 9–1
Current, Trailing, and Forward PE Ratios

TABLE 9.1 Summary Statistics: PE Ratios for U.S. Stocks

	CURRENT PE	TRAILING PE	FORWARD PE
Mean	31.30	28.49	27.21
Standard deviation	44.13	40.86	41.21
Median	14.47	13.68	11.52
Mode	12.00	7.00	7.50
10th percentile	5.63	5.86	5.45
90th percentile	77.87	63.87	64.98
Skewness	17.12	25.96	19.59

Looking at all three measures of the PE ratio, we see that the average is consistently higher than the median, reflecting the fact that PE ratios can be very high numbers but cannot be less than zero. This asymmetry in the distributions is captured in the skewness values. The current PE ratios are also higher than the trailing PE ratios, which, in turn, are higher than the forward PE ratios. This reflects the fact that earnings grew at a healthy rate during the period of our analysis.

Technology Stocks. Technology stocks generally have higher price-earnings ratios than other firms in the market. This is evident from Figure 9–2, which provides the distribution of PE ratios for technology stocks in the United States in July 2000.

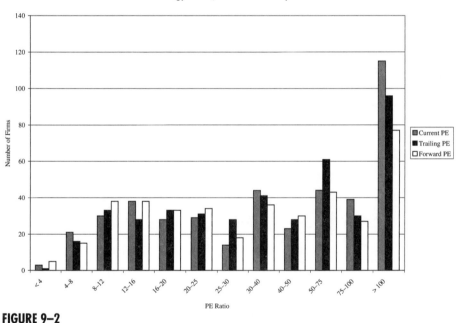

Technology Stocks, United States: July 2000

FIGURE 9–2
Current, Trailing, and Forward PE Ratios

Table 9.2 summarizes statistics on PE ratios for technology stocks, with the PE ratios capped at 200.

As in Table 9.1, the current PE ratio is lower than the trailing PE, which is lower than the forward PE. Illustrating the impact of outliers on the distribution, not capping the PE ratios at 200 would have yielded an average current PE ratio of 199, an average trailing PE of 190.84, and an average forward PE of 120.52. The PE ratios for technology stocks are also consistently higher than the PE ratios for the rest of the market.

TABLE 9.2 Summary Statistics: PE Ratios for U.S. Technology Stocks

	CURRENT PE	TRAILING PE	FORWARD PE
Mean	72.05	66.41	60.61
Standard deviation	67.14	62.56	62.06
Median	43.24	40.45	32.56
Mode	83.00	109.00	7.50
10th percentile	10.68	11.08	10.71
90th percentile	200.00	200.00	200.00
Skewness	7.99	11.49	19.59

The contrast between the PE ratios of technology stocks and other stocks is clear when you look at the percent of stocks that fall into each PE ratio class for the two groups in Figure 9–3.

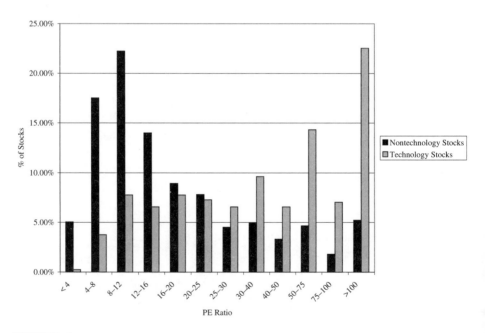

FIGURE 9–3
Trailing PE: Technology versus Nontechnology Stocks

A much higher proportion of technology stocks have PE ratios greater than 100 than do nontechnology stocks. In general, the distribution of PE ratios is skewed upward for technology stocks.

One final point should be made about the PE ratio, and that relates to the number of firms that had negative earnings and no meaningful PE ratios. A far greater proportion of technology stocks fell into this category than stocks in other sectors. Table 9.3 summarizes the statistics on the number of stocks in each group that had negative earnings and lists the biases introduced into the statistics as a result.

TABLE 9.3 Negative Earnings Companies

	TECHNOLOGY STOCKS	NONTECHNOLOGY STOCKS
Number of firms in sample	1103	4800
Number of firms with negative earnings	677	1456
% of firms with negative earnings	61.38%	30.33%
Average trailing PE	190.84	35.01
Market capitalization/earnings	263.45	39.06

If you average the PE ratio only across firms where the PE ratio can be estimated, you obtain an estimate of 190.84 for technology firms and 35.01 for nontechnology firms. If you divide the market capitalization of all firms in the group by the collective net income of these firms (including those with negative earnings), then the estimate of the PE ratio shifts upward. The shift is much larger for technology stocks.

 pedata.xls: A dataset on the Web summarizes price-earnings ratios and fundamentals, by industry group, in the United States for the most recent year.

DETERMINANTS OF THE PE RATIO

In Chapter 8, the fundamentals that determine multiples were extracted with a discounted cash flow model—an equity model like the dividend discount model for equity multiples and a firm value model for firm multiples. The price-earnings ratio, being an equity multiple, can be analyzed with an equity valuation model. In this section, the fundamentals that determine the price earnings ratio for a high-growth firm are analyzed.

A Discounted Cash Flow Model Perspective on PE Ratios. In Chapter 8, we derived the PE ratio for a stable growth firm from the stable-growth dividend discount model:

$$\frac{P_0}{EPS_0} = PE = \frac{Payout \ Ratio \times (1 + g_n)}{k_e - g_n}$$

If the PE ratio is stated in terms of expected earnings in the next time period, it can be simplified to:

$$\frac{P_0}{EPS_1} = Foreward \ PE = \frac{Payout \ Ratio}{k_e - g_n}$$

The PE ratio is an increasing function of the payout ratio and the growth rate, and a decreasing function of the riskiness of the firm.

The price-earnings ratio for a high-growth firm can also be related to fundamentals. In the special case of the two-stage dividend discount model, this relationship can be made explicit fairly simply. When a firm is expected to be in high growth for the next n years and stable growth thereafter, the dividend discount model can be written as follows:

$$P_0 = \frac{EPS_0 \times Payout\ Ratio \times (1+g) \times \left[1 - \frac{(1+g)^n}{(1+k_{e,hg})^n}\right]}{k_{e,hg} - g}$$

$$+ \frac{EPS_0 \times Payout\ Ratio_n \times (1+g)^n \times (1+g_n)}{(k_{e,st} - g_n)(1+k_{e,hg})^n}$$

where

EPS_0 = Earnings per share in year 0 (current year)
g = Growth rate in the first n years
$k_{e,hg}$ = Cost of equity in high-growth period
$k_{e,st}$ = Cost of equity in stable-growth period
Payout = Payout ratio in the first n years
g_n = Growth rate after n years forever (stable-growth rate)
$Payout_n$ = Payout ratio after n years for the stable firm

Bringing EPS_0 to the left side of the equation:

$$\frac{P_0}{EPS_0} = \frac{Payout\ Ratio \times (1+g) \times \left[1 - \frac{(1+g)^n}{(1+k_{e,hg})^n}\right]}{k_{e,hg} - g}$$

$$+ \frac{Payout\ Ratio_n \times (1+g)^n \times (1+g_n)}{(k_{e,st} - g_n)(1+k_{e,hg})^n}$$

The left side of the equation is the price-earnings ratio. It is determined by three factors:

a. *Payout ratio during the high-growth period and in the stable period:* The PE ratio increases as the payout ratio increases.

b. *Riskiness (through the discount rate r):* The PE ratio becomes lower as riskiness increases.

c. *Expected growth rate in earnings, in both the high-growth and stable phases:* In either period, the PE increases as the growth rate increases.

This formula is general enough to be applied to any firm, even one that is not paying dividends right now. In fact, the ratio of FCFE to earnings can be substituted for the payout ratio for firms that pay significantly less in dividends than they can afford to.

ILLUSTRATION 9.1

Estimating the PE Ratio for a High-Growth Firm in the Two-Stage Model

Assume that you have been asked to estimate the PE ratio for a firm that has the following characteristics:

Growth rate in first five years = 25%   Payout ratio in first five years = 20%
Growth rate after five years = 8%   Payout ratio after five years = 50%
Beta = 1.0   Risk-free rate = T-bond rate = 6%
Risk premium = 5.5%
Required rate of return[2] = 6% + 1(5.5%) = 11.5%

$$
PE = \frac{0.2 \times (1.25) \times \left[1 - \frac{(1.25)^5}{(1.115)^5}\right]}{(0.115 - 0.25)} + \frac{0.5 \times (1.25)^5 \times (1.08)}{(0.115 - 0.08)(1.115)^5} = 28.75
$$

The estimated PE ratio for this firm is 28.75.

ILLUSTRATION 9.2

Estimating a Fundamental PE Ratio for Motorola

The following is an estimation of the appropriate PE ratio for Motorola in July 2000. The assumptions on the growth period, growth rate, and cost of equity are identical to those used in the discounted cash flow valuation of Motorola in Chapter 6, "Estimating Firm Value." The assumptions are summarized in Table 9.4.

TABLE 9.4 Values for Estimation of PE Ratio

	HIGH-GROWTH PERIOD	STABLE GROWTH
Length	5 years	Forever after year 5
Cost of equity	10.85%	10.00%
Expected growth rate	13.63%	5%
Payout ratio	36.00%	66.67%

The current payout ratio of 36% is used for the entire high-growth period. After year five, the estimated payout ratio is based on the expected growth rate of 5% and a return on equity of 15% (based on industry averages):

Stable Period Payout Ratio = 1– Growth Rate / Return on Equity = 1– 5% / 15% = 66.67%

We base our estimate of the price-earnings ratio on these inputs:

$$PE = \frac{0.36 \times (1.1363) \times \left[1 - \frac{(1.1363)^5}{(1.1085)^5}\right]}{(0.1085 - 0.1363)}$$

$$+ \frac{0.6667 \times (1.1363)^5 \times (1.05)}{(0.10 - 0.05)(1.1085)^5} = 17.79$$

Based on its fundamentals, you would expect Motorola to be trading at 17.79 times earnings.

PE Ratios and Expected Extraordinary Growth. The PE ratio of a high-growth firm is a function of the expected extraordinary growth rate: the higher the expected growth, the higher the PE ratio for a firm. In Illustration 9.1, for instance, the PE ratio that was estimated to be 28.75, with a growth rate of 25%, will change as that expected growth rate changes. Figure 9–4 graphs the PE ratio as a function of the extraordinary growth rate during the high-growth period.

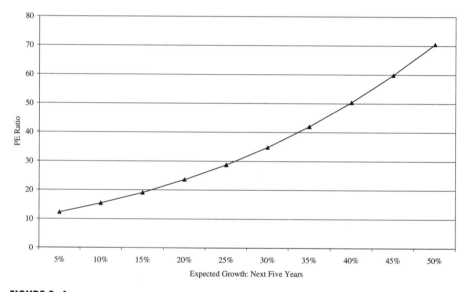

FIGURE 9–4
PE Ratios and Expected Growth

As the firm's expected growth rate in the first five years declines from 25% to 5%, the PE ratio for the firm also decreases from 28.75 to just above 10.

The effect of changes in the expected growth rate varies with the level of interest rates. In Figure 9–5, the PE ratios are estimated for different expected growth rates at four levels of riskless rates: 4%, 6%, 8%, and 10%.

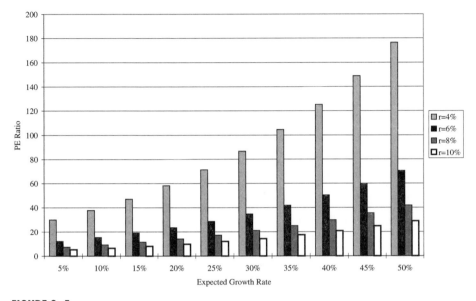

FIGURE 9–5
PE Ratios and Expected Growth: Interest Rate Scenarios

The PE ratio is much more sensitive to changes in expected growth rates when interest rates are low than when they are high. The reason is simple. Growth produces cash flows in the future, and the present value of these cash flows is much smaller at high interest rates. Consequently, the effect of changes in the growth rate on the present value tends to be smaller.

There is a possible link between this finding and how markets react to earnings surprises from technology firms. When a firm reports earnings that are significantly higher than expected (a positive surprise) or lower than expected (a negative surprise), investors' perceptions of the expected growth rate for this firm can change concurrently, leading to a price effect. You would expect to see much greater price reactions for a given earnings surprise, positive or negative, in a low-interest rate environment than you would in a high-interest rate environment.

PE Ratios and Risk. The PE ratio is a function of the perceived risk of a firm, and the effect shows up in the cost of equity. A firm with a higher cost of equity will trade at a lower multiple of earnings than a similar firm with a lower cost of equity.

Again, the effect of higher risk on PE ratios can be seen from the firm in Illustration 9.1. Recall that the firm, which has an expected growth rate of 25% for the next 5 years and 8% thereafter, has an estimated PE ratio of 28.75 if its beta is assumed to be 1.

$$PE = \frac{0.2 \times (1.25) \times \left[1 - \frac{(1.25)^5}{(1.115)^5}\right]}{(0.115 - 0.25)} + \frac{0.5 \times (1.25)^5 \times (1.08)}{(0.115 - 0.08)(1.115)^5} = 28.75$$

If you assume that the beta is 1.5, the cost of equity increases to 14.25%, leading to a PE ratio of 14.87:

$$PE = \frac{0.2 \times (1.25) \times \left[1 - \frac{(1.25)^5}{(1.1425)^5}\right]}{(0.1425 - 0.25)} + \frac{0.5 \times (1.25)^5 \times (1.08)}{(0.1425 - 0.08)(1.1425)^5} = 14.87$$

The higher cost of equity reduces the value created by expected growth.

In Figure 9–6, you can see the impact of changing the beta on the price-earnings ratio for four high-growth scenarios: 8%, 15%, 20%, and 25% for the next five years.

As the beta increases, the PE ratio decreases in all four scenarios. However, the difference between the PE ratios across the four growth classes is lower when the beta is very high and increases as the beta decreases. This would suggest that at very high risk levels, a firm's PE ratio is likely to increase more as the risk decreases than as growth increases. For many technology firms that are viewed as both very risky and having good growth potential, reducing risk may increase value much more than increasing expected growth.

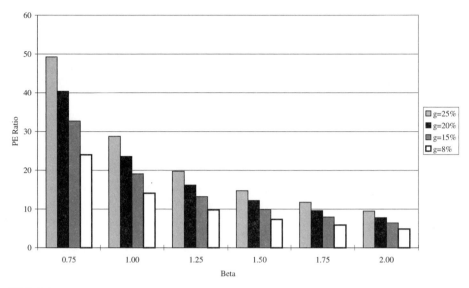

FIGURE 9–6
PE Ratios and Beta: Growth Rate Scenarios

 eqmult.xls: This spreadsheet enables you to estimate the price earnings ratio for a stable-growth or high-growth firm, given its fundamentals.

USING THE PE RATIO FOR COMPARISONS

Now that you have defined the PE ratio, looked at the cross-sectional distribution, and examined the fundamentals that determine the multiple, we can use PE ratios to make valuation judgments. In this section, we first use PE ratios to analyze firms within a sector, then expand the analysis to the entire market. In doing so, note that PE ratios vary across industries and across firms because of differences in fundamentals; higher growth, lower risk, and higher payout generally result in higher PE ratios. When comparisons are made across firms, you must control for these differences in risk, growth rates, and payout ratios.

Comparable Firms: Firms in the Same Business. The most common approach to estimating the PE ratio for a firm is to choose a group of comparable firms, to calculate the average PE ratio for this group, and to subjectively adjust this average for differences between the firm being valued and the comparable firms. This approach has several problems.

First, the definition of a "comparable" firm is essentially subjective. The use of other firms in the industry as the control group is often not the solution because firms within the same industry can have very different business mixes and risk and growth profiles. There is also plenty of potential for bias. One clear example of this is takeovers, where a high PE ratio for the target firm is justified by the price-earnings ratios of a control group of other firms that have been taken over. This group is designed to give an upward-biased estimate of the PE ratio and other multiples.

Second, even when a legitimate group of comparable firms can be constructed, differences will continue to persist in fundamentals between the firm being valued and this group. It is very difficult to subjectively adjust for differences across firms. Thus, knowing that a firm has much higher growth potential than other firms in the comparable firm list would lead you to estimate a higher PE ratio for that firm, but how much higher is an open question.

The alternative to subjective adjustments is to control explicitly for the one or two variables that you believe account for the bulk of the differences in PE ratios across companies in the sector in a regression. The regression equation can then be used to estimate predicted PE ratios for each firm in the sector, and these predicted values can be compared to the actual PE ratios to enable judgments to be made on whether stocks are under- or overpriced.

ILLUSTRATION 9.3

Estimating a PE Ratio for Cisco, Using Comparable Firms

Table 9.5 summarizes the trailing PE ratios for Cisco and a few of its comparable firms in June 2000, as well as measures of expected growth in earnings per share over the next five years (from analyst estimates) and the betas of the stocks.

TABLE 9.5 Trailing PE Ratios for Cisco and Comparable Firms

COMPANY NAME	PE	BETA	PROJECTED GROWTH (%)
3Com Corp.	37.20	1.35	11.00
ADC Telecom.	78.17	1.40	24.00
Alcatel ADR	51.50	0.90	24.00
Ciena Corp.	94.51	1.70	27.50
Cisco	133.76	1.43	35.20
Comverse Technology	70.42	1.45	28.88
E-TEK Dynamics	295.56	1.55	55.00
JDS Uniphase	296.28	1.60	65.00
Lucent Technologies	54.28	1.30	24.00
Nortel Networks	104.18	1.40	25.50
Tellabs, Inc.	52.57	1.75	22.00
Average	*115.31*	*1.44*	*31.00*

With a simple comparison, Cisco with a PE ratio of 133.76 could be viewed as overvalued, since the average for the sample is lower at 115.31. However, Cisco does have a higher growth rate than the average firm and should trade at higher multiple of earnings than the average firm in the group, but how much higher?

Regressing the PE ratio for the sector against the expected growth rate yields the following results:

PE Ratio = −64.85 + 579.34 (Expected Growth rate) $R^2 = 92.3\%$

Plugging in Cisco's expected growth rate of 35.2% in this regression yields a predicted PE ratio of:

Predicted PE Ratio = −64.85 + 579.34 (.352) = 139.08

At 133.76 times earnings, Cisco would be viewed as slightly undervalued.

Expanding the Comparable Firm List. In the last section, we narrowly defined comparable firms to be other firms in the same business. In this section, we consider ways in which to expand the number of comparable firms by looking at an entire sector or even the market. There are two advantages to this scrutiny. The first is that the estimates may become more precise as the number of comparable firms increases. The second is that you can pinpoint when firms in a small subgroup (say, e-tailers) are being under- or overvalued relative to the rest of the sector or the market. Since the differences across firms will increase when you loosen the definition of comparable firms, you have to adjust for these differences. The simplest way of adjusting is with a multiple regression, with the PE ratio as the dependent variable and proxies for risk, growth, and payout as the independent variables.

Past Studies

One of the earliest regressions of PE ratios against fundamentals across the entire market was done by Kisor and Whitbeck in 1963. Using data from the Bank of New York for 135 stocks as of June 1962, they arrived at the following regression:

P/E = 8.2 + 1.5 (Growth Rate in Earnings) + 6.7 (Payout Ratio)
   − 0.2 (Standard Deviation in EPS Changes)

Malkiel and Cragg followed up by estimating the coefficients for a regression of the price-earnings ratio on the growth rate, the payout ratio, and the beta for stocks for the time period from 1961 to 1965, as shown in Table 9.6.

TABLE 9.6 Regression Coefficients for U.S. Stocks from 1961–1965

Year	Equation	R^2
1961	P/E = 4.73 + 3.28 g + 2.05 π – 0.85 β	0.70
1962	P/E = 11.06 + 1.75 g + 0.78 π – 1.61 β	0.70
1963	P/E = 2.94 + 2.55 g + 7.62 π – 0.27 β	0.75
1964	P/E = 6.71 + 2.05 g + 5.23 π – 0.89 β	0.75
1965	P/E = 0.96 + 2.74 g + 5.01 π – 0.35 β	0.85

where

P/E = Price/earnings ratio at the start of the year
g = Growth rate in earnings
p = Earnings payout ratio at the start of the year
β = Beta of the stock

Malkiel and Cragg concluded that while such models were useful in explaining PE ratios, they were of little use in predicting performance. In both these studies, the three variables used—payout, risk, and growth—represent the three variables that were identified as the determinants of PE ratios in an earlier section.

The regressions were updated from 1987 to 1991 in Damodaran (1994), using a much broader sample of stocks.[3] The results are summarized in Table 9.7.

TABLE 9.7 Regression Coefficients for U.S. Stocks from 1987–1991

Year	Regression	R^2
1987	PE = 7.1839 + 13.05 Payout – 0.6259 Beta + 6.5659 EGR	0.9287
1988	PE = 2.5848 + 29.91 Payout – 4.5157 Beta + 19.9143 EGR	0.9465
1989	PE = 4.6122 + 59.74 Payout – 0.7546 Beta + 9.0072 EGR	0.5613
1990	PE = 3.5955 + 10.88 Payout – 0.2801 Beta + 5.4573 EGR	0.3497
1991	PE = 2.7711 + 22.89 Payout – 0.1326 Beta + 13.8653 EGR	0.3217

Note the volatility in the R^2 over time and the changes in the coefficients on the independent variables. For instance, the R^2 in the regressions reported above declines from 93% in 1987 to 32% in 1991, and the coefficients change dramatically over time. Part of the reason for these shifts is that earnings are volatile, and price-earnings ratios reflect this volatility. The low R^2 for the 1991 regression can be ascribed to the recession's effects on earnings in that year. These regressions are clearly not stable, and the predicted values are likely to be noisy.

Updated Market Regressions

The data needed to run market regressions is much more easily available today than it was for these earlier studies. In this section, the results of two regressions are presented. In the first regression, the trailing PE ratios of stocks in the technology sector are regressed against payout ratios, betas, and expected growth for these stocks in July 2000:[4]

PE = –29.28 + 210.69 (Expected Growth Rate) + 26.99 (Beta) – 20.41 (Payout Ratio)
     (2.19)   (8.82)   (2.46)   (–0.43)

$R^2 = 30.7\%$ *Number of Observations = 251*

The betas were estimated from five years of weekly returns, from July 1996 to June 2000. The payout ratios were based on dividends paid and earnings reported over the most recent four quarters, and the expected growth rate represents the consensus estimate of growth on the part of analysts following these stocks. This regression, with 251 firms, represents a significant expansion in terms of the number of firms over the regressions that were based on narrower definitions of comparable firms.

In the second regression, the PE ratio was regressed against payout ratios, betas, and expected growth for all firms in the market:

PE = –17.22 + 155.65 (Expected Growth Rate) + 16.44 (Beta) + 10.93 (Payout Ratio)
     (7.06)   (6.42)   (6.77)   (5.02)

$R^2 = 24.9\%$ *Number of Observations = 2498*

With the sample size expanding to about 2,500 firms, this regression represents the broadest measure of relative value.

Both regressions have low R^2 values, but it is more a reflection of the noise in PE ratios than it is of the regression methodology. As you will see, the market regressions for price-to-sales ratios tend to be better behaved and have higher R^2 values than do PE ratio regressions. The other disquieting finding is that the coefficients on the variables do not always have the signs you would expect them to have. For instance, higher-risk stocks (higher betas) have higher PE ratios, when fundamentals would lead you to expect the opposite.

Problems with the Regression Methodology

The regression methodology is a convenient way of compressing large amounts of data into one equation, capturing the relationship between PE ratios and financial fundamentals. But it does have its limitations. First, the independent variables are correlated with each other.[5] For example, high-growth firms tend to have high risk and low payout ratios, as is clear from Table 9.8, which summarizes the correlation between beta, growth, and payout ratios for all U.S. firms.

TABLE 9.8 Correlations between Independent Variables

	PE	GROWTH	BETA	PAYOUT RATIO
PE	1.000			
Growth rate	0.288	1.000		
Beta	0.141	0.292*	1.000	
Payout ratio	–0.087	–0.404*	–0.183*	1.000

* Significant at 1% level

Note the negative correlation between payout ratios and growth, and the positive correlation between beta and growth. This "multi-collinearity" makes the coefficients of the regressions unreliable and may explain the wrong signs on the coefficients and the large changes in these coefficients from period to period. Second, the regression is based on a linear relationship between PE ratios and the fundamentals, and that linearity might not be appropriate. An analysis of the residuals from a regression may suggest transformations of the independent variables (squared, natural logs) that work better in explaining PE ratios. Third, the basic relationship between PE ratios and financial variables itself might not be stable, and if it shifts from year to year, the predictions from the regression equation may not be reliable for extended periods. For all these reasons, the regression approach is useful, but we would view it as only one more tool in the search for true value.

ILLUSTRATION 9.4

Valuing Motorola, Using Broader Regressions

To value Motorola using the broader regressions, we first estimate the values, for Motorola, of the independent variables in the regression:

Motorola's beta = 1.21
Motorola's payout ratio = 35.62%
Motorola's expected growth rate = 13.63%

Note that these variables have been defined consistently with the variables in the regression. Thus, the growth rate over the next five years, the beta over the last five years, and the payout ratio over the most recent four quarters are used to make the prediction. Based on the price-earnings ratio regression for technology stocks reported above, we compute a predicted PE ratio:

$$
\begin{aligned}
\text{Predicted PE}_{Sector} &= -29.28 + 210.69 \text{ (Growth)} + 26.99 \text{ (Beta)} - 20.41 \text{ (Payout)} \\
&= -29.28 + 210.69 \text{ (.1363)} + 26.99 \text{ (1.21)} - 20.41 \text{ (.3563)} \\
&= 24.83
\end{aligned}
$$

Based on the sector regression, you would expect Motorola to be trading at 24.83 times earnings.

Based on the price-earnings ratio regression for all stocks in the market, we compute a predicted PE ratio of:

$$\text{Predicted PE}_{Mkt} = -17.22 + 155.65 \text{ (Growth)} + 16.44 \text{ (Beta)} + 10.93 \text{ (Payout)}$$
$$= -17.22 + 155.65 \text{ (.1363)} + 16.44 \text{ (1.21)} + 10.93 \text{ (.3563)}$$
$$= 27.78$$

Based on the market regression, you would expect Motorola to be trading at 27.78 times earnings, which is slightly higher than the predicted value you would obtain using just technology stocks.

 pereg.htm: This Web site reports the results of the latest regression of PE ratios against fundamentals, using all firms in the market.

THE PEG RATIO

Portfolio managers and analysts sometimes compare PE ratios to the expected growth rate to identify undervalued and overvalued stocks. In the simplest form of this approach, firms with PE ratios less than their expected growth rate are viewed as undervalued. In its more general form, the ratio of PE to growth is used as a measure of relative value, with a lower value believed to indicate that a firm is undervalued. For many analysts, especially those tracking firms in high-growth sectors, these approaches offer the promise of controlling for differences in growth across firms while preserving the inherent simplicity of a multiple.

DEFINITION OF THE PEG RATIO

The PEG ratio is defined to be the price-earnings ratio divided by the expected growth rate in earnings per share:

PEG Ratio = PE Ratio / Expected Growth Rate

For instance, a firm with a PE ratio of 20 and a growth rate of 10% is estimated to have a PEG ratio of 2. Consistency requires that the growth rate used in this estimate be the growth rate in earnings per share, rather than operating income, because this is an equity multiple.

Given the many definitions of the PE ratio, which one should you use to estimate the PEG ratio? The answer depends on the base on which the expected growth rate is computed. If the expected growth rate in earnings per share is based on earnings in the most recent year (current earnings), the PE ratio that should be used is the current PE ratio. If it is based on trailing earnings, the PE ratio used should be the trailing PE ratio. The forward PE ratio should never be used in this computation since it may result in a double-counting of growth. To see why, assume that you have a firm with a current price of $30 and current earnings per share of $1.50. The firm is expected to double its earnings per share over the next year (forward earnings per share will be $3.00) and then have an earnings growth of 5% a year for the following four years. An analyst estimating growth in earnings per share for this firm, with the current earnings per share as a base, will estimate a growth rate of 19.44%:

Expected Earnings Growth
$$= [(1 + \text{Growth Rate}_{yr}\,1)(1 + \text{Growth Rate}_{yrs\,2-5})]^{1/5} - 1$$
$$= (2.00\,(1.05)^4)^{1/5} - 1 = 0.1944$$

If you used the forward PE ratio and this estimate of earnings growth to estimate the PEG ratio, you would compute:

PEG Ratio Based on Forward PE
$$= \text{Forward PE} / \text{Expected Growth}_{\text{next 5 years}}$$
$$= (\text{Price} / \text{Forward EPS}) / \text{Expected Growth}_{\text{next 5 years}}$$
$$= (\$30 / \$3) / 19.44 = 0.51$$

Judged by the PEG ratio, this firm seems to be cheap. Note, however, that the growth in the first year has been counted twice—the forward earnings are high because of the doubling of earnings, leading to a low forward PE ratio, and the growth rate is high for the same reason. A consistent estimate of the PEG ratio would require using a current PE and the expected growth rate over the next five years:

PEG Ratio Based on Current PE

= (Price / Current EPS) / Expected Growth Rate$_{\text{next 5 years}}$

= ($30 / $1.50) / 19.44 = 1.03

Alternatively, you could compute the PEG ratio based on forward earnings per share and the growth rate from years two through five:

PEG Ratio Based on Forward PE

= (Price / Forward EPS) / Expected Growth$_{\text{yrs 2-5}}$

= ($30 / $3) / 5 = 2.0

If you use this approach, you must estimate the PEG ratio uniformly for all of the other comparable firms as well, using the forward PE and the expected growth rate from years two through five.

Building on the theme of uniformity, you estimate the PEG ratio by using the same growth estimates for all firms in the sample. You should not, for instance, use five-year growth rates for some firms and one-year growth rates for others. One way of ensuring uniformity is to use the same source for earnings growth estimates for all the firms in the group. For instance, I/B/E/S and Zacks both provide consensus estimates from analysts of earnings per share growth over the next five years for most U.S. firms.

CROSS-SECTIONAL DISTRIBUTION OF THE PEG RATIO

Now that the PEG ratio has been defined, the cross sectional distribution of PEG ratios across all U.S. firms is illustrated in Figure 9–7.

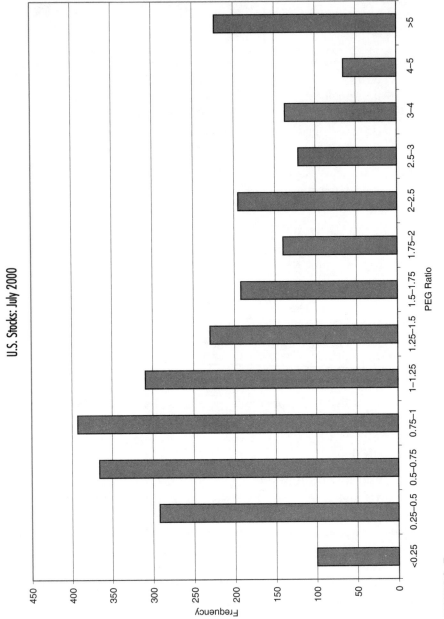

FIGURE 9–7
PEG Ratios

For estimation of these PEG ratios, the analyst estimates of growth in earnings per share over the next five years is used in conjunction with the current PE. Any firm, therefore, that has negative earnings per share or lacks an analyst estimate of expected growth is dropped from the sample. This may be a source of bias, since larger and more liquid firms are more likely to be followed by analysts.

Figure 9–8 contains the distribution of PEG ratios for technology stocks, using analyst estimates of growth again to arrive at the PEG ratios.

Note that of the 448 firms for which PE ratios were estimated, only 335 have PEG ratios available; the 113 firms for which analyst estimates of growth were not available have been dropped from the sample.

Finally, Table 9.9 includes the summary statistics for PEG ratios for technology stocks and nontechnology stocks.[6]

TABLE 9.9 PEG Ratios: Technology versus Nontechnology Stocks

	TECHNOLOGY STOCKS	NONTECHNOLOGY STOCKS	ALL STOCKS
Mean	5.83	2.99	3.31
Standard error	1.03	0.36	0.34
Median	2.03	1.13	1.18
Standard deviation	18.05	17.68	17.74
Skewness	7.81	22.09	20.33
Range	198.62	569.73	569.73
Minimum	0.08	0.00	0.00
Maximum	198.70	569.73	569.73
Number of firms	309	2454	2763

As with the PE ratio, the average PEG ratio for technology stocks is much higher than the average PEG ratio for nontechnology stocks. In addition, the average is much higher than the median for both groups.

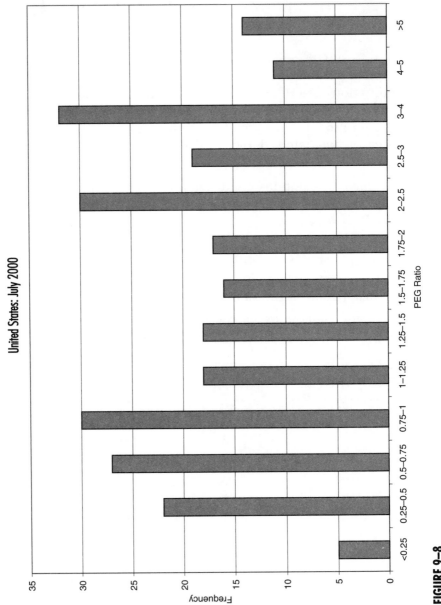

FIGURE 9–8
PEG Ratios for Technology Stocks

pedata.xls: This dataset summarizes the PEG ratios, by industry, for firms in the United States.

DETERMINANTS OF THE PEG RATIO

The determinants of the PEG ratio can be extracted by the same method used to estimate the determinants of the PE ratio. The value per share in a two-stage dividend discount model can be written as:

$$P_0 = \frac{EPS_0 \times Payout\ Ratio \times (1+g) \times \left[1 - \dfrac{(1+g)^n}{(1+k_{e,hg})^n}\right]}{k_{e,hg} - g}$$

$$+ \frac{EPS_0 \times Payout\ Ratio_n \times (1+g)^n \times (1+g_n)}{(k_{e,st} - g_n)(1+k_{e,hg})^n}$$

By first dividing both sides of the equation by the earnings per share (EPS_0) and then dividing that result by the expected growth rate over the high-growth period (g), you can estimate the PEG ratio:

$$PEG = \frac{Payout\ Ratio \times (1+g) \times \left[1 - \dfrac{(1+g)^n}{(1+k_{e,hg})^n}\right]}{g(k_{e,hg} - g)}$$

$$+ \frac{Payout\ Ratio_n \times (1+g)^n \times (1+g_n)}{g(k_{e,st} - g_n)(1+k_{e,hg})^n}$$

Even a cursory glance at this equation suggests that analysts who believe that using the PEG ratio neutralizes the growth effect are mistaken. Instead of disappearing, the growth rate becomes even more deeply entangled in the multiple. In fact, as the growth rate increases, there are both positive and negative effects on the PEG ratio and the net effect can vary according to the level of the growth rate.

ILLUSTRATION 9.5

Estimating the PEG Ratio for a Firm

Assume that you have been asked to estimate the PEG ratio for a firm that has the same characteristics as the firm described in Illustration 9.1, that is:

Growth rate in first five years = 25%   Payout ratio in first five years = 20%
Growth rate after five years = 8%   Payout ratio after five years = 50%
Beta = 1.0   Risk-free rate = T-bond rate = 6%
Risk premium = 5.5%
Required rate of return = 6% + 1(5.5%) = 11.5%

The PEG ratio can be estimated as follows:

$$PEG = \frac{0.2 \times (1.25) \times \left[1 - \frac{(1.25)^5}{(1.115)^5} \right]}{0.25(0.115 - 0.25)} + \frac{0.5 \times (1.25)^5 \times (1.08)}{0.25(0.115 - 0.08)(1.115)^5} = 1.15$$

The PEG ratio for this firm, based on fundamentals, is 1.15.

Exploring the Relationship with Fundamentals. Consider first the effect of changing the growth rate during the high-growth period (next five years) from 25%. Figure 9–9 presents the PEG ratio as a function of the expected growth rate.

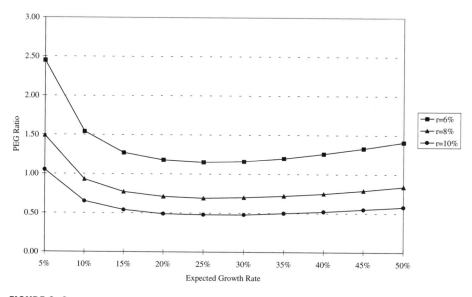

FIGURE 9–9
PEG Ratios, Expected Growth, and Interest Rates

As the growth rate increases, the PEG ratio initially decreases but then starts increasing again. Firms with very low and very high growth rates have high PEG ratios. This U-shaped relationship between PEG ratios and growth suggests that comparing PEG ratios across firms with widely different growth rates can be complicated.

Next, consider the effect of changing the riskiness (beta) of this firm on the PEG ratio. Figure 9–10 presents the PEG ratio as a function of the beta.

Here, the relationship is clear. As the risk increases, the PEG ratio of a firm decreases. When comparing the PEG ratios of firms with different risk levels, even within the same sector, you can infer that riskier firms should have lower PEG ratios than safer firms.

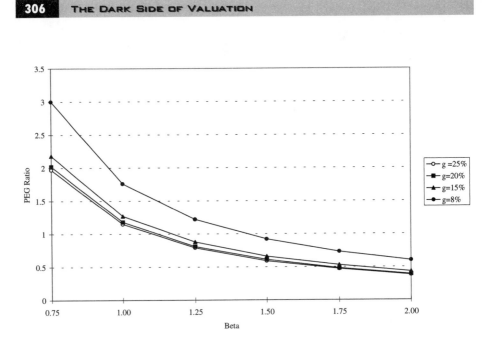

FIGURE 9–10
PEG Ratios and Beta: Different Growth Rates

Finally, not all growth is created equal. A firm that is able to grow at 20% a year while paying out 50% of its earnings to stockholders has higher-quality growth than that of another firm with the same growth rate that reinvests all of its earnings. Thus, the PEG ratio should increase as the payout ratio increases, for any given growth rate, as is evidenced in Figure 9–11.

The growth rate and the payout ratio are linked by the firm's return on equity. In fact, the expected growth rate of a firm can be written as:

Expected Growth Rate = Return on Equity (1 – Payout Ratio)

The PEG ratio should therefore be higher for firms with higher returns on equity for any given growth rate.

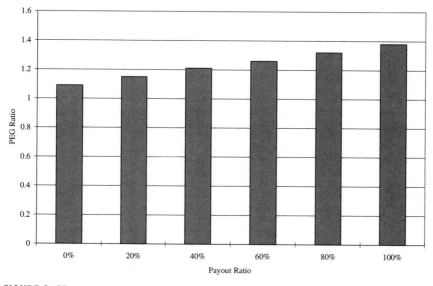

FIGURE 9–11
PEG Ratios and Payout Ratios

 eqmult.xls: This spreadsheet enables you to estimate the price earnings ratio for a stable-growth or high-growth firm, given its fundamentals.

USING THE PEG RATIO FOR COMPARISONS

As with the PE ratio, the PEG ratio is compared across firms that are in the same business. As noted in the last section, the PEG ratio is a function of the risk, growth potential, and the payout ratio of a firm. In this section, we look at ways of using the PEG ratio and examine some of the problems in comparing PEG ratios across firms.

Direct Comparisons. Most analysts who use PEG ratios compute them for firms within a business (or comparable firm group) and compare these ratios. Firms with lower PEG ratios are usually viewed as undervalued, even if growth rates are different across the firms being compared. This approach is based on the incorrect perception that PEG ratios control for differences in growth. In fact, direct comparisons of PEG ratios work only if firms are similar in terms of growth potential, risk, and payout ratios (or returns on equity). If this were the case, however, you could just as easily compare PE ratios across firms.

When PEG ratios are compared across firms with different risk, growth, and payout characteristics, and judgments are made about valuations based on this comparison, you will tend to find the following results ensue:

- Lower-growth firms will have higher PEG ratios and look more overvalued than higher-growth firms because PEG ratios tend to decrease as the growth rate decreases, at least initially (see Figure 9–9).
- Higher-risk firms will have lower PEG ratios and look more undervalued than lower-risk firms because PEG ratios tend to decrease as a firm's risk increases (see Figure 9–10).
- Firms with lower returns on equity (or lower payout ratios) will have lower PEG ratios and look more undervalued than firms with higher returns on equity and higher payout ratios (see Figure 9–11).

In short, firms that look undervalued upon direct comparison of the PEG ratios may, in fact, be firms with higher risk, higher growth, or lower returns on equity and may, in fact, be correctly valued.

Controlled Comparisons. When comparing PEG ratios across firms, then, it is important that you control for differences in risk, growth, and payout ratios when making the comparison. You can attempt to do this subjectively, but the complicated relationship between PEG ratios and these fundamentals can pose a challenge. A far more promising route is to use the regression approach suggested for PE ratios and to relate the PEG ratios of the firms being compared to measures of risk, growth potential, and the payout ratio.

As with the PE ratio, the comparable firms in this analysis can be defined narrowly (as other firms in the same business), more expansively (as firms in the same sector), or as all firms in the market. In running these regressions, all the caveats that were presented for the PE regression continue to apply. The independent variables continue to be correlated with each other, and the relationship is both unstable and likely to be nonlinear. In fact, Figure 9–12, which provides a scatter plot of PEG ratios against growth rates for all U.S. stocks in July 2000, indicates the degree of nonlinearity.

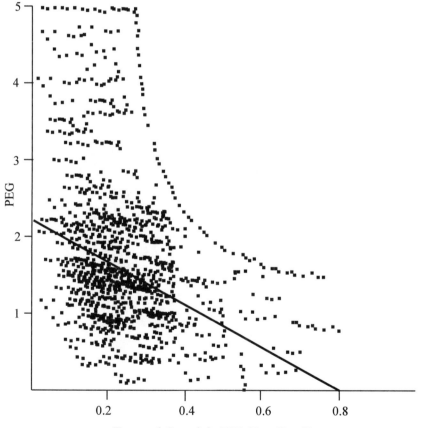

Expected Growth in EPS: Next Five Years

FIGURE 9–12
PEG Ratios versus Expected Growth Rates

In running the regression, especially when the sample contains firms with very different levels of growth, you should transform the growth rate to make the relationship more linear. Figure 9–13 shows that a scatter plot of PEG ratios against the natural log of the expected growth rate yields a much more linear relationship.

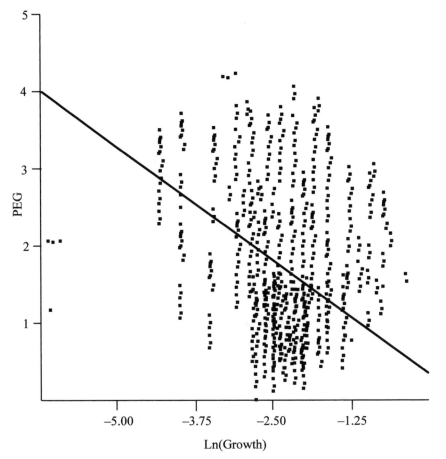

FIGURE 9–13
PEG Ratios versus Ln(Expected Growth Rate)

The results of the regression of PE ratios against ln(expected growth), beta, and payout ratio is reported below for the entire market and for technology stocks.

For the entire market:

PEG Ratio = –0.25 – 0.44 ln(Growth) + 0.95 (Beta) + 0.71 (Payout)
        (1.76) (10.40)   (9.66)   (7.95)
R^2 = 9.0%   *Number of Firms = 2594*

For technology stocks only:

PEG Ratio = 1.24 + 0.80 ln(Growth) + 2.45 (Beta) – 1.96 (Payout)
        (1.27) (2.20)   (4.15)   (0.73)
R^2 = 11.0%   *Number of Firms = 274*

The low R^2 is indicative of the problems with this multiple and the difficulties you will run into in using it for comparisons across firms.

ILLUSTRATION 9.6

Estimating and Using the PEG Ratio for Cisco

Table 9.10 summarizes the PEG ratios of the firms that are considered comparable to Cisco.

TABLE 9.10 PEG Ratios of Firms Comparable to Cisco

COMPANY NAME	PE	BETA	PROJECTED GROWTH (%)	PEG
3Com Corp.	37.20	1.35	11.00	3.38
ADC Telecom.	78.17	1.40	24.00	3.26
Alcatel ADR	51.50	0.90	24.00	2.15
Ciena Corp.	94.51	1.70	27.50	3.44
Cisco	133.76	1.43	35.20	3.80
Comverse Technology	70.42	1.45	28.88	2.44

(continued)

TABLE 9.10 *(Continued)*

COMPANY NAME	PE	BETA	PROJECTED GROWTH (%)	PEG
E-TEK Dynamics	295.56	1.55	55.00	5.37
JDS Uniphase	296.28	1.60	65.00	4.56
Lucent Technologies	54.28	1.30	24.00	2.26
Nortel Networks	104.18	1.40	25.50	4.09
Tellabs, Inc.	52.57	1.75	22.00	2.39
Average	*115.31*	*1.44*	*31.00*	*3.38*

Cisco, with a PEG ratio of 3.80, is trading at a higher PEG than the average for the sector, suggesting, at least on a preliminary basis, an overvalued stock. Regressing the PEG ratio against the ln(expected growth rate) in this sector yields:

PEG Ratio = 5.06 + 1.33 ln(Expected Growth Rate) $R^2 = 29.6\%$
         (6.46) (2.28)

For Cisco, with an expected growth rate of 35.20%, the predicted PEG ratio based on this regression is:

Predicted PEG Ratio = 5.06 + 1.35 ln(.352) = 3.68

Cisco's actual PEG ratio is very close to this predicted value.

You can also estimate the predicted PEG ratio for Cisco by using the broader regressions across the technology sector and the market, as reported in the last section:

Predicted PEG$_{Market}$ = −0.25 − 0.44 ln(.352) + 0.95 (1.43) + 0.71 (0) = 1.57
Predicted PEG$_{Technology}$ = 1.24 + 0.80 ln(.352) + 2.45 (1.43) − 1.96 (0) = 3.91

Cisco looks overvalued when compared with the rest of the market but is fairly valued when compared to just technology stocks.

pegreg.xls: This dataset summarizes the results of the most recent regression of PEG ratios against fundamentals for U.S. stocks.

OTHER EARNINGS MULTIPLES

While the PE ratio and the PEG ratio may be the most widely used earnings multiples, other earnings multiples are also used by analysts. In this section, we consider three variants. The first is a multiple of price to earnings in a future year (say five or ten years from now), the second is a multiple of price to earnings prior to R&D expenses, and the third is a multiple of value to EBITDA.

PRICE TO FUTURE EARNINGS

The price-earnings ratio cannot be estimated for firms with negative earnings per share. Since many younger technology firms, like Amazon, Ariba, and Rediff.com, are losing money, PE ratios cannot be estimated and used for these firms. Although other multiples such as the price-to-sales ratio can still be estimated for these firms, some analysts prefer the familiar ground of PE ratios. One way in which you can modify the price-earnings ratio for use in these firms is to use expected earnings per share in a future year in computing the PE ratio. For instance, assume that a firm has negative earnings per share currently of –$2.00 but is expected to report earnings per share in five years of $1.50 per share. You could divide the price today by the expected earnings per share in five years to obtain the PE ratio.

How would you use such a PE ratio? You would have to estimate the PE ratio for all of the comparable firms, using expected earnings per share in five years and compare the resulting values across firms. Assuming that all of the firms in the sample share the same risk, growth, and payout characteristics after year five, firms with low price-to-future-earnings ratios will be considered undervalued. An alternative approach is to estimate a target price for the negative earnings firm in five years by multiplying the forecasted earnings by an industry-average PE ratio, and discounting this price back to the present.

While this modified version of the PE ratio increases the reach of PE ratios to cover many firms that have negative earnings today, it is difficult to control for differences between the firm being valued and the comparable firms, since you are comparing firms at different points in time.

ILLUSTRATION 9.7

Analyzing Amazon, Using
Price to Future Earnings per Share

Amazon.com has negative earnings per share in the current year (2000). Based on consensus estimates, analysts expect it to lose $0.63 per share in 2001 but expect it to earn $1.50 per share in 2004. At its current price of $49 per share, this would translate into a price/future earnings per share of 32.67.

In the first approach, this multiple of earnings can be compared to the price/future earnings ratios of comparable firms. If you define comparable firms to be e-tailers, Amazon looks reasonably attractive since the average price/future earnings per share of e-tailers is 65.[7] If, on the other hand, you compared Amazon's price to future earnings per share to the average price to future earnings per share (in 2004) of specialty retailers, the picture is bleaker. The average price to future earnings for these firms is 12, which would lead to a conclusion that Amazon is overvalued. Implicit in both these comparisons is the assumption that in five years Amazon will have risk, growth, and cash flow characteristics similar to those of comparable firms. You could argue that Amazon will still have much higher growth potential than other specialty retailers after 2004 and that this could explain the difference in multiples. You could even use differences in expected growth after 2004 to adjust for the differences, but estimates of these growth rates are usually not made by analysts.

In the second approach, the current price-to-earnings ratio for specialty retailers, which is estimated to be 20.31, is compared to the earnings per share of Amazon in 2004 (which is estimated to be $1.50). This would yield a target price of $30.46. Discounting this price back to the present, using Amazon's cost of equity of 12.94%, results in a value per share:

$$\text{Value per Share} = \text{Target Price in Five Years} / (1 + \text{Cost of Equity})^5$$
$$= \$30.46 / 1.1294^5 = \$16.58$$

At its current price of $49, this result would again suggest an overvalued stock. Here again, though, you are assuming that Amazon in five years will resemble a specialty retailer today in terms of risk, growth, and cash flow characteristics.

The second approach can be modified to yield a more realistic PE ratio for the future by bringing in a regression estimate of PE that allows for differences in growth. For instance, regressing PE against expected growth for specialty retailers yields the following:

$$PE = 3.24 + 102.5(\text{Expected Growth in EPS}) \qquad R^2 = 29\%$$
$$(1.00) \ (6.79)$$

Assume that Amazon's expected growth rate, in earnings, beyond year five will be 30%. Plugging this value into the regression yields a predicted PE of:

$$PE = -3.24 + 102.5(0.30) = 27.51$$

Multiplying the forecasted EPS of $1.50 in five years by this PE results in a price per share of $41.26 in five years. Discounting back to the present at 12.94% gives us a value per share of $22.46.

PRICE TO EARNINGS BEFORE R&D EXPENSES

In the discussion of cash flows and capital expenditures in Chapter 4, "Cash Is King: Estimating Cash Flows," it was argued that research and development expenses should be capitalized since they represent investments for the future. Since accounting standards require that R&D be expensed rather than capitalized, the earnings of high-growth firms with substantial research expenses are likely to be understated, and the PE ratio is, therefore, likely to be overstated. This will especially be true if you are comparing technology firms, which have substantial research expenditures, to nontechnology firms, which usually do not. Even when you are comparing only across technology stocks, firms that are growing faster with larger R&D expenses will end up with lower earnings and higher PE ratios than more stable firms in the sector with lower R&D expenses. Some analysts argue that the PE ratio should be estimated with earnings prior to R&D expenses:

$PE_{\text{pre R\&D}}$ = Market Value of Equity / (Net Income + R&D Expenses)

The PE ratios that emerge from this calculation are likely to be much lower than the PE ratios obtained from conventional definitions of earnings per share.

While the underlying logic behind this approach is sound, adding back R&D to earnings represents only a partial adjustment. To complete the adjustment, you would need to capitalize R&D expenses and compute the amortization of R&D expenses, as was done in Chapter 4. The adjusted PE would then be:

$PE_{\text{R\&D Adjusted}}$ = Market Value of Equity
/ (Net Income + R&D Expenses – Amortization of R&D)

These adjusted PE ratios can then be computed across firms in the sample.

This adjustment to the PE ratio, while taking care of one problem—the expensing of R&D—will still leave you exposed to all of the other problems associated with PE ratios. Earnings will continue to be volatile and affected by accounting choices, and differences in growth, risk, and cash flow characteristics will still cause price-earnings ratios to be different across firms. In addition, you will also have to estimate expected growth in earnings (pre-R&D) on your own, since consensus estimates from analysts will not be available for this growth rate.

ENTERPRISE VALUE TO EBITDA

The enterprise value to EBITDA multiple relates the total market value of the firm, net of cash, to the earnings before interest, taxes, and depreciation of the firm:

EV / EBITDA
= (Market Value of Equity – Market Value of Debt – Cash) / EBITDA

Why is cash netted out of firm value for this calculation? Since the interest income from the cash is not counted as part of the EBITDA, not netting out the cash will result in an over-statement of the true value to EBITDA multiple. (The asset (cash) is added to value, but the income from the asset is excluded from the income measure (EBITDA).)

In the last two decades, this multiple has acquired a number of adherents among analysts, for a number of reasons. First, there are far fewer firms with negative EBITDA than there are firms with negative earnings per share, and thus fewer firms are lost from the analysis. Second, differences in depreciation methods across different companies—some might use straight line, while others use accelerated depreciation—can cause differences in operating income or net income but will not affect EBITDA. Third, this multiple can be compared far more easily across firms with different financial leverage—the numerator is firm value and the denominator is predebt earnings—than other earnings multiples. For all of these reasons, this multiple is particularly useful for firms in sectors that require large investments in infrastructure with long gestation periods. Good examples are cable firms in the 1980s and cellular firms in the 1990s.

The absence of debt and the low depreciation charges at technology firms result in value to EBITDA multiples that are very close to price to pre-tax equity earnings. To illustrate, the average PE ratio across technology stocks in July 2000 was 199.14, whereas the average value to EBITDA multiple was 185.17. In contrast, the average PE ratio for nontechnology stocks was 39.39, whereas the average value to EBITDA multiple was only 20.59. Consequently, far less is gained by the use of value-to-EBITDA in this sector.

SUMMARY

The price-earnings ratio and other earnings multiples, which are widely used in valuation, have the potential to be misused. These multiples are ultimately determined by the same fundamentals that determine the value of a firm in a discounted cash flow model: expected growth, risk, and cash flow potential. Firms with higher growth, lower risk, and higher payout ratios, other things remaining equal, should trade at much higher multiples of earnings than other firms. To the extent that there are differences in fundamentals across countries, across time, and across companies, the multiples will also be different. A failure to control for these differences in fundamentals can lead to erroneous conclusions if based solely on a direct comparison of multiples.

Earnings multiples can be used in valuation in several ways. One way is to compare earnings multiples across a narrowly defined group of comparable firms and to subjectively control for differences in growth, risk, and payout. Another is to expand the definition of a comparable firm to the entire sector (such as technology) or the market and to use statistical techniques to control for differences in fundamentals.

ENDNOTES

1. The mean and the standard deviation are the summary statistics that are most likely to be affected by these outliers.

2. For simplicity, the beta and cost of equity are estimated to be the same in both the high-growth and stable-growth periods. They could have been different.

3. These regressions look at all stocks listed on the COMPUSTAT database. The growth rate over the previous five years was used as the expected growth rate, and the betas were estimated from the CRSP tape.

4. The t statistics are reported in parentheses underneath the coefficients.

5. In a multiple regression, the independent variables should be independent of each other.

6. The PEG ratio is capped at 10.

7. The earnings per share in 2004 of e-tailers were obtained from consensus estimates of analysts following these firms, and the current price was divided by the expected earnings per share.

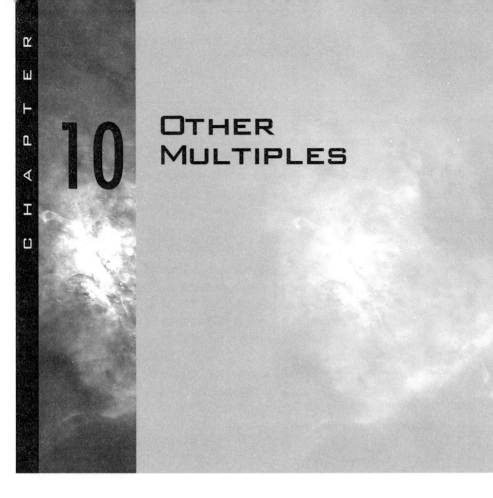

10

OTHER
MULTIPLES

While earnings multiples are intuitively appealing and widely used, analysts in recent years have increasing turned to alternative multiples to value companies. For new technology firms that have negative earnings, multiples of revenues have replaced multiples of earnings in many valuations. In addition, these firms are being valued on multiples of sector-specific measures such as the number of customers, subscribers, or even Web site visitors. In this chapter, we examine the reasons for the increased use of revenue multiples, then analyze the determinants of these multiples and look at how best to use them in valuation. Finally, we discuss the dangers of sector-specific multiples and the adjustments that might be needed to make them work.

REVENUE MULTIPLES

A revenue multiple measures the value of the equity or firm value of a business relative to the revenues that the business generates. As with other multiples, other things remaining equal, firms that trade at low multiples of revenues are viewed as cheap, relative to firms that trade at high multiples of revenues.

Revenue multiples have proved attractive to analysts for a number of reasons. First, unlike earnings and book value ratios, which can become negative for many firms and not meaningful, the revenue multiples are available even for the most troubled firms and for very young firms. Thus, the potential for bias created by eliminating firms in the sample is far lower. Second, unlike earnings and book value, which are heavily influenced by accounting decisions on depreciation, inventory, R&D, acquisition accounting, and extraordinary charges, revenue is relatively difficult to manipulate. Third, revenue multiples are not as volatile as earnings multiples and hence may be more reliable for use in valuation. For instance, the price-earnings ratio of a cyclical firm changes much more than its price-sales ratios because earnings are much more sensitive to economic changes than are revenues.

The biggest disadvantage of focusing on revenues is that doing so can lull you into assigning high values to firms that are generating high revenue growth while losing significant amounts of money. Ultimately, a firm has to generate earnings and cash flows in order to have value. While it is tempting to use price-sales multiples to value firms with negative earnings and book value, the failure to control for differences across firms in costs and profit margins can result in misleading valuations.

DEFINITION OF REVENUE MULTIPLE

As noted, two basic revenue multiples are in use. The first, and more popular one, is the multiple of the market value of equity to the revenues of a firm, termed the price-to-sales ratio. The second, and more robust, ratio is the multiple of the value of the firm (including both debt and equity) to revenues—this is the value-to-sales ratio.

$$\text{Price-to-Sales Ratio} = \frac{\text{Market Value of Equity}}{\text{Revenues}}$$

Enterprise Value-to-Sales Ratio =

$$\frac{(\text{Market Value of Equity} + \text{Market Value of Debt} - \text{Cash})}{\text{Revenues}}$$

Why is the value-to-sales ratio a more robust multiple than the price-to-sales ratio? Because it is internally consistent. It divides the total value of the firm by the revenues generated by that firm. The price-to-sales ratio divides an equity value by revenues that are generated for the firm. Consequently, it will yield lower values for more highly levered firms and may result in misleading conclusions when price-to-sales ratios are compared across firms in a sector with different degrees of leverage.

One of the advantages of revenue multiples is that fewer problems are associated with ensuring uniformity across firms. Accounting standards across different sectors and markets are fairly similar when it comes to how revenues are recorded. There have been firms in recent years, though, that have used questionable accounting practices in recording installment sales and intracompany transactions to make their revenues higher. Notwithstanding these problems, revenue multiples suffer far less than other multiples from differences across firms.

CROSS-SECTIONAL DISTRIBUTION

As with the price-earning ratio, the place to begin the examination of revenue multiples is with the cross-sectional distribution of price-to-sales and value-to-sales ratios across firms in the United States. Figure 10–1 summarizes this distribution.

Two things are worth noting in this distribution. The first is that revenue multiples are even more skewed toward positive values than are earnings multiples. The second is that the price-to-sales ratio is generally lower than the value-to-sales ratio, which should not be surprising since the former includes only equity whereas the latter considers firm value.

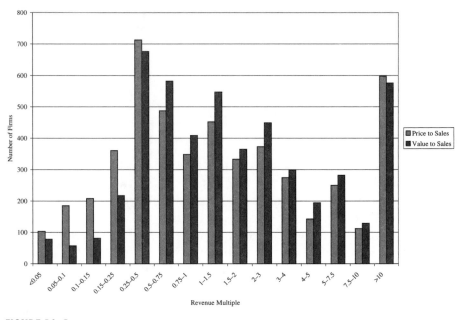

FIGURE 10–1
Revenue Multiples

Table 10.1 summarizes statistics on both the price-to-sales and the value-to-sales ratios.

TABLE 10.1 Summary Statistics on Revenue Multiples: July 2000[*]

	PRICE-TO-SALES RATIO	VALUE-TO-SALES RATIO
Number of firms	4940	4940
Average	11.63	13.89
Median	0.82	1.32
Standard deviation	116.90	127.26
10th percentile	0.13	0.27
90th percentile	7.45	12.89

* These statistics were computed with revenue multiples capped at 50; any firm with a revenue multiple greater than 50 was assigned a value of 50.

The price-to-sales ratio is slightly lower than the value-to-sales ratio, and the median values are much lower than the average values for both multiples.

The revenue multiples are presented only for technology firms in Figure 10–2.

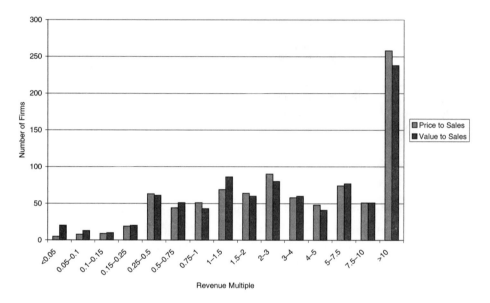

FIGURE 10–2
Revenue Multiples for Technology Firms: July 2000

In general, the values for both multiples are higher for technology firms than they are for the market.

Table 10.2 contrasts the price-to-sales ratios at technology firms with revenue multiples at nontechnology firms.

Technology firms trade at revenue multiples that are significantly higher than those of nontechnology firms. It is worth noting in closing that revenue multiples can be estimated for far more firms than can earnings multiples, and the potential for sampling bias is, therefore, much smaller.

TABLE 10.2 Price-to-Sales Ratios: Technology versus Nontechnology Firms

	TECHNOLOGY FIRMS	NONTECHNOLOGY FIRMS
Number of firms	944	4029
Average	25.65	11.63
Median	3.57	0.82
Standard deviation	181.51	116.90
10th percentile	0.44	0.13
90th percentile	34.98	7.45

 psdata.xls: A dataset on the Web that summarizes price-to-sales and value-to-sales ratios and fundamentals, by industry group, in the United States for the most recent year.

ANALYSIS OF REVENUE MULTIPLES

You can extract the variables that determine the revenue multiples by going back to the appropriate discounted cash flow models: dividend discount model (or other equity valuation model) for price-to-sales and a firm valuation model for value-to-sales ratios.

Price-to-Sales Ratios. The price-to-sales ratio for a stable firm can be extracted from a stable growth dividend discount model:

$$P_0 = \frac{DPS_1}{r - g_n}$$

where

P_0 = Value of equity
DPS_1 = Expected dividends per share next year
r = Required rate of return on equity
g_n = Growth rate in dividends (forever)

Substituting for $DPS_1 = EPS_0 (1 + g_n)$ (payout ratio), the value of the equity can be written as:

$$P_0 = \frac{EPS_0 \times Payout\ Ratio \times (1 + g_n)}{r - g_n}$$

Defining the profit margin = $EPS_0 \div$ Sales per share, the value of equity can be written as:

$$P_0 = \frac{Sales_0 \times Margin \times Payout\ Ratio \times (1 + g_n)}{r - g_n}$$

Rewriting in terms of the price-sales ratio,

$$\frac{P_0}{Sales_0} = PS = \frac{Net\ Profit\ Margin \times Payout\ Ratio \times (1 + g_n)}{r - g_n}$$

If the profit margin is based on expected earnings in the next time period, the preceding equation can be simplified to

$$\frac{P_0}{Sales_0} = PS = \frac{Net\ Profit\ Margin \times Payout\ Ratio}{r - g_n}$$

The PS ratio is an increasing function of the profit margin, the payout ratio, and the growth rate and is a decreasing function of the riskiness of the firm.

The price-sales ratio for a high-growth firm can also be related to fundamentals. In the special case of the two-stage dividend discount model, this relationship can be made explicit fairly simply. The value of equity of a high-growth firm in the two-stage dividend discount model can be written as:

P_0 = Present Value of Expected Dividend in High-Growth Period
+ Present Value of Terminal Price

With two stages of growth, a high-growth stage and a stable-growth phase, the dividend discount model can be written as follows:

$$P_0 = \frac{EPS_0 \times Payout\ Ratio \times (1+g) \times \left[1 - \dfrac{(1+g)^n}{(1+k_{e,hg})^n}\right]}{k_{e,hg} - g}$$

$$+ \frac{EPS_0 \times Payout\ Ratio_n \times (1+g)^n \times (1+g_n)}{(k_{e,st} - g_n)(1+k_{e,hg})^n}$$

where

g = Growth rate in the first n years
$k_{e,hg}$ = Cost of equity in high growth
Payout = Payout ratio in the first n years
g_n = Growth rate after n years forever (stable growth rate)
$k_{e,st}$ = Cost of equity in stable growth
$Payout_n$ = Payout ratio after n years for the stable firm

Rewriting EPS_0 in terms of the profit margin, $EPS_0 = Sales_0 \times$ Profit Margin, and bringing $Sales_0$ to the left side of the equation:

$$\frac{Price}{Sales} = Net\ Margin \left[\frac{Payout\ Ratio \times (1+g) \times \left(1 - \dfrac{(1+g)^n}{(1+k_{e,hg})^n}\right)}{k_{e,hg} - g}\right]$$

$$+ Net\ Margin_n \left[\frac{Payout\ Ratio_n \times (1+g)^n \times (1+g_n)}{(k_{e,st} - g_n)(1+k_{e,hg})^n}\right]$$

The left side of the equation is the price-sales ratio. It is determined by the following factors:

- *Net profit margin during the high-growth period and the stable period:* Net Income / Revenues. The price-sales ratio is an increasing function of the net profit margin.

- *Payout ratio during the high-growth period and in the stable period:* The PS ratio increases as the payout ratio increases.

- *Riskiness (through the discount rate $k_{e,hg}$ in the high-growth period and $k_{e,st}$ in the stable period):* The PS ratio becomes lower as riskiness increases.

- *Expected growth rate in earnings, in both the high-growth and stable phases:* In either period, the PS increases as the growth rate increases.

This formula is general enough to be applied to any firm, even one that is not paying dividends right now.

ILLUSTRATION 10.1

Estimating the PS Ratio for a High-Growth Firm in the Two-Stage Model

Assume that you have been asked to estimate the PS ratio for a firm that has the following characteristics:

Growth rate in first five years = 20% Payout ratio in first five years = 20%
Growth rate after five years = 8% Payout ratio after five years = 50%
Beta = 1.0 Risk-free rate = T-bond rate = 6%
Net profit margin = 10% Risk premium = 5.5%
Required rate of return = 6% + 1(5.5%) = 11.5%

This firm's price-to-sales ratio can be estimated as follows:

$$PS = 0.10 \times \left[\frac{0.2 \times (1.20) \times \left[1 - \frac{(1.20)^5}{(1.115)^5} \right]}{(0.115 - 0.20)} + \frac{0.50 \times (1.20)^5 \times (1.08)}{(0.115 - 0.08)(1.115)^5} \right]$$

$$= 2.35$$

Based on this firm's fundamentals, you would expect this firm to trade at 2.35 times revenues.

ILLUSTRATION 10.2

Estimating the Price-to-Sales Ratio for Cisco

You can estimate the price-to-sales ratio for Cisco by using the fundamentals you used to value it on a discounted cash flow basis. The fundamentals are summarized in Table 10.3.

TABLE 10.3 Estimating the Price-to-Sales Ratio for Cisco

	HIGH-GROWTH PERIOD	STABLE-GROWTH PERIOD
Length	12 years	Forever after year 12
Growth rate	36.39%	5%
Net profit margin	17.25%	15%
Beta	1.43	1.00
Cost of equity	11.72%	10%
Payout ratio	0%	80%

The risk-free rate used in the analysis is 6% and the risk premium is 4%.

$$PS = 0.1725 \times \frac{0 \times (1.3639) \times \left[1 - \frac{(1.3639)^{12}}{(1.1172)^{12}}\right]}{(0.1172 - 0.3639)}$$

$$+ 0.15 \times \frac{0.80 \times (1.3639)^{12} \times (1.05)}{(0.10 - 0.05)(1.1172)^{12}} = 27.72$$

Based on its fundamentals, you would expect Cisco to trade at 27.72 times revenues, which was approximately what it was trading at in July 2000.

Price-to-Sales Ratio and Net Profit Margins. The key determinant of price-sales ratios is the net profit margin. Firms involved in businesses that have high margins can expect to sell for high multiples of sales. A decline in profit margins has a twofold effect. First, the reduction in profit margins reduces the price-sales ratio directly. Second, the lower profit margin can lead to lower growth and hence lower price-sales ratios.

The profit margin can be linked to expected growth fairly easily if an additional term is defined—the ratio of sales to book value of equity, which is also called an equity turnover ratio. Using a relationship developed between growth rates and fundamentals, we can write the expected growth rate as:

Expected Growth Rate
= Retention Ratio × Return on Equity
= Retention Ratio × (Net Profit / Sales) × (Sales / BV of Equity)
= Retention Ratio × Profit Margin × (Sales / BV of Equity)

As the profit margin is reduced, the expected growth rate will decrease if the sales do not increase proportionately.

In fact, this relationship between profit margins, turnover ratios, and expected growth can be used to examine how different pricing strategies will affect value.

ILLUSTRATION 10.3

Estimating the Effect of Lower Margins of Price-Sales Ratios

Consider again the firm analyzed in Illustration 10.1. If the firm's profit margin declines and total revenue remains unchanged, the price-sales ratio for the firm will decline with the profit margin. For instance, if the firm's profit margin declines from 10% to 5% and the sales / BV remains unchanged:

New Growth Rate in First Five Years = Retention Ratio × Profit Margin × (Sales / BV)
$$= .8 \times .05 \times 2.50 = 10\%$$

The new price-sales ratio can then be calculated as follows:

$$PS = 0.05 \times \left[\frac{0.2 \times (1.10) \times \left[1 - \frac{(1.10)^5}{(1.115)^5} \right]}{(0.115 - 0.10)} + \frac{0.50 \times (1.10)^5 \times (1.08)}{(0.115 - 0.08)(1.115)^5} \right]$$

$$= 0.77$$

The relationship between profit margins and the price-sales ratio is illustrated more comprehensively in Figure 10–3. The price-sales ratio is estimated as a function of the profit margin, keeping the sales / book value of equity ratio fixed.

This linkage of price-sales ratios and profit margins can be used to analyze the value effects of changes in corporate strategy and the value of a brand name.

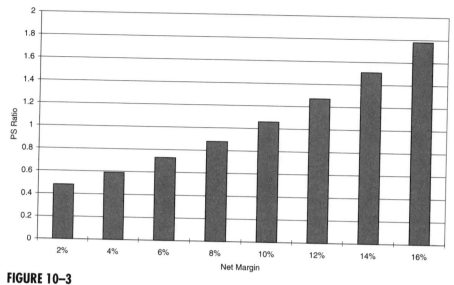

FIGURE 10–3
Price-Sales Ratios and Profit Margins

Value-to-Sales Ratio. To analyze the relationship between value and sales, consider the value of a stable growth firm:

$$\text{Firm Value}_0 = \frac{\text{EBIT}_1(1-t)(1-\text{Reinvestment Rate})}{\text{Cost of Capital} - g_n}$$

Dividing both sides by the revenue:

$$\frac{\text{Firm Value}_0}{\text{Sales}} = \frac{\text{EBIT}_1(1-t)(1-\text{Reinvestment Rate})}{\text{Cost of Capital} - g_n}$$

$$\frac{\text{Firm Value}_0}{\text{Sales}} =$$

$$\frac{\text{After -Tax Operating Margin } (1-\text{Reinvestment Rate})}{\text{Cost of Capital} - g_n}$$

Just as the price-to-sales ratio is determined by net profit margins, payout ratios, and costs of equity, the value-to-sales ratio is determined by after-tax operating margins, reinvestment rates, and the cost of capital. Firms with higher operating margins, lower reinvestment rates (for any given growth rate), and lower costs of capital will trade at higher value-to-sales multiples.

We can expand this equation to cover a firm in high growth by using a two-stage firm valuation model:

$$P_0 = AT\ Oper\ Margin \left[\frac{(1-RIR) \times (1+g) \times \left(1 - \frac{(1-g)^n}{(1+k_{c,hg})^n}\right)}{(k_{c,hg}-g)} \right]$$

$$+ AT\ Oper\ Margin_n \left[\frac{(1-RIR_n) \times (1+g)^n \times (1+g_n)}{(k_{c,st}-g_n)(1+k_{c,hg})^n} \right]$$

where

AT Oper Margin = After-tax operating margin (AT Oper Margin$_n$ is stable period margin)

RIR = Reinvestment Rate (RIR$_n$ is for stable-growth period)

k_c = Cost of capital (in high-growth and stable-growth periods)

g = Growth rate in operating income in high-growth and stable-growth periods

Note that the determinants of the value-to-sales ratio remain the same as they were in the stable growth model—the growth rate, the reinvestment rate, the operating margin, and the cost of capital—but the number of estimates increases to reflect the existence of a high-growth period.

firmmult.xls: This spreadsheet enables you to estimate the value-to-sales ratio for a stable-growth or
high-growth firm, given its fundamentals.

USING REVENUE MULTIPLES IN ANALYSIS

The key determinants of the revenue multiples of a firm
are its expected margins (net and operating), risk, cash flow,
and growth characteristics. To use revenue multiples in analysis and to make comparisons across firms, you would control
for differences on these characteristics. In this section, we
examine different ways of comparing revenue multiples across
firms.

Looking for Mismatches. Although growth, risk, and cash flow characteristics affect revenue multiples, the key determinants of
revenue multiples are profit margins—net profit margin for
equity multiples and operating margins for firm value multiples. Thus, it is not surprising to find firms with low profit margins and low revenue multiples, and firms with high profit
margins and high revenue ratios. However, firms with high revenue multiples and low profit margins as well as firms with low
revenue multiples and high profit margins should attract
investors' attention as potentially overvalued and undervalued
securities, respectively. In Figure 10–4, this analysis is presented in a matrix.

You can identify under- or overvalued firms in a sector or
industry by plotting them on this matrix and looking for
potential mismatches between margins and revenue multiples.

While intuitively appealing, this approach is accompanied
by at least three practical problems. The first problem is that
data is more easily available on historical (current) profit margins than on expected profit margins. If a firm's current margins are highly correlated with future margins—a firm that has
earned high margins historically will continue to do so, and
one that has earned low margins historically will also continue

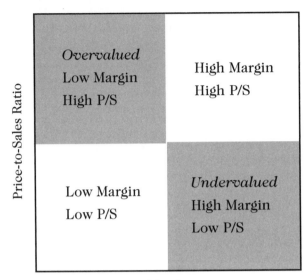

FIGURE 10–4
Price / Sales and Margins

to do so—using current margins and current revenue multiples to identify under- or overvalued securities is reasonable. If the current margins of firms are not highly correlated with expected future margins, it is no longer appropriate to argue that firms are overvalued just because they have low current margins and trade at high price-to-sales ratios. The second problem with this approach is that it assumes revenue multiples are linearly related to margins. In other words, as margins double, you would expect revenue multiples to double as well. The third problem is that this approach ignores differences of other fundamentals, especially risk. Thus, a firm that looks undervalued because it has a high current margin and is trading at a low multiple of revenues may in fact be a fairly valued firm with very high risk.

ILLUSTRATION 10.4

Revenue Multiples and Margins: Specialty Retailers

In the first comparison, we look at specialty retailers with positive earnings in the most recent financial year. In Figure 10–5, the value-to-sales ratios of these firms are plotted against the operating margins of these firms (with the stock symbols for each firm next to each observation).

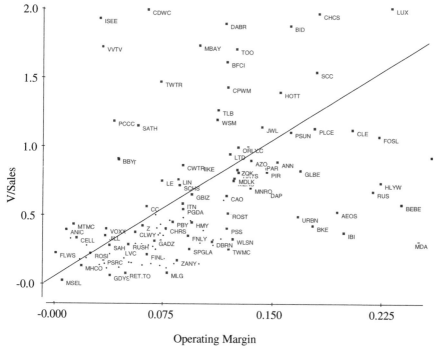

FIGURE 10–5
Value-to-Sales Ratios and Operating Margins

Firms with higher operating margins tend to have higher value-to-sales ratios, and firms with lower margins have lower value-to-sales ratios. Note, though, that even in this subset of firms, there is a considerable amount of noise in the relationship between value-to-sales ratios and operating margins.

ILLUSTRATION 10.5

Revenue Multiples and Margins: Internet Retailers

In the second comparison (Figure 10–6), the price-to-sales ratios of Internet retailers are plotted against the net margins earned by these firms in the most recent year.

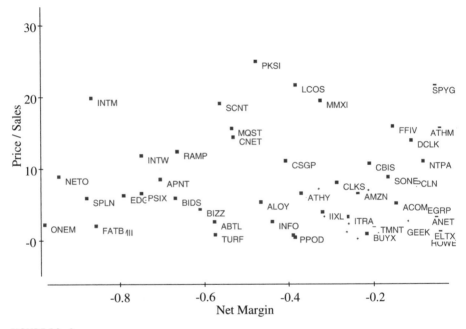

FIGURE 10–6
Price-to-Sales Ratios versus Net Margins: Internet Stocks

Here, there seems to be almost no relationship between price-to-sales ratios and net margins. This should not be surprising. Most Internet firms have negative net income and net margins. The market values of these firms are based not on what they earn now but on what they are expected to earn in the future, and there is little correlation between current and expected future margins.

Statistical Approaches. When analyzing price earnings ratios, we used regressions to control for differences in risk, growth, and payout ratios across firms. You could also use regressions to control for differences across firms to analyze revenue multiples. In this section, we begin by applying this approach to comparables defined narrowly as firms in the same business and then expanded to cover the entire sector and the market.

Comparable Firms in the Same Business

In the last section, you examined firms in the same business, looking for mismatches; firms with high margins and low revenue multiples were viewed as undervalued. In a simple extension of this approach, you could regress revenue multiples against profit margins across firms in a sector:

Price-to-Sales Ratio = a + b (Net Profit Margin)

Value-to-Sales Ratio = a + b (After-Tax Operating Margin)

These regressions can be used to estimate predicted values for firms in the sample, helping to identify under- and overvalued firms.

If the number of firms in the sample is large enough to allow for it, this regression can be extended to accommodate other independent variables. For instance, the standard deviation in stock prices or the beta can be used as an independent variable to capture differences in risk, and analyst estimates of expected growth can control for differences in growth. The regression can also be modified to account for nonlinear relationships between revenue multiples and any or all of these variables.

Can this approach be used for sectors such as the Internet where there seems to be little or no relationship between revenue multiples and fundamentals? It can, but only if you adapt it to consider the determinants of value in these sectors.

ILLUSTRATION 10.6

Regression Approach: Specialty Retailers

Consider again the scatter plot of value-to-sales ratios and operating margins for retailers in Illustration 10.4. There is clearly a positive relationship and a regression of value-to-sales ratios against operating margins for specialty retailers yields the following:

Value-to-Sales Ratio = 0.0563 + 6.6287 After-Tax Operating Margin $\qquad R^2= 39.9\%$
$\qquad\qquad\qquad\quad$ (0.72)$\quad$(10.39)

This regression has 162 observations; the t statisics are reported in parentheses. To estimate the predicted value-to-sales ratio for Talbot's, one of the specialty retailers in the group, which has a 11.22% after-tax operating margin:

Predicted Value-to-Sales Ratio = 0.0563 + 6.6287(.1122) = 0.80

With an actual value-to-sales ratio of 1.27, Talbot's can be consider overvalued.

This regression can be modified in two ways. One way is to regress the value-to-sales ratio against the ln(operating margins) to allow for the nonlinear relationship between the two variables:

Value-to-Sales Ratio = 1.8313 + 0.4339 ln(After-Tax Operating Margin) $\qquad R^2= 22.40\%$
$\qquad\qquad\qquad\quad$ (10.76)$\quad$(6.89)

The other way is to expand the regression to include proxies for risk and growth:

Value to Sales = −0.6209 + 7.21 (At Op Mgn) − 0.0209 σ_{OpInc} + 3.1460 Growth
$\qquad\qquad\quad$ (3.47)$\qquad$(10.34)$\qquad\qquad$(0.22)$\qquad\qquad$(4.92)

where
AT Op Mgn = After-tax operating margin
σ_{OpInc} = Standard deviation in operating income over previous five years
Growth = Expected growth rate in earnings over next five years

This regression has fewer observations (124) than the previous two but a higher R^2 of 50.09%. The predicted value-to-sales ratio for Talbot's with this regression is:

Predicted Value to Sales = −0.6209 + 7.21 (.1122) − 0.0209 (.7391) + 3.1460 (0.225)
$$= 0.88$$

Talbot's remains overvalued even after adjusting for differences in growth and risk.

___

ILLUSTRATION 10.7

Regression Approach: Internet Retailers

In the case of the Internet stocks graphed in Figure 10–6, the regression of price-to-sales ratios against net margins yields the following:

Price to Sales Ratio = 44.4495 − 0.7331 (Net Margin) $R^2 = 0.22\%$

Not only is the R^2 close to zero, the relationship between current net margins and price-to-sales ratios is negative. There is little relationship between the pricing of these stocks and their current profitability.

What variables might do a better job of explaining the differences in price-to-sales ratios across Internet stocks? Consider the following propositions.

- Since this sample contains some firms with very little in revenues and other firms with much higher revenues, you would expect the firms with less in revenues to trade at a much higher multiple of revenues than do firms with higher revenues. Thus, Amazon with revenues of almost $2 billion can be expected to trade at a lower multiple of this value than iVillage with revenues of less than $60 million.

- The probability is high that some or many of these Internet firms will not survive because they will run out of cash. A widely used measure of this potential for cash problems is the cash-burn ratio, which is the ratio of the cash balance to the EBITDA (usually a negative number). Firms with a low cash-burn ratio are at higher risk of running into a cash crunch and should trade at lower multiples of revenues.

- Revenue growth is a key determinant of value at these firms. Firms that are growing revenues more quickly are likely to reach profitability sooner, other things remaining equal.

The following regression relates price-to-sales ratios to the level of revenues (ln(Revenues)), the cash-burn ratio (absolute value of cash / EBITDA), and revenue growth over the last year for Internet firms:

$$\text{Price-to-Sales Ratio} = 37.18 - 4.34 \ln(\text{Revenue}) + 0.75 \text{ (Cash / EBITDA)} + 8.37 \text{ Growth}_{\text{Revenues}}$$
$$(1.85) \quad (0.95) \qquad\qquad (4.18) \qquad\qquad\qquad (1.06)$$

The regression has 117 observations and an R^2 of 13.83%. The coefficients all have the right signs but are of marginal statistical significance. You could obtain a predicted price-to-sales ratio for Amazon in this regression of:

$$PS_{\text{Amazon}} = 37.18 - 4.34 \ln(1,920) + 0.75 \,(2.12) + 8.37 \,(1.4810) = 18.34$$

Due to the low R^2 on the regression, this estimate would have a standard error of 3.85. At its actual price-to-sales ratio of 6.69, Amazon looks significantly undervalued relative to other Internet firms.

For Ariba, a similar analysis would yield:

$$PS_{\text{Ariba}} = 37.18 - 4.34 \ln(92.5) + 0.75 \,(6.36) + 8.37 \,(1.2694) = 32.91$$

At its actual price-to-sales ratio of 247.91, Ariba looks significantly overvalued relative to other Internet firms. This may reflect the fact that, from its business model, Ariba has better prospects of earning high margins in the future than do other Internet firms.

In either case, the regressions are much too noisy to lend much weight to the predictions. In fact, the low explanatory power with fundamentals and the huge differences in measures of relative value should sound a note of caution on the use of multiples in sectors such as this one, where firms are in transition and changing dramatically from period to period.

Market Regressions

If you can control for differences across firms by using a regression, you can extend this approach to look at much broader cross-sections of firms. Here, the cross-sectional data is used to estimate the price-to-sales ratio as a function of fundamental variables: profit margin, dividend payout, beta, and growth rate in earnings.

Consider first the technology sector. Regressing the price-to-sales ratio against net margins, growth rate in earnings, payout ratios, and betas in July 2000 yields the following result:

PS = –8.48 + 30.37 (Net Margin) + 20.98 (Growth Rate) + 4.68 Beta + 3.79 Payout
    (7.19)   (10.2)   (10.0)   (4.64)   (0.85)

There are 273 observations in this regression, and the R^2 is 53.8%.

This approach can be extended to cover the entire market. In Damodaran (1994), regressions of price-sales ratios on fundamentals—dividend payout ratio, growth rate in earnings, profit margin, and beta—were run for each year from 1987 to 1991, as summarized in Table 10.4.

TABLE 10.4 Regression of Price-Sales Ratio on Fundamentals

YEAR	REGRESSION	R^2
1987	PS = 0.7894 + .0008 – 0.2734 + 0.5022 EGR + 6.46	44.3%
1988	PS = 0.1660 + .0006 – 0.0692 + 0.5504 EGR + 10.31	78.6%
1989	PS = 0.4911 + .0393 – 0.0282 + 0.2836 EGR + 10.25	46%
1990	PS = 0.0826 + .0105 – 0.1073 + 0.5449 EGR + 10.36	88.9%
1991	PS = 0.5189 + .2749 – 0.2485 + 0.4948 EGR + 8.17	48.5%

where

PS = Price/sales ratio at the end of the year
Margin = Profit margin for the year = net income / sales for the year (in %)
Payout = Payout ratio = Dividends / Earnings ... at the end of the year
Beta = Beta of the stock
EGR = Earnings growth rate over the previous five years

This regression is updated for the entire market in July 2000 and presented below:

PS = –2.36 + 17.43 (Net Margin) + 8.72 (Growth Rate) + 1.45 Beta + 0.37 Payout
    (16.5)   (35.5)   (23.9)   (10.1)   (3.01)

We used analysts' estimates of expected growth in this regression. There are 2,235 observations in this regression, and the R^2 is 52.5%.

The regression can also be run in terms of the value-to-sales ratio, with the operating margin, standard deviation in operating income, and reinvestment rate used as independent variables:

VS = –1.67 + 8.82 (Operating Margin) + 7.66 (Growth Rate) + 1.50 σ_{oi} + 0.08 RIR
(14.4) (30.7)   (19.2)   (8.35)   (1.44)

This regression also has 2,235 observations, but the R^2 is slightly lower at 42%.

ILLUSTRATION 10.8

Valuing Cisco and Motorola with Sector and Market Regressions

These sector and market regressions can be used to estimate predicted price-to-sales ratios for Cisco and Motorola. In Table 10.5, the values of the independent variables are reported for both firms.

TABLE 10.5 Predicted Price-to-Sales Ratio for Cisco and Motorola

	CISCO	MOTOROLA
Net margin	17.25%	2.64%
Expected growth rate (analyst projection over five yrs)	36.39%	21.26%
Beta	1.43	1.21
Payout ratio	0	35.62%

Using these values, you can estimate predicted price-to-sales ratios for the two firms from the sector regression:

PS_{Cisco} = –8.48 + 30.37 (.1725) + 20.98 (.3639) + 4.68 (1.43) + 3.79 (0) = 11.09
$PS_{Motorola}$ = –8.48 + 30.37 (.0264) + 20.98 (.2126) + 4.68 (1.21) + 3.79 (0.3562) = 3.79

You can also estimate predicted price-to-sales ratios from the market regression:

$$PS_{Cisco} = -2.36 + 17.43\ (.1725) + 8.72\ (.3639) + 1.45\ (1.43) + 0.37\ (0) = 5.89$$
$$PS_{Motorola} = -2.36 + 17.43\ (.0264) + 8.72\ (.2126) + 1.45\ (1.21) + 0.37\ (0.3562) = 1.84$$

Cisco at its existing price-to-sales ratio of 27.77 looks significantly overvalued relative to both the market and the technology sector. In contrast, Motorola with a price-to-sales ratio of 2.27 is slightly overvalued relative to the rest of the market but is significantly undervalued relative to other technology stocks.

MULTIPLES OF FUTURE REVENUES

In Chapter 9, "Earnings Multiples," we examined the use of market value of equity as a multiple of earnings in a future year. Revenue multiples can also be measured in terms of future revenues. Thus, you could estimate the value of Amazon as a multiple of revenues five years from now. There are several advantages to doing this:

- For firms like Ariba and Rediff.com, which have little in revenues currently but are expected to grow rapidly over time, the revenues five years from now are likely to better reflect the firm's true potential than revenues today. Ariba's revenues grow from $93 million in the current year to almost $12 billion in five years, reflecting the high growth over the period.
- It is easier to estimate multiples of revenues when growth rates have leveled off and the firm's risk profile is stable. This is more likely to be the case five years from now than it is today.

Assuming that revenues five years from now are to be used to estimate value, what multiple should be used on these revenues? We have two choices.

One approach is to use the average multiples of value[1] (today) to revenues today of comparable firms to estimate a value five years from now and then to discount that value back to the present. Thus, if the average value-to-sales ratio of more mature comparable firms is 1.8, the computed value of Ariba can be computed as follows:

Revenues at Ariba in Five Years = $12,149 million

Value of Ariba in Five Years = $12,149 × 1.8 = $21,867

Value of Ariba Today = $21,867 / 1.1312^5 = $11,809 million

The value is discounted back at Ariba's cost of capital (13.12%).

The other approach is to forecast the expected revenue, in five years, for each of the comparable firms, and to divide these revenues by the current firm value. This multiple of current value to future revenues can be used to estimate the value today. To illustrate, if current value is 1.1 times revenues in five years for comparable firms, the value of Ariba can be estimated as follows:

Revenues at Ariba in Five Years = $12,149 million

Value Today
= Revenues in Five years × (Value Today / Revenues$_{\text{year five}}$)$_{\text{Comparable firms}}$
= 12,149 (1.1) = $13,363 million

Finally, you can adjust the multiple of future revenues for differences in operating margin, growth, and risk for differences between the firm you are valuing and comparable firms.

SECTOR-SPECIFIC MULTIPLES

The value of a firm can be standardized with a number of sector-specific multiples. For new technology firms, these multiples can range from value per subscriber for Internet service providers, to value per Web site visitor for Internet portals, to value per customer for Internet retailers. These sector-specific multiples enable analysts to compare firms for which other multiples cannot even be estimated. Analysts risk tunnel vision, however, if they narrowly focus on comparing the values of the multiples across a few firms in a sector and thus lose perspective on the true value.

DEFINITIONS OF SECTOR-SPECIFIC MULTIPLES

For Internet service providers (such as AOL) or information providers (such as TheStreet.com) that rely on subscribers for their revenues, the value of a firm can be stated in terms of the number of subscribers:

Value per Subscriber =

$$\frac{(\text{Market Value of Equity} + \text{Market Value of Debt})}{\text{Number of Subscribers}}$$

For retailers such as Amazon that generate revenue from customers who shop at their site, the value of the firm can be stated in terms of the number of regular customers:

Value per Customer =

$$\frac{(\text{Market Value of Equity} + \text{Market Value of Debt})}{\text{Number of Customers}}$$

For Internet portals that generate revenue from advertising revenues that are based on traffic to the site, the revenues can be stated in terms of the number of visitors to the site:

Value per Site Visitor =

$$\frac{(\text{Market Value of Equity} + \text{Market Value of Debt})}{\text{Number of Visitors to the Site}}$$

These are all multiples that can be estimated only for the subset of firms for which such statistics are maintained and are thus sector specific.

DETERMINANTS OF VALUE

What are the determinants of value for these sector-specific multiples? Not surprisingly, they are the same as the determinants of value for other multiples—cash flows, growth, and risk—though the relationship can be complex. You can derive the fundamentals that drive these multiples by going back to a discounted cash flow model stated in terms of these sector-specific variables.

Consider an Internet service provider that has NX existing subscribers, and assume that each subscriber is expected to remain with the provider for the next n years. In addition, assume that the firm will generate net cash flows per customer (revenues from each customer minus cost of serving the customer) of CFX per year for these n years.[2] The value of each existing customer to the firm can then be written as:

$$\text{Value per Customer} = VX = \sum_{t=1}^{t=n} \frac{CFX}{(1+r)^t}$$

The discount rate used to compute the value per customer can range from close to the riskless rate if the customer has signed a contract to remain a subscriber for the next n years, to the cost of capital if the estimate is just an expectation based on past experience.

Assume that the firm expects to continue to add new subscribers in future years and that the firm will face a cost (advertising and promotion) of C_t for each new subscriber added in period t. If the new subscribers (ΔNX_t) added in period t will generate a value VX_t per subscriber, then the value of this firm can be written as:

$$\text{Value of Firm} = NX \times VX + \sum_{t=1}^{t=\infty} \frac{\Delta NX_t (VX_t - C_t)}{(1+k_c)^t}$$

Note that the first term in this valuation equation represents the value generated by existing subscribers and that the second term is the value of expected growth. The subscribers added generate value only if the cost of adding a new subscriber (C_t) is less than the present value of the net cash flows generated by that subscriber for the firm.

Dividing both sides of this equation by the number of existing subscribers (NX) yields the following:

$$\text{Value per Existing Subscriber} = \frac{\text{Value of Firm}}{\text{NX}}$$

$$= VX + \frac{\displaystyle\sum_{t=1}^{t=\infty} \frac{\Delta NX_t(VX_t - C_t)}{(1 + k_c)^t}}{NX}$$

In the most general case, then, the value of a firm per subscriber is a function not only of the expected value that will be generated by existing subscribers but also by the potential for value creation from future growth in the subscriber base. If you assume a competitive market, where the cost of adding new subscribers (C_t) converges on the value that is generated by that customer, the second term in the equation drops out and the value per subscriber becomes just the present value of cash flows that will be generated by each existing subscriber.

$$\text{Value per Existing Subscriber}_{C=VX} = VX$$

A similar analysis can be done to relate the value of an Internet retailer to the number of customers it has, though it is generally much more difficult to estimate the value that will be created by a customer. Unlike subscribers who pay a fixed fee, retail customers have buying habits that are more difficult to predict.

In either case, you can see the problems associated with comparing these multiples across firms. Implicitly, you have to assume competitive markets and conclude that the firms with the lowest market value per subscriber are the most undervalued. Alternatively, you have to assume that the value of growth is the same proportion of the value generated by existing customers for all of the firms in your analysis, leading to the same conclusion.

Value can also be related to the number of site visitors, but only if the link between revenues and the number of site visitors is made explicit. For instance, if an Internet portal's advertising revenues are directly tied to the number of visitors at its site, the value of the Internet portal can be stated in terms of the number of visitors to the site. Since sites have to spend money (on advertising) to attract visitors, the net value generated by each visitor ultimately determines value.

ILLUSTRATION 10.9

Estimating the Value per Subscriber: Internet Portal

Assume that you are valuing GOL, an Internet service provider with one million existing subscribers. Each subscriber is expected to remain for three years, and GOL is expected to generate $100 in net after-tax cash flow (subscription revenues − costs of providing subscription service) per subscriber each year. GOL has a cost of capital of 15%. The value added to the firm by each existing subscriber can be estimated as follows:

$$\text{Value per Subscriber} = \sum_{t=1}^{t=3} \frac{100}{(1.15)^t} = \$228.32$$

Value of Existing Subscriber Base = $228.32 million

Furthermore, assume that GOL expects to add 100,000 subscribers each year for the next 10 years and that the value added by each subscriber will grow from the current level ($228.32) at the inflation rate of 3% every year. The cost of adding a new subscriber is $100 currently, assumed to be growing at the inflation rate. Table 10.6 summarizes the calculations.

TABLE 10.6 Value Added by New Subscribers

YEAR	VALUE ADDED/ SUBSCRIBER	COST OF ACQUIRING SUBSCRIBER	NUMBER OF SUBSCRIBERS ADDED	PRESENT VALUE AT 15%
1	$235.17	$103.00	100,000	$11,493,234
2	$242.23	$106.09	100,000	$10,293,940
3	$249.49	$109.27	100,000	$9,219,789
4	$256.98	$112.55	100,000	$8,257,724
5	$264.69	$115.93	100,000	$7,396,049
6	$272.63	$119.41	100,000	$6,624,287
7	$280.81	$122.99	100,000	$5,933,057
8	$289.23	$126.68	100,000	$5,313,956
9	$297.91	$130.48	100,000	$4,759,456
10	$306.85	$134.39	100,000	$4,262,817
				$73,554,309

The cumulative value added by new subscribers is $73.55 million. The total value of the firm is the sum of the value generated by existing customers and the value added by new customers:

Value of Firm = Value of Existing Subscriber Base + Value Added by New Customers
= $228.32 million + $73.55 million = $301.87 million

Value per Existing Subscriber = Value of Firm / Number of Subscribers
= $301.87 million / 1 million = $301.87 per Subscriber

Note, though, that a portion of this value per subscriber is attributable to future growth. As the cost of acquiring a subscriber converges on the value added by each subscriber, the value per subscriber will converge on $228.32.

ANALYSIS WITH SECTOR-SPECIFIC MULTIPLES

To analyze firms by using sector-specific multiples, you should control for the differences across firms on any or all of the fundamentals that you identified as affecting these multiples in the last part.

With value per subscriber, you must control for differences in the value generated by each subscriber. In particular:

- Firms that are more efficient in delivering a service for a given subscription price (resulting in lower costs) should trade at a higher value per subscriber than do comparable firms. This would also apply if a firm has significant economies of scale. In Illustration 10.9, the value per subscriber would be higher if each existing subscriber generated $120 in net cash flows for the firm each year instead of $100.
- Firms that can add new subscribers at a lower cost (advertising and promotion) should trade at a higher value per subscriber than do comparable firms.
- Firms with higher expected growth in the subscriber base (in percentage terms) should trade at a higher value per subscriber than do comparable firms.

You could make similar statements about value per customer.

With value per site visitor, you must control for the additional advertising revenue that is generated by each visitor— the greater the advertising revenue, the higher the value per site visitor—and the cost of attracting each visitor: the higher the costs, the lower the value per site visitor.

ILLUSTRATION 10.10

Comparing Value per Site Visitor

In Table 10.7, the market value per site visitor is presented for Internet firms that generate the bulk of their revenues from advertising. The number of visitors per site was collected from July 1, 2000 to July 31, 2000 and the market value is as of July 31, 2000.

TABLE 10.7 Value per Visitor

COMPANY NAME	FIRM VALUE	VISITORS	VALUE PER VISITOR
Lycos, Inc.	$5,396.00	5,858	$0.92
MapQuest.com Inc.	$604.80	6,621	$0.09
iVillage Inc.	$250.40	7,346	$0.03
CNET Networks	$1,984.30	10,850	$0.18
Ask Jeeves Inc.	$643.50	11,765	$0.05
Go2Net Inc.	$1,468.60	12,527	$0.12
LookSmart, Ltd.	$1,795.30	13,374	$0.13
About.com Inc.	$541.90	18,282	$0.03
Excite@Home	$7,008.20	27,115	$0.26
Yahoo! Inc.	$65,633.40	49,045	$1.34

(*Source:* Media Metrix, *www.mediametrix.com*, June 1, 2000, Media Metrix)

Note the differences in value per site visitor across Yahoo!, Excite, and Lycos. Excite looks much cheaper than either of the other two firms, but the differences could also be attributable to differences on the fundamentals across the firms. It could be that Yahoo! earns more than Excite and Lycos in advertising revenues and that its prospects of earning higher profits in the future are brighter.

SUMMARY

The price-to-sales and value-to-sales multiples are widely used to value technology firms and to compare value across these firms. An analysis of the fundamentals highlights the importance of profit margins in determining these multiples, in addition to the standard variables—the dividend payout ratio, the required rate of return, the expected growth rates for price to sales, and the reinvestment rate and risk for value to sales. Comparisons of revenue multiples across firms have to take into account differences in profit margins. One approach is to look for mismatches: low margins and high revenue multiples suggesting overvalued firms, and high margins and low revenue multiples suggesting undervalued firms. Another approach that controls for differences in fundamentals is the cross-sectional regression approach, where revenue multiples are regressed against fundamentals across firms in a business, an entire sector, or the market. Sector-specific multiples relate value to sector-specific variables, but they must be used with caution. It is often difficult to compare these multiples across firms without making stringent assumptions about their operations and growth potential.

ENDNOTES

1. As with price to future earnings, you could use a modified revenue multiple (to reflect differences in growth and margins) to arrive at a value.

2. For simplicity, assume that the cash flow is the same in each year. This can be generalized to allow cash flows to grow over time.

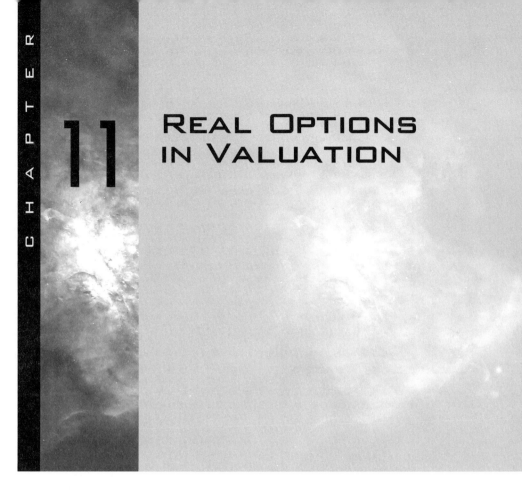

11 REAL OPTIONS IN VALUATION

In discounted cash flow valuation, the value of a firm is the present value of the expected cash flows from the assets of the firm. In recent years, this framework has come under some fire for failing to consider the options that are embedded in many firms. For instance, the discounted cash flow value of a young startup firm in a very large market may not reflect the possibility, small though it might be, that this firm may break out of the pack and become the next Microsoft or Cisco. Similarly, a firm with a patent or a license on a product may be undervalued with a discounted cash flow model because the expected cash flows do not consider the possibility that the patent could allow the firm to enter new markets.

In both the examples cited above, discounted cash flow valuation understates the value of the firm, not because the expected cash flows are too low—they reflect the probability of success—but because they ignore the options that these firms have to invest more in the future and take advantage of unexpected success in their businesses. These options are often called real options because the underlying assets are real investments, and they might explain, at least in some cases, why discounted cash flow valuations understate the value of technology firms.

This chapter begins with an introduction to options, the determinants of option value, and the basics of option pricing. The technicalities of option pricing are dealt with briefly, though some of the special issues that come up when valuing real options are presented. Two types of real options that are most likely to come up in the process of valuing technology firms are considered. The first is the option to delay investing in a proprietary technology that might not be viable today, and the second is the option to expand the firm to take advantage of unexpected opportunities that emerge in the market served by the firm. In the process, the question of when real options have significant value and have to be considered when valuing a firm is answered, as is the related question of when discounted cash flow valuation is sufficient.

BASICS OF OPTION PRICING

An option provides the holder with the right to buy or sell a specified quantity of an *underlying asset* at a fixed price (called a *strike price* or an *exercise price*) at or before the expiration date of the option. Since it is a right and not an obligation, the holder can choose not to exercise the right and allow the option to expire. There are two types of options: *call options* and *put options*.

CALL OPTIONS: DESCRIPTION AND PAYOFF DIAGRAMS

A call option gives the buyer of the option the right to buy the underlying asset at a fixed price, called the strike or the exercise price, any time prior to the expiration date of the option. The buyer pays a price for this right. If at expiration, the value of the asset is less than the strike price, the option is not exercised and expires worthless. If, on the other hand, the value of the asset is greater than the strike price, the option is exercised—the buyer of the option buys the stock at the exercise price, and the difference between the asset value and the exercise price constitutes the gross profit on the investment. The net profit on the investment is the difference between the gross profit and the price paid for the call initially.

A payoff diagram illustrates the cash payoff on an option at expiration. For a call, the net payoff is negative (and equal to the price paid for the call) if the value of the underlying asset is less than the strike price. If the price of the underlying asset exceeds the strike price, the gross payoff is the difference between the value of the underlying asset and the strike price, and the net payoff is the difference between the gross payoff and the price of the call. This is illustrated in Figure 11–1.

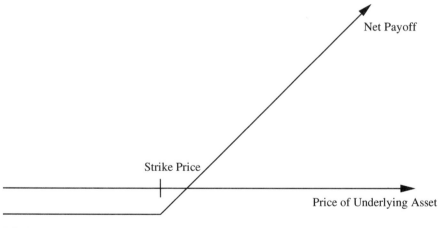

FIGURE 11–1
Payoff on Call Option

PUT OPTIONS: DESCRIPTION AND PAYOFF DIAGRAMS

A put option gives the buyer of the option the right to sell the underlying asset at a fixed price, again called the strike or exercise price, at any time prior to the expiration date of the option. The buyer pays a price for this right. If the price of the underlying asset is greater than the strike price, the option will not be exercised and will expire worthless. If, on the other hand, the price of the underlying asset is less than the strike price, the owner of the put option will exercise the option and sell the stock at the strike price, claiming the difference between the strike price and the market value of the asset as the gross profit—again, netting out the initial cost paid for the put yields the net profit from the transaction.

A put has a negative net payoff if the value of the underlying asset exceeds the strike price and has a gross payoff equal to the difference between the strike price and the value of the underlying asset if the asset value is less than the strike price. This is summarized in Figure 11–2.

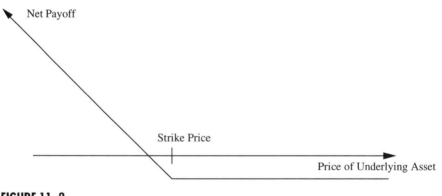

FIGURE 11–2
Payoff on Put Option

DETERMINANTS OF OPTION VALUE

The value of an option is determined by a number of variables relating to the underlying asset, the option itself, and financial markets.

- *Current value of the underlying asset:* Options are assets that derive value from an underlying asset. Consequently, changes in the value of the underlying asset affect the value of the options on that asset. Since calls provide the right to buy the underlying asset at a fixed price, an increase in the value of the asset will increase the value of the calls. Puts, on the other hand, become less valuable as the value of the asset increases.

- *Variance in value of the underlying asset:* The buyer of an option acquires the right to buy or sell the underlying asset at a fixed price. The higher the variance in the value of the underlying asset, the greater the value of the option. This is true for both calls and puts. While it may seem counterintuitive that an increase in a risk measure (variance) should increase value, options are different from other securities because buyers of options can never lose more than the price they pay for the options; in fact, the buyers have the potential to earn significant returns from large price movements.

- *Dividends paid on the underlying asset:* The value of the underlying asset can be expected to decrease if dividend payments are made on the asset during the life of the option. Consequently, the value of a call on the asset is a *decreasing* function of the size of expected dividend payments, and the value of a put is an *increasing* function of expected dividend payments. A more intuitive way of thinking about dividend payments for call options is as a cost of delaying exercise on in-the-money options. To see why, consider an option on a traded stock. Once a call option is in-the-money, exercising the call option will provide the holder with the stock and entitle him or her to the dividends on the stock in subsequent periods. Failing to exercise the option will mean that these dividends are foregone.

- *Strike price of option:* A key characteristic used to describe an option is the strike price. In the case of calls, where the holder acquires the right to buy at a fixed price, the value of the call will decline as the strike price increases. In the case of puts, where the holder has the right to sell at a fixed price, the value will increase as the strike price increases.

- *Time to expiration on option:* Both calls and puts become more valuable as the time to expiration increases. The reason is that the longer time to expiration provides more time for the value of the underlying asset to move, increasing the value of both types of options. Additionally, in the case of a call, where the buyer has to pay a fixed price at expiration, the present value of this fixed price decreases as the life of the option increases, further increasing the value of the call.

- *Riskless interest rate corresponding to life of option:* Since the buyer of an option pays the price of the option up front, an opportunity cost is involved. This cost depends on the level of interest rates and the time to expiration on the option. The riskless interest rate also enters into the valuation of options when the present value of the exercise price is calculated, since the exercise price does not have to be paid (received) until expiration on calls (puts). Increases in the interest rate will increase the value of calls and reduce the value of puts.

Table 11.1 summarizes the variables and their predicted effects on call and put prices.

TABLE 11.1 Summary of Variables Affecting Call and Put Prices

	EFFECT ON	
Factor	Call Value	Put Value
Increase in underlying asset's value	Increases	Decreases
Increase in strike price	Decreases	Increases
Increase in variance of underlying asset	Increases	Increases
Increase in time to expiration	Increases	Increases
Increase in interest rates	Increases	Decreases
Increase in dividends paid	Decreases	Increases

AMERICAN VERSUS EUROPEAN OPTIONS: VARIABLES RELATING TO EARLY EXERCISE

A primary distinction between American and European options is that American options can be exercised at any time prior to their expiration, whereas European options can be exercised only at expiration. The possibility of early exercise makes American options more valuable than otherwise similar European options; it also makes them more difficult to value. One compensating factor enables the former to be valued with models designed for the latter. In most cases, the time premium associated with the remaining life of an option and transaction costs makes early exercise suboptimal. In other words, the holders of in-the-money options generally profit much more by selling the option to someone else than by exercising the options.

Although early exercise is not optimal generally, there are at least two exceptions to this rule. One is a case where the *underlying asset pays large dividends*, thus reducing the value of the asset and any call options on that asset. In this case, call options can be exercised just before an ex-dividend date if the time premium on the options is less than the expected decline in asset value as a consequence of the dividend payment. The other exception arises when an investor holds both the underlying asset and *deep in-the-money puts* on that asset at a time when interest rates are high. In this case, the time premium on the put may be less than the potential gain from exercising the put early and earning interest on the exercise price.

OPTION PRICING MODELS

Option pricing theory has made vast strides since 1972, when Black and Scholes published their path-breaking paper that provides a model for valuing dividend-protected European options. Black and Scholes used a "replicating portfolio"—a portfolio composed of the underlying asset and the risk-free asset that had the same cash flows as the option being valued—to come up with their final formulation. Their derivation is mathematically complicated, but a simpler binomial model for valuing options draws on the same logic.

The Binomial Model. The *binomial option-pricing model* is based on a simple formulation for the asset price process, in which the asset, in any time period, can move to one of two possible prices. The general formulation of a stock price process that follows the binomial is shown in Figure 11–3 for a two-period process.

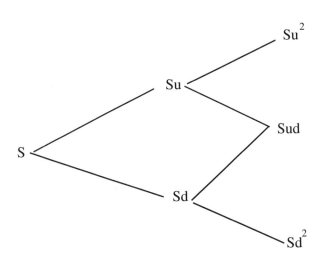

FIGURE 11–3
General Formulation for Binomial Price Path

In the figure, S is the current stock price; the price moves up to Su with probability p and down to Sd with probability 1 – p in any time period; the up movement is u and the down movement is d.

Creating a Replicating Portfolio. The objective in creating a replicating portfolio is to use a combination of risk-free borrowing/lending and the underlying asset to create the same cash flows as the option being valued. The principles of arbitrage apply here, and the value of the option must be equal to the value of the replicating portfolio. In the case of the general formulation above, where stock prices can either move up to Su or down to Sd in any time period, the replicating portfolio for a call with strike price K will involve borrowing $B and acquiring Δ of the underlying asset, where:

$$\Delta = \text{Number of units of the underlying asset bought}$$
$$= (C_u - C_d) / (Su - Sd)$$

where

C_u = Value of the call if the stock price is Su
C_d = Value of the call if the stock price is Sd

In a multiperiod binomial process, the valuation has to proceed iteratively; that is, starting with the last time period and moving backward in time until the current point in time. The portfolios replicating the option are created at each step and valued, providing the values for the option in that time period. The final output from the binomial option pricing model is a statement of the value of the option in terms of the replicating portfolio, composed of Δ shares (option delta) of the underlying asset and risk-free borrowing/lending.

Value of the Call = Current Value of Underlying Asset
                    × Option Delta
                    – Borrowing Needed to Replicate the Option

An Example of Binomial Valuation. Assume that the objective is to value a call with a strike price of 50, which is expected to expire in two time periods, on an underlying asset whose price currently is 50 and is expected to follow a binomial process, as shown in Figure 11–4.

Now assume that the interest rate is 11%. In addition, define

Δ = Number of shares in the replicating portfolio
B = Dollars of borrowing in replicating portfolio

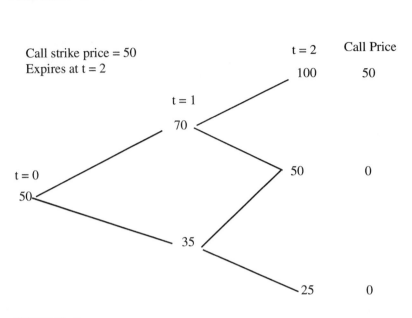

Call strike price = 50
Expires at t = 2

t = 2   Call Price
100   50

t = 1
70

t = 0
50

50   0

35

25   0

FIGURE 11–4
Example of Binomial Valuation

The objective is to combine Δ shares of stock and B dollars of borrowing to replicate the cash flows from the call with a strike price of $50. This replication can be done starting with the last period and working back through the binomial tree.

Step 1

Start with the end nodes and work backward (Figure 11–5). Thus, if the stock price is $70 at t = 1, borrowing $45 and buying one share of the stock will yield the same cash flows as buying the call. The value of the call at t = 1, if the stock price is $70, is therefore:

Value of Call = Value of Replicating Position = 70 Δ – B = 70 – 45 = 25

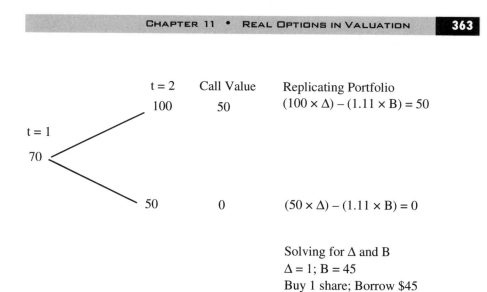

FIGURE 11–5
Replicating Portfolios at t = 1, Price = $70

Consider the other leg of the binomial tree at t = 1 as in Figure 11–6.

If the stock price is $35 at t = 1, then the call is worth nothing.

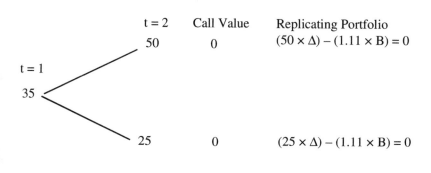

FIGURE 11–6
Replicating Portfolios at t = 1, Price = $35

Step 2

Move backward to the earlier time period and create a replicating portfolio that provides the cash flows the option provides, as shown in Figure 11–7.

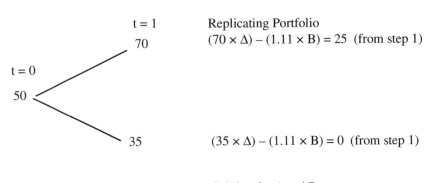

FIGURE 11–7
Replicating Portfolios at t = 0

In other words, borrowing $22.5 and buying 5/7 of a share provides the same cash flows as a call with a strike price of $50. The value of the call, therefore, has to be the same as the value of this position.

Value of Call = Value of Replicating Position
$$= 5/7 \times \text{Current Stock Price} - \$22.5 = \$13.20$$

The Determinants of Value. The binomial model provides insight into the determinants of option value. The value of an option is not determined by the expected price of the asset but by its current price, which, of course, reflects expectations about the future. This is a direct consequence of arbitrage. If the option value deviates from the value of the replicating portfolio, investors can create an arbitrage position, that is, one that requires no investment, involves no risk, and delivers positive returns. To illustrate, if the portfolio that replicates the call costs more than the call does in the market, an investor could buy the call, sell the replicating portfolio, and be guaranteed the difference as a profit. The cash flows on the two positions offset each other, leading to no cash flows in subsequent periods. The option value also increases as the time to expiration is extended, as the price movements (u and d) increase, and with increases in the interest rate.

The Black-Scholes Model. While the binomial model provides an intuitive feel for the determinants of option value, it requires a large number of inputs, in terms of expected future prices at each node. The Black-Scholes model is not an alternative to the binomial model; rather, it is one limiting case of the binomial.

The binomial model is a discrete-time model for asset price movements, including a time interval (t) between price movements. As the time interval is shortened, the limiting distribution as t approaches 0 can take one of two forms. If, as t approaches 0, price changes become smaller, the limiting distribution is the normal distribution, and the price process is a continuous one. If, as t approaches 0, price changes remain large, the limiting distribution is the Poisson distribution, that is, a distribution that allows for price jumps. The Black-Scholes model applies when the limiting distribution is the normal distribution,[1] and it explicitly assumes that the price process is continuous and that there are no jumps in asset prices.

The Model. The version of the model presented by Black and Scholes was designed to value European options, which were dividend protected. Thus, neither the possibility of early exercise nor the payment of dividends affects the value of options in this model.

The value of a call option in the Black-Scholes model can be written as a function of the following variables:

S = Current value of the underlying asset
K = Strike price of the option
t = Life to expiration of the option
r = Riskless interest rate corresponding to the life of the option
σ^2 = Variance in the ln(value) of the underlying asset

The model itself can be written as:

$$\text{Value of Call} = S\,N\,(d_1) - K\,e^{-rt}\,N(d_2)$$

where

$$d_1 = \frac{\ln\left(\frac{S}{K}\right) + \left(r + \frac{\sigma^2}{2}\right)t}{\sigma\sqrt{t}}$$

$$d_2 = d_1 - \sigma\sqrt{t}$$

The process of valuation of options with the Black-Scholes model involves the following steps:

Step 1

Use the inputs to the Black-Scholes to estimate d_1 and d_2.

Step 2

Estimate the cumulative normal distribution functions, $N(d_1)$ and $N(d_2)$, corresponding to these standardized normal variables.

Step 3

Estimate the present value of the exercise price, using the continuous time version of the present value formulation:

$$\text{Present Value of Exercise Price} = K\,e^{-rt}$$

Step 4

Estimate the value of the call from the Black-Scholes model.

The Replicating Portfolio in the Black-Scholes Model. The determinants of value in the Black-Scholes are the same as those in the binomial: the current value of the stock price, the variability in stock prices, the time to expiration on the option, the strike price, and the riskless interest rate. The principle of replicating portfolios that is used in binomial valuation also underlies the Black-Scholes model. In fact, embedded in the Black-Scholes model is the replicating portfolio.

$$\text{Value of Call} = S \, N \, (d_1) - K \, e^{-rt} \, N(d_2)$$

$$\underbrace{\qquad}_{\text{Buy } N(d_1) \text{ Shares}} \qquad \underbrace{\qquad}_{\text{Borrow } K \, e^{-rt} \, N(d_2)}$$

$N(d1)$, which is the number of shares that are needed to create the replicating portfolio, is called the *option delta*. This replicating portfolio is self-financing and has the same value as the call at every stage of the option's life.

Model Limitations and Fixes. The version of the Black-Scholes model presented above does not take into account the possibility of early exercise or the payment of dividends, both of which impact the value of options. Adjustments exist, which, while not perfect, provide partial corrections to value.

Dividends

The payment of dividends reduces the stock price. Consequently, call options become less valuable and put options more valuable as dividend payments increase. One approach to dealing with dividends is to estimate the present value of expected dividends paid by the underlying asset during the option life and subtract that value from the current value of the asset to use as S in the model. Since this approach becomes impractical as the option life becomes longer, you can use an alternate approach. If the dividend yield (y = dividends ÷ current value of the asset) of the underlying asset is expected to remain unchanged during the life of the option, you can modify the Black-Scholes model to take dividends into account:

$$C = S\ e^{-yt}\ N(d_1) - K\ e^{-rt}\ N(d_2)$$

where

$$d_1 = \frac{\ln\left(\dfrac{S}{K}\right) + \left(r - y + \dfrac{\sigma^2}{2}\right)t}{\sigma\sqrt{t}}$$

$$d_2 = d_1 - \sigma\sqrt{t}$$

From an intuitive standpoint, the adjustments have two effects. First, the value of the asset is discounted back to the present at the dividend yield to take into account the expected drop in value from dividend payments. Second, the interest rate is offset by the dividend yield to reflect the lower carrying cost from holding the stock (in the replicating portfolio). The net effect will be a reduction in the value of calls, with the adjustment, and an increase in the value of puts.

Early Exercise

The Black-Scholes model is designed to value European options, that is, options that cannot be exercised until the expiration day. Most of the options analyzed are American options, which can be exercised any time before expiration. Without working through the mechanics of valuation models, an American option should always be worth at least as much, and generally more, than a European option because of the early exercise option.

There are three basic approaches for dealing with the possibility of early exercise. The first is to continue to use the unadjusted Black-Scholes model and regard the resulting value as a floor or conservative estimate of the true value. The second approach is to value the option to each potential exercise date. With options on stocks, this approach basically requires that you value options to each ex-dividend day and choose the maximum of the estimated call values. The third approach is to use a modified version of the binomial model to consider the possibility of early exercise.

It is difficult to estimate the prices for each node of a binomial, but there is a way in which variances estimated from historical data can be used to compute the expected up and down movements in the binomial. To illustrate, if σ^2 is the variance in ln(stock prices), the up and down movements in the binomial can be estimated as follows:

$$u = \text{Exp}\,[(r - \sigma^2/2)(T/m) + \sqrt{(\sigma^2 T/m)}\,]$$

$$d = \text{Exp}\,[(r - \sigma^2/2)(T/m) - \sqrt{(\sigma^2 T/m)}\,]$$

where u and d are the up and down movements per unit time for the binomial, T is the life of the option, and m is the number of periods within that lifetime. Multiplying the stock price at each stage by u and d yields the up and the down prices. These can then be used to value the asset.

The Impact of Exercise on the Value of the Underlying Asset

The derivation of the Black-Scholes model is based on the assumption that exercising an option does not affect the value of the underlying asset. This may be true for listed options on stocks, but it is not true for other types of options. For instance, the exercise of warrants increases the number of shares outstanding and brings fresh cash into the firm, both of which will affect the stock price.[2] The expected negative impact (dilution) of exercise decreases the value of warrants compared to otherwise similar call options. The adjustment for dilution in the Black-Scholes to the stock price is fairly simple. The stock price is adjusted for the expected dilution from the exercise of the options. In the case of warrants, for instance:

$$\text{Dilution-Adjusted } S = (S\,n_s + W\,n_w) / (n_s + n_w)$$

where

S = Current value of the stock
n_s = Number of shares outstanding
W = Market value of warrants outstanding
n_w = Number of warrants outstanding

When the warrants are exercised, the number of shares outstanding increases, reducing the stock price. The numerator reflects the market value of equity, including both stocks and warrants outstanding. The reduction in S will reduce the value of the call option.

There is an element of circularity in this analysis: the value of the warrant is needed to estimate the dilution-adjusted S, and the dilution-adjusted S is needed to estimate the value of the warrant. You can resolve this problem by starting the process with an estimated value of the warrant (say, the exercise value) and then iterating with the new estimated value for the warrant until there is convergence.

Valuing Puts. The value of a put can be derived from the value of a call with the same strike price and the same expiration date through an arbitrage relationship that specifies that

$$C - P = S - K\,e^{-rt}$$

where C is the value of the call and P is the value of the put (with the same life and exercise price).

This arbitrage relationship can be derived fairly easily and is called *put-call parity*. To see why put-call parity holds, consider creating the following portfolio:

(a) Sell a call and buy a put with exercise price K and the same expiration date t.

(b) Buy the stock at current stock price S.

As you can see in Table 11.2, the payoff from this position is riskless and always yields K at expiration (t). To see this, assume that the stock price at expiration is S^*.

TABLE 11.2 Arbitrage and Put-Call Parity

POSITION	PAYOFFS AT T IF S* > K	PAYOFFS AT T IF S* < K
Sell call	$-(S^* - K)$	0
Buy put	0	$K - S^*$
Buy stock	S^*	S^*
Total	K	K

Since this position yields K with certainty, its value must be equal to the present value of K at the riskless rate ($K e^{-rt}$).

$$S + P - C = K e^{-rt}$$

$$C - P = S - K e^{-rt}$$

This relationship can be used to value puts. Substituting the Black-Scholes formulation with the dividend adjustment for the value of an equivalent call:

$$\text{Value of Put} = S\,e^{-yt}\,(N(d_1) - 1) - K\,e^{-rt}\,(N(d_2) - 1)$$

where

$$d_1 = \frac{\ln\left(\frac{S}{K}\right) + \left(r - y + \frac{\sigma^2}{2}\right)t}{\sigma\sqrt{t}}$$

$$d_2 = d_1 - \sigma\sqrt{t}$$

 optlt.xls: This spreadsheet enables you to estimate the value of an option, using the dividend-adjusted Black-Scholes model.

A FEW CAVEATS ON APPLYING OPTION PRICING MODELS

The option pricing models described in the preceding chapter can be used to value any asset that has the characteristics of an option, with some caveats. In subsequent sections, option pricing theory is applied in a variety of contexts. In many of the cases described, the options being valued are not on traded assets (such as stocks or commodities) but are real options (such as those on projects). There are a few caveats on the application of option pricing models to these cases, and some adjustments might need to be made to these models.

- *The underlying asset is not traded.* Option pricing theory, as presented in both the binomial and the Black-Scholes models, is built on the premise that a replicating portfolio can be created by the underlying asset and riskless lending or borrowing. While this is a perfectly justifiable assumption in the context of listed options on traded stocks, it becomes less defensible when the underlying asset is not traded and arbitrage is, therefore, not feasible. When the options valued are on assets that are not traded, the values from option pricing models must be interpreted with caution.
- *The price of the asset follows a continuous process.* As noted earlier, the Black-Scholes option pricing model is derived under the assumption that the underlying asset's price process is continuous (i.e., there are no price jumps). If this assumption is violated, as it is with many real options, the model will underestimate the value of deep out-of-the-money options. One solution is to use higher variance estimates to value deep out-of-the-money options and lower variance estimates for at-the-money or in-the-money options; another is to use an option pricing model that explicitly allows for price jumps, though the inputs to these models are often difficult to estimate.[3]

■ *The variance is known and does not change over the life of the option.* In most option pricing models, the variance is both known and constant over the option lifetime. This is not an unreasonable assumption when you are valuing a three-month or six-month option. When option pricing models are used to value long-term real options, however, there are problems with this assumption, since the variance is unlikely to remain constant over extended periods of time and may, in fact, be difficult to estimate in the first place. Again, there are modified versions of the option pricing model that allow for changing variances, but they require that the process by which variance changes be modeled explicitly.

■ *Exercise is instantaneous.* The option pricing models are based on the premise that the exercise of an option is instantaneous. This assumption may be difficult to justify with real options, however; exercise may require building a plant or constructing an oil rig, for example, actions that do not happen in an instant. The fact that exercise takes time also implies that the true life of a real option is often less than the stated life. Thus, while a firm may own the rights to an oil reserve for the next 10 years, the fact that it takes several years to extract the oil reduces the life of the natural resource option the firm owns.

BARRIER, COMPOUND, AND RAINBOW OPTIONS

So far in the discussion of option pricing, the more complicated options that often arise in analysis have not been considered. In this section, we examine three variations on the simple option. The first is a *barrier option*, where the option value is capped if the price of the underlying asset exceeds a prespecified level. The second is the *compound option*, which is an option on an option. The third is a *rainbow option*, for which more than one source of uncertainty affects the value of the option.

Capped and Barrier Options. Assume that you have a call option with a strike price of $25 on an asset. In an unrestricted call option, the payoff on this option will increase as the underlying asset's price increases above $25. Assume, however, that if the price reaches $50, the payoff is capped at $25. The payoff diagram on this option is shown in Figure 11–8.

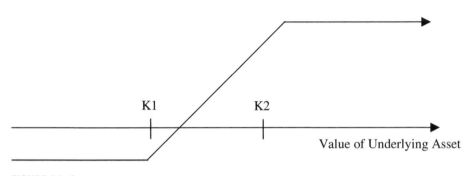

FIGURE 11–8
Payoff on Capped and Barrier Options

This option is called a *capped call*. Notice, also, that once the price reaches $50, no time premium is associated with the option anymore and that the option will therefore be exercised. Capped calls are part of a family of options called *barrier options*, where the payoff on and the life of the option is a function of whether the underlying asset reaches a certain level during a specified period. Caps are commonly found in convertible bonds (where bondholders are forced to exercise at a certain price), and floating rate bonds often have both caps and floors on interest rates.

The value of a capped call will always be lower than the value of the same call without the payoff limit. You can obtain a simple approximation of this value by valuing the call twice, once with the given exercise price and once with the cap, and taking the difference in the two values. In the above example, then, the value of the call with an exercise price of K_1 and a cap at K_2 can be written as:

Value of Capped Call = Value of Call $(K = K_1)$ – Value of Call $(K = K_2)$

Barrier options can take many forms. In a *knockout option*, an option ceases to exist if the option reaches a certain price. In the case of a call option, this knockout price is usually set below the strike price; this option is called a *down-and-out option*. In the case of a put option, the knockout price will be set above the exercise price; this option is called an *up-and-out option*. Like the capped call, these options will be worth less than their unrestricted counterparts. Many real options have limits on potential upside or knockout provisions, and ignoring these limits can result in the overstatement of the value of these options.

Compound Options. Some options derive their value, not from an underlying asset, but from other options. These options are called *compound options*. Compound options can take any of four forms: a call on a call, a put on a put, a call on a put, and a put on a call. Geske (1979) developed the analytical formulation for valuing compound options by replacing the standard normal distribution used in a simple option model with a bivariate normal distribution in the calculation.

In the context of real options, the compound option process can get complicated. Consider, for instance, the option to expand a project considered in the next section. While this option is valued with a simple option pricing model, in reality, there could be multiple stages in expansion, with each stage representing an option for the following stage. In this case, you value the option by considering it as a compound rather than a simple option.

Notwithstanding this discussion, the valuation of compound options becomes progressively more difficult as more options are added to the chain. In this case, rather than wreck the valuation on the shoals of estimation error, it may be better to accept the conservative estimate that is provided with a simple valuation model as a floor on the value.

Rainbow Options. In a simple option, the only source of uncertainty is the price of the underlying asset. There are some options that derive their value from two or more sources of uncertainty; these options are called *rainbow options*. Using the simple option pricing model to value such options can lead to biased estimates of value. As an example, consider an undeveloped oil reserve as an option, where the firm that owns the reserve has the right to develop the reserve. Here, there are two sources of uncertainty. The first is obviously the price of oil, and the second is the quantity of oil that is in the reserve.

To value this undeveloped reserve, we simply assume that the quantity of the reserves is known with certainty. In reality, however, uncertainty about the quantity will affect the value of this option and make the decision to exercise more difficult.[4]

THE OPTION TO DELAY

Projects are typically analyzed on the basis of their expected cash flows and discount rates at the time of the analysis; the net present value computed on that basis is a measure of its value and acceptability at that time. Expected cash flows and discount rates change over time, however, and so does the net present value. Thus, a project that now has a negative net present value may have a positive net present value in the future. In a competitive environment in which individual firms have no special advantages over their competitors in taking projects, this may not seem significant. In an environment in which a project can be taken by only one firm (because of legal restrictions or other barriers to entry to competitors), however, the changes in the project's value over time give it the characteristics of a call option.

THE PAYOFF DIAGRAM ON THE OPTION TO DELAY

In the abstract, assume that a project requires an initial up-front investment of X and that the present value of expected cash inflows computed right now is V. The net present value of this project is the difference between the two:

$$NPV = V - X$$

Now, assume that the firm has exclusive rights to this project for the next n years and that the present value of the cash inflows may change over that time because of changes in either the cash flows or the discount rate. Thus, the project may have a negative net present value right now, but it may still become a good project if the firm waits. Defining V^* again as the present value of the cash flows, the firm's decision rule on this project can be summarized as follows:

- If $V^* > X$, invest in the project: project has positive net present value.
- If $V^* < X$, do not invest in the project: project has negative net present value.

If the firm does not invest in the project, it incurs no additional cash flows, though it will lose what it originally invested in the project. This relationship can be presented in a payoff diagram of cash flows on this project, as shown in Figure 11–9, assuming that the firm holds out until the end of the period for which it has exclusive rights to the project.

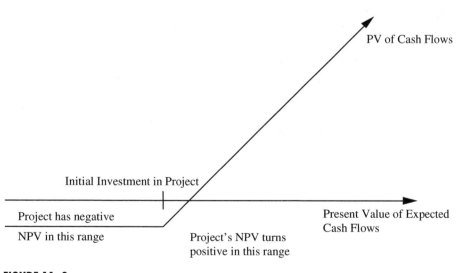

FIGURE 11–9
The Option to Delay a Project

Note that this payoff diagram is that of a call option—the underlying asset is the project, the strike price of the option is the investment needed to take the project, and the life of the option is the period for which the firm has rights to the project. The present value of the cash flows on this project and the expected variance in this present value represent the value and variance of the underlying asset.

VALUING THE OPTION TO DELAY

On the surface, the inputs needed to apply the option pricing model to valuing the option to delay are the same as those needed for any option. The inputs include the following: the value of the underlying asset, the variance in that value, the time to expiration on the option, the strike price, the riskless rate, and the equivalent of the dividend yield (cost of delay). Actually estimating these inputs for valuing an option to delay can be difficult.

Value of the Underlying Asset. In the case of options to delay a project, the underlying asset is the project itself. The current value of this asset is the present value of expected cash flows from initiating the project now, not including the up-front investment, which you can obtain by doing a standard capital budgeting analysis. There is likely to be a substantial amount of noise in the cash flow estimates and the present value, however. Rather than being viewed as a problem, this uncertainty should be viewed as the reason for why the project delay option has value. If the expected cash flows on the project were known with certainty and were not expected to change, there would be no need to adopt an option pricing framework, since there would be no value to the option.

Variance in the Value of the Asset. As noted in the prior section, there is likely to be considerable uncertainty associated with the cash flow estimates and the present value that measures the value of the asset now, partly because the potential market size for the product may be unknown, and partly because technological shifts can change the cost structure and profitability of the product. The variance in the present value of cash flows from the project can be estimated in one of three ways.

- If similar projects have been introduced in the past, the variance in the cash flows from those projects can be used as an estimate. This may be the way that a firm like Intel might estimate the variance associated with introducing a new computer chip.

- Probabilities can be assigned to various market scenarios, cash flows estimated under each scenario, and the variance estimated across present values. Alternatively, the probability distributions can be estimated for each of the inputs into the project analysis—the size of the market, the market share, and the profit margin, for instance—and simulations used to estimate the variance in the present values that emerge. This approach tends to work best when there are only one or two sources[5] of significant uncertainty about future cash flows.

- The variance in firm value of firms involved in the same business (as the project being considered) can be used as an estimate of the variance. Thus, the average variance in firm value of firms involved in the software business can be used as the variance in present value of a software project.

The value of the option is largely derived from the variance in cash flows; the higher the variance, the higher the value of the project delay option. Thus, the value of an option to invest in a project in a stable business will be less than the value of one in an environment where technology, competition, and markets are all changing rapidly.

Exercise Price on Option. A project delay option is exercised when the firm owning the rights to the project decides to invest in it. The cost of making this investment is the exercise price of the option. The underlying assumption is that this cost remains constant (in present value dollars) and that any uncertainty associated with the product is reflected in the present value of cash flows on the product.

Expiration of the Option and the Riskless Rate. The project delay option expires when the rights to the project lapse; investments made after the project rights expire are assumed to deliver a net present value of zero as competition drives returns down to the required rate. The riskless rate to use in pricing the option should be the rate that corresponds to the expiration of the option. While the life of the option can be estimated easily when firms have the explicit right to a project (through a license or a patent, for instance), it becomes far more difficult to obtain when firms only have a competitive advantage to take a project. Since competitive advantages fade over time, the number of years for which the firm can be expected to have these advantages is the life of the option.

Cost of Delay (Dividend Yield). There is a cost to delaying taking a project, once the net present value turns positive. Since the project rights expire after a fixed period and excess profits (which are the source of positive present value) are assumed to disappear after that time as new competitors emerge, each year of delay translates into one less year of value-creating cash flows.[6] If the cash flows are evenly distributed over time and the life of the patent is n years, the cost of delay can be written as:

$$\text{Annual Cost of Delay} = \frac{1}{n}$$

Thus, if the project rights are for 20 years, then the annual cost of delay works out to 5% a year. Note, though, that this cost of delay rises each year, to 1/19 in year two, 1/18 in year three, and so on, making the cost of delaying exercise larger over time.

optvar.xls: A dataset on the Web that summarizes standard deviations in equity and firm value, by industry, for firms in the United States.

ILLUSTRATION 11.1

Valuing the Option to Delay a Project

Assume that you have, or are interested in acquiring, the exclusive rights to market a new product that will make it easier for people to access their e-mail on the road. If you do acquire the rights to the product, you estimate that it will cost you $500 million up front to set up the infrastructure needed to provide the service. Based on your current projections, you believe that the service will generate only $100 million in after-tax cash flows each year. In addition, you expect to operate without serious competition for the next five years.

You compute the net present value of this project by taking the present value of the expected cash flows over the next five years. Assuming a discount rate of 15% (based on the riskiness of this project), you obtain the following net present value for the project:

NPV of Project = –$500 million + $100 million (PV of Annuity, 15%, 5 Years)
= –$500 million + $335 million = –$165 million

This project has a negative net present value.

The biggest source of uncertainty on this project is the number of people who will be interested in this product. Current market tests indicate that you will capture a relatively small number of business travelers as your customers, but the tests also indicate a possibility that the potential market could get much larger over time. In fact, a simulation of the project's cash flows yields a standard deviation of the 42% in the present value of the cash flows, with an expected value of $335 million.

To value the exclusive rights to this project, you first define the inputs to the option pricing model:

Value of the underlying asset (S) = PV of cash flows from project if introduced now
= $335 million

Strike price (K) = Initial investment needed to introduce the product = $500 million

Variance in underlying asset's value = $0.42^2 = 0.1764$

Time to expiration = Period of exclusive rights to product = 5 years

Dividend yield = 1 / life of the patent = 1 / 5 = 0.20

Assume that the 5-year riskless rate is 5%. The value of the option can be estimated as follows:

Call Value = 335 exp$^{(-0.2)(5)}$ (0.2250) − 500 (exp$^{(-0.05)(5)}$ (0.0451) = $10.18 million

The rights to this product, which has a negative net present value if introduced today, is $10.18 million.

PRACTICAL CONSIDERATIONS

While it is quite clear that the option to delay is embedded in many projects, several problems are associated with the use of option pricing models to value these options. First, *the underlying asset in this option, which is the project, is not traded*, making it difficult to estimate its value and variance. The value can be estimated from the expected cash flows and the discount rate for the project, albeit with error. The variance is more difficult to estimate, however, since you are attempting to estimate a variance in project value over time.

Second, *the behavior of prices over time may not conform to the price path assumed by the option pricing models.* In particular, the assumption that value follows a continuous process and that the variance in value remains unchanged over time may be difficult to justify in the context of a project. For instance, a sudden technological change may dramatically change the value of a project, either positively or negatively.

Third, *there may be no specific period for which the firm has rights to the project.* Unlike the example above, in which the firm had exclusive rights to the project for 20 years, often the firm's rights may be less clearly defined, both in terms of exclusivity and time. For instance, a firm may have significant advantages over its competitors, which may, in turn, provide it with the virtually exclusive rights to a project for a period of time. The rights are not legal restrictions, however, and could erode faster than expected. In such cases, the expected life of the project itself is uncertain and only an estimate. In the valuation of the rights to the product in the previous section, a life of five years was used for the option, but competitors could, in fact, enter sooner than anticipated. Alternatively, the barriers to entry may turn out to be greater than expected and allow the firm to earn excess returns for longer than five years. Ironically, uncertainty about the expected life of the option can increase the variance in present value and, through it, the expected value of the rights to the project.

 delay.xls: This spreadsheet enables you to estimate the value of the option to delay a project.

IMPLICATIONS FOR PROJECT ANALYSIS AND VALUATION

Several interesting implications emerge from the analysis of the option to delay a project as an option, especially in the context of technology firms.

First, a project may have a negative net present value based on expected cash flows currently, but the rights to that project may still be valuable because of the option characteristics.

Second, a project may have a positive net present value but still not be accepted right away—the firm may gain by waiting and accepting the project in a future period, for the same reasons that investors do not always exercise an option just because it is in-the-money. This is more likely to happen if the firm has the rights to the project for a long time and the variance in project inflows is high. To illustrate, assume that a firm has the patent rights to produce a new type of disk drive for computer systems and that building a new plant will yield a positive net present value right now. If the technology for manufacturing the disk drive is in flux, however, the firm may delay taking the project in the hopes that the improved technology will increase the expected cash flows and, consequently, the value of the project. It has to weigh this prospect against the cost of delaying taking the project, which will be the cash flows that will be forsaken by not taking the project.

Third, factors that can make a project less attractive in a static analysis can actually make the rights to the project more valuable. As an example, consider the effect of uncertainty about how long the firm will be able to operate without competition and earn excess returns. In a static analysis, increasing this uncertainty increases the riskiness of the project and may make it less attractive. When the project is viewed as an option, an increase in the uncertainty may actually make the option more valuable, not less.

What are the implications for discounted cash flow valuation? Consider a firm that owns the rights to a specific technological product (hardware or software) that is not viable today, but is expected to become viable in the future. On a discounted cash flow basis, these rights are worthless and add no value to the firm. Considered as options, however, these rights have value and you should consider them when valuing the firm. In the next section, we look at patents in this light and attempt to assign a value to them.

VALUING A PATENT

A product patent provides a firm with the right to develop and market a product. The firm will do so only if the present value of the expected cash flows from the product sales exceeds the cost of development, as shown in Figure 11–10. If this does not occur, the firm can shelve the patent and not incur any further costs. If I is the present value of the costs of developing the product and V is the present value of the expected cash flows from development, the payoffs from owning a product patent can be written as:

$$
\text{Payoff from Owning a Product Patent} = V - I \quad \text{if } V > I
$$
$$
= 0 \quad \text{if } V = I
$$

Thus, a product patent can be viewed as a call option, where the product is the underlying asset, as in Figure 11–10.

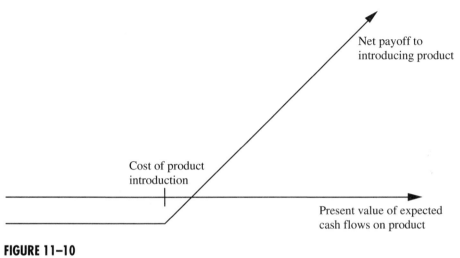

FIGURE 11–10
Payoff to Introducing a Product

ILLUSTRATION 11.2

Valuing a Patent: Avonex in 1997

Biogen is a biotechnology firm with a patent on a drug called Avonex, which has passed FDA approval to treat multiple sclerosis. Assume that you are trying to value the patent to Biogen and that you arrive at the following estimates for use in the option pricing model:

- An internal analysis of the drug today, based on the potential market and the price that the firm can expect to charge, yields a present value of cash flows of $3.422 billion, prior to consideration of the initial development cost.

- The initial cost of developing the drug for commercial use is estimated to be $2.875 billion if the drug is introduced today.

- The firm has the patent on the drug for the next 17 years, and the current long-term treasury bond rate is 6.7%.

- Although it is difficult to reasonably simulate the cash flows and present values, the average variance in firm value for publicly traded biotechnology firms is 0.224.

- It is assumed that the potential for excess returns exists only during the patent life and that competition will wipe out excess returns beyond that period. Thus, any delay in introducing the drug once it becomes viable will cost the firm one year of patent-protected excess returns. (For the initial analysis, the cost of delay will be 1/17, next year it will be 1/16, the year after 1/15, and so on.)

Based on these assumptions, you obtain the following inputs to the option pricing model.

Present value of cash flows from introducing the drug now = S = $3.422 billion

Initial cost of developing drug for commercial use (today) = K = $2.875 billion

Patent life = t = 17 years

Riskless rate = r = 6.7% (17-year T-bond rate)

Variance in expected present values = $\sigma^2 = 0.224$

Expected cost of delay = y = 1/17 = 5.89%

These yield the following estimates for d and N(d):

d1 = 1.1362   N(d1) = 0.8720

d2 = −0.8512   N(d2) = 0.2076

Plugging back into the option pricing model:

Value of the Patent =

$3,422^{(-0.0589)(17)} (0.8720) - 2,875\ exp^{(-0.067)(17)} (0.2076) = \$907$ million

Contrast this result with the net present value of this project:

NPV = $3,422 million – $2,875 million = $547 million

The time premium on this option suggests that the firm will be better off waiting rather than developing the drug immediately, the cost of delay notwithstanding.[7] However, the cost of delay will increase over time and make exercise (development) more likely.

 product.xls: This spreadsheet enables you to estimate the value of a patent, using an option pricing model.

FROM PATENT VALUE TO FIRM VALUE

If the patents owned by a firm can be valued as options, how can this estimate be incorporated into firm value? The value of a firm that derives its value primarily from commercial products that emerge from its patents can be written as a function of three variables:

- The cash flows it derives from patents that it has already converted into commercial products
- The value of the patents that it already possesses that have not been commercially developed
- The expected value of any patents that the firm can be expected to generate in future periods from new patents that it might obtain as a result of its research

Value of Firm =
Value of Commercial Products + Value of Existing Patents
+ (Value of New Patents That Will Be Obtained in the Future – Cost of Obtaining These Patents)

You can estimate the value of the first component by using traditional cash flow models. The expected cash flows from existing products can be estimated for their commercial lives and discounted back to the present at the appropriate cost of capital to arrive at the value of these products. The value of the second component can be obtained with the option pricing model described earlier to value each patent. The value of the third component will be based on perceptions of a firm's research capabilities. In the special case, where the expected cost of research and development in future periods is equal to the value of the patents that will be generated by this research, the third component will become zero. In the more general case, firms such as Cisco and Pfizer that have a history of generating value from research will derive positive value from this component as well.

How would the estimate of value obtained from this approach contrast with the estimate obtained in a traditional discounted cash flow model? In traditional discounted cash flow valuation, the second and the third components of value are captured in the expected growth rate in cash flows. Firms such as Cisco are allowed to grow at much higher rates for longer periods because of the technological edge they possess and their research prowess. In contrast, the approach described in this section looks at each patent separately and allows for the option component of value explicitly.

The biggest limitation of the option-based approach is the information that is needed to put it in practice. To value each patent separately, you need access to proprietary information that is usually available only to managers of the firm. In fact, some of the information, such as the expected variance to use in option pricing, may not even be available to insiders and will have to be estimated for each patent separately.

Given these limitations, the real option approach should be used to value small firms with one or two patents and little in terms of established assets. A good example would be Biogen in 1997, which was valued in the last section. For firms such as Cisco and Lucent that have significant assets in place and dozens of patents, discounted cash flow valuation is a more pragmatic choice. Viewing new technology as options provides insight into Cisco's successful growth strategy over the last decade. Cisco has been successful at buying firms with nascent and promising technologies (options) and converting them into commercial success (exercising these options).

ILLUSTRATION 11.3

Valuing Biogen as a Firm

In Illustration 11.2, the patent that Biogen owns on Avonex was valued as a call option and the estimated value was $907 million. To value Biogen as a firm two other components of value are considered:

- Biogen had two commercial products (a drug to treat Hepatitis B and Intron) that it had licensed to other pharmaceutical firms at the time of this valuation. The license fees on these products were expected to generate $50 million in after-tax cash flows each year for the next 12 years. To value these cash flows, which were guaranteed contractually, the riskless rate of 6.7% was used:

Present Value of License Fees = $50 million $(1 - (1.067)^{-12}) / 0.067 = $403.56 million

- Biogen continued to fund research into new products, spending about $100 million on R&D in the most recent year. These R&D expenses were expected to grow 20% a year for the next 10 years, and 5% thereafter. While it was difficult to forecast the specific patents that would emerge from this research, it was assumed that every dollar invested in research would create $1.25 in value in patents[8] (valued using the option pricing model described above) for the next 10 years, and break even after that (i.e., generate $1 in patent value for every $1 invested in R&D). There was a significant amount of risk associated with this component, and the cost of capital was estimated to be 15%.[9] The value of this component was then estimated as follows:

$$\text{Value of Future Research} = \sum_{t=1}^{T=\infty} \frac{\text{Value of Patents}_t - \text{R\&D}_t}{(1+r)^t}$$

Table 11.3 summarizes the value of patents generated each period and the R&D costs in that period. Note no surplus value is created after the tenth year.

TABLE 11.3 Value of New Research

YEAR	VALUE OF PATENTS GENERATED	R&D COST	EXCESS VALUE	PRESENT VALUE AT 15%
1	$150.00	$120.00	$30.00	$26.09
2	$180.00	$144.00	$36.00	$27.22
3	$216.00	$172.80	$43.20	$28.40
4	$259.20	$207.36	$51.84	$29.64
5	$311.04	$248.83	$62.21	$30.93
6	$373.25	$298.60	$74.65	$32.27
7	$447.90	$358.32	$89.58	$33.68
8	$537.48	$429.98	$107.50	$35.14
9	$644.97	$515.98	$128.99	$36.67
10	$773.97	$619.17	$154.79	$38.26
				$318.30

The total value created by new research is $318.3 million.

The value of Biogen as a firm is the sum of all three components: the present value of cash flows from existing products, the value of Avonex (as an option), and the value created by new research:

Value = CF: Commerical Products + Value: Undeveloped Patents + Value: Future R&D
= $403.56 million + $907 million + $318.30 million = $1628.86 million

Since Biogen had no debt outstanding, this value was divided by the number of shares outstanding (35.50 million) to arrive at a value per share:

Value per Share = $1,628.86 million / 35.5 = $45.88

THE OPTION TO EXPAND

In some cases, firms invest in projects because doing so allows them either to invest in other projects or to enter other markets in the future. In such cases, it can be argued that the initial projects are options allowing the firm to invest in other projects and the firm should therefore be willing to pay a price for such options. A firm might accept a negative net present value on the initial project because of the possibility of high positive net present values on future projects.

To examine this option with the framework developed earlier, assume that the present value of the expected cash flows, as estimated today, from entering the new market or taking the new project is V, and the total investment needed to enter this market or take this project is X. Further, assume that the firm has a fixed time horizon, at the end of which it has to make the final decision on whether to take advantage of this expansion opportunity. Finally, assume that the firm cannot move forward on this opportunity if it does not take the initial project. This scenario implies the option payoffs shown in Figure 11–11.

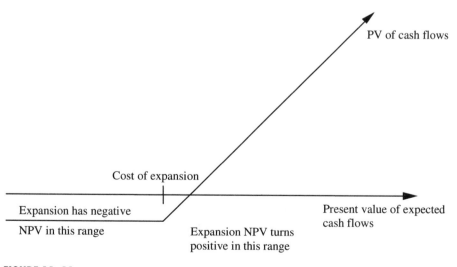

FIGURE 11–11
The Option to Expand a Project

At the expiration of the fixed-time horizon, the firm will enter the new market or take the new project if the present value of the expected cash flows at that point in time exceeds the cost of entering the market. If the expansion opportunity never has positive net present value, the firm loses the cost of acquiring the option, which is the negative net present value on the initial investment.

ILLUSTRATION 11.4

Valuing an Option to Expand: Amazon

Assume that Amazon is considering creating a Spanish version of its Web site and expanding into the Mexican market. It is estimated that the cost of creating this site will be $500 million and that the present value of the expected cash flows from the investment will be only $300 million. In other words, this venture considered on a stand-alone basis has a negative net present value of $200 million.

Assume, however, that by investing in this site and expanding into Mexico today, Amazon acquires the option to expand into the much larger Latin American market any time over the next 10 years. The cost of expansion will be $1 billion, and it will be undertaken only if the present value of the expected cash flows exceeds this value. At the moment, the present value of the expected cash flows from the expansion is believed to be only $850 million; thus, the expansion would not make economic sense today. Amazon still does not know much about the Latin American market, and there is considerable uncertainty about this estimate of present value. The variance in this estimate, based on the variance of publicly traded Internet ventures in Latin America, is 0.20.

You can estimate the value of the option to expand by defining the inputs to the option pricing model as follows:

> Value of the underlying asset (S) =
> PV of cash flows from expansion into Latin America, if done now = $850 million
>
> Strike price (K) = cost of expansion into Latin America = $1,000 million
>
> Variance in underlying asset's value = 0.20

Time to expiration = Period for which expansion option applies = 10 years

Assume that the ten-year riskless rate is 6%. The value of the option can be estimated as follows:

Call Value = 850 (0.8453) − 1000 (exp$^{(-0.06)(10)}$ (0.3454) = $528.94 million

This value can be added on to the net present value of the original project under consideration.

NPV of Mexican Venture = −$500 million + $300 million = −$200 million

Value of Option to Expand = $528.94 million

NPV of Investment with Expansion Option =
−$200 million + $528.94 million = $328.94 million

Amazon should invest in the Mexican venture even though it has a negative net present value because the option to expand into Latin America that emerges from the investment has such high value.

PRACTICAL CONSIDERATIONS

The practical considerations associated with estimating the value of the option to expand are similar to those associated with valuing the option to delay. In most cases, firms with options to expand have no specific time horizon by which they have to make an expansion decision, making these open-ended options or, at best, options with uncertain lives. Even in those cases where a life can be estimated for the option, neither the size nor the potential market for the product may be known, and estimating either can be problematic. To illustrate, consider the Amazon example discussed above. At the end of 10 years, it is assumed that Amazon has to decide whether or not to expand into Latin America. It is entirely possible that this time frame is not specified at the time the initial investment is made. Furthermore, it is assumed that both the cost and the present value of expansion can be estimated initially.

In reality, the firm may not have good estimates for either input before making the first investment, since it does not have much information on the underlying market.

IMPLICATIONS FOR VALUATION

Is there an option to expand embedded in some firms that can lead these firms to trade at a premium over their discounted cash flow values? At least in theory, there is a rationale for making this argument for a small, high-growth firm in a large and evolving market. The discounted cash flow valuation is based on expected cash flows and expected growth, and these expectations should reflect the probability that the firm could be hugely successful (or a huge failure). What the expectations might fail to consider is that, in the event of success, the firm could invest more, add new products, or expand into new markets and augment this success. This is the real option that is creating the additional value.

If the value of this option to expand is estimated, the value of a firm can be written as the sum of two components—a discounted cash flow value based on expected cash flows and a value associated with the option to expand:

Value of Firm = Discounted Cash Flow Value + Option to Expand

The option pricing approach adds rigor to this argument by estimating the value of the option to expand, and it also provides insight into those occasions when it is most valuable. In general, the option to expand is clearly more valuable for more volatile businesses with higher returns on projects (such as biotechnology or computer software) than in stable businesses with lower returns (such as housing, utilities, or automobile production).

Again, though, you have to be careful not to double-count the value of the option. If you use a higher growth rate than would be justified by expectations because of the option to expand, you have already counted the value of the option in the discounted cash flow valuation. Adding an additional component to reflect the value of the option would be double-counting.

ILLUSTRATION 11.5

Considering the Value of the Option to Expand

Consider the discounted cash flow valuation of Rediff.com presented in Chapter 6, "Estimating Firm Value." Rediff.com was valued at $474 million, based on its expected cash flows in the Internet portal business. Assume that in buying Rediff.com, you are in fact buying an option to expand in the online market in India. This market is a small one now but could potentially be much larger in 5 or 10 years.

In more specific terms, assume that Rediff.com has the option to enter the Internet retailing business in India in the future. The cost of entering this business is expected to be $1 billion, and based on current expectations, the present value of the cash flows that would be generated by entering this business today is only $500 million. Based on current expectations of the growth in the Indian e-commerce business, this investment clearly does not make sense.

There is substantial uncertainty about both future growth in online retailing in India and the overall performance of the Indian economy. If the economy booms and the online market grows faster than expected over the next five years, Rediff.com might be able to create value from entering this market. If you leave the cost of entering the online retailing business at $1 billion, the present value of the cash flows would have to increase above this value for Rediff to enter this business and add value. The standard deviation in the present value of the expected cash flows (which is currently $500 million) is assumed to be 50%.

The value of the option to expand into Internet retailing can now be estimated with an option pricing model, with the following parameters:

S = Present value of the expected cash flows from entering market today
= $500 million

K = Cost of entering the market today = $1 billion

σ^2 = Variance in the present value of expected cash flows = $0.5^2 = 0.25$

r = 5.8% (this is a five-year Treasury bond rate: the analysis is being done in U.S. dollar terms)

t = 5 years

The value of the option to expand can be estimated as follows:

Option to Expand = 500 (0.5786) − 1000 (exp$^{(-0.058)(5)}$ (0.1789) = $155.47 million

Why does the option expire in five years? If the online retail market in India expands beyond this time, it is assumed that there will be other potential entrants into this market and that Rediff.com will have no competitive advantages and hence no good reason for entering this market. If the online retail market in India expands sooner than expected, it is assumed that Rediff.com, as one of the few recognized names in the market, will be able to parlay its brand name and the visitors to its portal to establish competitive advantages.

The value of Rediff.com as a firm can now be estimated as the sum of the discounted cash flow value of $474 million and the value of the option to expand into the retail market ($155 million). It is true that the discounted cash flow valuation is based on a high growth rate in revenues, but all of this growth is assumed to occur in the Internet portal business and not in online retailing.

In fact, the option to enter online retailing is only one of several options available to Rediff. Another path on which it might embark is to become a development exchange for resources — software developers and programmers in India looking for programming work in the United States and other developed markets. The value of this option can also be estimated with an approach similar to the one shown above.

expand.xls: This spreadsheet enables you to estimate the value of the option to expand an investment or project.

WHEN ARE REAL OPTIONS VALUABLE? SOME KEY TESTS

The argument that some or many investments have valuable strategic or expansion options embedded in them has great allure, and there is a danger that this argument will be used to justify poor investments. In fact, acquirers have long justified huge premiums on acquisitions on synergistic and strategic grounds. To prevent real options from falling into the same black hole, you need to be more rigorous in your assessment of the value of real options.

QUANTITATIVE ESTIMATION

When real options are used to justify a decision, the justification has to be in more than qualitative terms. In other words, managers who argue for taking a project with poor returns or for paying a premium on an acquisition on the basis of real options should be required to value these real options and show, in fact, that the economic benefits exceed the costs. Two arguments will be made against this requirement. The first is that real options cannot be easily valued, since the inputs are difficult to obtain and often noisy. The second argument is that the inputs to option pricing models can be easily manipulated to back up whatever the conclusion might be. While both arguments have some merit, an estimate with error is better than no estimate at all, and the process of quantitatively trying to estimate the value of a real option is, in fact, the first step to understanding what drives its value.

KEY TESTS

Not all investments have options embedded in them, and not all options, even if they do exist, have value. To assess whether an investment creates valuable options that need to be analyzed and valued, you need affirmative answers to three key questions:

- *Is the first investment a prerequisite for the later investment/expansion? If not, how necessary is the first investment for the later investment/expansion?*

Consider the earlier analysis of the value of a patent. A firm cannot generate patents without investing in research or paying another firm for the patents.

Clearly, the initial investment here (spending on R&D or acquiring the patent from someone else) is required for the firm to have the second investment. Now, consider the Amazon investment in its Mexican venture and the option to expand into the Latin American market later. The initial investment allows Amazon to build a Spanish Web site and learn more about this market, but it does not give them exclusive rights to expand into the larger market. Unlike the patent illustration, the initial investment is not a prerequisite for the second, though management might view it as such.

The connection gets even weaker when you look at one firm acquiring another to have the option to enter a large market. Acquiring an Internet service provider to gain a foothold in the Internet retailing market would be an example of such a transaction.

■ *Does the firm have an exclusive right to the later investment/expansion? If not, does the initial investment provide the firm with significant competitive advantages on subsequent investments?* The value of the option ultimately derives not from the cash flows generated by the second and subsequent investments but from the excess returns generated by these cash flows. The greater the potential for excess returns on the second investment, the greater the value of the option in the first investment. The potential for excess returns is closely tied to how much competitive advantage the first investment provides the firm when it takes subsequent investments.

At one extreme, again, consider investing in research and development to acquire a patent. The patent gives the firm that owns it the exclusive rights to produce that product, and if the market potential is large, the right to the excess returns from the project. At the other extreme, the firm might gain no competitive advantages on subsequent investments, in which case, it is questionable whether there can be any excess returns on these investments. In reality, most investments will fall in the continuum between these two extremes, with greater competitive advantages being associated with higher excess returns and larger option values.

■ *How sustainable are the competitive advantages?* In a competitive marketplace, excess returns attract competitors, and competition drives out excess returns. The more sustainable the competitive advantages possessed by a firm, the greater will be the value of the options embedded in the initial investment. The sustainability of competitive advantages is a function of two forces. The first is the *nature of the competition*; other things remaining equal, competitive advantages fade much more quickly in sectors where there are aggressive competitors. The second is the *nature of the competitive advantage*. If the resource controlled by the firm is finite and scarce (as is the case with natural resource reserves and vacant land), the competitive advantage is likely to be sustainable for longer periods.

Alternatively, if the competitive advantage comes from being the first mover in a market or technological expertise, it will come under assault far sooner. The most direct way of reflecting this potential in the value of the option is in its life; the life of the option can be set to the period of competitive advantage, and only the excess returns earned over this period count toward the value of the option.

These are tough tests, and you can see that using a real option argument to justify paying large premiums for new technology firms is questionable. You do not need to buy a dot.com firm to partake in the e-commerce market in the future, and there is no clear competitive advantage that dot.com firms existing today are likely to have in this future market. It is true that firms like Yahoo! and Amazon.com will be much better known than other firms in the e-commerce market five or ten years from now (assuming that they survive that long) and that this may give them a brand name component that may allow them to earn excess returns. The question is whether these excess returns can be sustained, given how easy it is for competition to emerge online from both upstart new ventures and established brick-and-mortar businesses.

There might be a stronger rationale for using a real option argument to justify a premium for a small B2B like Ariba or a telecomm company like Qualcomm, where a first mover may be able to get its technology adopted as the baseline technology for the business. You could argue that investing in these firms today allows you to share in the expansion opportunities that will emerge if this occurs, and that the winning firm will be have a competitive advantage over others in the market.

SUMMARY

The value of a firm or an investment in a traditional discounted cash flow framework is the present value of the expected cash flows. In the process, however, you might ignore the options to delay or expand that are often embedded in firms.

Two types of options can influence the value of a technology firm. The first is the option to delay investing in a technology or project. When a firm has the exclusive rights to a project, even one with a negative net present value, it can hold back on investing until the project becomes an attractive one and can choose not to invest if this never happens. Consequently, the value of the rights to invest in this type of investment will often exceed the discounted cash flow value of the investment and can be estimated with an option pricing model. In fact, the value of a patent or patents owned by a firm can be estimated with the same approach and added on to the value of the cash flows generated by the more conventional assets of the firm to arrive at firm value.

The second type of option is the option to expand into a new product, market, or business as a consequence of an initial investment. In this case, the estimated value of the option to expand can be based on the expected volatility in the cash flows from expansion and the cost of the expansion. In some cases, the option to expand can have sufficient value to allow firms to invest in projects that have negative net present value. In fact, this argument has been used by some analysts as a justification for paying premiums over discounted cash flow values for technology stocks and large premiums on acquisitions.

While real options can exist and have substantial value, we should be cautious in using them as justification for large premiums over traditional value measures. In particular, a real option will have substantial value only if the first investment is a prerequisite for the second investment and if it creates significant and sustainable competitive advantages on the second investment. A new technology firm indeed has the option to expand into the e-commerce market, but it has neither exclusive rights to do so nor any significant and sustainable competitive advantages over others who might decide to come into the market later. In such a case, the real option to expand has little or no value.

ENDNOTES

1. Stock prices cannot drop below zero because of the limited liability of stockholders in publicly listed firms. Hence, stock prices, by themselves, cannot be normally distributed, since a normal distribution requires some probability of infinitely negative values. The distribution of the natural logs of stock prices is assumed to be log-normal in the Black-Scholes model. This is why the variance used in this model is the variance in the log of stock prices.

2. Warrants are call options issued by firms, either as part of management compensation contracts or to raise equity.

3. Jump process models that incorporate the Poisson process require inputs on the probability of price jumps, the average magnitude, and the variance, all of which can be estimated, but with a significant amount of noise.

4. The analogy to a listed option on a stock would be the case where you do not know for certain what the stock price is when you exercise the option. The more uncertain you are about the stock price, the more margin for error you have to give yourself when you exercise the option, to ensure that you are in fact earning a profit.

5. In practical terms, the probability distributions for inputs like market size and market share can often be obtained from market testing.

6. A value-creating cash flow is one that adds to the net present value because it is in excess of the required return for investments of equivalent risk.

7. This decision could change if the firm believes that one of its competitors is close to obtaining approval for a rival drug to treat MS. In that case, the cost of delay will rise, making early exercise (commercially developing the product) more likely.

8. To be honest, this is not an estimate based on any significant facts other than Biogen's history of success in coming up with new products.

9. This discount rate was estimated from the costs of equity of young, publicly traded biotechnology firms with little or no revenue from commercial products.

CHAPTER

12 VALUE
ENHANCEMENT

I n all the valuations so far in this book, we have taken the perspective of an investor valuing a firm from the outside. The question we have asked is: Given how their existing management run Cisco, Motorola, Amazon, Ariba, and Rediff, what value would you assign them? In this chapter, we look at valuation from the perspective of the managers of the firms. Unlike investors, who have to take the firm's actions and policies as given, managers can change the way a firm is run. We examine how the actions and decisions of a firm can enhance value.

For an action to create value, it has to affect one of four inputs into the valuation model: the cash flows generated from existing investments; the expected growth rate in earnings, which determines the cash flows looking forward; the period for which the firm can sustain above-normal growth (and excess returns); and the cost of capital that gets applied to discount these cash flows. In the first half of this chapter, we look at the different approaches to value enhancement and the link to management actions, with an emphasis on technology firms. In the second half of the chapter, we look at economic value added (EVA) and cash flow return on investment (CFROI), which are the two most widely used value enhancement tools, and examine their strengths and weaknesses in the context of technology firms.

VALUE CREATION: A DISCOUNTED CASH FLOW (DCF) PERSPECTIVE

In this section, we explore the requirements for an action to be value creating and then examine the different ways in which a firm can create value. In the process, we also examine the role that marketing decisions, production decisions, and strategic decisions have in value creation. In each section, we also look at the potential for each of these actions to create value at Cisco, Motorola, Amazon, Ariba, and Rediff.

VALUE-CREATING AND VALUE-NEUTRAL ACTIONS

The value of a firm is the present value of the expected cash flows from both assets in place and future growth, discounted at the cost of capital. For an action to create value, it has to do one or more of the following:

- Increase the cash flows generated by existing investments
- Increase the expected growth rate in these cash flows in the future
- Increase the length of the high-growth period
- Reduce the cost of capital that is applied to discount the cash flows

Conversely, an action that does not affect cash flows, the expected growth rate, the length of the high-growth period, or the cost of capital cannot affect value.

While this might seem obvious, a number of value-neutral actions taken by firms receive disproportionate attention from both managers and analysts. Consider four examples.

■ Technology firms often announce stock splits to keep their stock trading in a desirable price range. In 1999, both Cisco and Amazon announced stock splits: Cisco splitting each share into two, and Amazon converting each share into three. Stock dividends and stock splits change the number of units of equity in a firm but do not affect cash flows, growth, or value.

■ Accounting changes in inventory valuation and depreciation methods that are restricted to the reporting statements and do not affect tax calculations have no effect on cash flows, growth, or value. In recent years, technology firms, in particular, have spent an increasing amount of time on the management and smoothing of earnings and seem to believe that there is a value payoff to doing this.

■ When making acquisitions, firms often try to structure the deal in such a way that they can pool their assets and not show the market premium paid in the acquisition. When they fail and are forced to show the difference between market value and book value as goodwill, their earnings are reduced by the amortization of the goodwill over subsequent periods. This amortization is generally not tax deductible, however, and thus does not affect the cash flows of the firm. So, the accounting approach a firm adopts, whether purchase or pooling, and the length of time it takes to write off the goodwill should not really make any difference to value. The same can be said about the practice of writing off in-process R&D, adopted by many technology firms, to eliminate or reduce the goodwill charges in future periods.

■ The number of firms that have issued tracking stock on their high-growth divisions has surged. For instance, the New York Times announced that it would issue tracking stock on its online unit. Since these divisions remain under the complete control of the parent company, the issue of tracking stock, by itself, should not create value.

Some analysts take issue with this proposition. When a stock splits or a firm issues tracking stock, they argue, the stock price often goes up.[1] While this may be true, it is price, not value, that is affected by these actions. These actions could possibly change market perceptions about growth or cash flows and thus act as signals. Alternatively, they might provide more information about undervalued assets owned by the firm, and the price may react as a consequence. In some cases, these actions may lead to changes in operations; tying the compensation of managers to the price of stock tracking the division in which they work may improve efficiency and thus increase cash flows, growth, and value.

WAYS OF INCREASING VALUE

Clearly, some actions that firms take affect their cash flow, growth, and discount rates, and consequently the value. In this section, we consider how actions taken by a firm on a variety of fronts can have a value effect.

Increase Cash Flows from Existing Investments. The first place to look for value is in the firm's existing assets. These assets represent investments the firm has already made, and they generate the current operating income for the firm. To the extent that these investments earn less than their cost of capital or are earning less than they could if optimally managed, there is potential for value creation.

Keep, Divest, or Liquidate Poor Investments

Every firm has some investments that earn less than necessary to break even (the cost of capital) and sometimes even lose money. At first sight, it would seem to be a simple argument to make that investments that do not earn their cost of capital should either be liquidated or divested. If, in fact, the firm could get back the original capital invested on liquidation, this statement would be true. But that assumption is not generally true, and you need to consider three different measures of value for an existing investment.

- The *continuing value*, which reflects the present value of the expected cash flows from continuing the investment through the end of its life.
- The *liquidation or salvage value*, which is the net cash flow that the firm will receive if it terminated the project today.
- The *divestiture value*, which is the price that will be paid by the highest bidder for this investment.

Whether a firm should continue with an existing project, liquidate the project, or sell it to someone else depends on which of the three measures is highest. If the continuing value is the highest, the firm should continue with the project to the end of the project life, even though it might be earning less than the cost of capital. If the liquidation or divestiture value is higher than the continuing value, there is potential for an increase in value from liquidation or divestiture. The value increment can then be summarized:

If liquidation is optimal:
Expected Value Increase = Liquidation Value – Continuing Value

If divestiture is optimal:
Expected Value Increase = Divestiture Value – Continuing Value

Improve Operating Efficiency

A firm's operating efficiency determines its operating margin and, thus, its operating income; more efficient firms have higher operating margins, other things remaining equal, than do less efficient firms in the same business. If a firm can increase its operating margin on existing assets, it will generate additional value. There are a number of indicators of the potential to increase margins; the most important is a measure of how much a firm's operating margin deviates from its industry.

Firms whose current operating margins are well below their industry average must locate the source of the difference and try to fix it. In some cases, the problem may lie in a firm's cost structure, in which case, the first step in value enhancement takes the form of cost cutting and layoffs. These actions are value enhancing only if the resources that are pruned do not contribute sufficiently either to current operating income or to future growth. Companies can easily show increases in current operating income by cutting back on expenditures (such as research and development), but they may sacrifice future growth in doing so. In other cases, the problem may lie in the fact that the firm does not differentiate its product adequately from its competition, thus reducing its pricing power and margins. Here, value enhancement requires a long-term strategy focused on increasing product differentiation and pricing power.

Reduce the Tax Burden

The value of a firm is the present value of its *after-tax* cash flows. Thus, any action that can reduce the tax burden on a firm for a given level of operating income will increase value. Although some aspects of the tax code offer no flexibility to the firm, the tax rate can be reduced over time by doing any or all of the following:

- Multinational firms that generate earnings in different markets may be able to *move income* from high-tax locations to low-tax or no-tax locations. For instance, the prices that divisions of these firms charge each other for intracompany sales (transfer prices) can allow profits to be shifted from one part of the firm to another.[2]

- A firm may be able to acquire *net operating losses* that can be used to shield future income. In fact, this might be why a profitable firm acquires an unprofitable one.

- A firm can use risk management to reduce the average tax rate paid on income over time because the marginal tax rate on income tends to rise, in most tax systems, as income increases. By using risk management to smooth income over time, firms can make their incomes more stable and reduce their exposure to the highest marginal tax rates.[3] This is especially the case when a firm faces a windfall or supernormal profit tax.

Reduce Net Capital Expenditures on Existing Investments

The net capital expenditure is the difference between capital expenditures and depreciation, and, as a cash outflow, it reduces the free cash flow to the firm. Part of the net capital expenditure is designed to generate future growth, but a part, called maintenance capital expenditure, is to maintain existing assets. If a firm can reduce its maintenance capital expenditures without negative consequences, it will increase value.

There is generally a trade-off between capital maintenance expenditures and the life of existing assets. A firm that does not make any maintenance capital expenditures will generate much higher after-tax cash flows from these assets, but the assets will have a far shorter life. At the other extreme, a firm that reinvests all the cash flows it gets from depreciation into capital maintenance may be able to extend the life of its assets in place significantly. Firms often ignore this trade-off when they embark on cost cutting and reduce or eliminate capital maintenance expenditures. Although these actions increase current cash flows from existing assets, the firm might actually lose value as it depletes these assets at a faster rate.

Reduce Noncash Working Capital

As noted in the earlier chapters, the noncash working capital in a firm is the difference between noncash current assets, generally inventory and accounts receivable, and the nondebt portion of current liabilities, generally accounts payable. Money invested in noncash working capital is tied up and cannot be used elsewhere; thus, increases in noncash working capital are cash outflows, whereas decreases are cash inflows.

The path to value creation seems simple. Reducing noncash working capital as a percent of revenues should increase cash flows and, therefore, value. This assumes, however, that there are no negative consequences for growth and operating income. Firms generally maintain inventory and provide credit because it allows them to sell more. If cutting back on one or both causes lost sales, the net effect on value may be negative.

ILLUSTRATION 12.1

Potential for Value Creation from Existing Investments

We begin this analysis by estimating how much of the value of the firms we are analyzing comes from existing investments. One way of doing this is to assume that the current operating earnings of the firm are generated by existing assets and that these earnings would continue in perpetuity with no growth, as long as the firm reinvests the depreciation on those assets (capital maintenance = depreciation).

$$\text{Value of Existing Assets} = \frac{\text{EBIT (1 − Tax Rate)}}{\text{Cost of Capital}}$$

This value will become negative if the operating earnings are negative, as they are for Amazon, Ariba, and Rediff.com, and will be set to zero. The difference between the total value of the firm, estimated in Chapter 6, "Estimating Firm Value," with the discounted cash flow model and the value of existing assets can then be attributed to the growth potential of the firm. Table 12.1 summarizes the estimates of value for the five firms under consideration.

The table also summarizes the return on capital and cost of capital of the firms, as well as the industry average return on capital. To the extent that you trust the return on capital as a measure of the earning power of existing assets, it provides a snapshot on whether the existing investments of the firm are earning a sufficient return.

Of the five firms that you are analyzing, Rediff.com has almost no existing investments, and hence there is little potential for value creation from this source for the firm. Amazon and Ariba have existing investments that are also a negligible proportion of their total value, and managing them better can provide only a minor boost in value. Does the negative return on capital on existing investments at these firms suggest that the existing investments of the firm are poor investments? That conclusion is not justified because these firms are young, and the returns on existing investments are being measured early in the investment life cycle. To the extent that returns improve as projects mature, the negative returns could reverse over time. In addition, the operating income at young firms, especially technology-based ones, is misstated because many capital expenses are treated as operating expenses. While we have adjusted for some of these expenses (R&D at Ariba, SG&A at Rediff.com), the current operating income at these firms may not be a good measure of the profitability of existing investments at these firms.

TABLE 12.1 Investments in Existing Assets

	AMAZON	ARIBA	CISCO	MOTOROLA	REDIFF
EBIT with adjustments	$(276)	$(164)	$3,455	$3,216.00	$(6.92)
Tax rate	0.00%	0.00%	35.00%	35.00%	0.00%
EBIT (1 – t)	–$276	–$164	$2,246	2090.4	–$6.92
Cost of capital	12.56%	13.11%	11.71%	10.39%	25.82%
Value of assets in place	$0	$0	$19,184	$20,115	$0
Value of operating assets	$13,971	$17,816	$310,124	$66,139	$463
Assets in place/ value	0.00%	0.00%	6.19%	30.41%	0.00%
Growth potential/ value	100.00%	100.00%	93.81%	69.59%	100.00%
Firm's return on capital	–7.18%	–218.10%	34.07%	12.18%	–73.69%
Industry average return on capital	16.94%	23.86%	16.52%	15.03%	NMF

Cisco does have significant existing investments, but the potential for value creation from this source is likely to be small for two reasons. First, while these investments might be substantial in terms of absolute value, they represent a small proportion of the total value of the firm—only 6.19%. Second, Cisco earns a return on these investments that is not only well in excess of its cost of capital but is much higher than that of its competitors. This would suggest that it is managing these investments optimally already.

Motorola offers the most promise for value creation from existing investments, getting almost a third of its value from these investments. Its return on capital has been on a downward trend recently, and it has investments in diverse businesses. Table 12.2 breaks down the operating income, operating margin, and return on capital and cost of capital in Motorola's telecomm and semi-conductor businesses.

TABLE 12.2 Motorola: Segment Analysis

SEGMENT	REVENUES	% OF TOTAL	EBIT	EBIT (1 − T)	CAPITAL INVESTED	ROC	INDUSTRY AVERAGE
Telecomm	$25,042	77.26%	$947	$616	$5,016	12.27%	13.82%
Semiconductors	$7,370	22.74%	$619	$402	$3,344	12.03%	18.09%

While Motorola is earning more than its cost of capital in both segments, it is earning less than its competitors in both. To the extent that it can move its margins and returns toward the industry averages, there is potential for value added.

Reductions in maintenance capital expenditures or noncash working capital offer little promise in terms of cash flows for the firms being analyzed. Much of the maintenance capital expenditure is in intangible assets (R&D or brand name), and the noncash working capital investments of the firms are similar or lower than those of the industry, as shown in Table 12.3.

TABLE 12.3 Noncash Working Capital Investments

	AMAZON	ARIBA	CISCO	MOTOROLA	REDIFF.COM
Firm	−25.53%	−41.57%	6.75%	8.23%	26.02%
Industry average	8.26%	3.05%	22.68%	20.06%	22.35%

In summary, there is some potential for value creation from existing assets at Motorola, but very little at the other firms in the analysis.

Increase Expected Growth. A firm with low or negative current cash flows can still have high value if it is able to grow quickly and earn high cash flows in the future. In Chapter 5, "Looking Forward: Estimating Growth," we considered two categories of firms. For the first category, which includes firms like Cisco and Motorola that have profitable investments, higher growth arises either from increases in reinvestment or a higher return on capital. For the second category, which includes money-losing firms such as Amazon, Ariba, and Rediff, the expected cash flows in the future are determined by the expected growth rate in revenues, the expected operating margin, and the sales-to-capital ratio (determining the reinvestment needs of the firm).

Profitable Firms: The Reinvestment Rate/ Return on Capital Analysis

For a firm that has positive operating earnings, the expected growth rate in operating earnings is the product of the reinvestment rate and the after-tax return on capital on new investments (marginal return on investment):

$$\text{Expected Growth}_{\text{Operating Income}} = \text{Reinvestment Rate} \times \text{Marginal Return on Capital}$$

The expected growth rate can be increased by an increase in either the reinvestment rate or the marginal return on capital or both.

The trade-off from increasing the reinvestment rate is listed in Table 12.4. The positive effect of reinvesting more—higher growth—has to be compared to the negative effect of reinvesting more, the drop in free cash flows.

TABLE 12.4 Trade-Off on Reinvestment Rate

NEGATIVE EFFECTS	POSITIVE EFFECTS
Reduces free cash flow to firm: FCFF = EBIT (1 − Tax Rate) (1 − Reinvestment Rate)	Increases expected growth: Expected Growth = Reinvestment Rate × Return on Capital

You could work through the entire valuation and determine whether the present value of the additional cash flows created by higher growth is greater than the present value of the actual reinvestments made, in cash flow terms. There is, however, a far simpler test to determine the effect on value. The net present value of a project measures the value added by the project to overall firm value, and the net present value is positive only if the internal rate of return on the project exceeds the cost of capital. If we assume that the accounting return on capital on a project is a reasonable estimate for the internal rate of return, then increasing the reinvestment rate will increase value if and only if the return on capital is greater than the cost of capital. If the return on capital is less than the cost of capital, the positive effects of growth will be less than the negative effects of making the reinvestment.

Note that the return on capital that we are talking about is the marginal return on capital, that is, the return on capital earned on the actual reinvestment rather than the average return on capital. Given that firms tend to accept their most attractive investments first and their less attractive investments later, the average returns on capital tend to be greater than the marginal returns on capital. Thus, a firm with a return on capital of 18% and a cost of capital of 12% may really be earning only 11% on its marginal projects. In addition, the marginal return on capital will be much lower if the increase in the reinvestment rate is substantial. So, we should be cautious about assuming large increases in the reinvestment rate while keeping the current return on capital constant.

A firm that is able to increase its return on capital while keeping the cost of capital fixed will increase its value. If, however, the increase in return on capital comes from the firm entering new businesses that are far riskier than its existing business, there might be an increase in the cost of capital that offsets the increase in growth. The general rule for value creation remains simple, however. As long as the projects, no matter how risky they are, have a marginal return on capital that exceeds their cost of capital, they will create value.

ILLUSTRATION 12.2

Reinvestment Rates, Return on Capital, and Value

In Table 12.5, the base case assumptions about reinvestment rates, returns on capital, and cost of capital, and the estimates of value are listed for Cisco and Motorola.

TABLE 12.5 Reinvestment Rate, Return on Capital, and Value for Cisco and Motorola

	CISCO	MOTOROLA
Reinvestment rate	106.81%	52.99%
Marginal return on capital	34.07%	17.22%
Expected growth	36.39%	9.12%
Cost of capital	11.71%	10.39%
Value of operating assets	$310,124	$66,138.81
Value per share	$44.92	$32.39

If Cisco and Motorola could increase their reinvestment rates without affecting their returns on capital, the value per share would increase because they are both earning excess returns. In Figure 12–1, the impact on the value of equity of changing the reinvestment rate at both firms is summarized, keeping the cost of capital fixed.

To illustrate, the reinvestment rate at Cisco was reduced from 106.81% to 76.81%, and the percentage effect on value of equity was examined; the value per share dropped 42.81%. The effect of a similar change at Motorola was a drop in value per share of 12.38%. The effect of changes in the reinvestment rate were more dramatic at Cisco for every change because one firm earns higher excess returns. In fact, as the excess return converges on zero, the reinvestment rate effect will disappear.

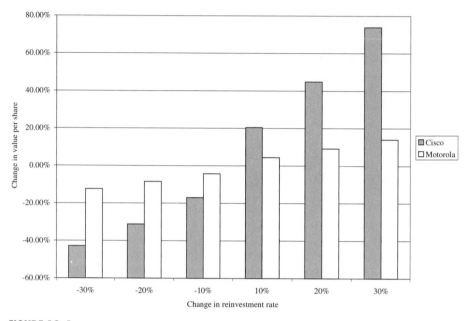

FIGURE 12–1
Reinvestment Rate and Value per Share

Negative Earnings Firms

For the negative earnings firms in the analysis—Amazon, Ariba, and Rediff.com—expected future cash flows are derived from assumptions made about three variables: the expected growth rate in revenues, the target operating margin, and the sales-to-capital ratio. The first two variables determine the operating earnings in future years, and the last variable determines reinvestment needs. Figure 12–2 summarizes the impact of each of these variables on the cash flows.

Other things remaining equal, the expected cash flows in future years will be higher if any of the three variables—revenue growth, target margins, and sales-to-capital ratios—increase. Increasing revenue growth and target margins will increase operating earnings; increasing the sales-to-capital ratio will reduce reinvestment needs.

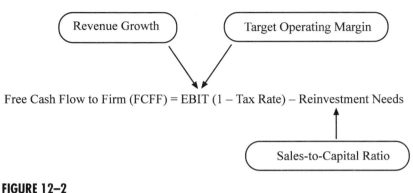

FIGURE 12–2
Determinants of Growth

In reality, though, firms have to trade off between higher revenue growth and higher margins. When firms increase prices for their products, they improve operating margins but reduce revenue growth. Michael Porter, one of the leading thinkers in corporate strategy, suggests that when it comes to pricing strategy, a firm can take two basic routes.[4] It can choose to be a *volume leader*, reducing price and hoping to increase revenues sufficiently to compensate for the lower margins. For this strategy to work, the firm needs a cost advantage over its competitors to prevent pricing wars that may make all firms in the industry worse off. Alternatively, it can attempt to be a *price leader*, increasing prices and hoping that the effect on volume will be smaller than the increased margins. The extent to which revenue growth will drop depends on how elastic the demand for the product is and how competitive the overall product market is. The net effect will determine value.

While a higher sales-to-capital ratio reduces reinvestment needs and increases cash flow, there are both internal and external constraints on the process. As the sales-to-capital ratio increases, the return on capital on the firm in future years will also increase. If the return on capital substantially exceeds the cost of capital, new competitors will enter the market, making it more difficult to sustain the expected operating margins and revenue growth.

ILLUSTRATION 12.3

Revenue Growth, Operating Margins, and Sales-to-Capital Ratios

In Table 12.6, the expected compounded revenue growth rate (over the next 10 years), the target margins, and sales-to-capital ratios are summarized for Ariba, Amazon, and Rediff.com.

TABLE 12.6 Growth Assumptions: Amazon, Ariba, and Rediff.com

	AMAZON	ARIBA	REDIFF.COM
Growth rate in revenues	40.00%	82.39%	104.57%
Target operating margin	9.32%	16.36%	40.00%
Sales-to-capital ratio	3.02	2.50	1.00
Return on capital (in terminal year)	16.94%	20.00%	25.00%
Value of operating assets	$13,971	$17,816	$463

In addition, the return on capital 10 years from now is also reported for each of the firms.

For all three firms, higher revenue growth translates into higher values per share. Figure 12–3 graphs the change in value per share for each of the firms as a function of the change in expected growth rate in revenues.

Thus, Amazon's value per share is almost doubled when the compounded revenue growth rate increases 20% from the base case of 40% to 60%. The changes in value per share tend to be smaller for Ariba and Rediff because the base case compounded growth rate in revenues is much higher for these firms. A 10% change in that growth rate thus has a smaller effect on value per share.

For all three firms, higher margins also translate into higher values per share. Figure 12–4 shows the value per share as a function of percentage changes in the target margin.

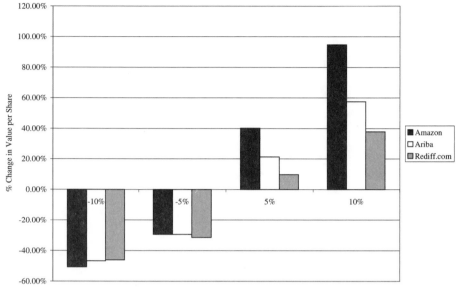

FIGURE 12–3
Revenue Growth and Value per Share

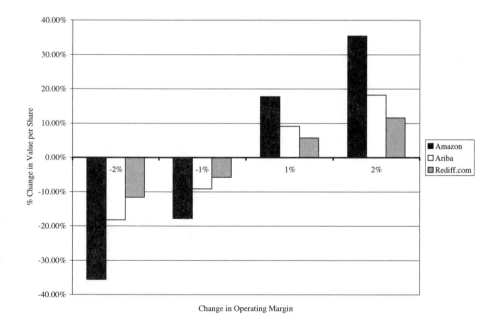

FIGURE 12–4
Change in Margin and Value per Share

Here again, the effects of changes in the margin are greatest for Amazon, where the base case margin is the lowest, and least for Rediff.com, where the base case margin is the highest.

For Amazon, the trade-off between revenue growth and margins is made more explicit in Table 12.7, which shows value per share as a function of both variables.

TABLE 12.7 Margin versus Revenue Growth: Amazon Value per Share

		TARGET OPERATING MARGIN (IN 10 YEARS)				
		6%	8%	10%	12%	14%
COMPOUNDED REVENUE GROWTH OVER NEXT 10 YEARS	30%	$6.91	$12.28	$17.62	$22.94	$28.24
	40%	$14.37	$25.02	$35.63	$46.22	$56.80
	50%	$28.42	$48.87	$69.27	$89.67	$110.05
	60%	$53.85	$91.83	$129.78	$167.73	$205.66

Amazon's value varies widely, depending on the combination of revenue growth and margins that you assume. In practical terms, this also provides Amazon with a sense of the trade-off between higher revenue growth and lower target margins.

Finally, a higher sales-to-capital ratio (which translates into a higher return on capital in 10 years) leads to a higher value per share for all three firms. Figure 12–5 presents the effects on value per share of assuming a different sales-to-capital ratio over the high-growth period for Amazon.

As the sales-to-capital ratio (and the terminal return on capital) increases, the value per share of Amazon also increases.

While the relationship between value and these three drivers of value is direct, it is not clear whether there is potential for value creation in any of these firms, given the favorable assumptions that have been made about each of the variables in the base case valuation. It is conceivable that Amazon could increase its revenue growth rate beyond the estimated 40%, but can it do so with 10% pre-tax margins? Ariba might be able to have higher sales-to-capital ratio, but will it be able to earn more than the assumed 20% return on capital in perpetuity?

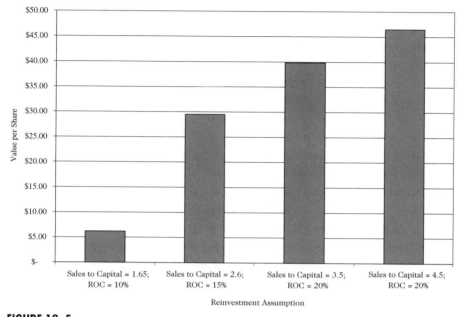

FIGURE 12–5
Effects of Changing Sales-to-Capital Ratio: Amazon

Lengthen the Period of High Growth

Every firm, at some point in the future, will become a stable growth firm, growing at a rate equal to or less than that of the economy in which it operates. In addition, growth creates value only if the firm earns excess returns on its investments. With excess returns, the longer the high-growth period lasts, other things remaining equal, the greater the value of the firm. No firm should be able to earn excess returns forever in a competitive product market, since competitors will be attracted to the business by the excess returns. Thus, implicit in the assumption of high growth with excess returns is the assumption that there also exist some barriers to entry that prevent competing firms from entering the market and eliminating the excess returns that prevail.

One way firms can increase value is by increasing existing barriers to entry and erecting new ones. In other words, companies earning excess returns have significant competitive advantages. Nurturing these advantages can increase value. In fact, every successful company can point to one or more competitive advantages as the source of its success: Nokia to its technology and market savvy, Cisco to its capacity to make acquisitions work, and Dell to its distribution system and cost advantages.

The Brand Name Advantage

When valuing firms, analysts are often accused of overlooking intangible assets such as brand name value in their estimations. This accusation is unfounded, since the inputs to the traditional discounted cash flow valuation incorporate the effects of brand name. In particular, firms with more valuable brand names are either able to charge higher prices than the competition for the same products (leading to higher margins) or sell more than the competitors at the same price (leading to higher turnover ratios). They usually have higher returns on capital and greater value than their competitors in the industry.

Creating a brand name is a difficult and expensive process that may take years to achieve, but firms can often build on existing brand names and make them valuable. Consider the extraordinary success that Coca Cola has had in increasing its market value over the last two decades. Some attribute its success to its high return on equity or capital, yet these returns are not the cause of its success but the consequence of it. The high returns can be traced to the company's relentless focus on making its brand name more valuable globally.[5] Conversely, the managers of a firm who take over a valuable brand name and then dissipate its value will reduce the values of the firm substantially. The near-death experience of Apple Computers in 1996 and 1997 and the travails of Quaker Oats after the Snapple acquisition suggest that managers can quickly squander the advantage that comes from valuable brand names.

New technology firms are cognizant of the value of a powerful brand name, and much of their advertising and promotion is driven as much by the desire to make their brand names recognizable to customers as it is directed at attracting customers today. Firms like Yahoo!, AOL, and Amazon have had some success in creating recognizable brand names, but the true test ultimately is whether they can use these brand names to earn higher returns in the future.

Patents, Licenses, and Other Legal Protection

The second competitive advantage that companies can possess is a legal one. Firms may enjoy exclusive rights to produce and market a product because they own the patent rights on the product, as is often the case in the pharmaceutical industry. Alternatively, firms may have exclusive licensing rights to service a market, as is the case with regulated utilities in the United States.

The key to value enhancement is not just to preserve but to increase any competitive advantages that the firm possesses. If the competitive advantage comes from its existing patents, the firm has to work at developing new patents that allow it to maintain this advantage over time. While spending more money on research and development (R&D) is clearly one way, the efficiency of the reinvestment also matters. The companies that have the greatest increases in value are not necessarily those that spend the most on R&D, but those that have the most productive R&D departments not only in generating patents but also in converting patents into commercial products.

The competitive advantage from exclusive licensing or a legal monopoly is a mixed blessing and may not lead to value enhancement. When a firm is granted these rights by another entity, say, the government, that entity usually preserves the right to control the prices charged and margins earned through regulation. In the United States, for instance, much of the regulation of power and phone utilities was driven by the objective of ensuring that these firms did not earn excess returns. In these circumstances, firms may actually gain in value by giving up their legal monopolies if they get pricing freedom in return. You could argue that this has already occurred, in great part, in the airline and long-distance telecommunications businesses and will occur in the future in other regulated businesses. In the aftermath of deregulation, the firms that retain competitive advantages will gain value at the expense of others in the business.

Switching Costs

There are some businesses where neither brand name nor a patent provides adequate protection against competition. Products have short life cycles, competition is fierce, and customers develop little loyalty to companies or products. This outlook describes the computer software business in the 1980s, and it still applies to a significant portion of that business today. How, then, did Microsoft succeed so well in establishing its presence in the market? Although many would attribute its success entirely to its ownership of the operating system needed to run the software, there is another reason. Microsoft recognized earlier than most firms that the most significant barrier to entry in the software business is the cost to the end user of switching from one product to a competitor. In fact, Microsoft Excel, early in its life, had to overcome the obstacle that most users were working with Lotus spreadsheets and did not want to bear the switching cost. Microsoft made it easy for end users to switch to its products (by allowing Excel to open Lotus spreadsheets, for instance) and it made it more and more expensive for them to switch to a competitor by creating the Microsoft Office Suite. Thus, users who have Microsoft Office installed on their system and who want to try to switch from Microsoft Word to WordPerfect must overcome multiple barriers. Will the conversion work well on the hundreds of Word files that exist already? Will the user still be able to cut and paste from Microsoft Excel and Power-Point into Word documents? The end result, of course, is that it becomes very difficult for competitors who do not have Microsoft's resources to compete with it in this arena.

There are a number of other businesses where the switching cost concept can be used to augment an argument for value enhancement or debunk it. For instance, there are many who argue that the high valuations of Internet companies such as Amazon.com and eToys reflect their first-mover advantage, that is, the fact that they are pioneers in the online business. However, the switching costs in online retailing seem to be minimal, and these companies have to come up with a way of increasing switching costs if they want to earn high returns in the future.

Cost Advantages

Firms can establish a cost advantage over their competitors and use it as a barrier to entry in several ways:

- In businesses where scale can be used to reduce costs, economies of scale can give bigger firms advantages over smaller firms.
- Owning or having exclusive rights to a distribution system can provide firms with a cost advantage over their competitors.
- Having access to lower-cost labor or resources can also provide cost advantages.

These cost advantages will influence value in one of two ways: The firm with the cost advantage can charge the same price as its competitors but have a much higher operating margin. Or, the firm can charge lower prices than its competitors and have a much higher capital turnover ratio. In fact, the net effect of increasing margins or turnover ratios (or both) will increase the return on capital and, through it, expected growth.

The cost advantage of economies of scale can create high capital requirements that prevent new firms from entering the business. In businesses such as aerospace and automobiles, the competition is almost entirely among existing competitors. The absence of new competitors may allow these firms to maintain above-normal returns, though the competition between existing firms will constrain the magnitude of these returns.

ILLUSTRATION 12.4

Potential for Increasing the Length of the High-Growth Period

The competitive advantages are different for the five firms being analyzed in this book, and the potential for building on these advantages is different as well.

- Cisco's most significant differential advantage seems to be its capacity to generate much larger excess returns on its new investments than its competitors can generate. Since most of these investments take the form of acquisitions of other firms, Cisco's excess returns rest on whether it can continue to maintain its success in this area. The primary challenge, however, is that as Cisco continues to grow, it will need to acquire even more acquisitions each year to maintain the growth rate it had the previous year. There might be both external and internal constraints on this process. The number of firms that are potential takeover targets is limited, and the firm may not have the resources to replicate its current success if the number of acquisitions doubles or triples.

- Motorola's research capabilities and the patents that emerge from the research represent its most significant competitive advantage. However, it is not viewed as the technological leader in either of the two businesses that it operates in. Firms like Nokia are viewed as more innovative when it comes to mobile communications (cellular phones), and Intel is considered the leading innovator among large semiconductor manufacturers.

- Amazon has two significant advantages associated with it. The first is that it is a pioneer in Internet retailing, giving it a first-mover advantage over Barnes and Noble, Border's, and other brick-and-mortar firms that came later. The second is the brand name value that Amazon has acquired in the few years that it has been in existence. It is clearly one of the more recognized names in e-commerce and has also acquired a reputation for good service in a sector (online retailing) where the gap between promise and practice has been large. It is one of the few online retailers that has invested as much in building a distribution and order fulfillment system as it has in promoting sales, and this investment has paid off in a reputation for reliability. The challenge for Amazon is to convert these two advantages into high profit margins. Given the ease of entry into the online retailing business, meeting the challenge will take substantial work.

■ Ariba is a pioneer in the B2B business, but it also has a technological component to its success. If Ariba can make its technology the default for the business, it will be able to capture a large portion of a huge market. Whether it will succeed in this endeavor will be partially in its own hands, partially in the hands of its competitors (like Commerce One), and partially in the minds of customers who are required to switch to new technologies.

■ Rediff.com's largest advantage comes from the market that it serves — the Indian online market. This market is a small one but potentially could have very high growth. Rediff's strength lies in its ability to deal with the linguistic and regional differences in the Indian market and to take advantage of changes in this market. Rediff's knowledge of the market can also help catapult it into bigger and more lucrative businesses, such as online retailing or becoming an online exchange for businesses that want to trade resources.[6] To build on this strength, it has to continue to accumulate information about the market that will give it an edge over its competition.

For each of these firms, the payoff from a successful strategy can be very large. For instance, Motorola, which has a value per share of $32.39 with a high-growth period of five years, would be able to increase its value to about $40 if it were able to grow longer (see Figure 12–6).

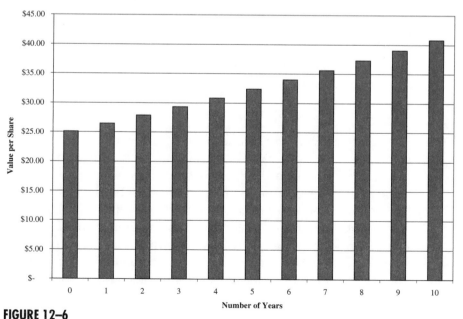

FIGURE 12–6
Length of Growth Period and Value per Share: Motorola

For Cisco, where a growth period of 12 years has been assumed, the risk is that the firm's competitive advantages may not be sustainable and that the value per share will drop off accordingly.

Reduce the Cost of Financing. The cost of capital for a firm is a composite cost of debt and equity financing. The cash flows generated over time are discounted to the present at the cost of capital. Holding the cash flows constant, reducing the cost of capital will increase the value of the firm. In this section, we explore the ways in which a firm can reduce its cost of capital, or more generally, increase its firm value by changing both financing mix and type.

Change Operating Risk

The operating risk of a firm is a direct function of the kinds of products or services it provides and the degree to which these products or services are discretionary to the customer. The more discretionary they are, the greater the operating risk faced by the firm. Both the cost of equity and cost of debt of a firm are affected by the operating risk of the business or businesses in which it operates. In the case of equity, only that portion of the operating risk that is not diversifiable affects value. Firms can reduce their operating risk by making their products and services less discretionary to their customers. Advertising clearly plays a role; finding new uses for a product or service is another.

Reduce Operating Leverage

The operating leverage of a firm measures the proportion of its costs that are fixed. Other things remaining equal, the greater the proportion of the costs of a firm that are fixed, the more volatile its earnings will be and the higher its cost of capital. Reducing the proportion of the costs that are fixed will make firms much less risky and reduce their cost of capital. Firms can reduce their fixed costs by using outside contractors for some services; if business does not measure up, the firm is not stuck with the costs of providing this service. They can also tie expenses to revenues; for instance, tying wages paid to revenues made will reduce the proportion of costs that are fixed. There is a trade-off here, though, that has to be acknowledged. Using outside employees and consultants can become expensive in the long term and can also cause morale to sag among regular employees. Furthermore, outside consultants are more likely to move on to competitors and take their expertise (and what they know about a firm) with them.

This basic idea of tying expenses to revenues is often described as *making the cost structure more flexible*. A more flexible cost structure influences three inputs in a valuation. It leads to a lower unlevered beta (due to the lower operating leverage), reduces the cost of debt (because of the reduction in default risk), and increases the optimal debt ratio. All three reduce the cost of capital and increase firm value.

Change the Financing Mix

A third way to reduce the cost of capital is to change the mix of debt and equity used to finance the firm. As noted in Chapter 4 in the discussion of cost of capital, debt is always cheaper than equity, partly because lenders bear less risk and partly because of the tax advantage associated with debt. This benefit has to be weighed against the additional risk of bankruptcy created by the borrowing; this higher risk increases both the beta for equity and the cost of borrowing. The net effect will determine whether the cost of capital will increase or decrease as the firm takes on more debt.

Note, however, that a firm's value will increase as the cost of capital decreases if and only if the operating cash flows are unaffected by the higher debt ratio. If, as the debt ratio increases, the riskiness of the firm increases and this, in turn, affects the firm's operations and cash flows, then the firm value may decrease even as cost of capital declines. If such is the case, the objective function when designing the financing mix for a firm has to be restated in terms of firm value maximization rather than cost of capital minimization.

ILLUSTRATION 12.5

The Effect of Financing Mix on Value

To analyze the effect of changing the financing mix on value, you estimate the costs of equity and debt at each debt ratio. In Table 12.8, the costs of equity and debt are estimated for Motorola for debt ratios from 0% to 90%.

TABLE 12.8 Cost of Capital and Firm Value: Motorola

DEBT RATIO	BETA	COST OF EQUITY	BOND RATING	INTEREST RATE ON DEBT	TAX RATE	COST OF DEBT (AFTER-TAX)	WACC	FIRM VALUE (G)
0%	1.16	10.63%	AAA	6.20%	35.00%	4.03%	10.63%	$74,912
10%	1.24	10.96%	A-	7.25%	35.00%	4.71%	10.33%	$80,253
20%	1.34	11.38%	B-	10.25%	35.00%	6.66%	10.43%	$78,348
30%	1.48	11.91%	CC	12.00%	35.00%	7.80%	10.68%	$73,986
40%	1.72	12.90%	C	13.50%	26.34%	9.94%	11.72%	$59,716
50%	2.07	14.28%	C	13.50%	21.07%	10.66%	12.47%	$52,238
60%	2.63	16.54%	D	16.00%	14.82%	13.63%	14.79%	$37,161
70%	3.51	20.05%	D	16.00%	12.70%	13.97%	15.79%	$32,881
80%	5.27	27.07%	D	16.00%	11.11%	14.22%	16.79%	$29,394
90%	10.54	48.14%	D	16.00%	9.88%	14.42%	17.79%	$26,498

Note that the estimated cost of equity is based on the levered beta. As the debt ratio increases, the beta increases as well.[7] The estimated cost of debt is based on a synthetic rating that is determined by the interest coverage ratio at each debt ratio. As the debt ratio increases, the interest expense increases, leading to a drop in the ratings and higher costs of debt. As Motorola moves from a 0% debt ratio to a 10% debt ratio, the cost of capital decreases (and firm value increases). Beyond 10%, though, the trade-off operates against debt because the cost of capital increases as the debt ratio increases.

Similar analyses were done for Cisco, Amazon, Ariba, and Rediff.com; the results on the actual and optimal debt ratios are summarized in Table 12.9.

TABLE 12.9 Actual versus Optimal Debt Ratios

	AMAZON	ARIBA	CISCO	MOTOROLA	REDIFF.COM
			Current		
Debt Ratio	7.81%	0.15%	0.18%	6.86%	0.00%
Cost of Capital	12.56%	13.12%	11.71%	10.39%	13.60%
			Optimal		
Debt Ratio	0.00%	0.00%	0.00%	10.00%	0.00%
Cost of Capital	12.40%	13.11%	11.71%	10.33%	13.60%
Change in value per share	$1.37	$0.03	($0.09)	$0.52	$0.00

The optimal debt ratio is 0% for all of the firms except Motorola. For the three firms that have negative operating income currently, this should not be surprising. A firm that is reporting operating losses cannot afford to add the additional charge of interest payments, and gets no tax benefit to boot. For Cisco, which does make more than $3 billion in operating income, the absence of excess debt capacity may seem puzzling. Note, however, that the operating income (and EBITDA) is a small percentage of the market value of Cisco as a firm:

$$\text{EBITDA} / \text{Market Value of Firm}_{Cisco} = \$3,941 / 446,989 = 0.89\%$$

Why does this matter? The debt ratio that is being assessed is a market value debt ratio. Even at a 10% debt ratio, Cisco would have $44.7 billion in debt outstanding, and the interest expense on this debt would push Cisco to a D rating.

Change Financing Type

A fundamental principle in choosing what kind of financing a firm should use to fund its operations is that the financing of a firm should be designed to ensure, as far as possible, that the cash flows on debt match as closely as possible the cash flows on the asset. By matching cash flows on debt to cash flows on the asset, a firm reduces its risk of default and increases its capacity to carry debt, which, in turn, reduces its cost of capital and increases value.

Firms that mismatch cash flows on debt and cash flows on assets (by using short-term debt to finance long-term assets, debt in one currency to finance assets in a different currency, or floating-rate debt to finance assets whose cash flows tend to be adversely impacted by higher inflation) will have higher default risk, higher costs of capital, and lower firm value. Firms can use derivatives and swaps to reduce these mismatches and, in the process, increase firm value. Alternatively, they can replace their existing debt with debt that is more closely matched to their assets. Finally, they can use innovative securities that allow them to pattern cash flows on debt to cash flows on investments.

The potential for value enhancement from this source is likely to be small for technology firms since they tend not to have much debt to begin with and little debt capacity to exploit. As they mature, though, this situation will change, and they should consider using debt that best fits their cash flow characteristics.

THE VALUE ENHANCEMENT CHAIN

You can categorize the range of actions firms can take to increase value in several ways. One is in terms of whether an action affects cash flows from assets in place, growth, the cost of capital, or the length of the growth period. There are two other parameters by which you can distinguish between actions that create value:

- *Does an action create a value trade-off, or is it a pure value creator?* Very few actions increase value without any qualifications. Among these are the divestitures of assets when the divestiture value exceeds the continuing value, and the elimination of deadweight costs that contribute nothing to the firm's earnings or future growth. Most actions have both positive and negative effects on value, and it is the net effect that determines whether these actions are value enhancing. In some cases, the trade-off is largely internal, and the odds are much better for value creation. An example is a firm changing its mix of debt and equity to reduce the cost of capital. In other cases, however, the net effect on value will be a function of how competitors react to a firm's actions. As an example, changing pricing strategy to increase margins may not work as a value enhancement measure if competitors react and change prices as well.

■ *How quickly do actions pay off?* Some actions generate an immediate increase in value. Among these are divestitures and cost cutting. Many actions, however, are designed to create value in the long term. Thus, building up a respected brand name clearly creates value in the long term but may not affect near-term cash flows.

ILLUSTRATION 12.6

A Value-Enhancement Plan

Reviewing the discussion of value enhancement at Amazon, Ariba, Cisco, Motorola, and Rediff.com, we see that the following conclusions seem to hold:

■ For Cisco, there seems to be little potential for enhancing value beyond the initial estimate. The firm earns high excess returns on its existing investments, nurtures its competitive advantage zealously, and has a financing mix (100% equity) that befits its cash flows. Upholding the old adage of doing no harm, Cisco is obviously doing things right and needs to maintain rather than change the way it is run.

■ For Amazon, Ariba, and Rediff.com, firms that have little in terms of existing investments, the agenda for value enhancement is clear. The firms should focus on increasing revenue growth while keeping reinvestment needs in check. In the process, they need to lay the groundwork for the competitive advantages that will allow them to earn high margins on their revenues in the future. These competitive advantages range from brand name for Amazon to technology for Ariba to localized knowledge (about the Indian market) for Rediff.com.

■ Motorola seems to offer the most promise for value enhancement. Its returns on existing investments lag behind its competitors, its competitive advantages in technology are small and need augmenting, and the firm does have some excess debt capacity. If you could increase the return on capital on existing investments to industry averages, improve the firm's research capabilities, and use its debt capacity, you could substantially increase the value of Motorola.

ALTERNATIVES TO THE TRADITIONAL VALUATION MODEL

The traditional discounted cash flow model provides for a rich and thorough analysis of all the different ways in which a firm can increase value, but it can become complex as the number of inputs increases. It is also very difficult to tie management compensation systems to a discounted cash flow model, since many of the inputs need to be estimated and can be manipulated to yield the results management wants.

If you assume that markets are efficient, you can replace the unobservable value from the discounted cash flow model with the observed market price and reward or punish managers on the basis of the stock performance. Thus, a firm whose stock price has gone up is viewed as having created value, whereas one whose stock price has fallen has destroyed value. Compensation systems based on the stock price, including stock grants and warrants, have become a standard component of most management compensation packages.

While market prices have the advantage of being up to date and observable, they are also noisy. Even if markets are efficient, stock prices tend to fluctuate around the true value, and markets sometimes do make mistakes. Thus, a firm may see its stock price go up and reward its top management even as they destroy value. Conversely, the managers of a firm may be penalized as the firm's stock price drops, even though the managers may have taken actions that increase firm value. The other problem with stock prices as the basis for compensation is that they are available only for the entire firm. Thus, stock prices cannot be used to analyze the managers for their performance at individual divisions of a firm or for their relative performance.

In the last decade, even as firms have become more focused on value creation, they have remained suspicious of financial markets. They might understand the notion of discounted cash flow value but be unwilling to tie compensation to a value that is based on dozens of estimates. In this environment, there is a ready market for new mechanisms for measuring value that are simple to estimate and use, do not depend too heavily on market movements, and do not require a lot of estimation. The two mechanisms that seem to have made the most impact are:

- *Economic value added*, which measures the dollar surplus value created by a firm on its existing investment
- *Cash flow return on investment*, which measures the percentage return made by a firm on its existing investments

In this section, we look at how each is related to discounted cash flow valuation. We also look at the conditions under which firms using these approaches to judge performance and evaluate managers may end up making decisions that destroy value rather than create it.

ECONOMIC VALUE ADDED

The *economic value added* (EVA) is a measure of the dollar surplus value created by an investment or a portfolio of investments. It is computed as the product of the excess return made on an investment or investments and the capital invested in that investment or investments:

Economic Value Added =
(Return on Capital Invested – Cost of Capital) (Capital Invested)

In this section, we begin by looking at the measurement of economic value added, then consider EVA's links to discounted cash flow valuation, and close with a discussion of the limitations of EVA as a value enhancement tool.

Calculating EVA. The definition of economic value added outlines three basic inputs you need for its computation: the return on capital earned on investments, the cost of capital for those investments, and the capital invested in them. In measuring each of these, you make many of the same adjustments discussed in the context of discounted cash flow valuation.

How much *capital is invested* in existing assets? One obvious answer is to use the market value of the firm, but market value includes capital invested not just in assets in place but in expected future growth.[8] Since you want to evaluate the quality of assets in place, you need a measure of the market value of just these assets. Given the difficulty of estimating market value of assets in place, it is not surprising that we turn to the book value of capital as a proxy for the market value of capital invested in assets in place.

The book value, however, is a number that reflects not just the accounting choices made in the current period, but also accounting decisions made over time on how to depreciate assets, value inventory, and deal with acquisitions. At a minimum, the three adjustments we made to capital invested in the discounted cash flow valuation—converting operating leases into debt, capitalizing R&D expenses, and eliminating the effect of one-time or cosmetic charges—we must make when computing EVA as well. The older the firm, the more extensive the adjustments that have to be made to book value of capital to get to a reasonable estimate of the market value of capital invested in assets in place. Since this requires that you know and take into account every accounting decision over time, there are cases where the book value of capital is too flawed to be fixable. Here, it is best to estimate the capital invested from the ground up, starting with the assets owned by the firm, estimating the market value of these assets, and cumulating this market value.

To evaluate the return on this invested capital, you need an estimate of the *after-tax operating income* earned by a firm on these investments. Again, the accounting measure of operating income must be adjusted for operating leases, R&D expenses, and one-time charges to compute the return on capital.

The third and final component needed to estimate EVA is the *cost of capital*. The estimated cost of capital should be based on the market values of debt and equity in the firm, rather than on the book value. There is no contradiction between using book value for purposes of estimating capital invested and using market value for estimating cost of capital, since a firm has to earn more than its market value cost of capital to generate value. From a practical standpoint, using the book value cost of capital will tend to understate cost of capital for most firms and will understate it more for more highly levered firms than for lightly levered firms. Understating the cost of capital will lead to overstating the EVA.

ILLUSTRATION 12.7

Estimating Economic Value Added

In this illustration, we estimate the EVA by Amazon, Ariba, Cisco, Motorola, and Rediff.com in the most recent year. To make these estimates, we use the operating income from that year in conjunction with the book value (adjusted for operating leases and R&D expenses) from the previous year in Table 12.10.

TABLE 12.10 Economic Value Added

	AMAZON	ARIBA	CISCO	MOTOROLA	REDIFF.COM
EBIT $(1-t)$	–$276.00	–$163.70	$2,245.75	$2,090.40	–$6.92
Capital invested	$1,746.94	$152.24	$9,944.43	$25,542.60	$5.67
Return on capital	–7.18%	–218.10%	34.07%	12.18%	–73.69%
Cost of capital	12.56%	13.11%	11.71%	10.39%	25.82%
EVA	–$344.79	–$351.99	$2,224.39	$455.49	–$5.64

The results are not surprising. The firms with negative operating earnings had negative EVA last year. Both Cisco and Motorola reported positive EVA last period, but Cisco's high return on capital results in a much higher EVA for the firm.

eva.xls: A dataset on the Web summarizes economic value added (EVA), by industry group, in the United States for the most recent year.

Economic Value Added, Net Present Value, and Discounted Cash Flow Valuation. One of the foundations of investment analysis in traditional corporate finance is the net present value rule. The net present value (NPV) of a project, which reflects the present value of expected cash flows on a project netted against any investment needs, is a measure of dollar surplus value on the project. Thus, investing in projects with positive NPV will increase the value of the firm, and investing in projects with negative NPV will reduce the value. EVA is a simple extension of the NPV rule. The NPV of the project is the present value of the economic value added by that project over its life:[9]

$$NPV = \sum_{t=1}^{t=n} \frac{EVA_t}{(1+k_c)^t}$$

where EVA_t is the economic value added by the project in year t, and the project has a life of n years.

This connection between EVA and NPV enables us to link the value of a firm to the economic value added by that firm. To see this, begin with a simple formulation of firm value in terms of the value of assets in place and expected future growth:

Firm Value = Value of Assets in Place + Value of Expected Future Growth

Note that in a discounted cash flow model, the values of both assets in place and expected future growth can be written in terms of the NPV created by each component:

Firm Value = Capital Invested$_{\text{Assets in Place}}$

$$+ \text{NPV}_{\text{Assets in Place}} + \sum_{t=1}^{t=\infty} \text{NPV}_{\text{Future Projects, } t}$$

Substituting the EVA version of NPV into this equation, you get:

Firm Value = Capital Invested$_{\text{Assets in Place}}$

$$+ \sum_{t=1}^{t=\infty} \frac{\text{EVA}_{t, \text{ Assets in Place}}}{(1 + k_c)^t} + \sum_{t=1}^{t=\infty} \frac{\text{EVA}_{t, \text{ Future Projects}}}{(1 + k_c)^t}$$

Thus, the value of a firm can be written as the sum of three components: the capital invested in assets in place, the present value of the EVA by these assets, and the expected present value of the economic value that will be added by future investments.

 fcffeva.xls: This spreadsheet enables you to value a firm on the basis of expected EVA in future years and compares it to a discounted cash flow value estimate of value.

EVA and Market Value. Will increasing economic value added cause market value to increase? Not necessarily: the market value has built into it expectations of future EVA. Thus, a firm like Microsoft is priced on the assumption that it will earn large and increasing EVA over time. Whether a firm's market value increases or decreases on the announcement of higher EVA will depend in large part on the expected change in EVA. For mature firms, where the market might have expected no increase or even a decrease in EVA, the announcement of an increase will be good news and cause the market value to increase. For firms that are perceived to have good growth opportunities and are expected to report an increase in EVA, the market value will decline if the announced increase in EVA does not measure up to expectations. This should be no surprise to investors, who have recognized this phenomenon with earnings per share for decades; the earnings announcements of firms are judged against expectations, and the earnings surprise is what drives prices.

You would, therefore, not expect any correlation between the magnitude of the EVA and stock returns, or even between the change in EVA and stock returns. Stocks that report the biggest increases in EVA should not necessarily earn high returns for their stockholders.[10] These hypotheses are confirmed by a study done by Richard Bernstein at Merrill Lynch, who examined the relationship between EVA and stock returns:

- A portfolio of the 50 firms that had the highest absolute levels[11] of economic value added earned an annual return of 12.9% between February 1987 and February 1997, while the S&P index returned 13.1% a year over the same period.
- A portfolio of the 50 firms that had the highest growth rates[12] in economic value added over the previous year earned an annual return of 12.8% over the same time period.

Economic Value Added at Technology Firms. The fact that the value of a firm is a function of the capital invested in assets in place, the present value of economic value added by those assets, and the economic value added by future investments points to some of the dangers of using it as a measure of success or failure for technology firms. Firms can increase their EVA from assets in place, and see their value decrease in these circumstances:

- The increase in EVA is the result of a shrinking of the capital invested in the firm. Note that restructuring charges and stock buybacks can reduce capital invested and make the EVA a much larger number, while yielding no gain in value or even a reduction in value.

■ The increase in EVA from existing assets is generated by sacrificing future investments and the economic value that would have been added by those investments.

■ The increase in EVA is accompanied by an increase in risk and cost of capital. In this case, the negative effect (of a higher discount rate) can more than offset the positive effect of a higher EVA.

Finally, it is unlikely that there will be much correlation between actual changes in EVA at technology firms and changes in market value. The market value is based on expectations of EVA in future periods, and investors expect a firm like Cisco to report an EVA that grows substantially each year. Thus, if Cisco's EVA increases, but by less than expected, you could see its market value drop on the report.

ILLUSTRATION 12.8

Analyzing Economic Value Added

Consider again the economic value added estimates for the five firms that are being analyzed. Cisco and Motorola have positive economic value added, and the other three firms, Amazon, Ariba, and Rediff.com, have negative EVA. Is this an indication of good management at the first two firms and poor management in the last three? Not necessarily. Even if you assume that the operating income measures the earnings from existing investments and that the book capital measures the capital invested in these assets, the EVA is a measure of the performance of these assets in one period. To the extent that asset cash flows change over their life, Amazon, Ariba, and Rediff.com might have value-creating investments that are currently losing money.

In fact, it would be dangerous to push the managers of these firms to increase the EVA and to reward them on that basis. Consider a firm like Cisco. Its existing investments earn attractive returns, but the bulk of the firm's value still comes from growth potential in the future. If managers sacrifice even a small portion of the latter to increase the EVA from existing assets, the firm might become a less valuable firm.

CASH FLOW RETURN ON INVESTMENT

Unlike economic value added, which is a dollar value, the CFROI is a percentage rate of return on existing investments. In fact, the CFROI is the internal rate of return on existing investments, based on real cash flows, and it is compared to the real cost of capital in judgments about the quality of these investments.

Calculating CFROI. The cash flow return on investment for a firm is calculated from four inputs. The first is the *gross investment* (GI) the firm has in its existing assets, obtained by adding back cumulated depreciation and inflation adjustments to the book value. The second input is the *gross cash flow* (GCF) earned in the current year on that asset, which is usually defined as the sum of the after-tax operating income of a firm and the non-cash charges against earnings, such as depreciation and amortization. The third input is *the expected life of the assets* (n) in place at the time of the original investment, which varies from sector to sector but reflects the earning life of the investments in question. The *expected value of the assets* (SV) at the end of this life, in current dollars, is the final input. SV is usually assumed to be the portion of the initial investment, such as land and building, that is not depreciable, adjusted to current dollar terms. The CFROI is the internal rate of return of these cash flows, that is, the discount rate that makes the net present value of the gross cash flows and salvage value equal to the gross investment; CFROI can thus be viewed as a composite internal rate of return in current dollar terms.

An alternative formulation of the CFROI allows for setting aside an annuity to cover the expected replacement cost of the asset at the end of the project life. This annuity is called the economic depreciation and is computed as follows:

Economic Depreciation =

$$\frac{\text{Replacement Cost in Current Dollars } (k_c)}{((1 + k_c)^n - 1)}$$

Where n is the expected life of the asset and the expected replacement cost of the asset is defined in current dollar terms to be the difference between the gross investment and the salvage value. The CFROI for a firm or a division can then be written as follows:

$$\text{CFROI} = \frac{\text{Gross Cash Flow} - \text{Economic Depreciation}}{\text{Gross Investment}}$$

For instance, assume that you have existing assets with a book value of $2,431 million, a gross cash flow of $390 million, an expected salvage value (in today's dollar terms) of $607.8 million, and a life of 10 years. The conventional measure of CFROI is 11.71%, and the real cost of capital is 8%. The estimate with the alternative approach is computed below:

$$\text{Economic Depreciation} = \frac{(\$2.431 \text{ billion} - \$0.6078 \text{ billion})(0.08)}{(1.08^{10} - 1)}$$

$$= \$125.86 \text{ million}$$

$$\text{CFROI} = (\$390.00 \text{ million} - \$125.86 \text{ million}) \div \$2,431 \text{ million} = 10.87\%$$

The differences in the reinvestment rate assumption account for the difference in CFROI estimated with the two methods. In the first approach, intermediate cash flows are reinvested at the internal rate of return; in the second approach, at least the portion of the cash flows that are set aside for replacement are reinvested at the cost of capital. In fact, if you estimated the economic depreciation by using the internal rate of return of 11.71%, the two approaches would yield identical results.[13]

cfroi.xls: This spreadsheet enables you to estimate the CFROI for an investment or a firm.

Cash Flow Return on Investment, Internal Rate of Return, and Discounted Cash Flow Value. If net present value provides the genesis for the EVA approach to value enhancement, the internal rate of return is the basis for the CFROI approach. In investment analysis, the internal rate of return on a project is computed from the initial investment on the project and all cash flows over the project's life, as shown in Figure 12–7.

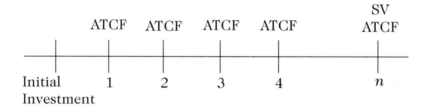

FIGURE 12–7
Internal Rate of Return on a Project

In the figure, ATCF is the after-tax cash flow on the project and SV is the expected salvage value of the project assets. This analysis can be done entirely either in nominal terms, in which case the internal rate of return is a nominal IRR and is compared to the nominal cost of capital, or in real terms, in which case it is a real IRR and is compared to the real cost of capital.

At first sight, the CFROI seems to do the same thing. It uses the gross investment in the project (in current dollars) as the equivalent of the initial investment, assumes that the gross current-dollar cash flow is maintained over the project life, and computes a real internal rate of return. There are, however, some significant differences.

■ The internal rate of return does not require the after-tax cash flows to be constant over a project's life, even in real terms. The CFROI approach assumes that real cash flows on assets do not increase over time. This may be a reasonable assumption for investments in mature companies but will understate project returns if there is real growth. Note, however, that the CFROI approach can be modified to allow for real growth.

■ The second difference is that the internal rate of return on a project or asset is based on incremental future cash flows. It does not consider cash flows that have occurred already, since these are viewed as "sunk." The CFROI, on the other hand, tries to reconstruct a project or asset, using both cash flows that have occurred already and cash flows that are yet to occur.

To link the cash flow return on investment with firm value, begin with a simple discounted cash flow model for a firm in stable growth:

$$\text{Firm Value} = \frac{\text{FCFF}_1}{(k_c - g_n)}$$

where FCFF is the expected free cash flow to the firm, k_c is the cost of capital, and g_n is the stable growth rate. Note that this can be rewritten, approximately, in terms of the CFROI as follows:

$$\text{Firm Value} = \frac{(\text{CFROI} \times \text{GI} - \text{DA})(1 - t) - ((\text{CX} - \text{DA}) - \Delta\text{WC})}{(k_c - g_n)}$$

where CFROI is the cash flow return on investment, GI is the gross investment, DA is the depreciation and amortization, CX is the capital expenditure, and ΔWC is the change in working capital.

To illustrate, consider a firm with a CFROI of 30%, a gross investment of $100 million, capital expenditures of $15 million, depreciation of $10 million, and no working capital requirements. If you assume a 10% cost of capital, a 40% tax rate, and a 5% stable growth rate, CFROI would be valued as follows:

$$\text{Firm Value} = \frac{(0.30 \times 100 - 10)(1 - 0.4) - ((15 - 10) - 0)}{(0.10 - 0.05)}$$

$$= \$140 \text{ million}$$

More important than the mechanics, however, is the fact that firm value, while a function of the CFROI, is also a function of the other variables in the equation—the gross investment, the tax rate, the growth rate, the cost of capital, and the firm's reinvestment needs.

Again, sophisticated users of CFROI do recognize the fact that value comes from the CFROI not just on assets in place but also on future investments. In fact, Holt Associates, one of CFROI's leading proponents, allows for a fade factor in CFROI, where the current CFROI fades toward the real cost of capital over time. They estimate the fade factor empirically by looking at firms in different CFROI classes and tracking them over time. Thus, a firm that has a current CFROI of 20% and real cost of capital of 8% will be projected to have lower CFROI over time. The value of the firm, in this more complex format, can then be written as a sum of the following:

■ The present value of the cash flows from assets in place over their remaining life, which can be written as

$$\sum_{t = 1}^{t = n} \frac{\text{CFROI}_{aip} \times \text{GI}_{aip}}{(1 + k_c)^t}$$

where CFROI_{aip} is the CFROI on assets in place, GI_{aip} is the gross investment in assets in place, and k_c is the real cost of capital.

■ The present value of the excess cash flows from future investments, which can be written in real terms as

$$\sum_{t=1}^{t=\infty} \frac{CFROI_{t,NI} \times \Delta GI_t}{(1+k_c)^t} - \Delta GI_t$$

where $CFROI_{t,NI}$ is the CFROI on new investments made in year t and ΔGI_t is the new investment made in year t. Note that if $CFROI_{t,NI} = k_c$, then this present value is equal to zero.

Thus, a firm's value will depend on the CFROI it earns on assets in place and the speed with which this CFROI fades toward the cost of capital. Thus, a firm can potentially increase its value by doing any of the following:

■ Increase the CFROI from assets in place, for a given gross investment

■ Reduce the speed at which the CFROI fades toward the real cost of capital

■ Reduce the abruptness with which CFROI fades toward the cost of capital

Note that this is no different from the earlier analysis of firm value in the discounted cash flow approach, in terms of cash flows from existing investments (increase current CFROI), the length of the high-growth period (reduce fade speed), and the growth rate during the growth period (keep excess returns from falling as steeply).

CFROI and Firm Value: Potential Conflicts. The relationship between CFROI and firm value is less intuitive than the relationship between EVA and firm value, partly because it is a percentage return. Notwithstanding this fundamental weakness, managers can take actions that increase CFROI while reducing firm value.

■ *Reduce gross investment*: If the gross investment in existing assets is reduced, the CFROI may be increased. Since the product of CFROI and gross investment determines value, it is possible for a firm to increase CFROI and end up with a lower value.

■ *Sacrifice future growth*: CFROI, even more than EVA, is focused on existing assets and does not look at future growth. To the extent that managers increase CFROI at the expense of future growth, the value can decrease while CFROI goes up.

■ *Trade-off risk*: While the CFROI is compared to the real cost of capital to pass judgment on whether a firm is creating or destroying value, it represents only a partial correction for risk. The value of a firm is still the present value of expected future cash flows. Thus, a firm can increase its spread between the CFROI and cost of capital but still end up losing value if the present value effect of having a higher cost of capital dominates the higher CFROI.

In general, then, an increase in CFROI does not, by itself, indicate that the firm value has increased, since it might have come at the expense of lower growth or higher risk.

CFROI and Market Value. CFROI and market value are related. Firms with high CFROI generally have high market value. This is not surprising, since it mirrors what was noted about economic value added earlier. However, it is *changes* in market value that create returns, not market value per se. When it comes to market value changes, the relationship between CFROI changes and value changes tends to be much weaker. Since market values reflect expectations, there is no reason to believe that firms that have high CFROI will earn excess returns.

The relationship between changes in CFROI and excess returns is more intriguing. To the extent that any increase in CFROI is viewed as a positive surprise, firms with the biggest increases in CFROI should earn excess returns. In reality, however, the actual change in CFROI has to be measured against expectations. If CFROI increases, but less than expected, then the market value should drop; if CFROI drops but by less than expected, then the market value should increase.

CFROI at Technology Firms. The cash flow return on investment, like economic value added, tends to work better at firms with significant assets in place. Technology firms get a substantial portion of their value from future growth potential, and it is not clear whether the CFROI on existing assets provides much information about this potential. In addition, the emphasis placed on the gross investment to estimate CFROI makes it easier to use for a manufacturing firm with tangible assets and more difficult to analyze for a technology firm whose biggest assets might emerge from their research.

You would also expect much lower correlation between changes in CFROI and changes in market value at technology firms because the expectation for these firms is that the CFROI will change over time. Thus, Motorola might report a higher CFROI next year than it reports this year, but the market value of Motorola may drop on the report if the increase does not match expectations. Cisco, on the other hand, might report a lower CFROI but it might see its market value go up because the drop was less than expected.

SUMMARY

The value of a firm has three components. The first is the firm's capacity to generate cash flows from existing assets, with higher cash flows translating into higher value. The second component is the firm's willingness to reinvest to create future growth and the quality of these reinvestments. Other things remaining equal, firms that reinvest well and earn significant excess returns on these investments will have higher value. The final component of value is the cost of capital, with higher costs of capital resulting in lower firm values. To create value, then, a firm must do the following:

- Generate higher cash flows from existing assets, without affecting its growth prospects or its risk profile
- Reinvest more and with higher excess returns, without increasing the riskiness of its assets

■ Reduce the cost of financing its assets in place or future growth, without lowering the returns made on these investments

All value enhancement measures are variants on these simple themes. Whether these approaches measure dollar excess returns, as does EVA or percentage excess returns, like CFROI, they have acquired followers because they seem simpler and less subjective than discounted cash flow valuation. This simplicity comes at a cost, since these approaches make subtle assumptions about other components of value that are often not visible or not recognized by many users. Approaches that emphasize EVA and reward managers for increasing EVA often assume that increases in EVA are not being accomplished at the expense of future growth or by increasing risk. Practitioners whose judgments of performance are based on the cash flow return on investment make similar assumptions.

As you look at various approaches to value enhancement, you should consider a few facts. The first is that no value enhancement mechanism will work at generating value unless managers commit to making value maximization their primary objective. If managers put other goals first, there will be no value enhancements. Conversely, if managers truly care about value maximization, they can make almost any mechanism work in their favor. The second consideration is that while it is sensible to connect your choice of value enhancement measurement to management compensation, there is a down side. Managers, over time, will tend to focus their attention on making themselves look better on that measure even if that goal can be accomplished only by reducing firm value. Finally, there are no magic bullets that create value. Value creation is hard work in competitive markets and almost always involves a trade-off between costs and benefits. Everyone has a role in value creation, and it certainly is not the sole domain of financial analysts. In fact, the value created by financial engineers is smaller and less significant than the value created by good strategic marketing, production, or personnel divisions.

ENDNOTES

1. This argument is backed up empirically. Stock prices do tend to increase, on average, when stocks are split.

2. Taxes are only one aspect of transfer pricing. Brickley, Smith, and Zimmerman (1995) look at the broader issue of how best to set transfer prices.

3. Stulz (1996) makes this argument for risk management. He also presents other ways in which risk management can be value enhancing.

4. *Competitive Strategy*, Michael Porter (1998).

5. Companies like Coca Cola have taken advantage of the global perception that they represent American culture and have used it to grow strong in other markets.

6. As an example, U.S. technology companies may be able to use Rediff as an online exchange for seeking out programming and development help from small Indian technology firms or entrepreneurs.

7. Levered Beta =
Unlevered Beta $(1 + (1 - \text{tax rate}) (\text{Debt} \div \text{Equity}))$

8. As an illustration, computing the return on capital at Microsoft by using the market value of the firm, instead of book value, results in a return on capital of about 3%. It would be a mistake to view this a sign of poor investments on the part of the firm's managers.

9. This definition holds, though, only if the expected present value of the cash flows from depreciation is assumed to be equal to the present value of the return of the capital invested in the project. A proof of this equality can be found in my paper on value enhancement in *The Contemporary Finance Digest* in 1999.

10. Kramer and Pushner (1997) found that differences in operating income (NOPAT) explained differences in market value better than did differences in EVA. O'Byrne (1996), however, finds that changes in EVA explain more than 55% of changes in market value over five-year periods.

11. See *Quantitative Viewpoint*, Merrill Lynch, December 19, 1997.

12. See *Quantitative Viewpoint*, Merrill Lynch, February 3, 1998.

13. With an 11.71% rate, the economic depreciation works out to $105.37 million, and the CFROI to 11.71%.

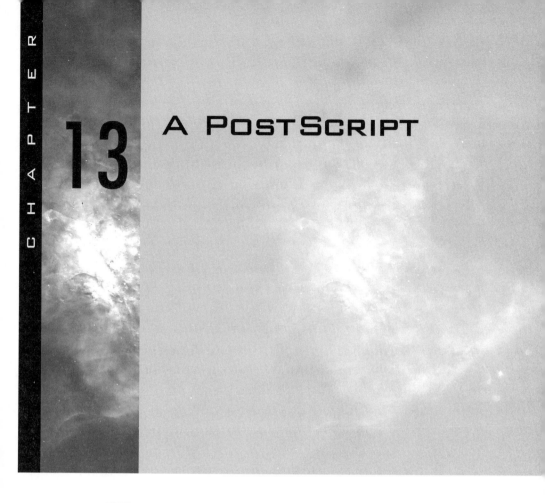

13 A PostScript

Both discounted cash flow models and relative valuation approaches can be used to value technology firms, though the challenges in estimating the inputs can be significant, especially for new technology firms with negative earnings and limited history. Many analysts do not share this view. They argue that discounted cash flow valuation will not work at technology firms for a number of reasons: there is too much uncertainty about the future, or too much of the value comes from the terminal value. They suggest new paradigms for valuing these firms that often deviate significantly from what we would view as first principles in traditional valuation models. In this chapter, we confront four fundamental propositions about valuation in technology firms and draw general lessons for both investors and managers.

FUNDAMENTALS DON'T CHANGE

Three fundamentals determine the value of a business: a firm's capacity to generate cash flows from existing investments, the expected growth in these cash flows over time, and the uncertainty about whether or not these cash flows will be generated in the first place. These fundamentals remain the same no matter what type of firm you are valuing—large or small, manufacturing or service, and technology or non-technology—though the emphasis placed on each may be different for different firms.

CASH FLOW, GROWTH, AND RISK

At the risk of repeating a mantra often stated in this book, consider again how the three determinants of value interact with value.

- Firms that generate *higher cash flows* from existing investments should be *worth more* than firms that generate lower or negative cash flows.
- Firms that *expect to grow faster* in the future should have *higher value* than firms that have lower growth rates.
- *Less uncertainty about future cash flows* should translate into *higher value* for firms.

In discounted cash flow valuations, the relationship between fundamental variables and value was made explicit through assumptions about each, with uncertainty showing up in the discount rate. In relative valuations, the relationship is implicit and often shows up in the form of adjustments made to multiples when firms are compared to each other.

It is true that the cash flows from existing investments are negative for some new technology firms, but that changes little that has been said here. These firms usually have to generate much higher positive cash flows in the future to compensate for their current negative cash flows. The uncertainty about these cash flows for these firms can compound this effect.

LESSONS FOR INVESTORS

With technology firms, the allure of high growth often blinds investors to the other fundamentals that determine value. Even though higher growth generally does justify assigning a higher value for a firm, we should add three qualifiers:

- *Cash flows matter:* It is not growth in revenues or earnings but growth in cash flows generated for investors that creates value. There are firms that generate astounding growth in revenue but never make it to profitability, and still other firms that make it to profitability but have little or no cash flows to show because of their reinvestment needs.

- *Value growth reasonably:* Higher expected growth in cash flows, other things remaining equal, can be used to justify a higher price for an asset but not any price. The term "growth at a reasonable price" is used commonly to justify the prices paid for technology stocks but seems to be ignored just as often by investors who are willing to pay any price for high growth.

- *Don't forget the other fundamentals:* Risk and cash flow generating capacity continue to determine value, even for the highest-growth firms. Investors who choose to ignore these fundamentals do so at their own peril.

You cannot avoid dealing with fundamentals by choosing to do relative valuation. Investors often compare a multiple (such as price to sales) at which a firm is trading to the average for other firms in the sector and use that comparison as justification for a stock being under- or overvalued. They should realize that they are making implicit assumptions about the risk, growth, and cash flow characteristics of the firms being compared when they do this.

LESSONS FOR MANAGERS

The fact that the value of a firm is determined by its fundamentals means that managers sometimes will be placed in the unenviable position of having to choose between what is good for the firm and what some investors and analysts want to see.

Manage for value, not for analysts: This may come as a surprise to some managers, but analysts do not determine stock prices. In fact, the evidence seems to suggest that analysts follow the market rather than lead it; buy recommendations on a stock often proliferate after a stock has gone up, and sell recommendations, rare though they might be, often show up after a stock has gone down. Notwithstanding this, the managers of some technology firms seem to run their firms with the singular objective of pleasing equity research analysts who follow their firms. These managers focus on meeting quarterly earning targets or delivering revenue growth or whatever else analysts consider important at the moment, often ignoring fundamentals in the process. While this approach may deliver short-term rewards in the form of favorable recommendations from analysts, these managers may be putting their enterprises at risk and destroying value.

Focus on fundamentals: Good management requires that the emphasis return to fundamentals, even if it makes analysts unhappy in the short term. Thus, an action that increases target operating margins in the long term at the expense of short-term revenue growth may disappoint some analysts, but it will increase value. The stock price may even drop, as a consequence, but the value will increase, and markets have to be trusted to recognize their mistakes over time.

GROW, GROW, GROW...

While cash flows, growth, and risk remain the determinants of value for all firms, growth plays a disproportionately large role in determining the values of technology firms. Not surprisingly, both investors and managers in these firms consider higher growth to be the key to higher value.

GROWTH AND VALUE

The first lesson that emerges from the last chapter on value enhancement is that it is not growth that creates value, but growth with excess returns. Thus, firms can grow at high rates and create no value or even destroy value, because they earn less than is required (the cost of capital) on their new investments.

The second lesson is that the relationship between growth and value is generally not linear. As the expected growth rate in cash flows doubles or triples, the value of the firm will generally not change proportionately.

LESSONS FOR INVESTORS

The fact that much of the value of technology firms comes from future growth has important implications for investors.

Screen for growth effects: Every action taken by these firms must be screened for potential effects, not just on current earnings but, more importantly, on future growth. Actions that increase current earnings but reduce future growth prospects can do significant damage to firm value. Technology firms are particularly susceptible to making this trade-off for two reasons.

Small earnings surprises, where the actual earnings exceed analyst earnings estimates by a few cents, can result in large increases in stock prices.

The fact that research and development expenses are treated as operating expenses gives firms some discretionary power over reported earnings. A technology firm, faced with earnings estimates that it will not be able to beat, may be tempted to reduce R&D expenses or resort to other accounting shenanigans to beat these estimates.

Don't forget the excess returns: When technology firms announce acquisitions or investments, the key question that you should have for these firms is: What effect will this action have on this firm's capacity to generate growth with excess returns? If this effect is negative, investors should weight this a great deal more than whether the announcement will have a positive or a negative effect on earnings. The same can be said of earnings reports. Earnings reports can be misleading, especially when reinvestment costs are expensed (as is the case with research, development, and long-term marketing expenses). Thus, when a firm with high-growth potential and poor earnings reports a significant improvement in earnings, investors should examine the report for causes. If the earnings are improving because the costs of generating current revenues are coming down (due to economies of scale or pricing power), this is clearly good news. If, however, the earnings are increasing because the firm has reduced or eliminated discretionary reinvestment expenditures (such as development costs), the net effect on value can be very negative, since future growth is being put at risk.

LESSONS FOR MANAGERS

Managers in growth firms often focus on increasing growth at the expense of all else in the firm. Actions that increase growth are viewed as good, whereas actions that decrease growth are viewed negatively. This is simplistic, because three factors must be considered in growth management.

- Increasing the growth rate in revenues is the easier half of the equation. Increasing target operating margins and returns on capital is much more difficult, but if accomplished, much more important in value creation.
- When a significant or substantial portion of firm value comes from expected growth, increasing firm value may mean investing more back into the firm. If the investment takes the form of research and development expenses, the earnings reported by the firm may fall below expectations. In order to increase their long-term value, firms may have to disappoint analysts (and investors) who are focused on current accounting earnings.
- As the firm matures, managers change with the firm. A greater proportion of firm value will come from existing assets, and reinvestment needs must be reduced as the growth rate decreases.

The emphasis on growth also points to the limitations in the mechanisms that are used to judge firm performance and to compensate management. In Chapter 12, we saw that neither EVA nor CFROI work well with technology firms, and using either may result in managers taking actions that lower the value of a firm. A good compensation mechanism in technology firms will reward managers for high-quality growth (growth with excess returns) and not for growth per se.

THE EXPECTATIONS GAME

As the proportion of value determined by future growth increases, expectations become a more critical determinant of how markets react to new information. In fact, the expectations game largely explains why stock prices change in ways that do not seem consistent with the news being announced (good earnings news leads to stock price drops, bad earnings news results in stock price increases) and the volatility of technology stocks, in general.

EXPECTATIONS, INFORMATION, AND VALUE

The value of a firm is the present value of the expected cash flows on the firm, and implicit in these expected cash flows and the discount rates used to discount the cash flows are investors' views about the firm, its management, and the potential for excess returns. While this is true for all firms, the larger proportion of value that comes from future growth potential at technology firms makes them particularly vulnerable to shifts in expectations about the future.

Consider the valuations in this book. In valuing Cisco, it was assumed that the firm would continue to make acquisitions at a rate comparable to last year's rate and make excess returns similar to those earned last year for the next six years. In fact, more than 90% of the value that was estimated for Cisco comes from these expectations about future success. For Motorola, the expectations were set lower, but the assumption that the firm's return on capital will improve over the next five years toward industry averages is responsible for almost a third of the value. For Amazon, Ariba, and Rediff, you could argue that almost the entire value is determined by expectations for the future.

How were these expectations formed? While the past history of these firms and industry averages were used as the basis for the estimates, three of the five firms valued have been in existence for less than five years and the industries themselves have both evolved and changed over those years. The fact that the information is both noisy and limited suggests that expectations can change relatively quickly and in response to small shifts in information. An earnings announcement by Cisco, for instance, which suggests that one of its acquisitions is not working as well as anticipated may lead to a reassessment of the likelihood of success of its entire strategy.

LESSONS FOR INVESTORS

The power of expectations in determining the value of a stock has to be considered when investors choose stocks for their portfolios and when they assess new information about the firm. There are several important implications:

- *Risk is measured relative to expectations.* The risk in a firm does not come from whether it performs well or badly but from how it does relative to expectations. Thus, a firm that reports earnings growth of 35% a year when it was expected to grow 50% a year is delivering bad news and will probably see its stock price drop. In contrast, a firm that reports a 20% drop in earnings when it was expected to report a 40% drop will generally see its stock price increase. In fact, you could argue that investors are more exposed to risk when they buy Cisco, because expectations have been set so high, than when they buy Motorola, where expectations are lower.

- *Good companies do not always make good investments.* It is not how well or badly a company is managed that determines stock returns, it is how well or badly managed it is, relative to expectations. A company that meets every financial criteria for excellence may be a poor investment, if markets are expecting too much of it. Conversely, a firm that is universally viewed as a poorly managed, poorly run company may be a good investment, if expectations have been set too low.[1]

- *Small news leads to big price jumps.* As noted in the last section, you should expect to see what seem like disproportionate stock price responses to relatively small pieces of information. A report from Motorola that earnings in the most recent quarter were two cents less than expected may lead investors to question whether Motorola can improve its return on capital toward industry averages and lead to a significant drop in the stock price.

■ *Focus on information about value drivers.* On a positive note, investors can assess what it is that drives value the most at a firm, and get a sense of what they should focus on when looking at new information. For instance, the key value drivers for Cisco are its capacity to continue to make acquisitions and to earn excess returns on them, while the value drivers for Amazon are revenue growth and operating margins. Looking past the aggregate earnings numbers for information on these variables may provide clues of both upcoming trouble and potential promise.

LESSONS FOR MANAGERS

If the expectation game affects investors, it is even more critical to managers at technology firms. One of the ironies that emerges from this game is that it is far easier to manage a firm that is perceived to be a poor performer than it is to manage one that is perceived to be a star.[2]

■ *Find out what is expected of you:* If you are going to be judged against expectations, it is critical that you gauge what these expectations are. While this translates, for many firms, into keeping track of what analysts are estimating earnings per share to be in the next quarter, there is more to it than this. Understanding why investors value your firm the way they do, and what they think are your competitive advantages, is much more important in the long term.

■ *Learn to manage expectations:* When firms first go public, managers and insiders sell the idea that their firm has great potential and should be valued highly. While this is perfectly understandable, managers have to change roles after they go public and learn to manage expectations. Specifically, they have to talk down expectations when they feel that their firm is being set up to do things that it cannot accomplish. Again, though, some firms damage their credibility when they talk down expectations incessantly, even when they know the expectations are reasonable.[3]

- *Do not delay the inevitable:* No matter how well a firm manages expectations, there are times when managers realize that they cannot meet expectations any more, because of changes in the sector or the overall economy. While the temptation is strong to delay revealing this to financial markets, often by shifting earnings from future periods into the current one or using accounting ploys, it is far better to deal with the consequences immediately. This may mean reporting lower earnings than expected and a lower stock price, but firms that delay their day of reckoning tend to be punished much more.

LIVE WITH NOISE

There are no precise valuations. Anyone who has valued a business knows that the inputs into a valuation are estimates and that the value that emerges is, therefore, an estimate as well. With technology firms, with short product life cycles and volatile technologies, the estimated value will have even more error associated with it.

NOISE IN THE VALUATION OF TECHNOLOGY FIRMS

The valuation of a technology firm will have substantial estimation error, and the noise in the valuation will be magnified if you are valuing a new technology firm with negative earnings and a limited history. One way to present this noise is in terms of a range in estimated value, and the range on the value of technology firms will be large. This is often used as an excuse by analysts who do not want to go through the process of valuing such firms. It also provides critics with a simplistic argument against trusting the numbers that emerge from these models.

You should take a different view. The noise in the valuation is not a reflection of the quality of the valuation model or the analyst using it, but of the underlying real uncertainty about the future prospects of the firm. This uncertainty is a fact of life when it comes to investing in technology firms. In a discounted cash flow valuation, you attempt to grapple with this uncertainty and make your best estimates about the future. Note that those who disdain valuation models for their potential errors end up using far cruder approaches, such as comparing price-sales ratios across firms.

IMPLICATIONS FOR INVESTORS

From a valuation perspective, a number of useful lessons emerge from the discussion above for investors in technology firms.

■ *Diversify*: This age-old rule of investing becomes even more critical when investing in stocks that derive the bulk of their value from uncertain future growth. The antidote to estimation noise is a more diversified portfolio both across firms and across sectors. Investors who choose to concentrate their bets on a few technology stocks are asking for trouble. Even if they have done their homework and the firms are undervalued, the noise in the process is so great that they could end up losing large portions of their portfolio.

■ *Keep your eyes on the prize*: Focus on sustainable margins and survival, rather than quarter-to-quarter or even year-to-year swings in profitability in your firm. Understanding what a firm's operating margins will look like when it reaches financial health might be the single most important determinant of whether you are successfully investing, in the long term, in such firms. Separating those firms that have a greater chance of surviving and reaching financial health is a closely connected second determinant. After all, most startup firms never survive to enjoy their vaunted growth prospects.

■ *Be ready to be wrong*: The noise in these valuations is such that no matter how much information is brought into the process and how carefully a valuation is done, the value obtained is an estimate. Thus, investors in technology stocks will be spectacularly wrong sometimes, and it is unfair to judge them on individual valuations. They will also be spectacularly right in other cases, and all that you can hope for is that with time as an ally, the successes outweigh the failures.

There are two other points to make about precision in the valuation of technology stocks. First, even if a valuation is imprecise, it provides a powerful tool to answer the question of what has to occur for the current market price of a firm to be justified. Investors can then decide whether they are comfortable with these assumptions and make their decisions on buying and selling stock in these firms. Second, even if individual valuations are noisy, portfolios constructed on the basis of these valuations will be more precisely valued. Thus, an investor who buys 40 stocks that he or she has found to be undervalued by traditional valuation models, albeit with significant noise, should find noise averaging out across the portfolio. The ultimate performance of the portfolio, then, should reflect the valuation skills, or the absence of them, of the analyst.

IMPLICATIONS FOR MANAGERS

If the future growth potential for a firm is uncertain, what are the implications for managers? The first is that the uncertainty about future growth will almost certainly translate into more uncertainty in traditional investment analysis. It is far more difficult to estimate cash flows and discount rates for individual projects in technology firms than in more stable sectors. While the reaction of some managers at these firms is to give up and fall back on more intuitive approaches, the managers who persevere and attempt to estimate cash flows will have a much better sense of what they need to do to make new investments pay off.

The second implication is that the uncertainty, which generally increases cost of capital, also increases the value of the options owned by the firm. It is entirely possible that the value of real options will be higher at higher levels of uncertainty, while existing investments become less valuable.

SUMMARY

The first principles of valuation do not change as you move from valuing manufacturing to valuing technology firms. Firms with higher cash flows from existing assets, higher expected growth, and lower uncertainty about the future should be worth more than firms without these characteristics. Technology firms that have negative cash flows from existing investments may seem like exceptions to this rule, but they are not; the fundamentals matter just as much, if not more, for these firms.

Growth is a key driver on value at technology firms, and both managers and investors in these firms sometimes fall into the trap of assuming that higher growth will always lead to higher value. If you accept the proposition that it is growth with excess returns that creates value, not growth per se, you can see that it is possible for firms to grow and destroy value simultaneously. When technology firms report earnings or new investments, investors have to consider the implications for both expected growth rates and excess returns. Thus, announcements that seem to contain good news (in the form of higher earnings or acquisitions that seem to make sense from a strategic standpoint) may, in fact, have negative consequences for value.

Finally, noise is a fact of life when you are valuing a technology firm. While the uncertainty about the future does increase the range of value that you may assign the firm, it does not make the valuation less useful. Investors should hedge their bets more by diversifying when investing in technology firms, because of the uncertainty. Managers must consider ways in which they can take advantage of uncertainty to create value.

ENDNOTES

1. The empirical evidence backs up this proposition. Studies of investments seem to indicate that companies that are viewed as well managed underperform companies that are less well regarded.

2. Steve Job's job at Apple Computer was far easier when he took over in 1998 (when the stock price had hit a ten-year low) than it was two years later, when he had succeeded in changing investor perceptions of the company (and pushed the stock price up tenfold, in the process).

3. Steve Ballmer at Microsoft has developed a reputation for talking down expectations and then beating them on a consistent basis.

REFERENCES

Many of the articles that are listed below are not directly referenced in the book, but they have influenced my thinking substantially. The articles are categorized by chapters.

CHAPTER 2 • SHOW ME THE MONEY: THE FUNDAMENTALS OF DISCOUNTED CASH FLOW VALUATION

Copeland, T. E., T. Koller, and J. Murrin, 1996, *Valuation: Measuring and Managing the Value of Companies*, John Wiley & Sons.

Damodaran, A., 1994, *Investment Valuation*, John Wiley & Sons.

CHAPTER 3 • THE PRICE OF RISK: ESTIMATING DISCOUNT RATES

FOR MORE ON RISK AND RETURN MODELS

Bernstein, P., 1996, *Against the Gods*, John Wiley & Sons, New York.

Bernstein, P., 1992, *Capital Ideas*, The Free Press, New York.

Fama, E. F., and K. R. French, 1992, The Cross-Section of Expected Returns, *Journal of Finance* [47: 427–466].

Lintner, J., 1965, The Valuation of Risk Assets and the Selection of Risky Investments in Stock Portfolios and Capital Budgets, *Review of Economics and Statistics* [47: 13–37].

Markowitz, Harry M., 1991, Foundations of Portfolio Theory, *Journal of Finance* [46: 469–478].

Roll, R., 1977, A Critique of the Asset Pricing Theory's Tests: Part I: On Past and Potential Testability of Theory, *Journal of Financial Economics* [4: 129–176].

Ross, Stephen A., 1976, The Arbitrage Theory of Capital Asset Pricing, *Journal of Economic Theory* [13: 341–360].

Sharpe, W. F., 1964, Capital Asset Prices: A Theory of Market Equilibrium under Conditions of Risk, *Journal of Finance* [19: 425–442].

FOR ESTIMATION ISSUES

Booth, L., 1999, Estimating the Equity Risk Premium and Equity Costs: New Way of Looking at Old Data, *Journal of Applied Corporate Finance* [12(1): 100–112].

Bruner, R. F., K. M. Eades, R. S. Harris, and R. C. Higgins, 1998, Best Practices in Estimating the Cost of Capital: Survey and Synthesis, *Financial Practice and Education* [8: 14–28].

Chan, K. C., G. A. Karolyi, and R. M. Stulz, 1992, Global Financial Markets and the Risk Premium on U.S. Equity, *Journal of Financial Economics* [32: 132–167].

Godfrey, S., and R. Espinosa, 1996, A Practical Approach to Calculating the Cost of Equity for Investments in Emerging Markets, *Journal of Applied Corporate Finance* [9(3): 80–81].

Hamada, R. S., The Effect of the Firm's Capital Structure on the Systematic Risk of Common Stocks, *Journal of Finance* [27: 435–452].

Ibbotson, R., and G. Brinson, 1993, *Global Investing*, McGraw-Hill, New York.

Indro, D. C., and W. Y. Lee, 1997, Biases in Arithmetic and Geometric Averages as Estimates of Long-run Expected Returns and Risk Premium, *Financial Management* [26: 81–90].

Pettit, J., 1999, Corporate Capital Costs: A Practitioner's Guide, *Journal of Applied Corporate Finance* [12(1): 113–120].

Siegel, J., 1999, Stocks, Bonds, Bills and Inflation, Ibbotson Associates.

CHAPTER 4 • CASH IS KING: ESTIMATING CASH FLOWS

Stickney, C. P., 1993, *Financial Statement Analysis*, Dryden, Fort Worth, TX.

White, G. I, A. Sondhi, and D. Fried, 1997, *The Analysis and Use of Financial Statements*, John Wiley & Sons, New York.

Williams, J. R., 1998, *GAAP Guide*, Harcourt Brace, New York.

CHAPTER 5 • LOOKING FORWARD: ESTIMATING GROWTH

Damodaran, A., 1994, *Investment Valuation*, John Wiley & Sons, New York.

Little, I. M. D., 1962, *Higgledy Piggledy Growth*, Institute of Statistics, Oxford.

Crichfield, T., T. Dyckman, and J. Lakonishok, 1978, An Evaluation of Security Analysts Forecasts, *Accounting Review* [5: 651–668].

O'Brien, P., 1988, Analyst's Forecasts as Earnings Expectations, *Journal of Accounting and Economics* [10: 53–83].

Cragg, J. G., and B. G. Malkiel, 1968, The Consensus and Accuracy of Predictions of the Growth of Corporate Earnings, *Journal of Finance* [23: 67–84].

Vander Weide, J. H., and W. T. Carleton, 1988, Investor Growth Expectations: Analysts vs. History, *Journal of Portfolio Management* [14: 78–83].

CHAPTER 6 • ESTIMATING FIRM VALUE

Damodaran, A., 2000, Dealing with Cash, Marketable Securities and Cross Holdings in Valuation, www.stern.nyu.edu/~adamodar/ New_Home_Page/papers.html

CHAPTER 7 • MANAGEMENT OPTIONS, CONTROL, AND LIQUIDITY

Carpenter , J. , 1998, The Exercise and Valuation of Executive Stock Options, *Journal of Financial Economics* [48: 127–158].

Lease, R. C., J. J. McConnell, and W. H. Mikkelson, 1983, The Market Value of Control in Publicly-Traded Corporations, *Journal of Financial Economics* [11: 439–471].

Silber, W. L., 1991, Discounts on Restricted Stock: The Impact of Illiquidity on Stock Prices, *Financial Analysts Journal* [47: 60–64].

CHAPTERS 8–10

THE RELATIONSHIP BETWEEN PE AND GROWTH

Leibowitz, M. L., and S. Kogelman, 1992, Franchise Value and the Growth Process, *Financial Analysts Journal* [48: 53–62].

THE FIRST REGRESSIONS OF PE RATIOS AGAINST FUNDAMENTALS

Kisor, M., Jr., and V. S. Whitbeck, 1963, A New Tool in Investment Decision-Making, *Financial Analysts Journal* [19: 55–62].

Cragg, J. G., and B. G. Malkiel, 1968, The Consensus and Accuracy of Predictions of the Growth of Corporate Earnings, *Journal of Finance* [23: 67–84].

CHAPTER 11 • REAL OPTIONS IN VALUATION

Black, F., and M. Scholes, 1972, The Valuation of Option Contracts and a Test of Market Efficiency, *Journal of Finance* [27: 399–417].

Cox, J. C., and S. A. Ross, 1976, The Valuation of Options for Alternative Stochastic Processes, *Journal of Financial Economics* [3: 145–166].

Cox, J. C., S. A. Ross, and M.Rubinstein, 1979, Option Pricing: A Simplified Approach, *Journal of Financial Economics* [7: 229–264].

Geske, R., 1979, The Valuation of Compound Options, *Journal of Finance* [7: 63–82].

Merton, R. C., 1976, Option Pricing When the Underlying Stock Returns Are Discontinuous, *Journal of Financial Economics* [3: 125–144].

Merton, R. C., 1973, The Theory Of Rational Option Pricing, *Bell Journal of Economics* [4: 141–183].

FOR MORE ON OPTION PRICING

Hull, J. C., 1999, *Options, Futures and Other Derivatives*, Prentice Hall, Upper Saddle River, NJ.

FOR MORE ON REAL OPTIONS

Brennan, M. J., and L. Trigeorgis, 1999, *Project Flexibility, Agency and Competition: New Developments in the Theory and Applications of Real Options*, Oxford University Press, New York.

CHAPTER 12 • VALUE ENHANCEMENT

Bernstein, R., 1997, *EVA and Market Returns*, Merrill Lynch, December 19, 1997.

Bernstein, R., 1997, *EVA and Market Returns*, Merrill Lynch, February 3, 1998.

Brickley, J., C. Smith, and J. Zimmerman, 1995, Transfer Pricing and the Control of Internal Corporate Transactions, *Journal of Applied Corporate Finance* [8(2): 60–67].

Kramer, J. R., and G. Pushner, 1997, An Empirical Analysis of Economic Value Added As a Proxy for Market Value Added, *Financial Practice and Education* [7: 41–49].

O'Byrne, S. F., 1996, EVA and Market Value, *Journal of Applied Corporate Finance* [9(1): 116–125].

Stulz, R., 1996, Rethinking Risk Management, *Journal of Applied Corporate Finance* [9(3): 8–24].

FOR MORE ON ECONOMIC VALUE ADDED

Stewart, M. L., 1990, *The Quest for Value*, Harper, New York.

FOR MORE ON CFROI

Madden. B. L., 1998, *CFROI Cash Flow Return on Investment Valuation: A Total System Approach to Valuing a Firm*, Butterworth-Heinemann, Woburn, MA.

INDEX

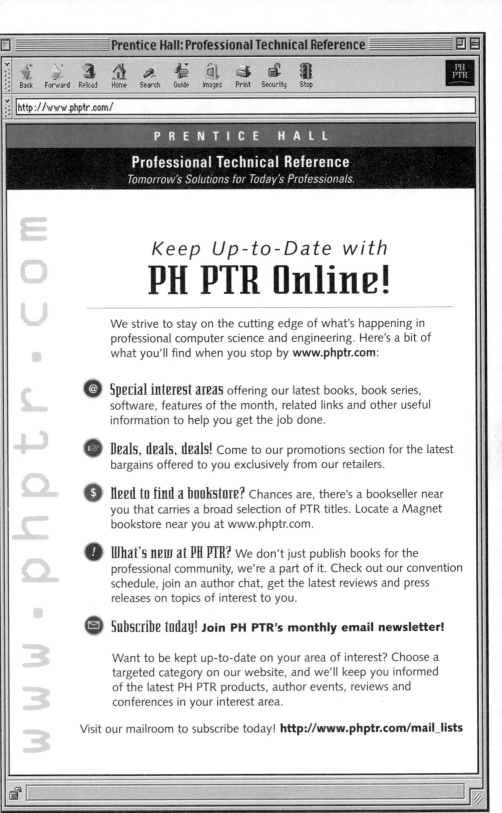